THE QUEEN'S KNIGHT

The Queen's Knight Vol. 7
created by Kim Kang Won

Translation - Sora Han
Retouch and Lettering - Gloria Wu
Production Artist - Mike Estacio
Cover Design - Monalisa De Asis

Editor - Troy Lewter
Digital Imaging Manager - Chris Buford
Managing Editor - Vy Ngyuen
Pre-Production Supervisor - Erika Terriquez
Art Director - Anne Marie Horne
Production Manager - Elisabeth Brizzi
VP of Production - Ron Klamert
Editor in Chief - Rob Tokar
Publisher - Mike Kiley
President and C.O.O. - John Parker
C.E.O. and Chief Creative Officer - Stuart Levy

A  Manga

TOKYOPOP Inc.
5900 Wilshire Blvd. Suite 2000
Los Angeles, CA 90036

E-mail: info@TOKYOPOP.com
Come visit us online at www.TOKYOPOP.com

ISBN: 1-59532-263-9

First TOKYOPOP printing: October 2006
10 9 8 7 6 5 4 3 2 1
Printed in the USA

THE QUEEN'S KNIGHT

Volume 7

by Kim Kang Won

HAMBURG // LONDON // LOS ANGELES // TOKYO

THE QUEEN'S KNIGHT

Yuna is a normal girl who visits her mother in Germany and endures a terrible disaster. After she returns home from her accident, she begins to have strange dreams. In her dream, a knight who calls himself "Rieno" tells Yuna that she is his Queen and that he is her knight. Yuna's brothers send her back to Germany, where she meets the knight from her dreams--who then promptly kidnaps her, taking her to Phantasma.

Phantasma is a world covered entirely with snow, and Yuna is forced to live with Rieno. But just when Yuna was getting used to being with him, spring arrives, and Yuna is taken to Elysian to be properly installed as the Queen of Phantasma. Once there, Yuna befriends the Queen's Guardian Knights, Ehren, Leon and Schiller, and meets the hateful Chancellor Kent, as well as the Queen's rival, Princess Libera.

However, when Yuna secretly leaves the castle with Schiller and Leon, they are unexpectedly robbed and branded as fugitives. While on the run, Yuna learns that the early arrival of spring means that she is indeed in love. This, predictably, stirs the coals of jealousy in the hearts of her knights, as they each wonder who has secretly won Yuna's favor.

But matters of love are the least of their problems when Yuna and the knights return to the castle to confront Chancellor Kent in regards to his political scheming. In a desperate attempt to maintain control in the wake of Libera and Kent's alliance, Yuna repeals the taxes and declares slavery illegal. In another bold move, Yuna insists on participating in the Forest of Darkness hunt.

However, little does she know that Libera's hired bandits plan to ambush Yuna and her hunting party. But when their first arrow strikes Yuna's pony, the frightened animal goes into a frenzied run that carries Yuna deep within the bowels of the demon-infested Forest...

The Queen's Knight

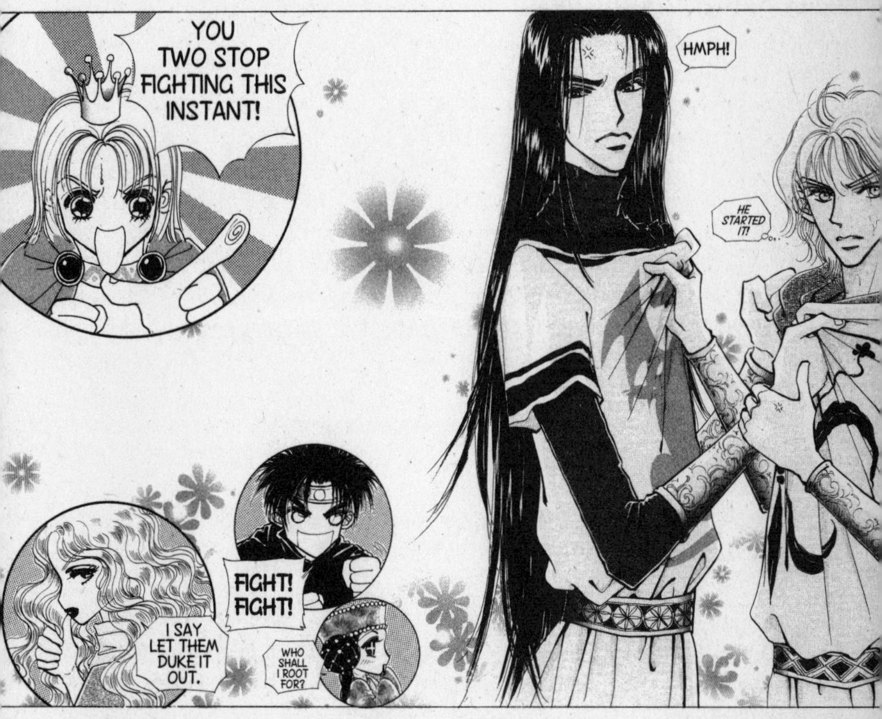
YOU TWO STOP FIGHTING THIS INSTANT!
HMPH!
HE STARTED IT!
FIGHT! FIGHT!
I SAY LET THEM DUKE IT OUT.
WHO SHALL I ROOT FOR?

Volume 7

Kim Kang Won

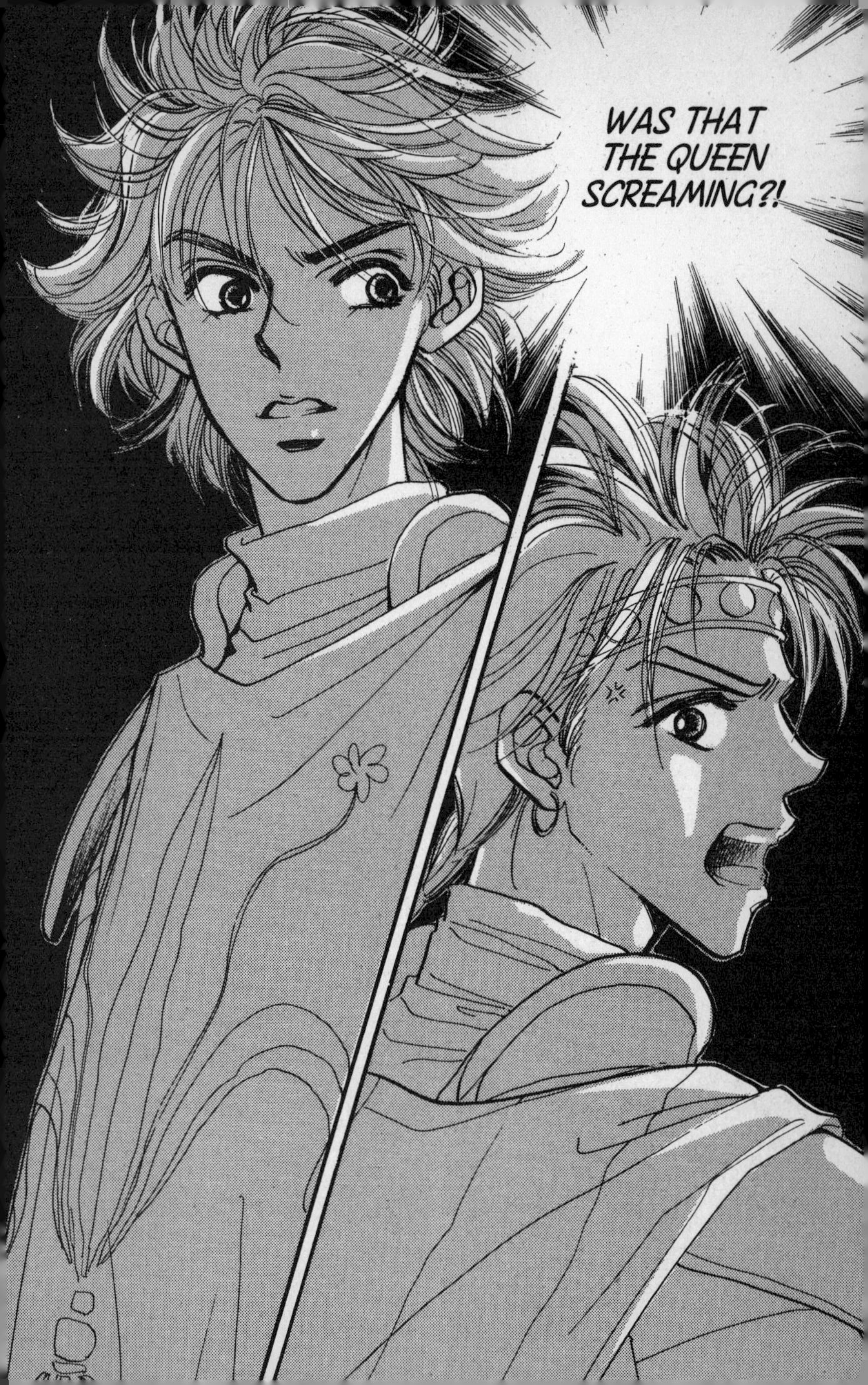
WAS THAT
THE QUEEN
SCREAMING?!

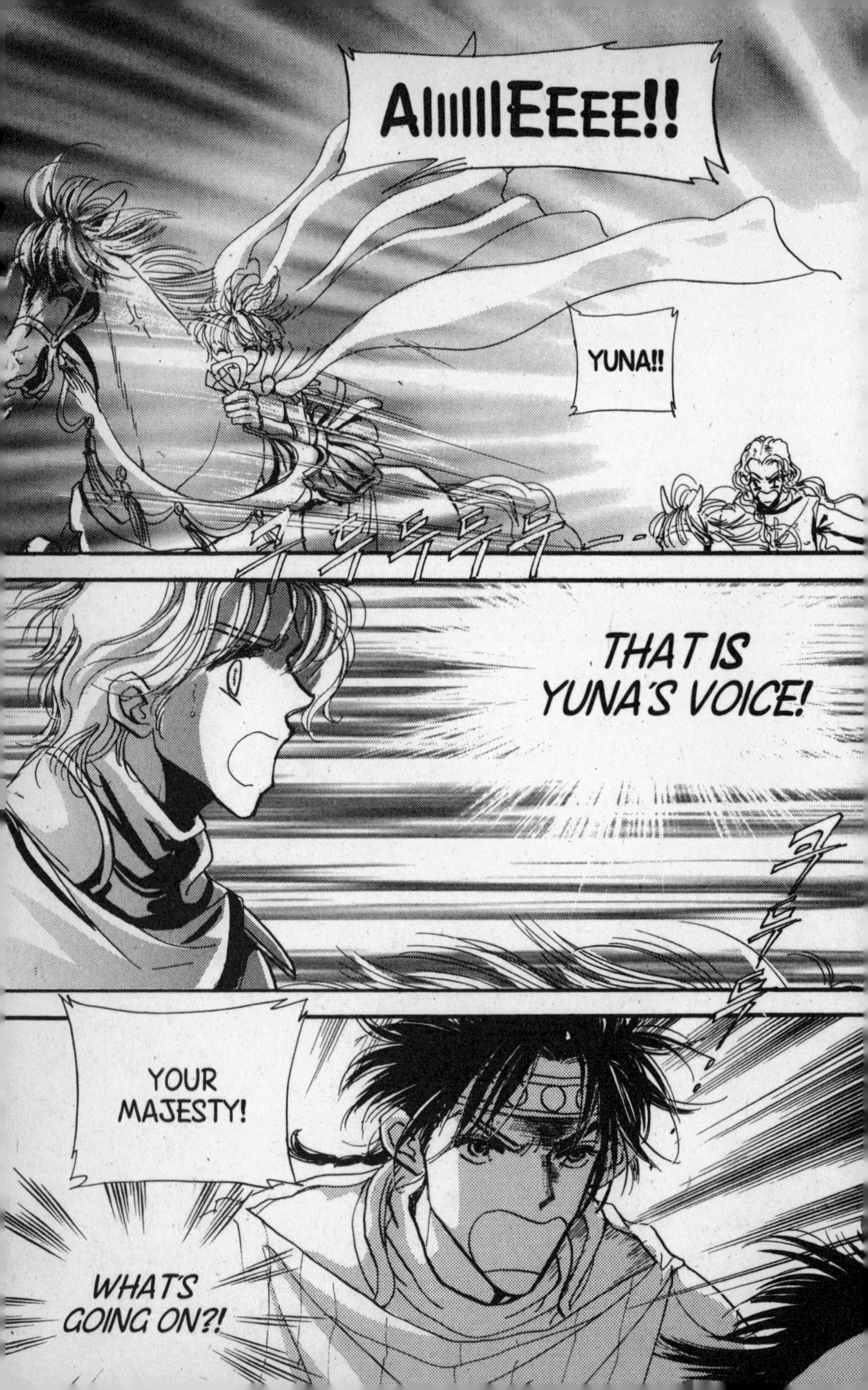
AIIIIIEEEE!!
YUNA!!
THAT IS YUNA'S VOICE!
YOUR MAJESTY!
WHAT'S GOING ON?!

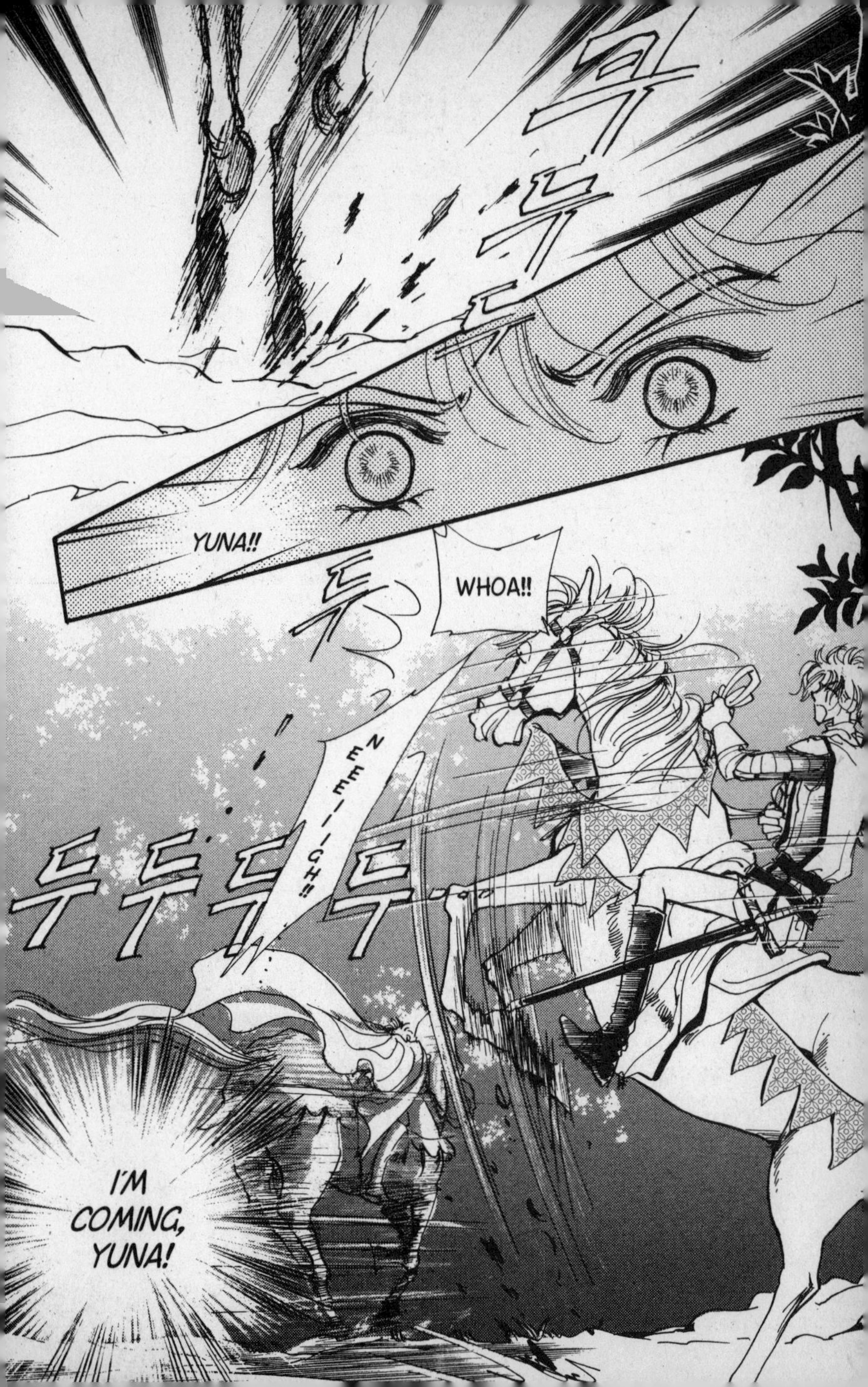
YUNA!!
WHOA!!
NEEEIIGH!!
I'M COMING, YUNA!

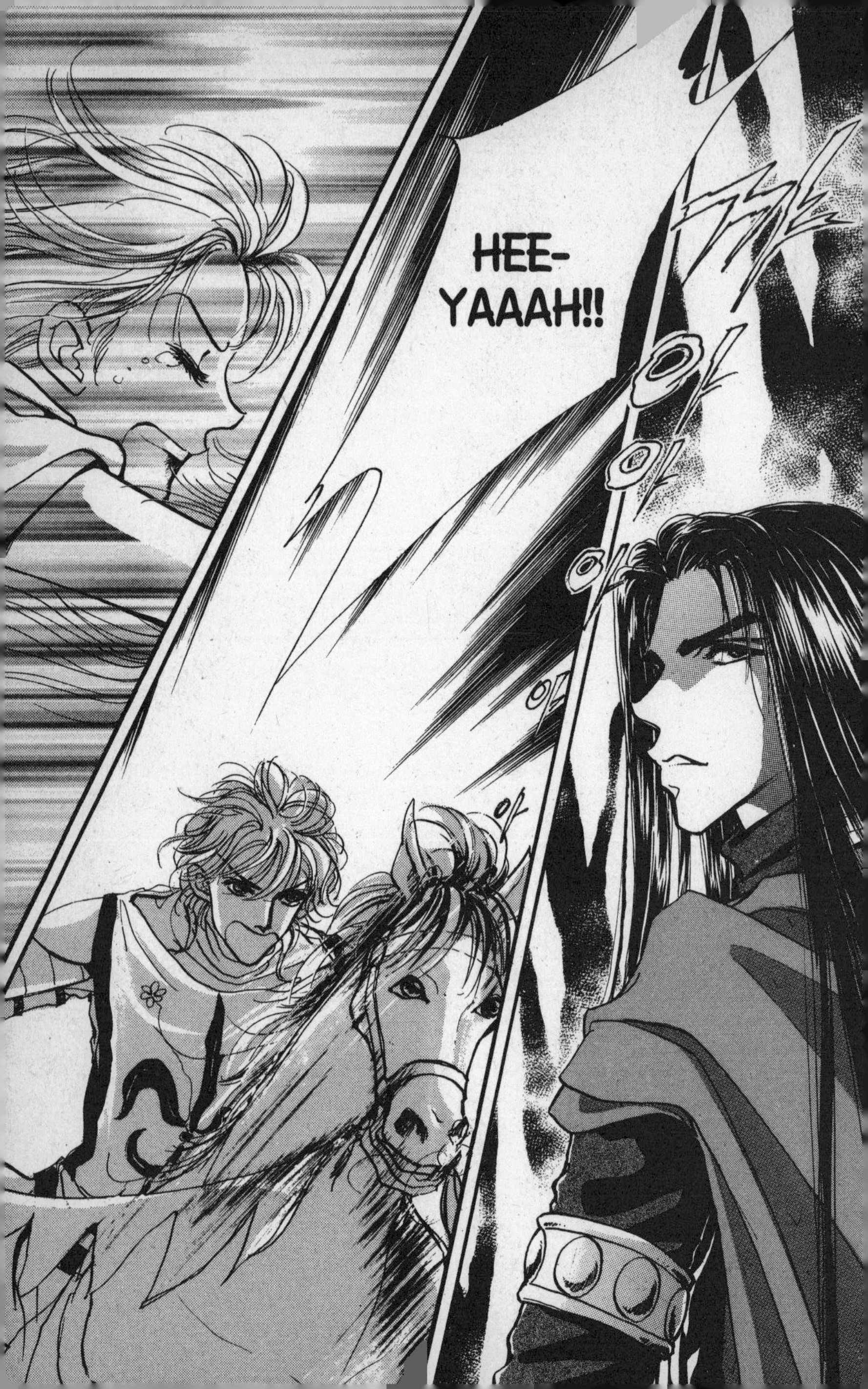
HEE-
YAAAH!!

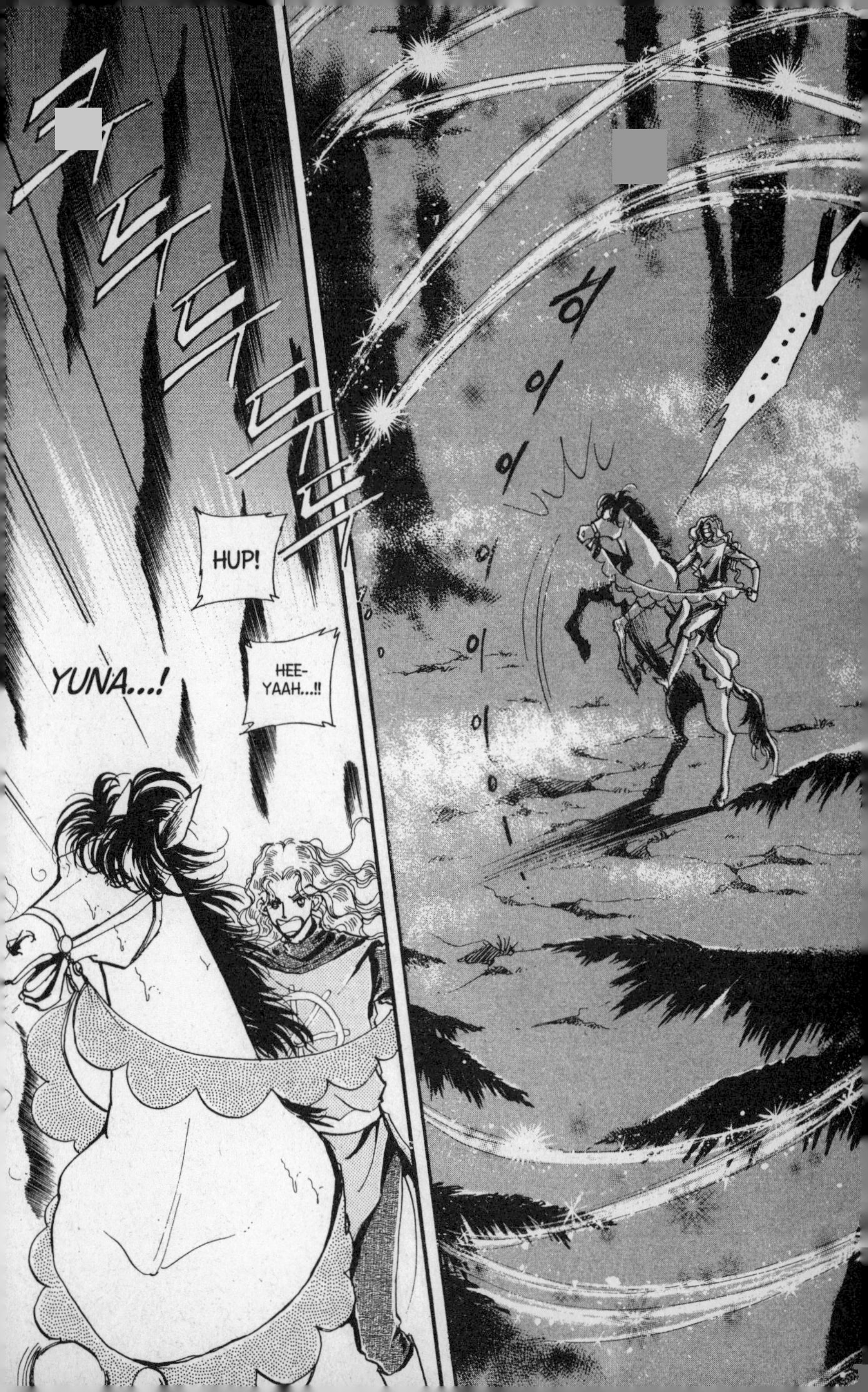
HUP!
YUNA...!
HEE-YAAH...!!

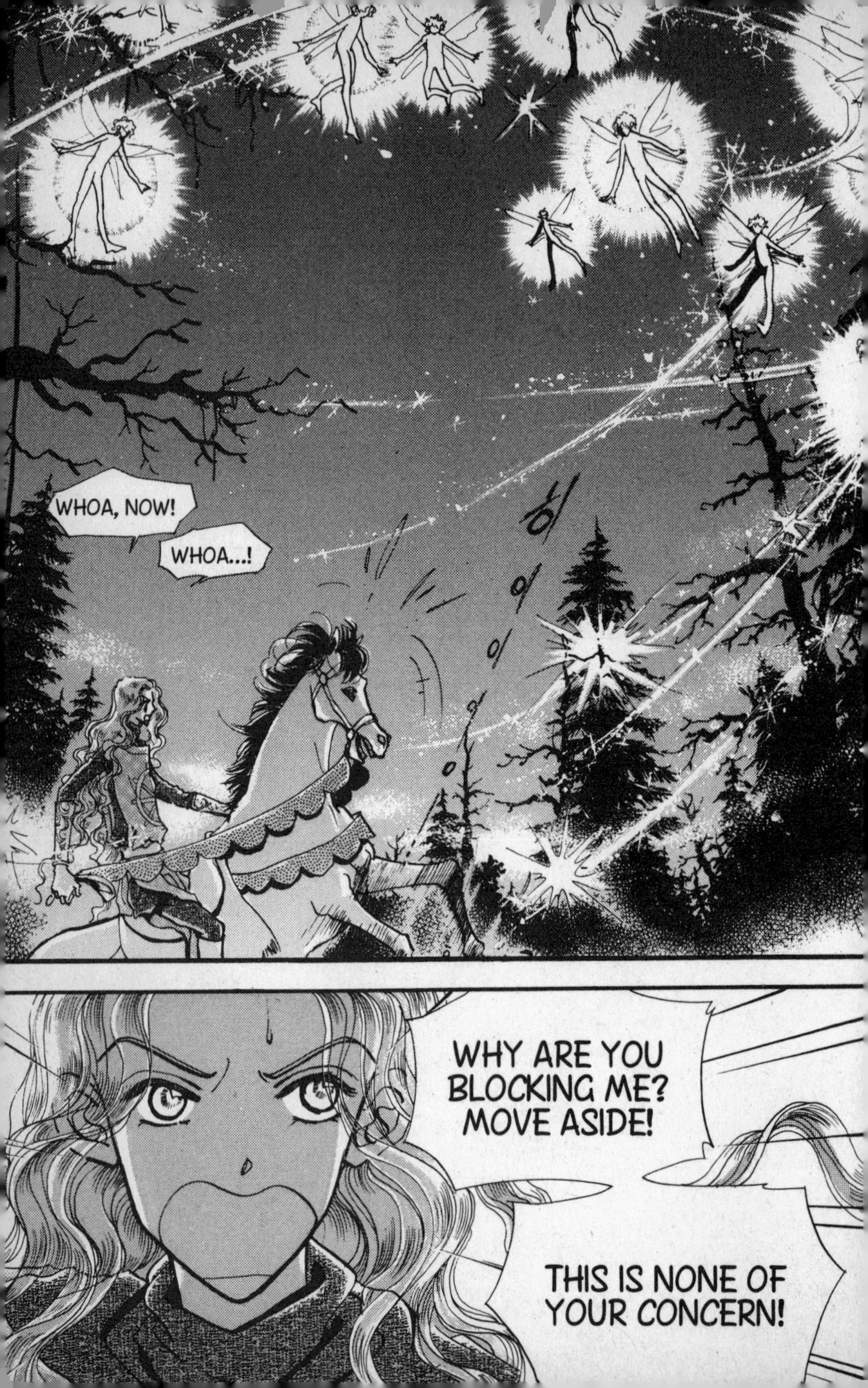
WHOA, NOW!
WHOA...!
WHY ARE YOU BLOCKING ME? MOVE ASIDE!
THIS IS NONE OF YOUR CONCERN!

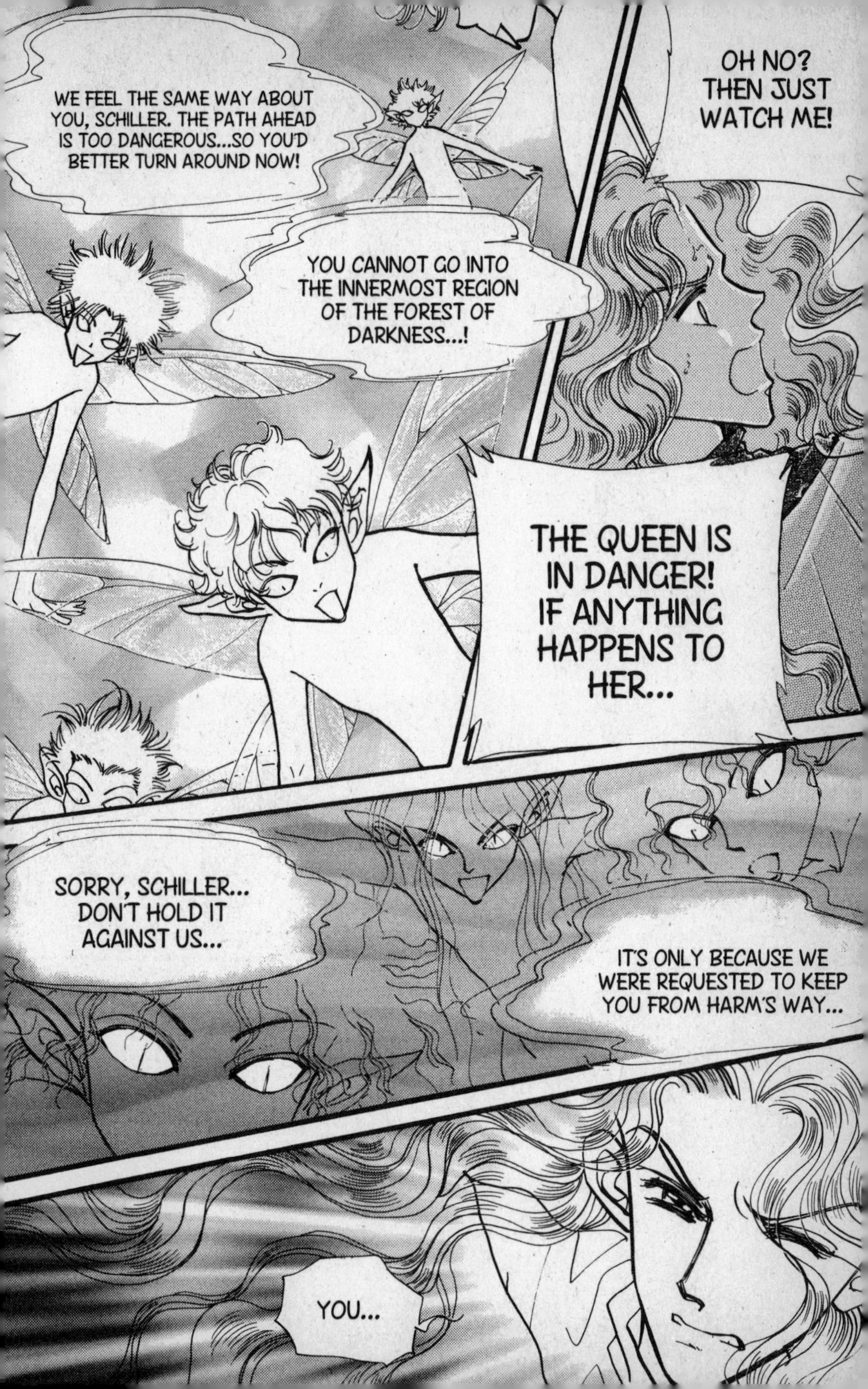
WE FEEL THE SAME WAY ABOUT YOU, SCHILLER. THE PATH AHEAD IS TOO DANGEROUS...SO YOU'D BETTER TURN AROUND NOW!
YOU CANNOT GO INTO THE INNERMOST REGION OF THE FOREST OF DARKNESS...!
THE QUEEN IS IN DANGER! IF ANYTHING HAPPENS TO HER...
OH NO? THEN JUST WATCH ME!
SORRY, SCHILLER... DON'T HOLD IT AGAINST US...
IT'S ONLY BECAUSE WE WERE REQUESTED TO KEEP YOU FROM HARM'S WAY...
YOU...

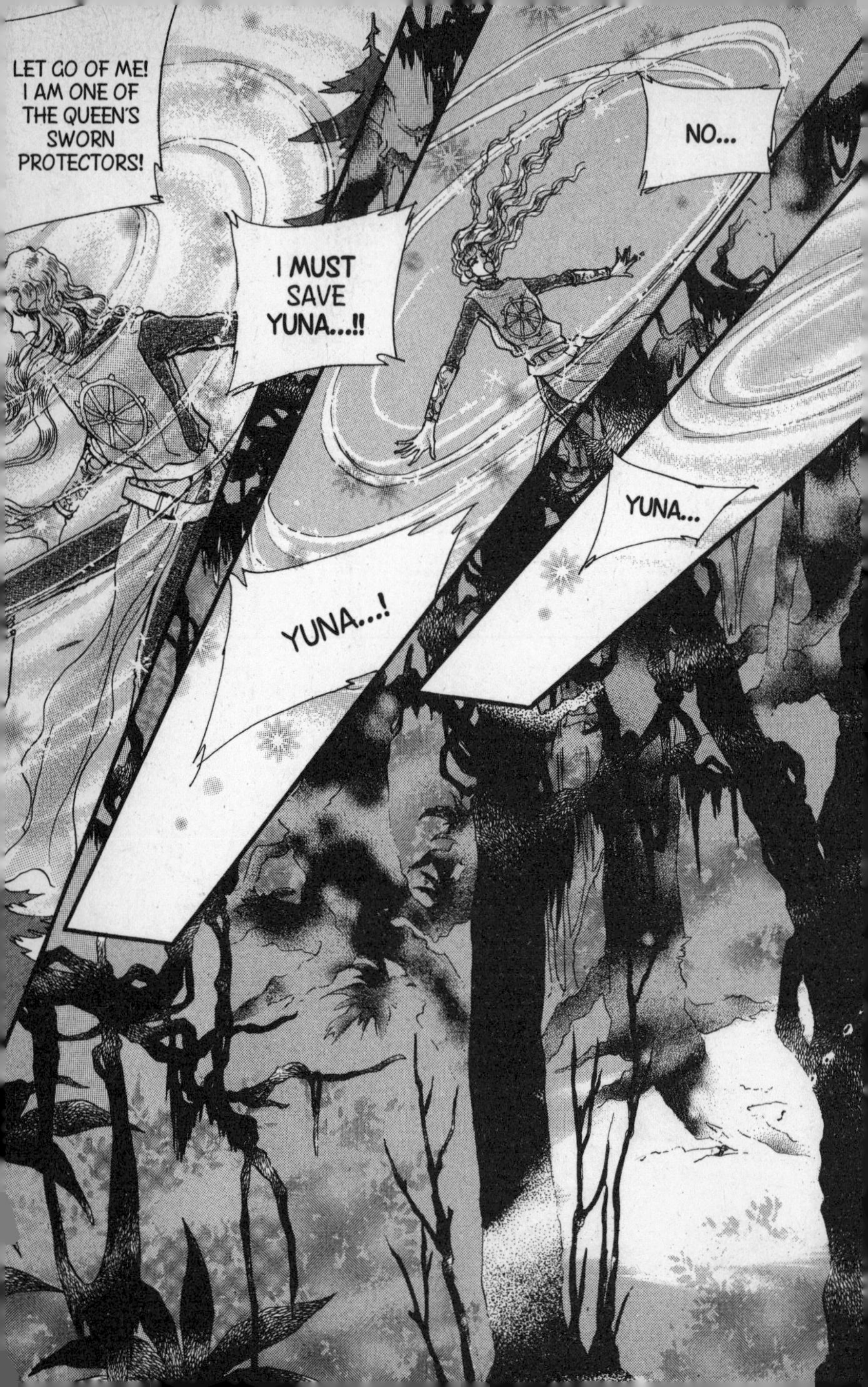
LET GO OF ME! I AM ONE OF THE QUEEN'S SWORN PROTECTORS!
I MUST SAVE YUNA...!!
NO...
YUNA...!
YUNA...

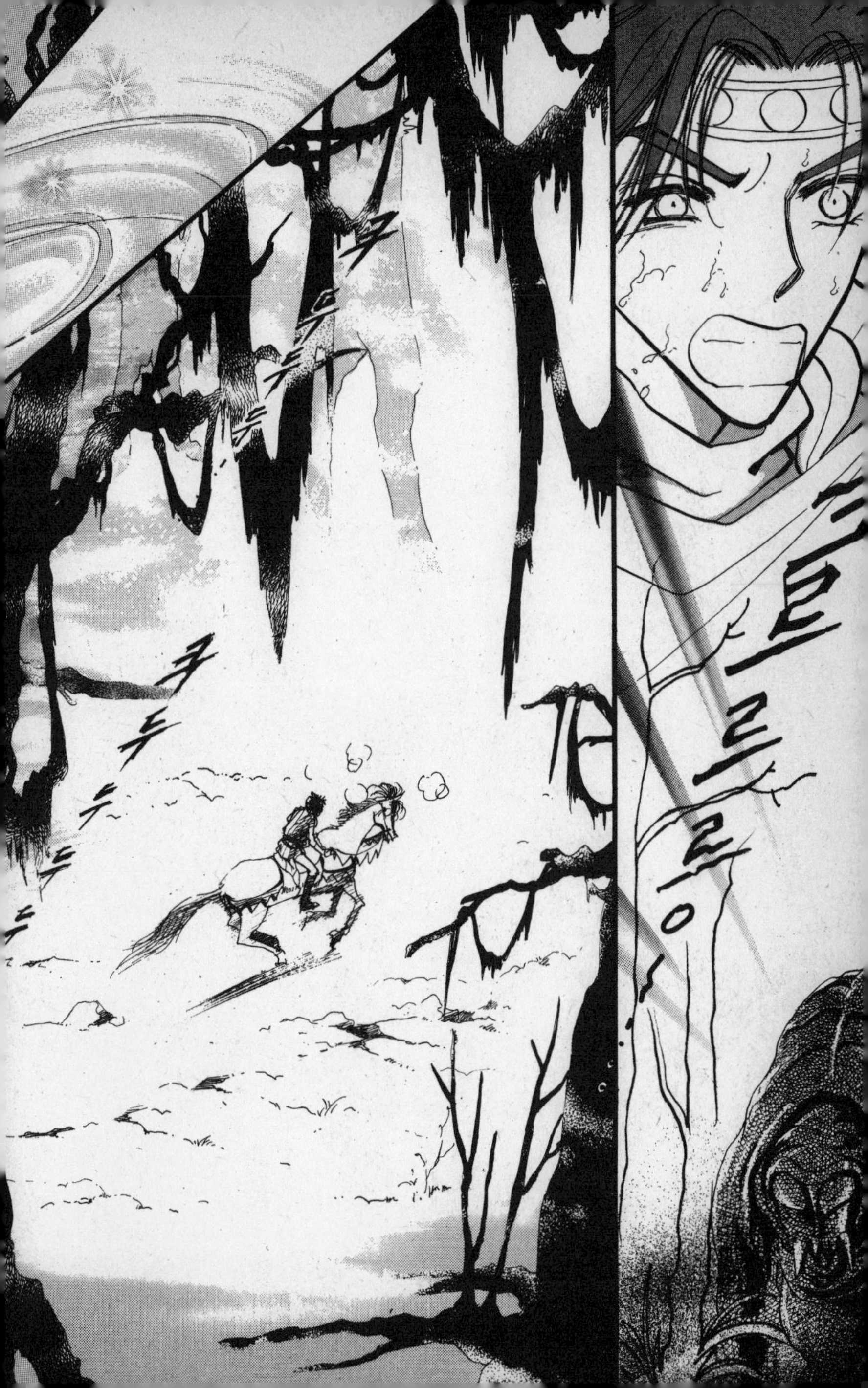
쿠두두두
쿠두두두두
크르르르으

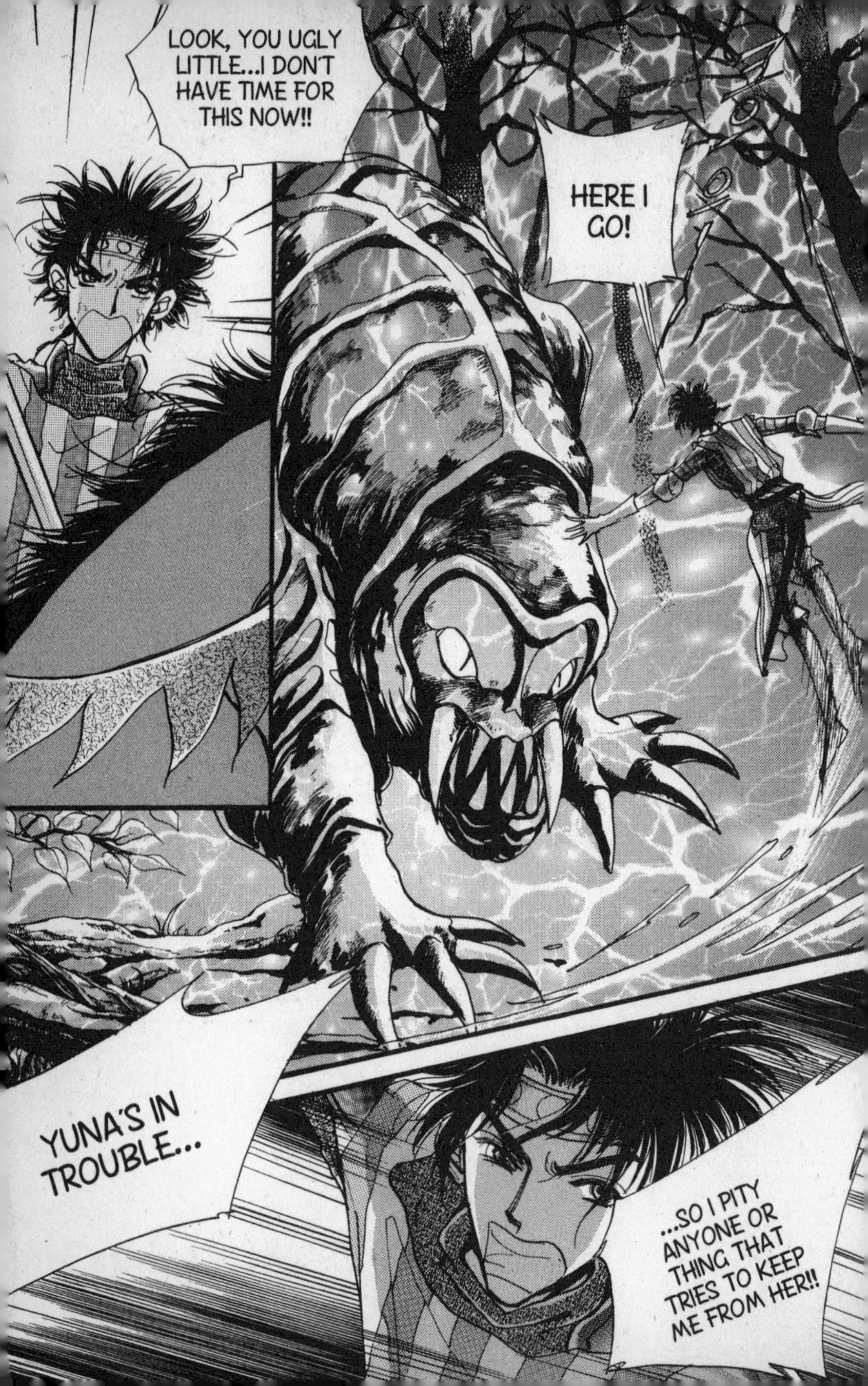
LOOK, YOU UGLY LITTLE...I DON'T HAVE TIME FOR THIS NOW!!
HERE I GO!
YUNA'S IN TROUBLE...
...SO I PITY ANYONE OR THING THAT TRIES TO KEEP ME FROM HER!!

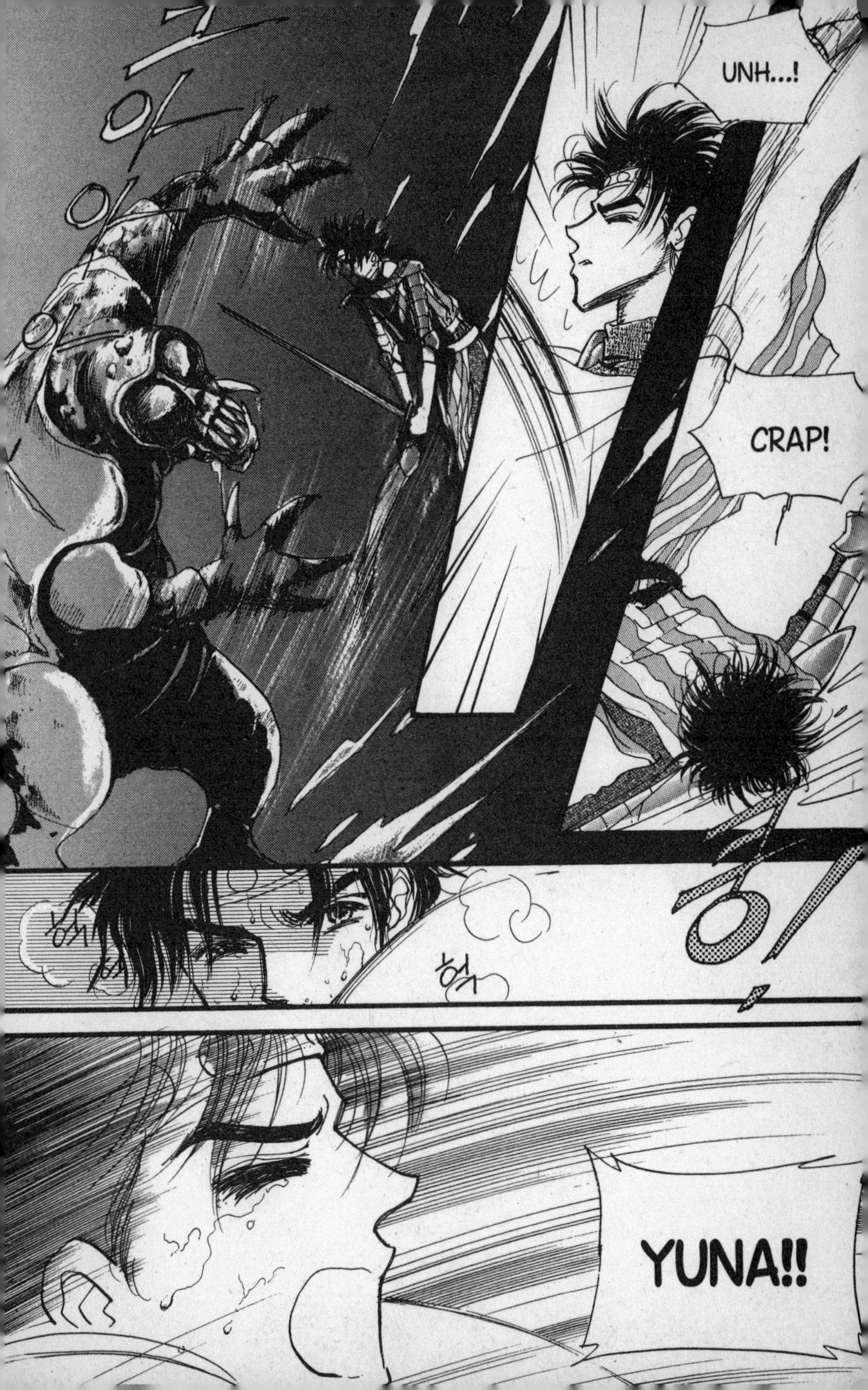
UNH...!
CRAP!
헉
헉
헉
YUNA!!

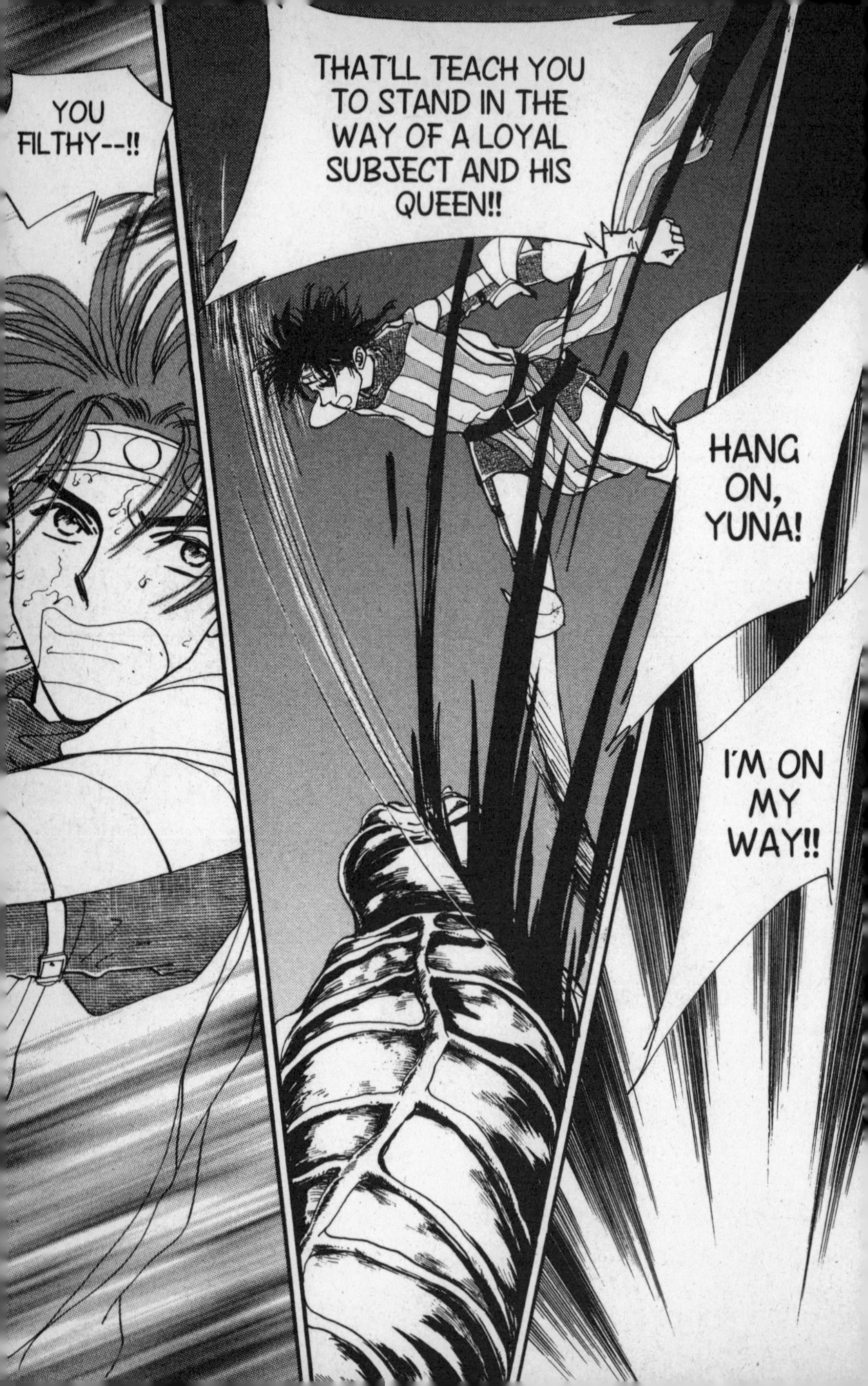
YOU FILTHY--!!
THAT'LL TEACH YOU TO STAND IN THE WAY OF A LOYAL SUBJECT AND HIS QUEEN!!
HANG ON, YUNA!
I'M ON MY WAY!!

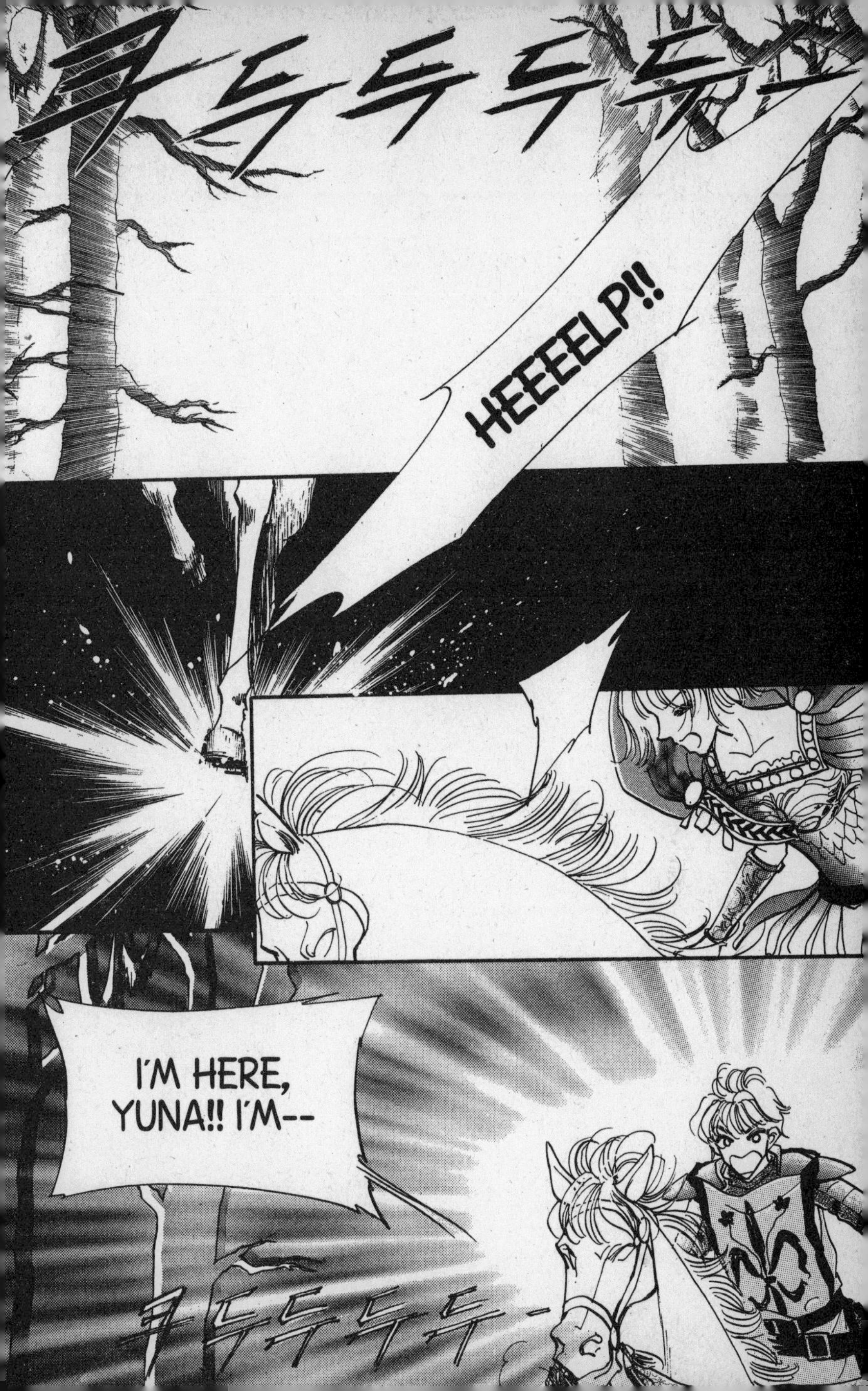
쿠두두두두-
HEEEELP!!
I'M HERE, YUNA!! I'M--
쿠두두두두-

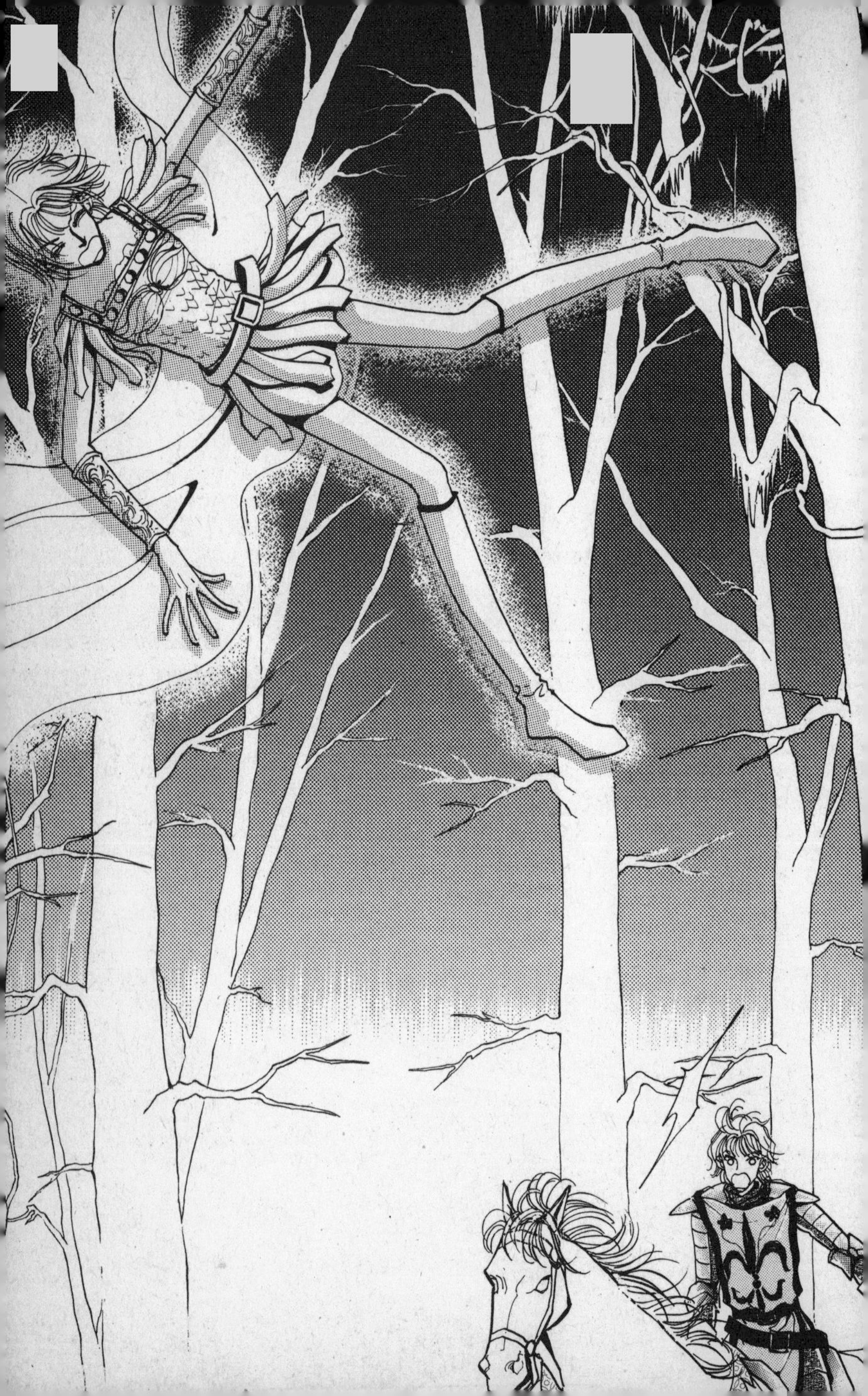

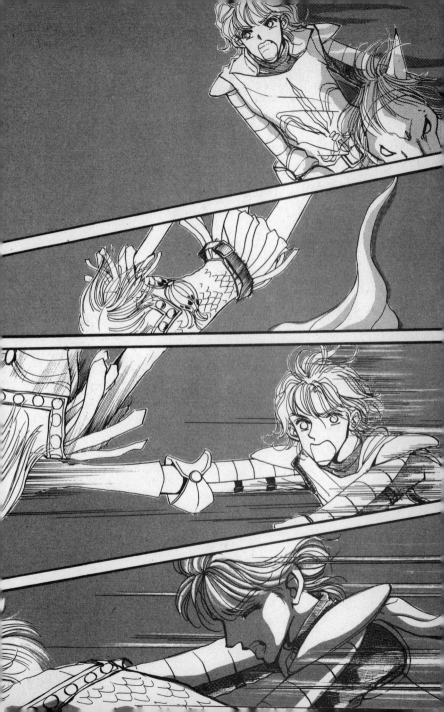

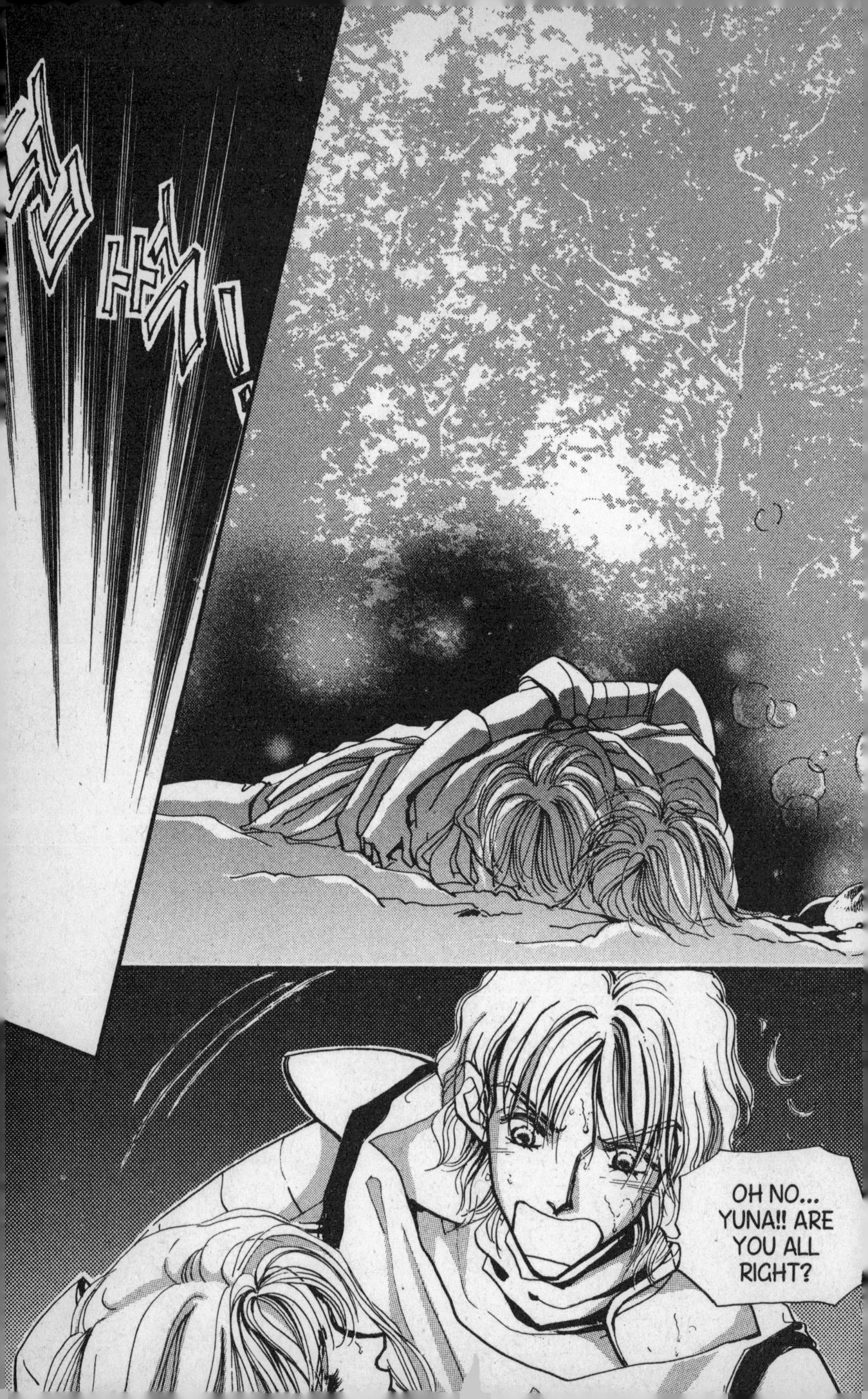
OH NO... YUNA!! ARE YOU ALL RIGHT?

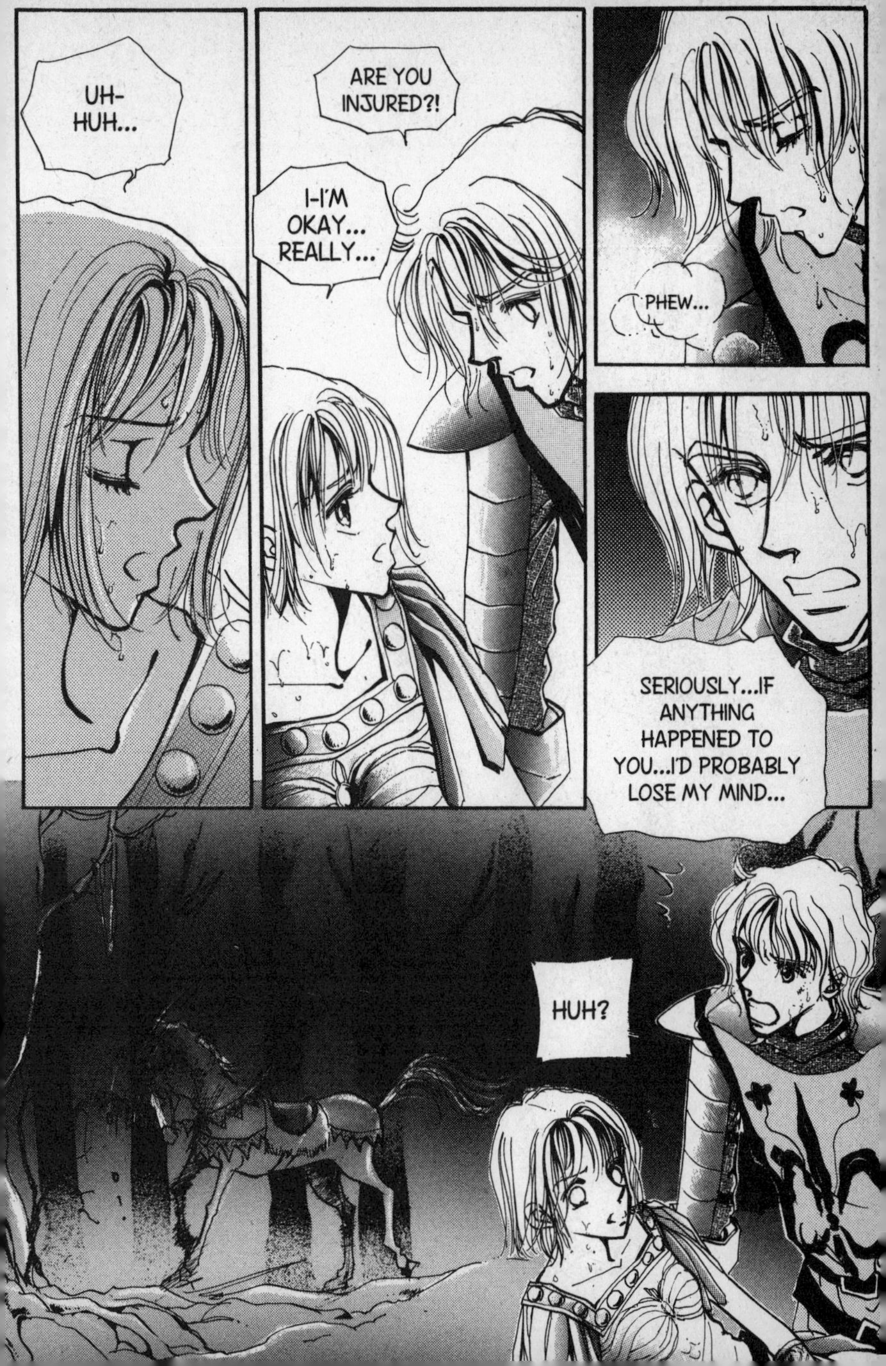
UH-HUH...
ARE YOU INJURED?!
I-I'M OKAY... REALLY...
PHEW...
SERIOUSLY...IF ANYTHING HAPPENED TO YOU...I'D PROBABLY LOSE MY MIND...
HUH?

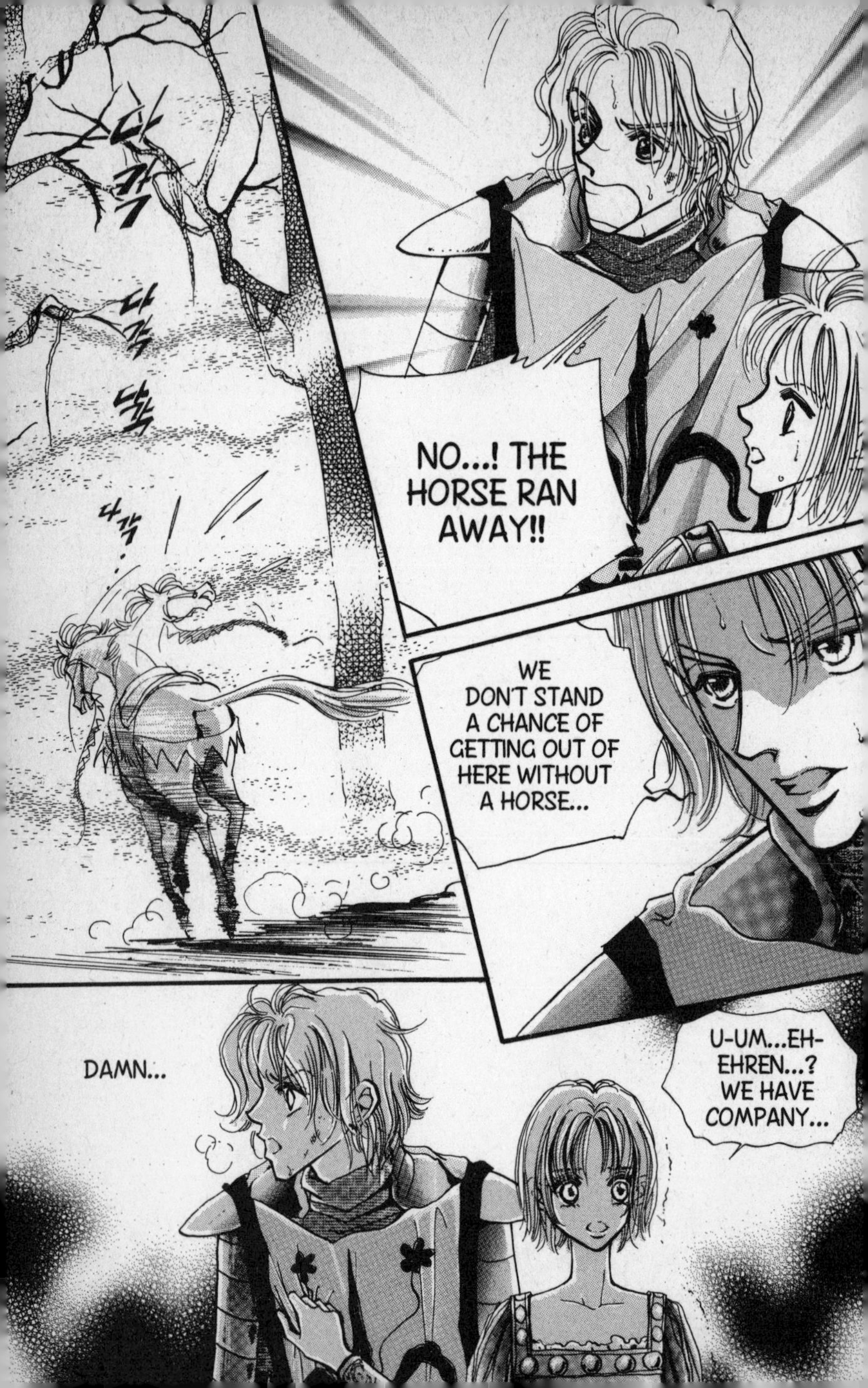
다각
다각
다각
다각
NO...! THE HORSE RAN AWAY!!
WE DON'T STAND A CHANCE OF GETTING OUT OF HERE WITHOUT A HORSE...
DAMN...
U-UM...EH-EHREN...? WE HAVE COMPANY...

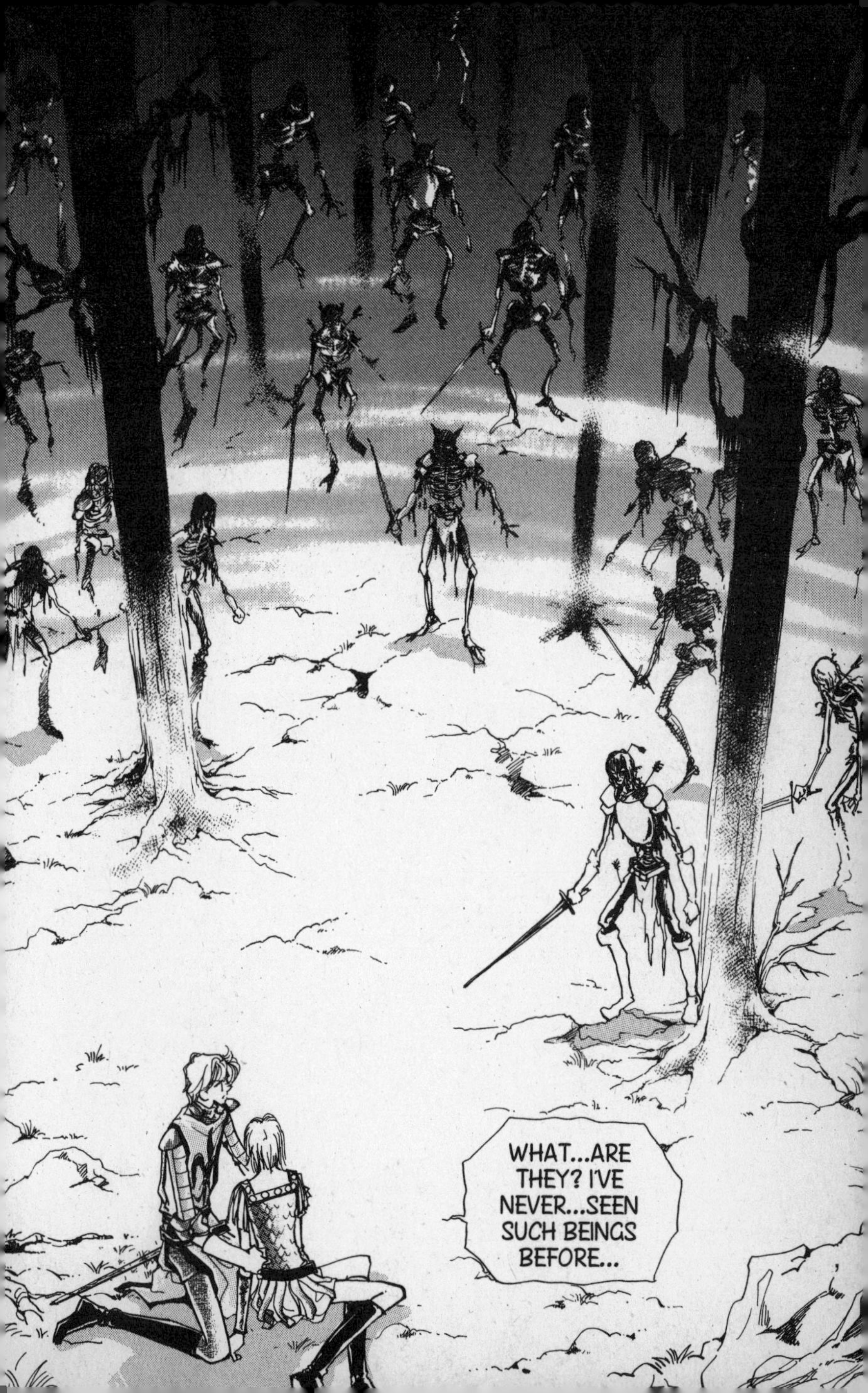
WHAT...ARE THEY? I'VE NEVER...SEEN SUCH BEINGS BEFORE...

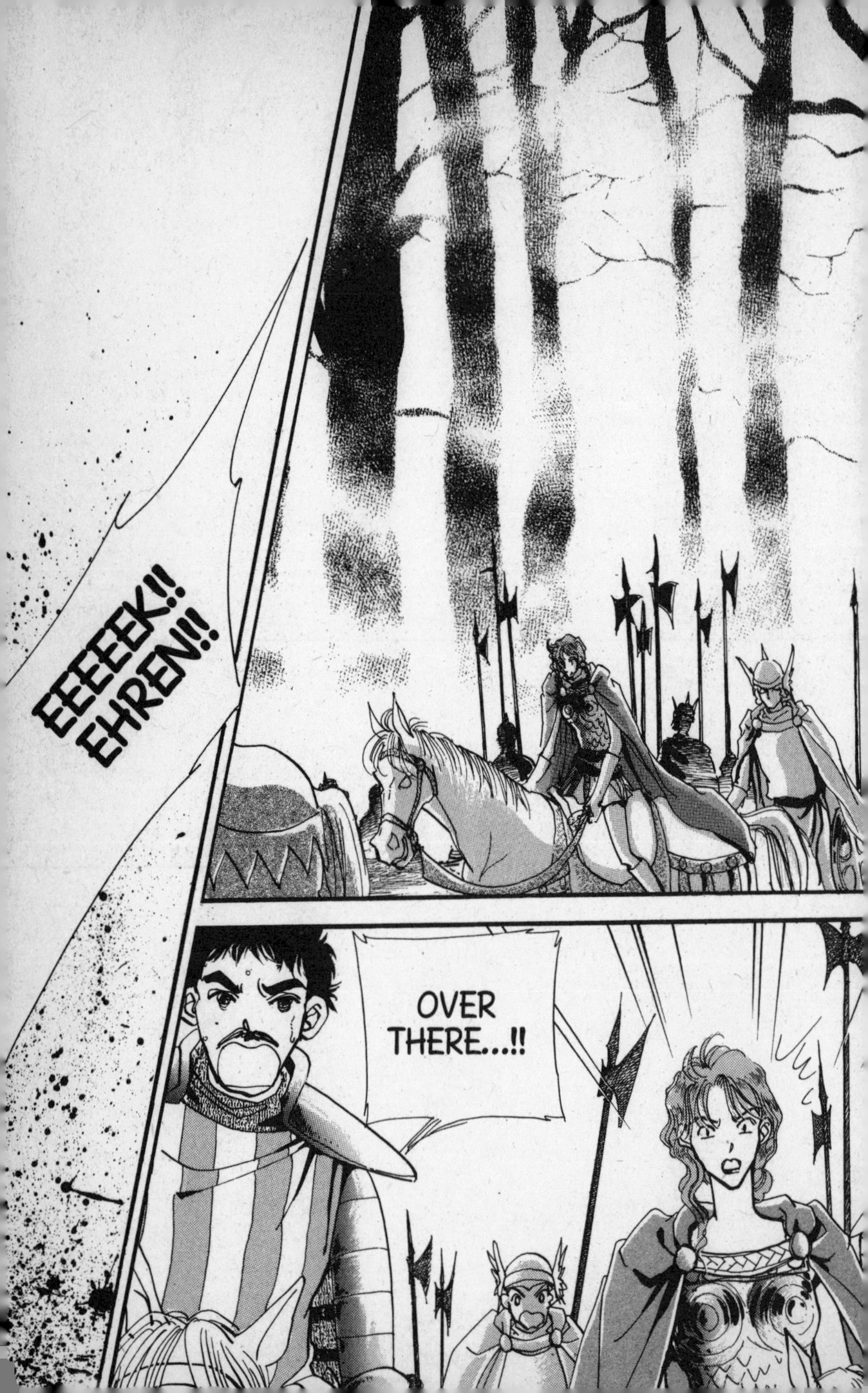
EEEEEK!!
EHREN!!
OVER THERE...!!

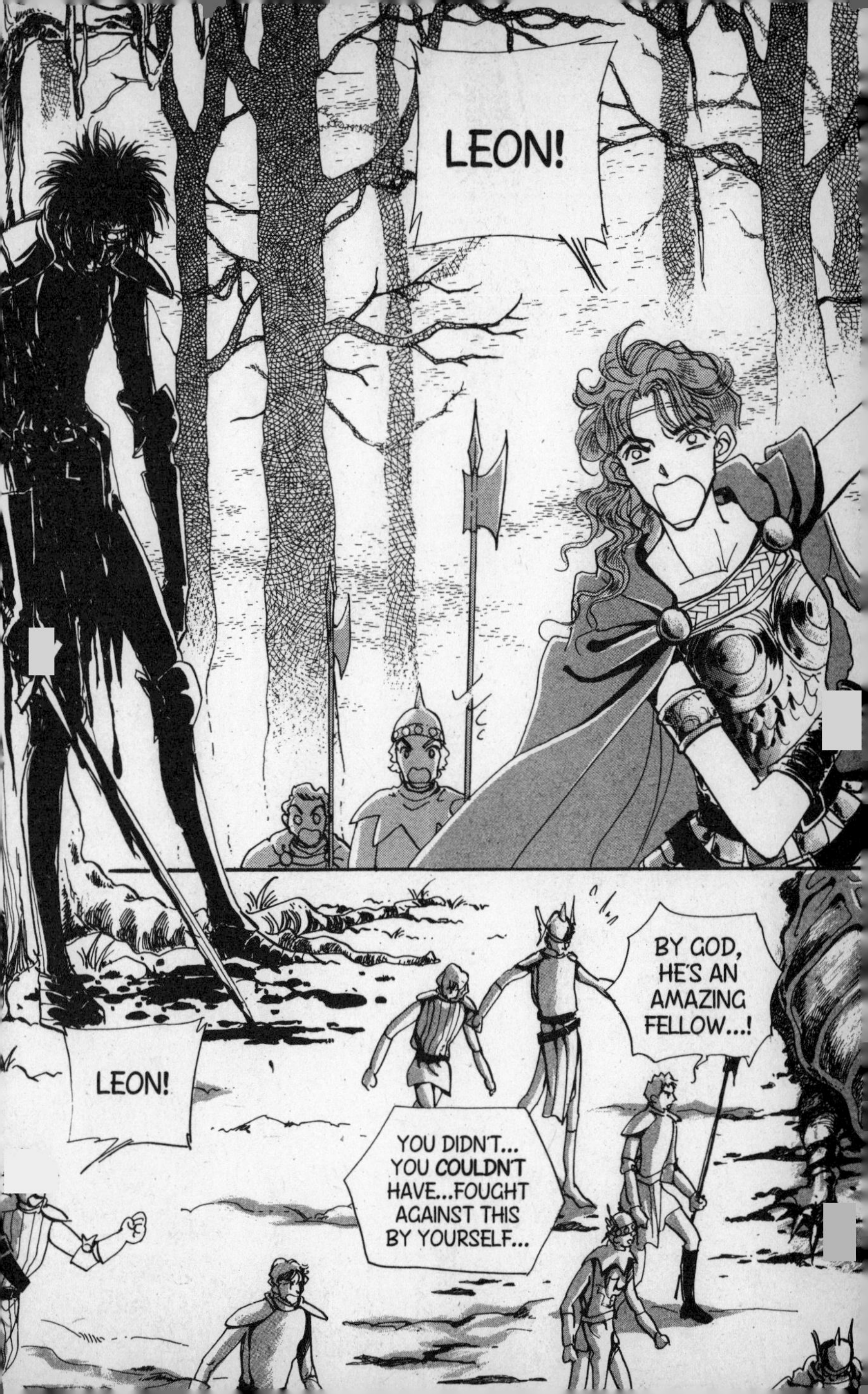
LEON!
LEON!
BY GOD, HE'S AN AMAZING FELLOW...!
YOU DIDN'T... YOU COULDN'T HAVE...FOUGHT AGAINST THIS BY YOURSELF...

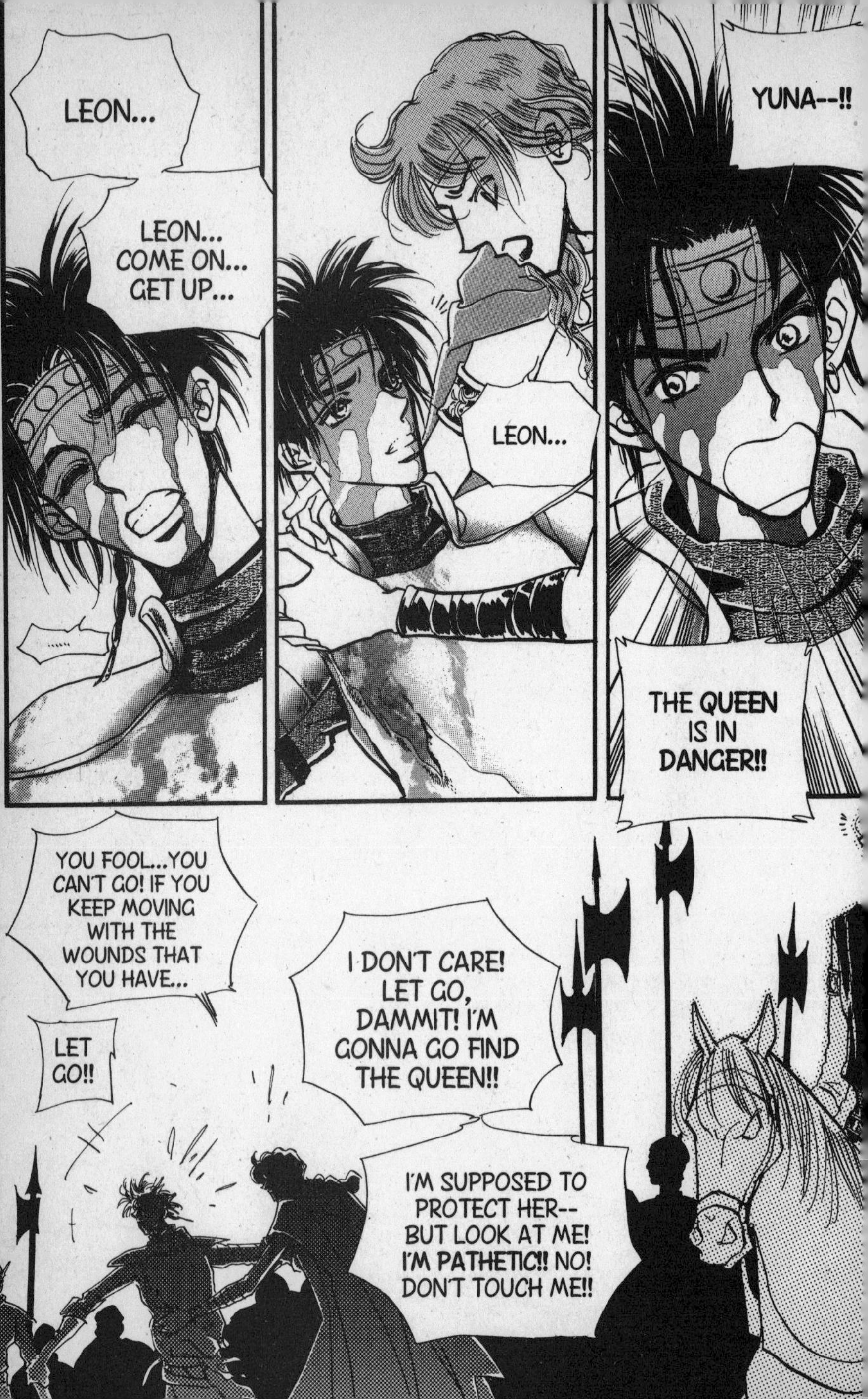
LEON...
LEON... COME ON... GET UP...
......
LEON...
YUNA--!!
THE QUEEN IS IN DANGER!!
YOU FOOL...YOU CAN'T GO! IF YOU KEEP MOVING WITH THE WOUNDS THAT YOU HAVE...
LET GO!!
I DON'T CARE! LET GO, DAMMIT! I'M GONNA GO FIND THE QUEEN!!
I'M SUPPOSED TO PROTECT HER-- BUT LOOK AT ME! I'M PATHETIC!! NO! DON'T TOUCH ME!!

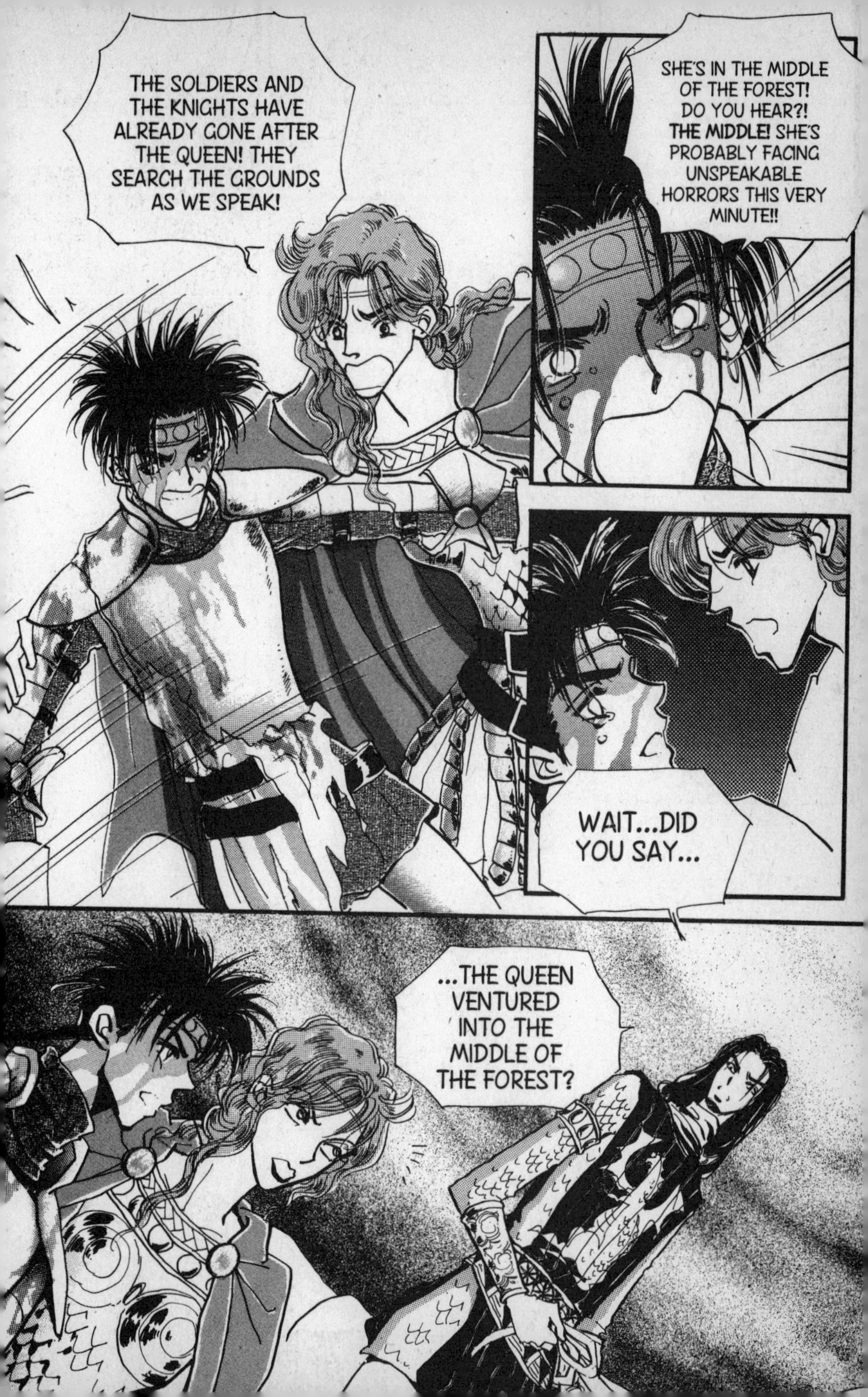
THE SOLDIERS AND THE KNIGHTS HAVE ALREADY GONE AFTER THE QUEEN! THEY SEARCH THE GROUNDS AS WE SPEAK!
SHE'S IN THE MIDDLE OF THE FOREST! DO YOU HEAR?! **THE MIDDLE!** SHE'S PROBABLY FACING UNSPEAKABLE HORRORS THIS VERY MINUTE!!
WAIT...DID YOU SAY...
...THE QUEEN VENTURED INTO THE MIDDLE OF THE FOREST?

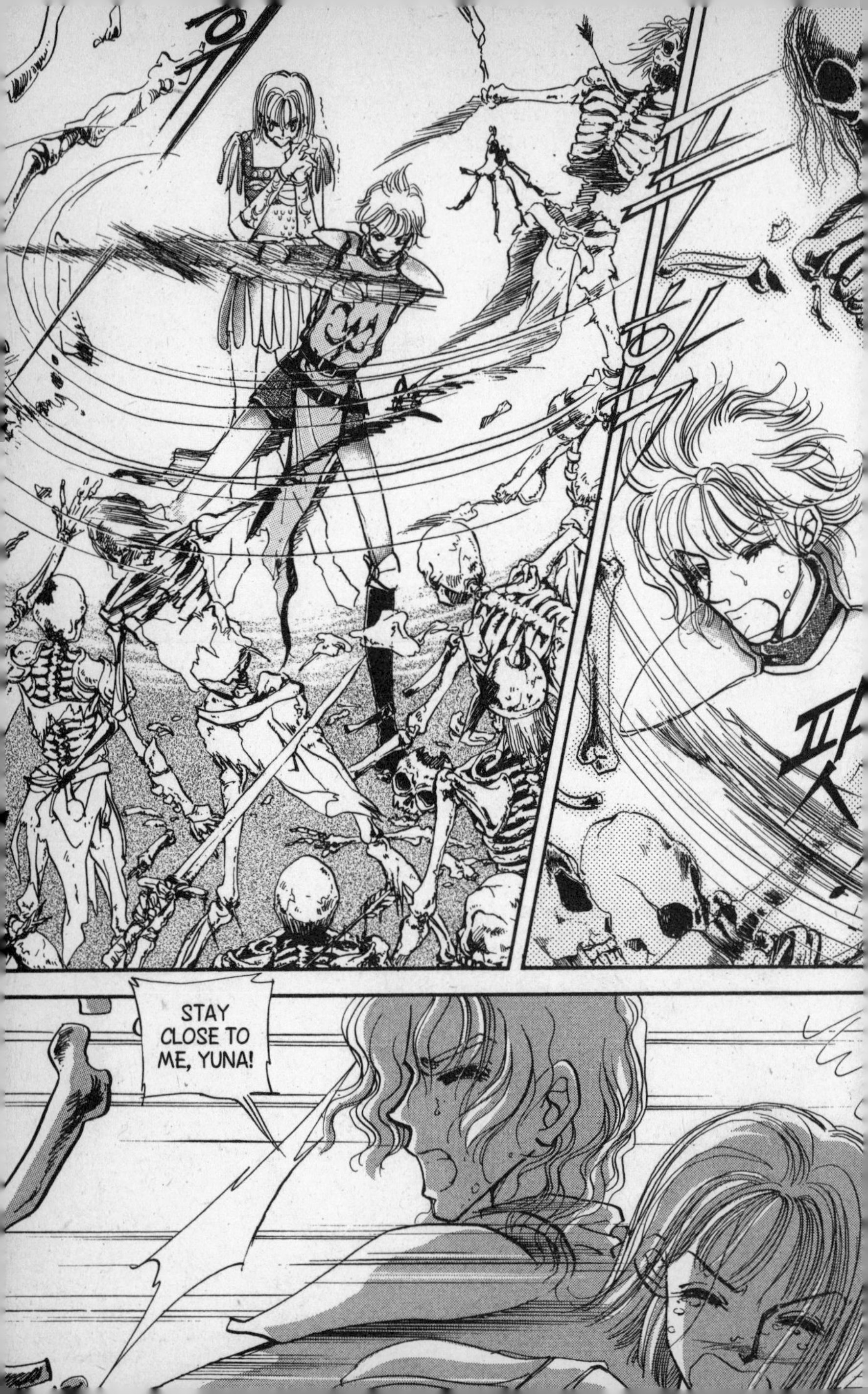
STAY CLOSE TO ME, YUNA!

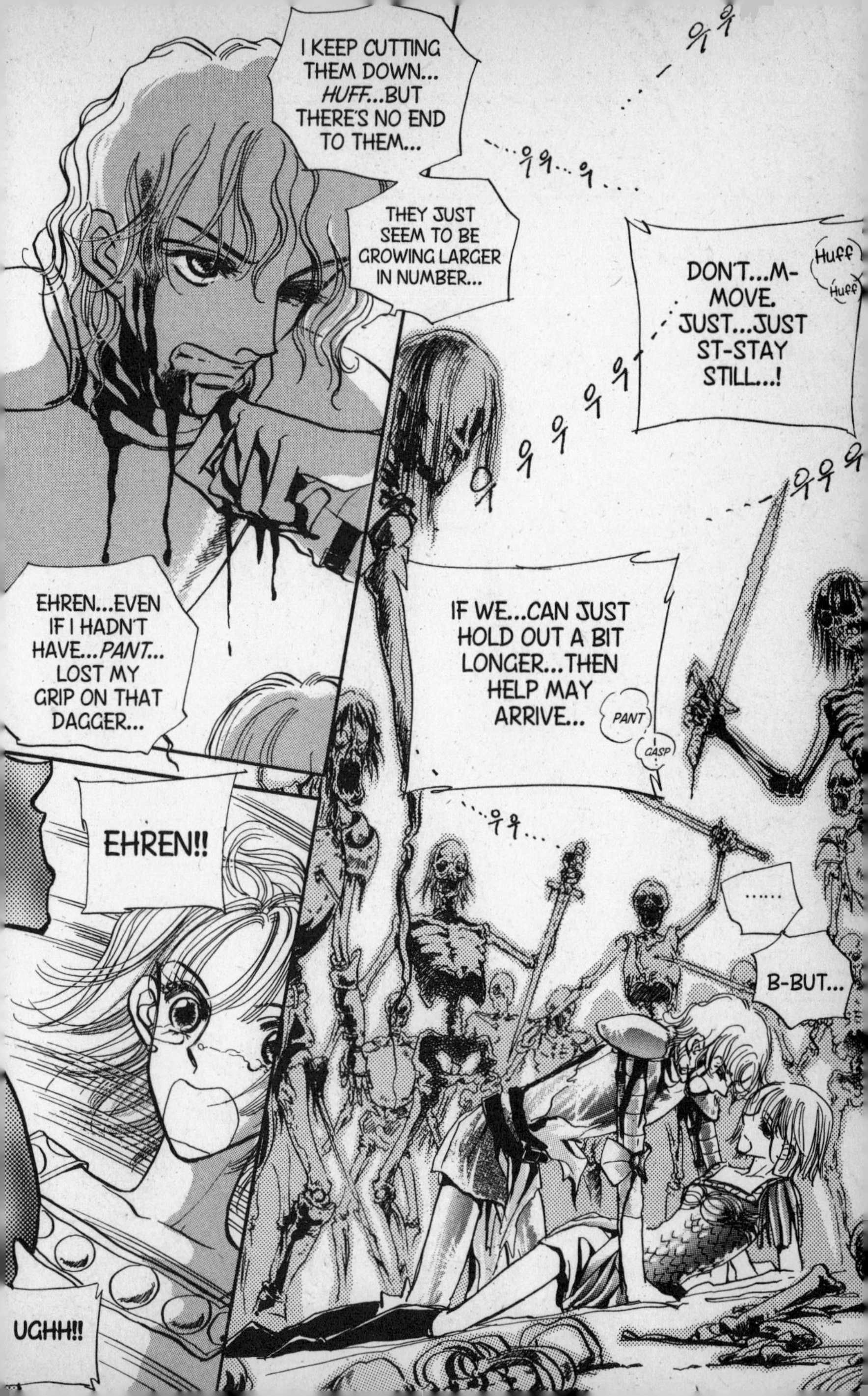
I KEEP CUTTING THEM DOWN... *HUFF*...BUT THERE'S NO END TO THEM...
THEY JUST SEEM TO BE GROWING LARGER IN NUMBER...
DON'T...M-MOVE. JUST...JUST ST-STAY STILL...!
Huff
Huff
EHREN...EVEN IF I HADN'T HAVE...*PANT*... LOST MY GRIP ON THAT DAGGER...
IF WE...CAN JUST HOLD OUT A BIT LONGER...THEN HELP MAY ARRIVE...
PANT
GASP
EHREN!!
UGHH!!
......
B-BUT...

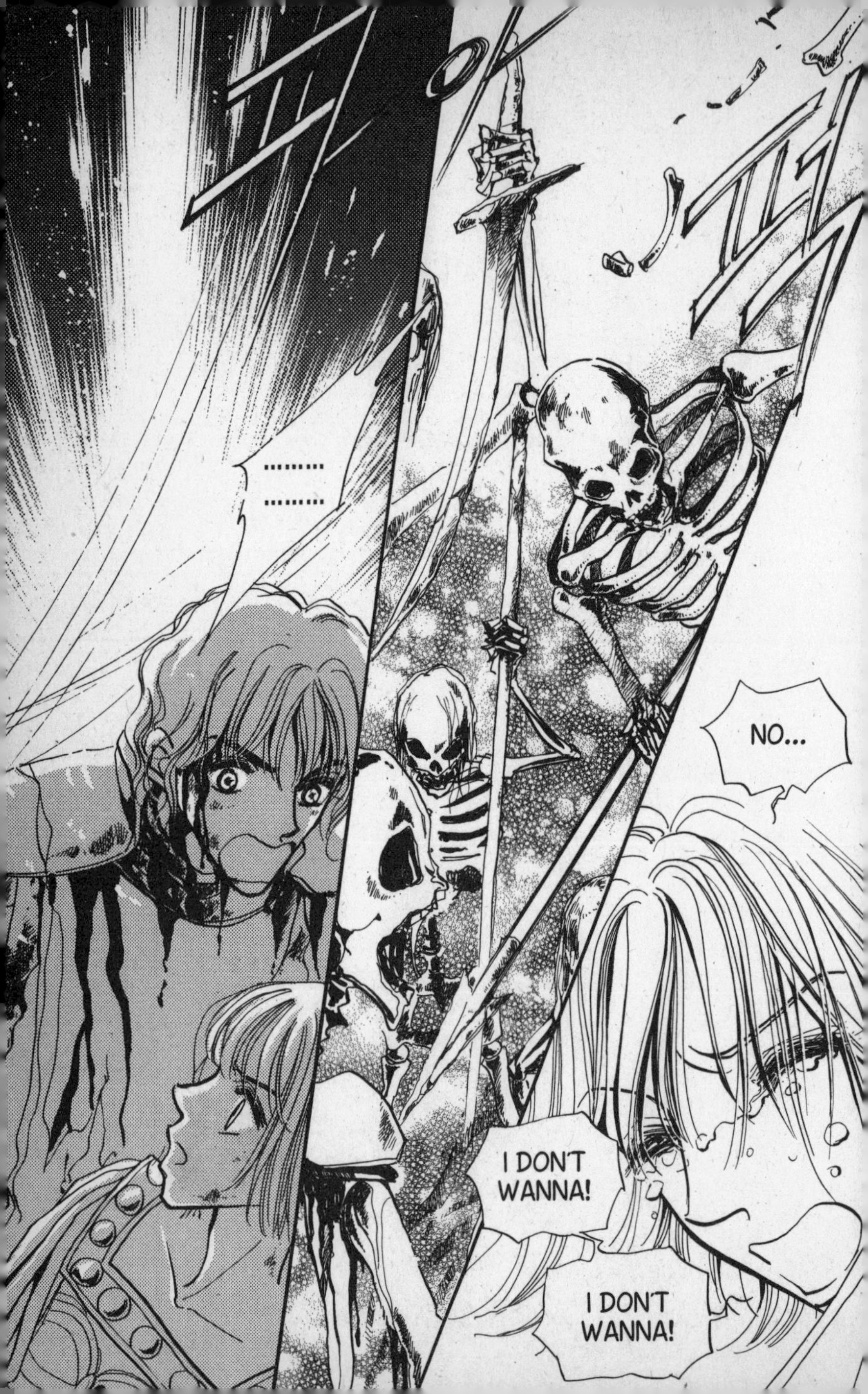

....
....
NO...
I DON'T WANNA!
I DON'T WANNA!

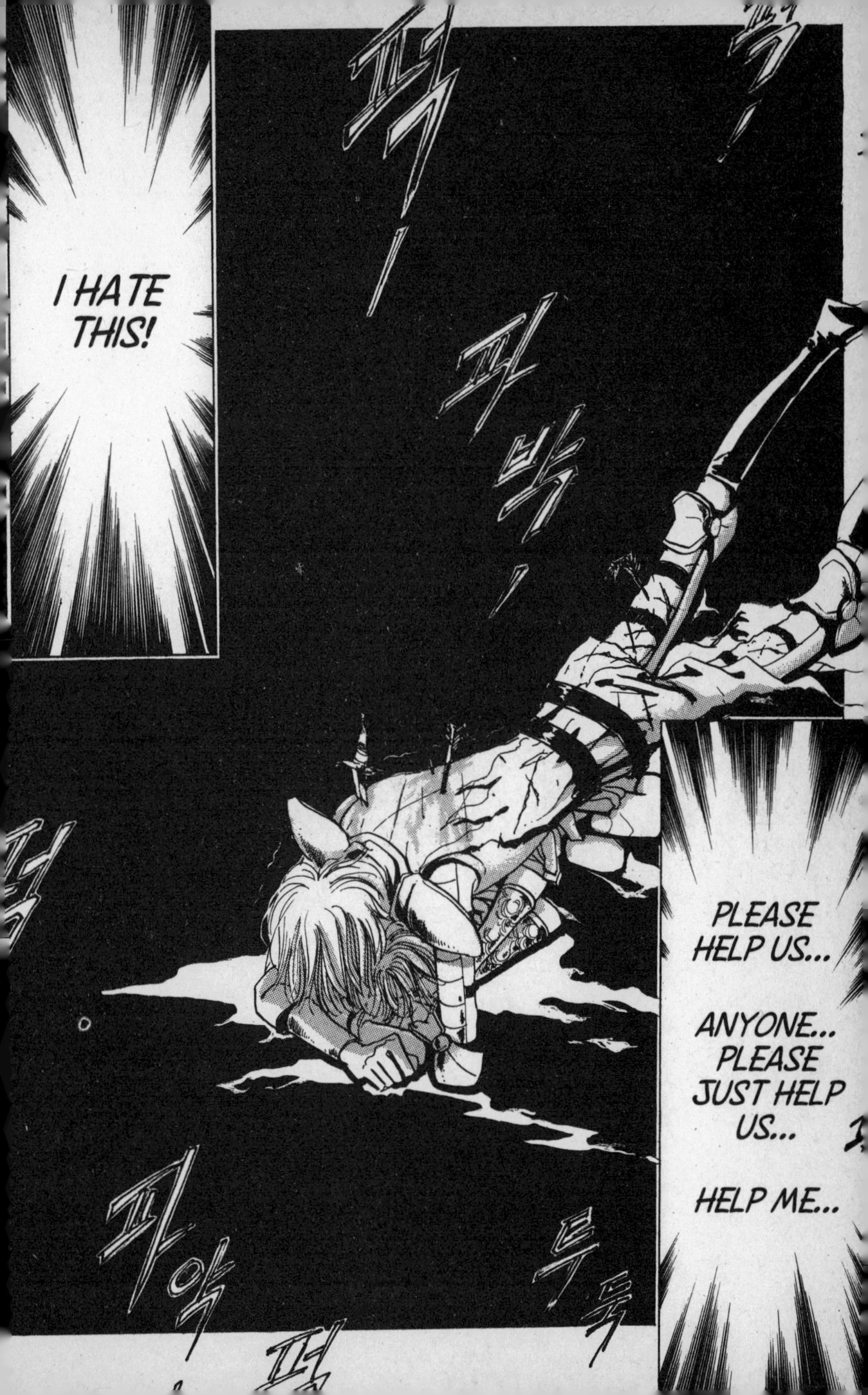
I HATE THIS!
PLEASE HELP US...
ANYONE... PLEASE JUST HELP US...
HELP ME...

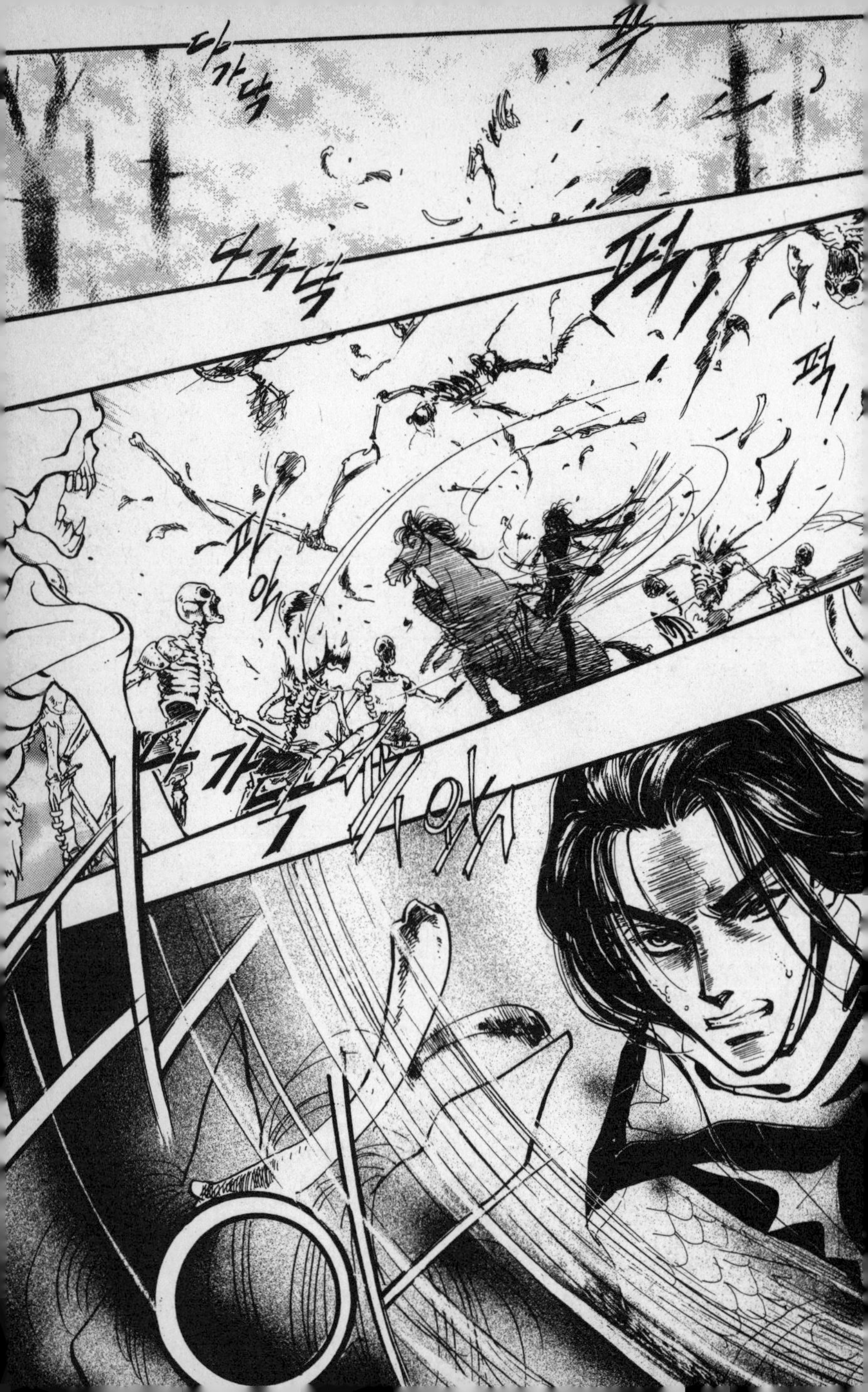

다가닥
퍽
다가닥
퍽!
퍽!
파앗
다가닥

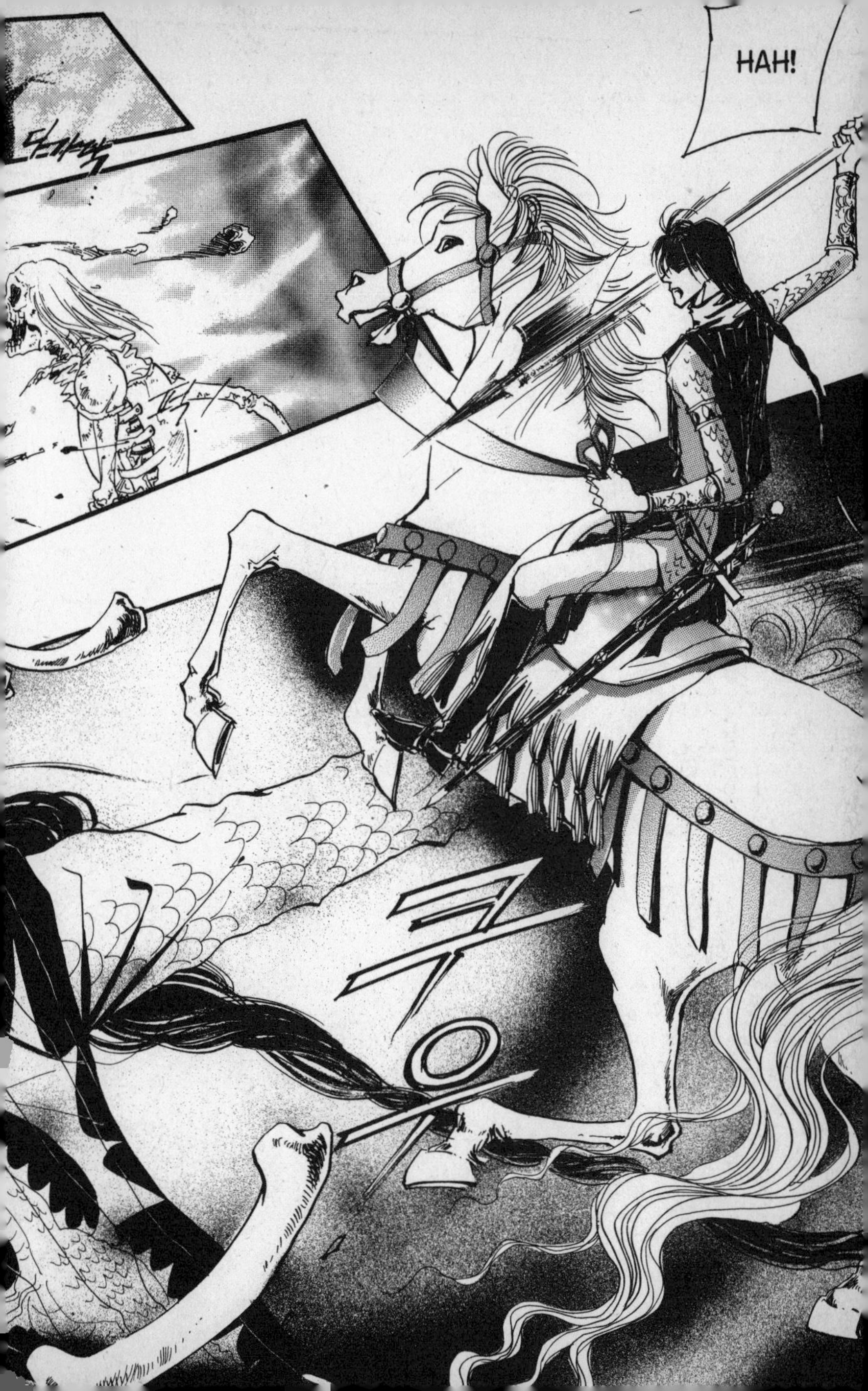
HAH!

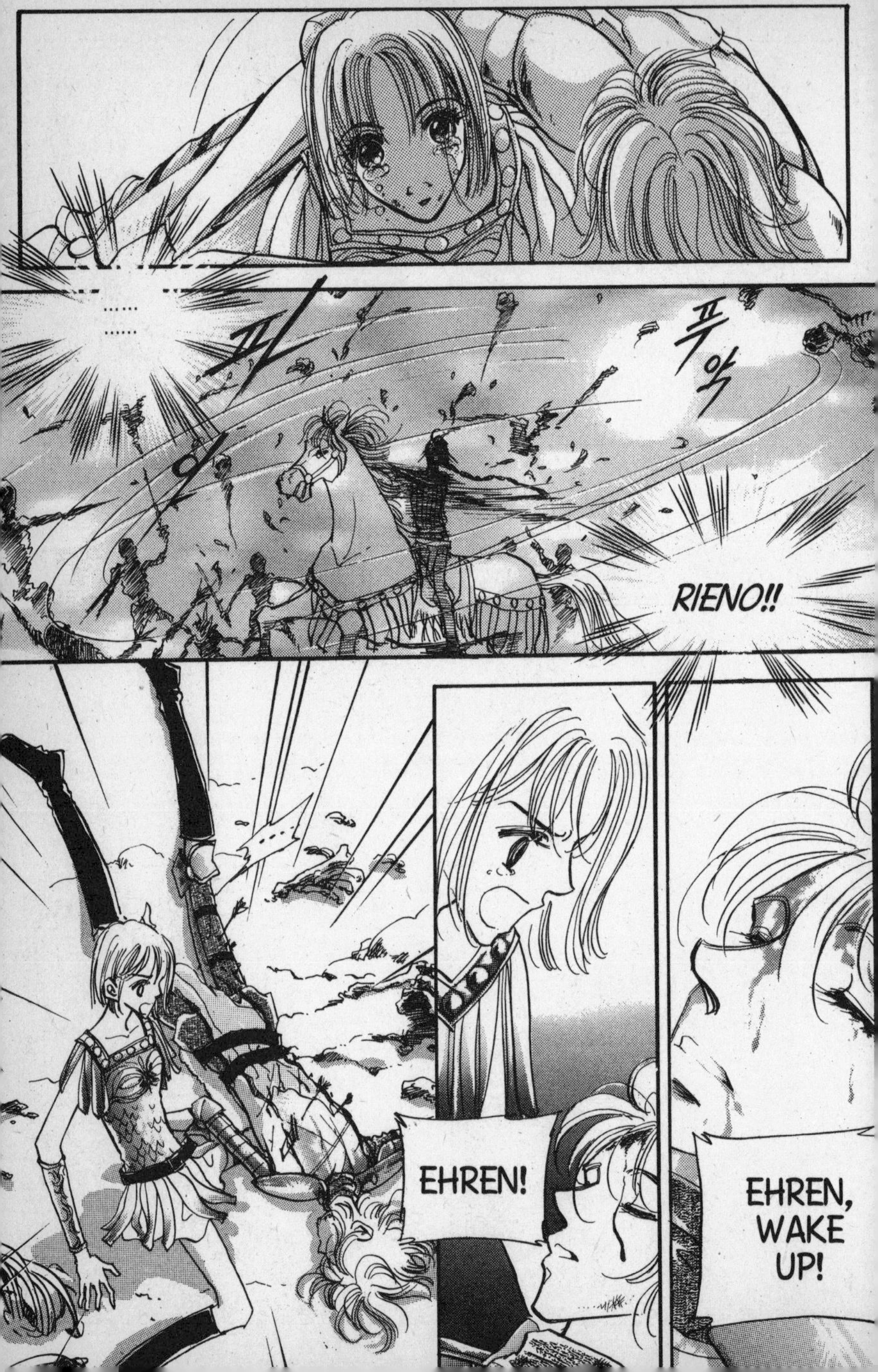
......
......
푸악
RIENO!!
...
EHREN!
EHREN, WAKE UP!

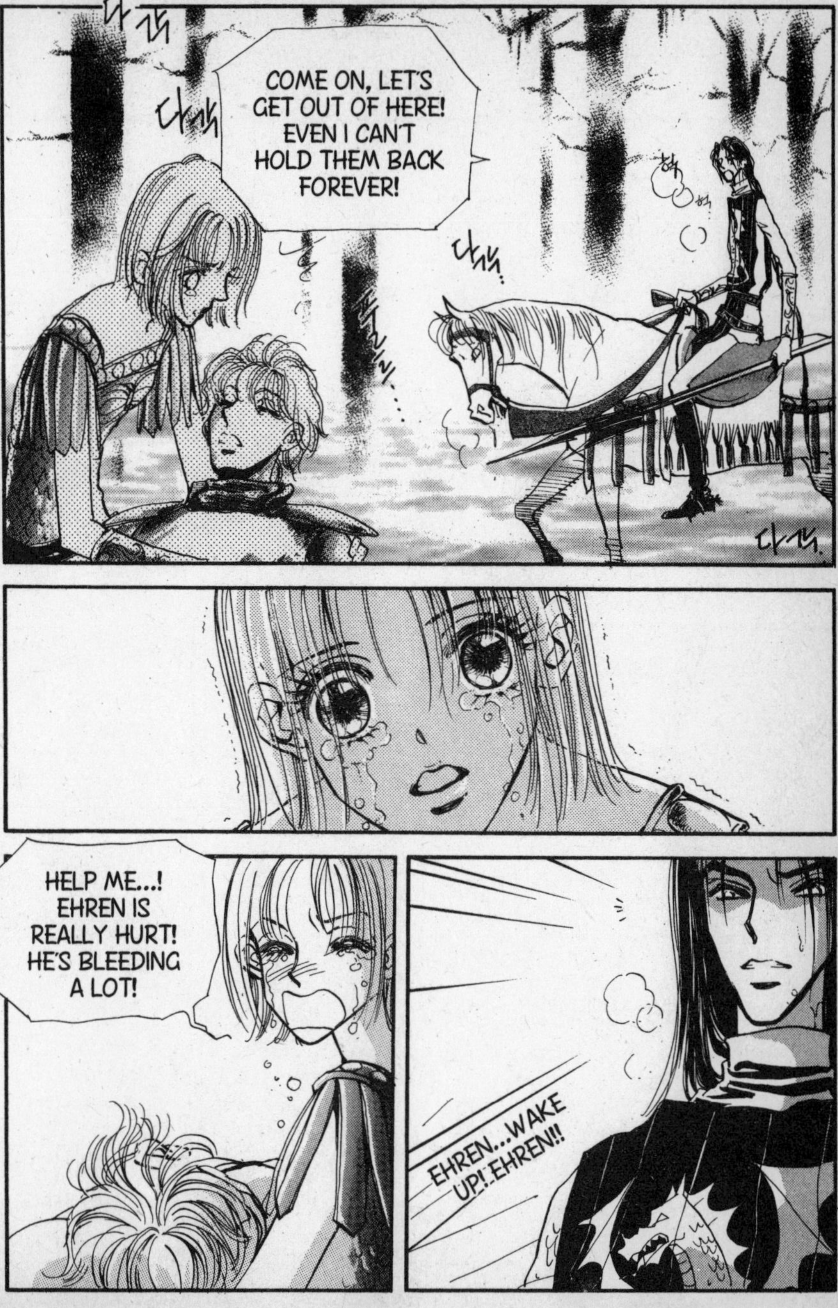
COME ON, LET'S GET OUT OF HERE! EVEN I CAN'T HOLD THEM BACK FOREVER!
HELP ME...! EHREN IS REALLY HURT! HE'S BLEEDING A LOT!
EHREN...WAKE UP!. EHREN!!

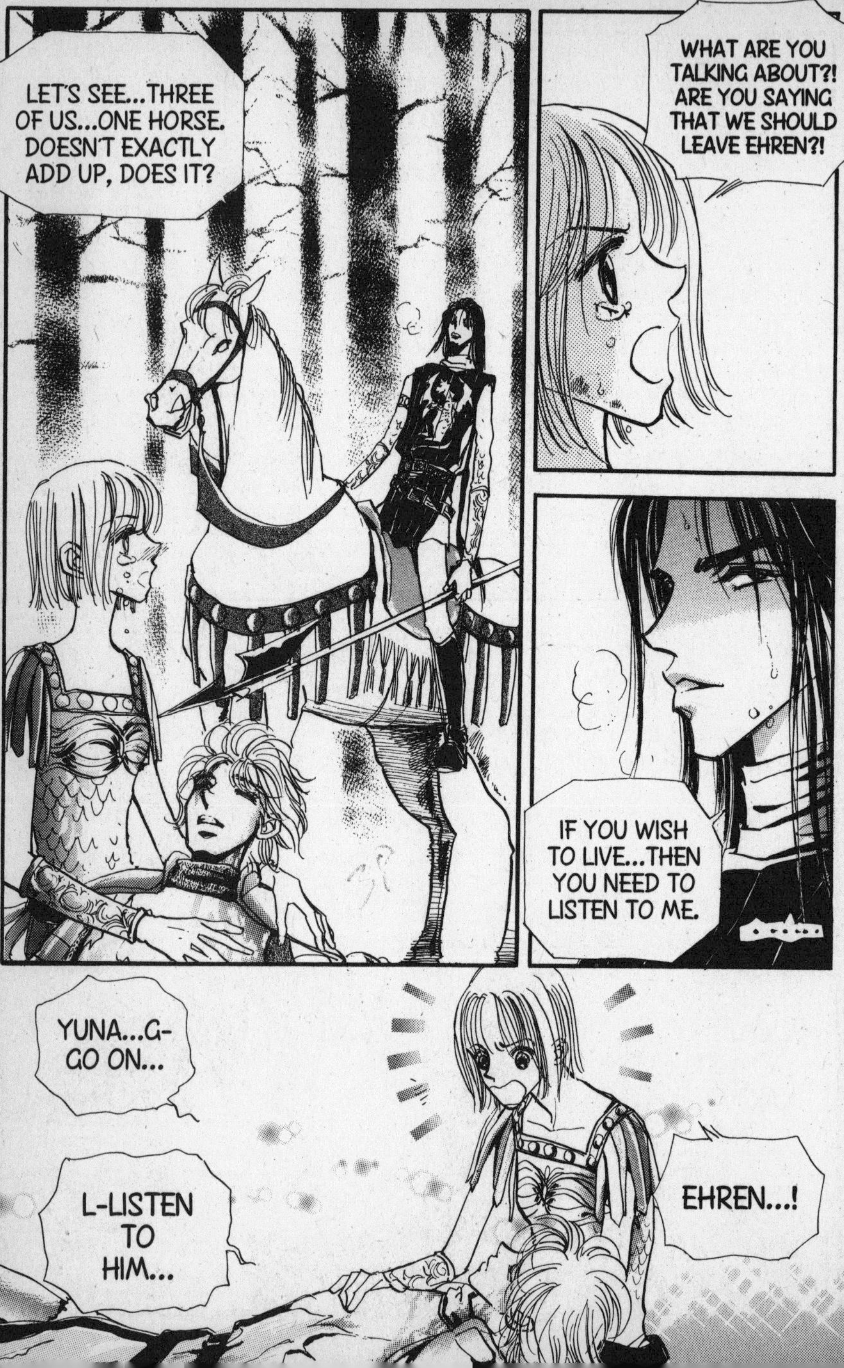
LET'S SEE...THREE OF US...ONE HORSE. DOESN'T EXACTLY ADD UP, DOES IT?
WHAT ARE YOU TALKING ABOUT?! ARE YOU SAYING THAT WE SHOULD LEAVE EHREN?!
IF YOU WISH TO LIVE...THEN YOU NEED TO LISTEN TO ME.
YUNA...G-GO ON...
L-LISTEN TO HIM...
EHREN...!

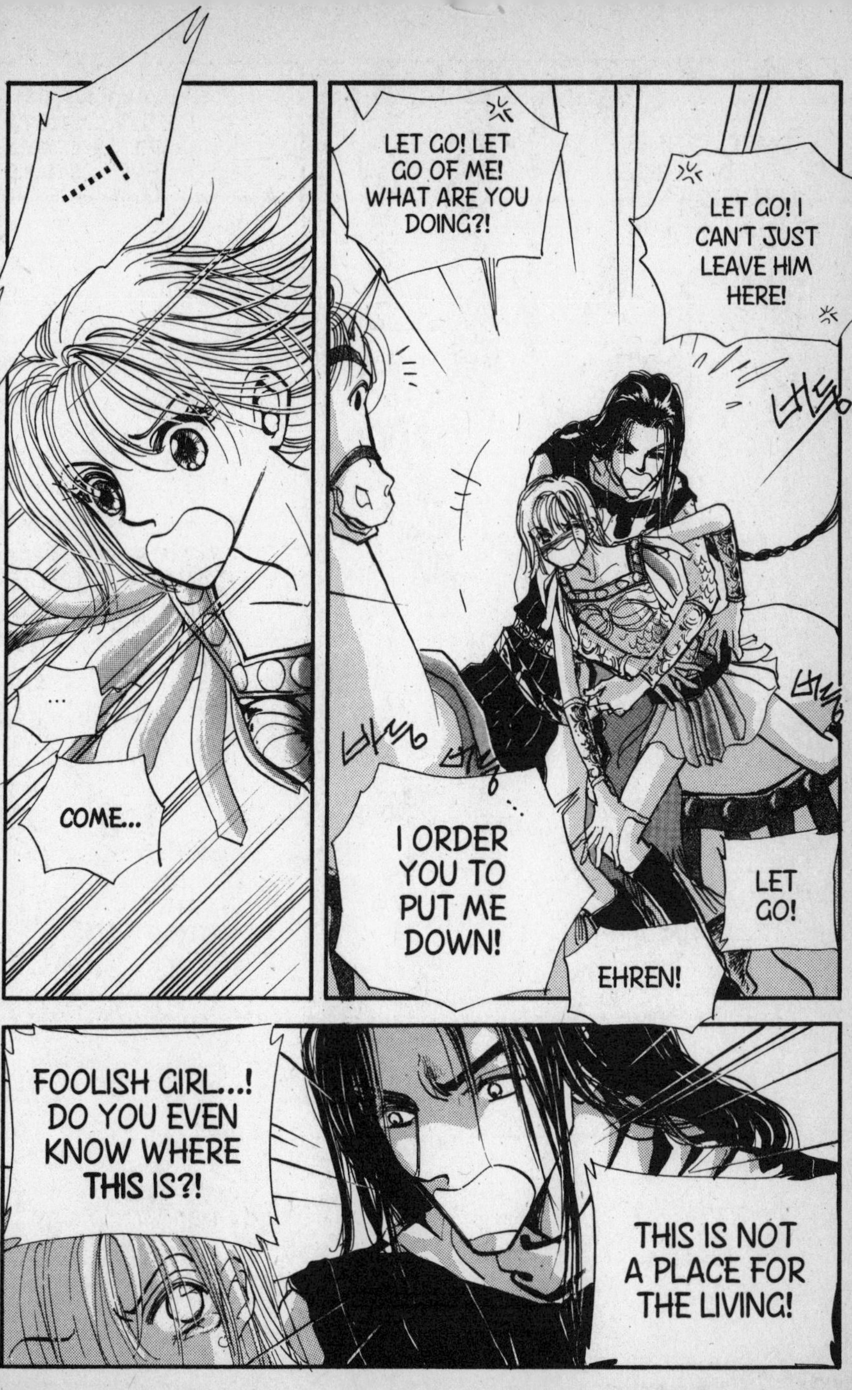
.....!
...
COME...
LET GO! LET GO OF ME! WHAT ARE YOU DOING?!
LET GO! I CAN'T JUST LEAVE HIM HERE!
I ORDER YOU TO PUT ME DOWN!
EHREN!
LET GO!
FOOLISH GIRL...! DO YOU EVEN KNOW WHERE THIS IS?!
THIS IS NOT A PLACE FOR THE LIVING!

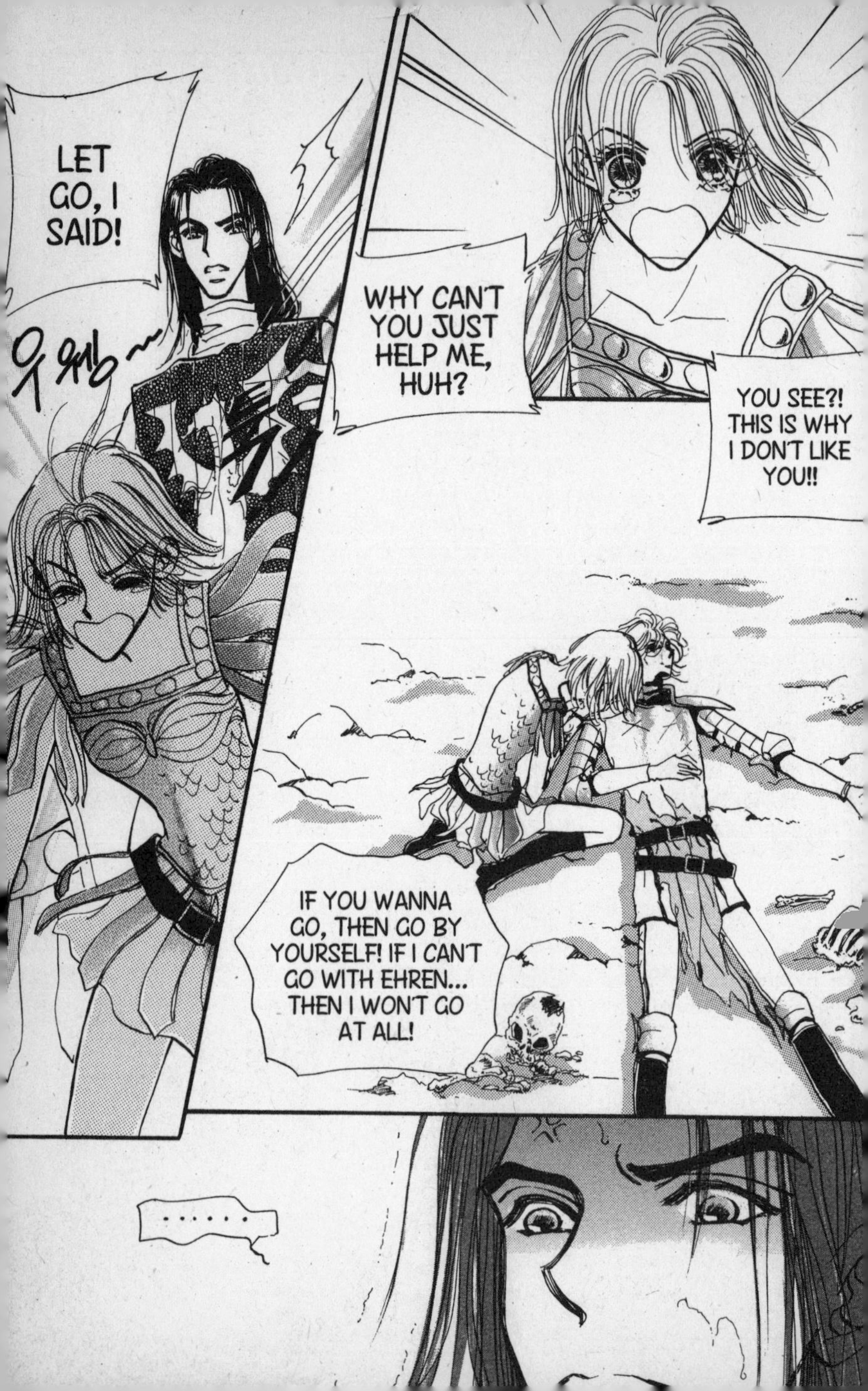
LET GO, I SAID!
WHY CAN'T YOU JUST HELP ME, HUH?
YOU SEE?! THIS IS WHY I DON'T LIKE YOU!!
IF YOU WANNA GO, THEN GO BY YOURSELF! IF I CAN'T GO WITH EHREN... THEN I WON'T GO AT ALL!
......

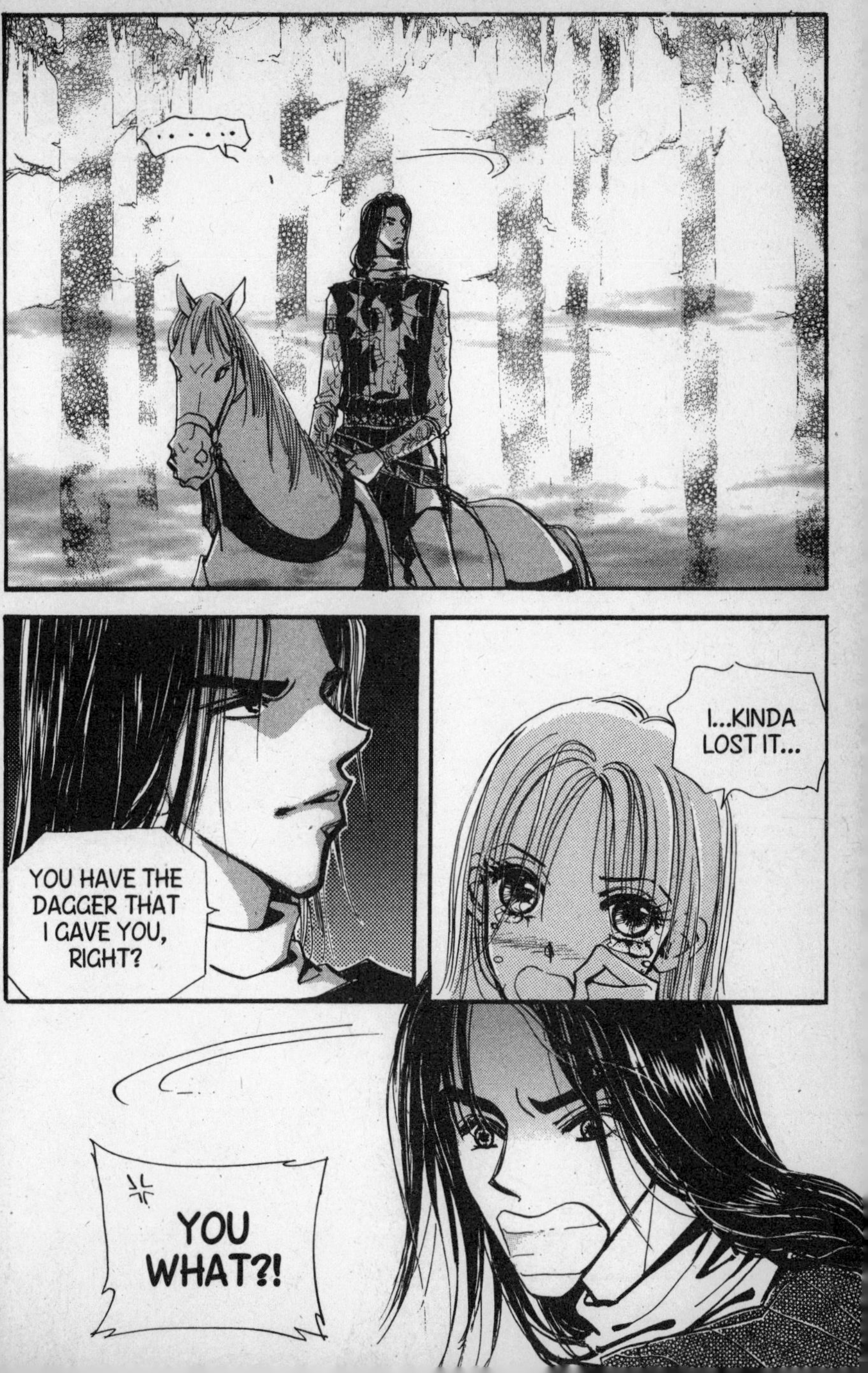
......
YOU HAVE THE DAGGER THAT I GAVE YOU, RIGHT?
I...KINDA LOST IT...
YOU WHAT?!

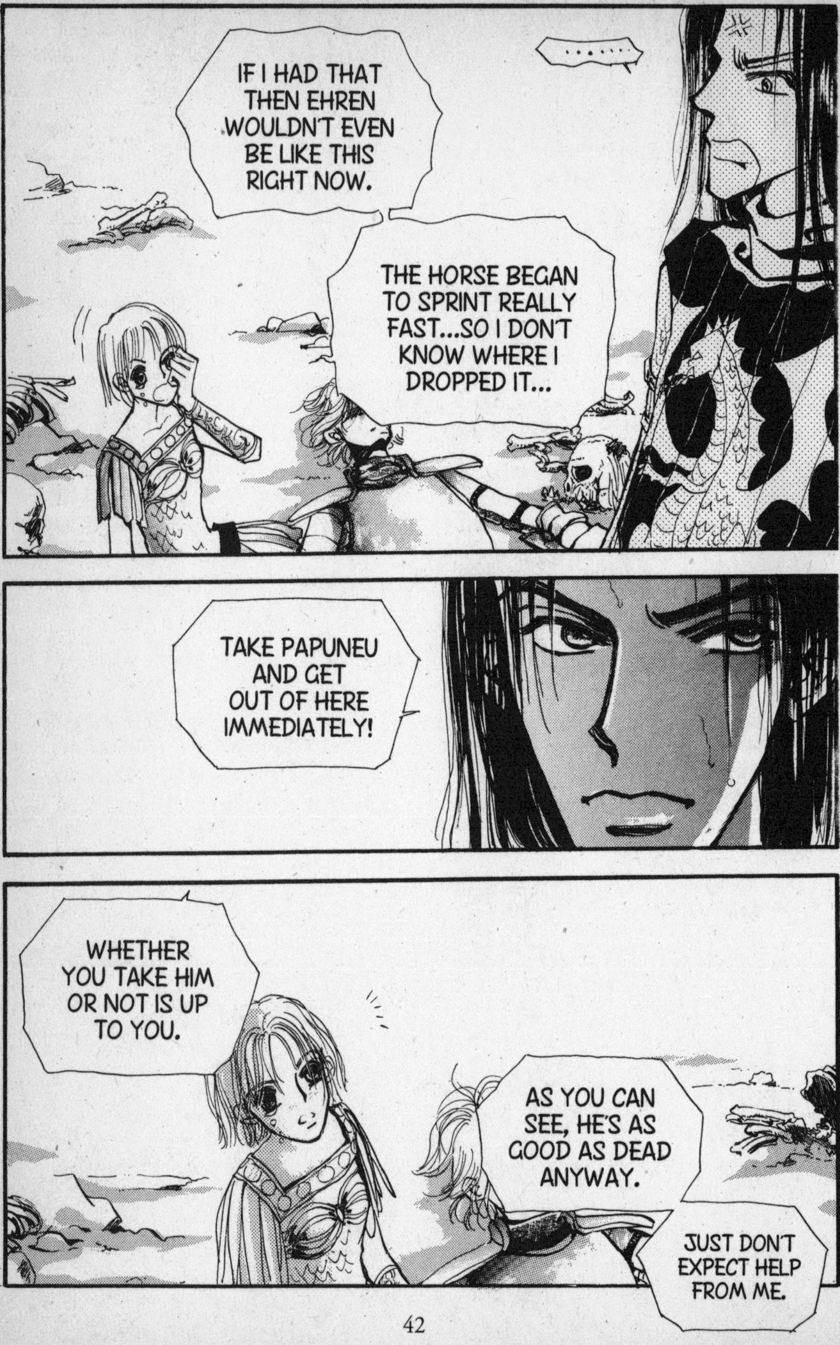
IF I HAD THAT THEN EHREN WOULDN'T EVEN BE LIKE THIS RIGHT NOW.
THE HORSE BEGAN TO SPRINT REALLY FAST...SO I DON'T KNOW WHERE I DROPPED IT...
....
TAKE PAPUNEU AND GET OUT OF HERE IMMEDIATELY!
WHETHER YOU TAKE HIM OR NOT IS UP TO YOU.
AS YOU CAN SEE, HE'S AS GOOD AS DEAD ANYWAY.
JUST DON'T EXPECT HELP FROM ME.

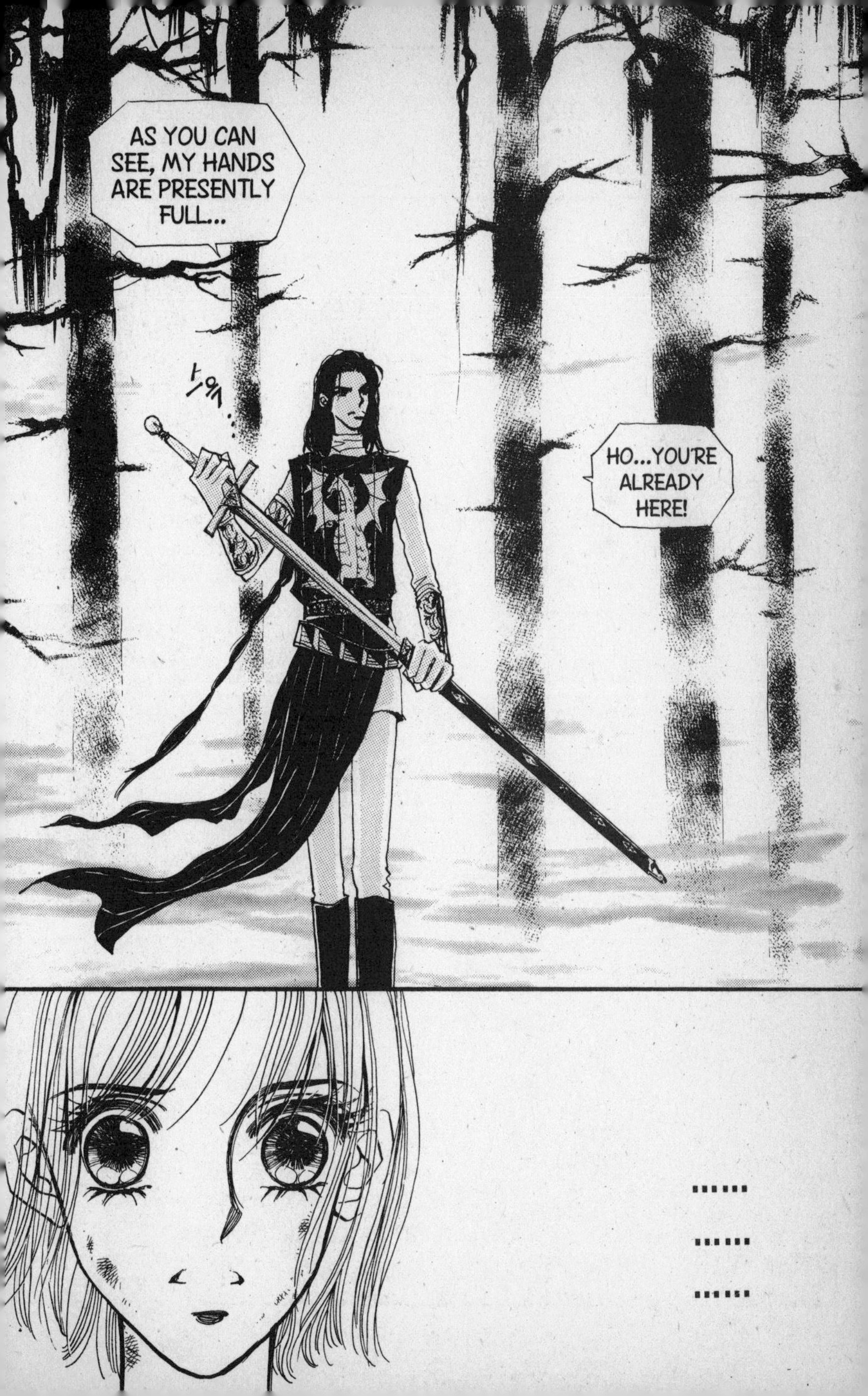
AS YOU CAN SEE, MY HANDS ARE PRESENTLY FULL...
HO...YOU'RE ALREADY HERE!
......
......
......

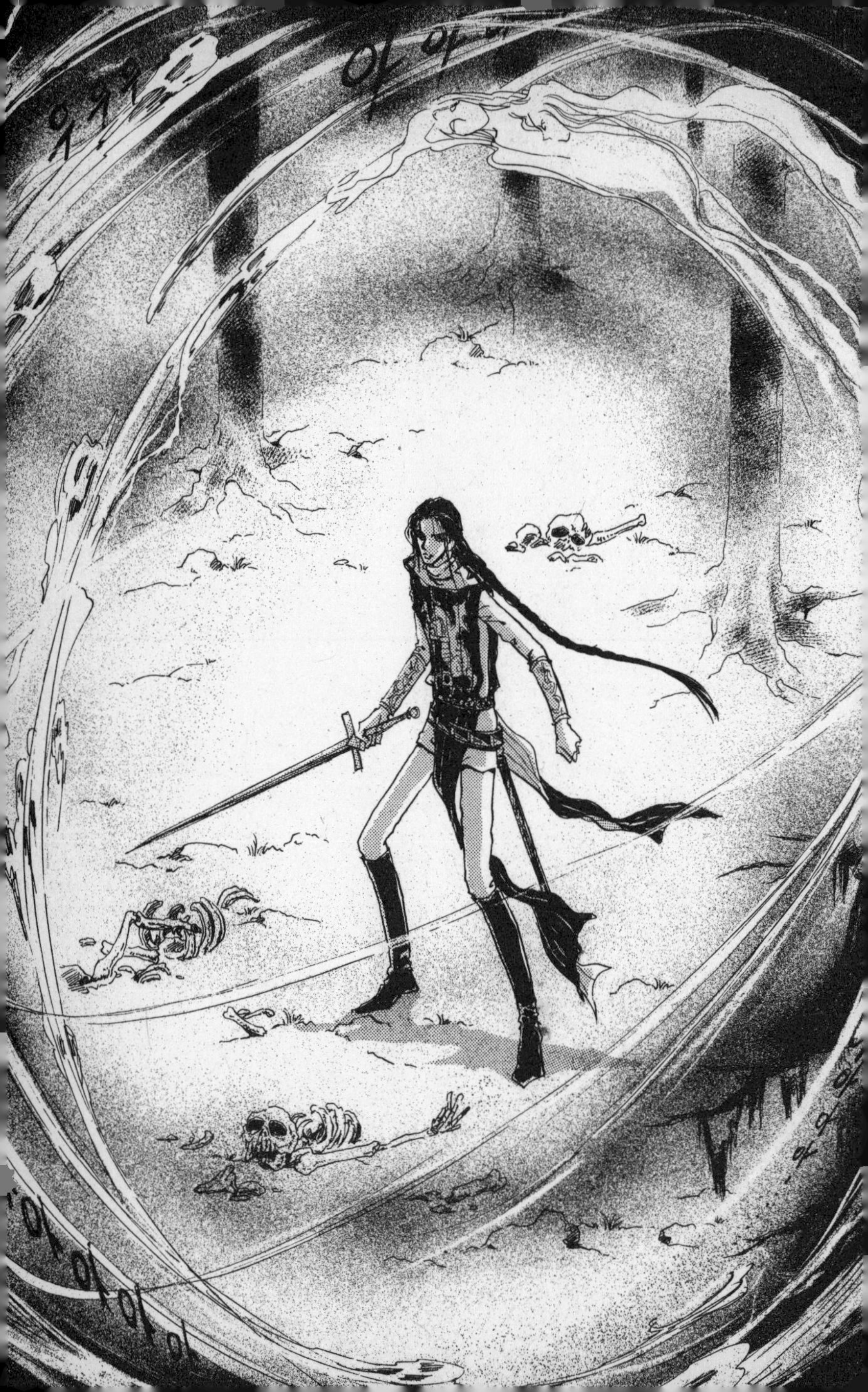

아 아
아아아아아

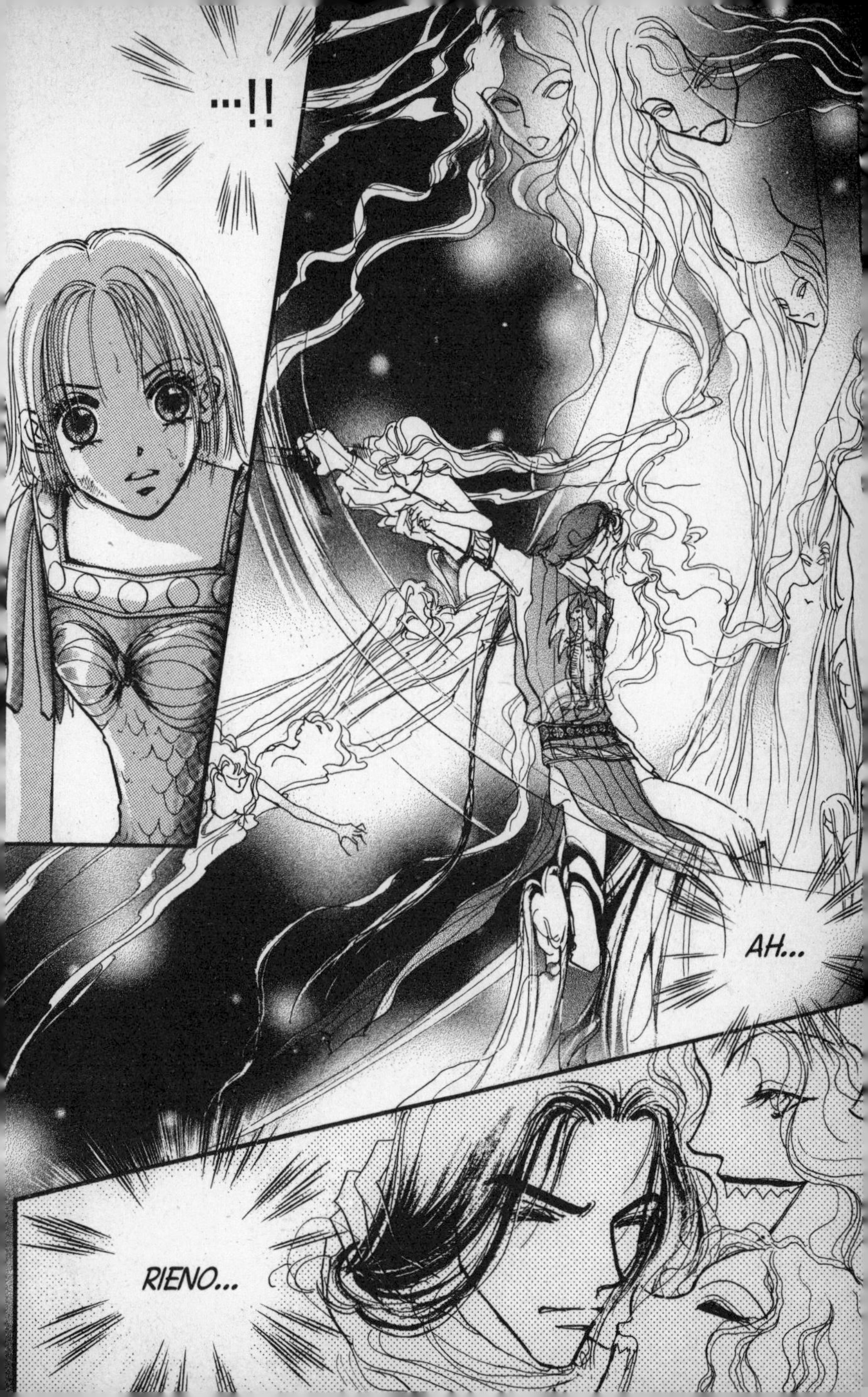
…!!
AH...
RIENO...

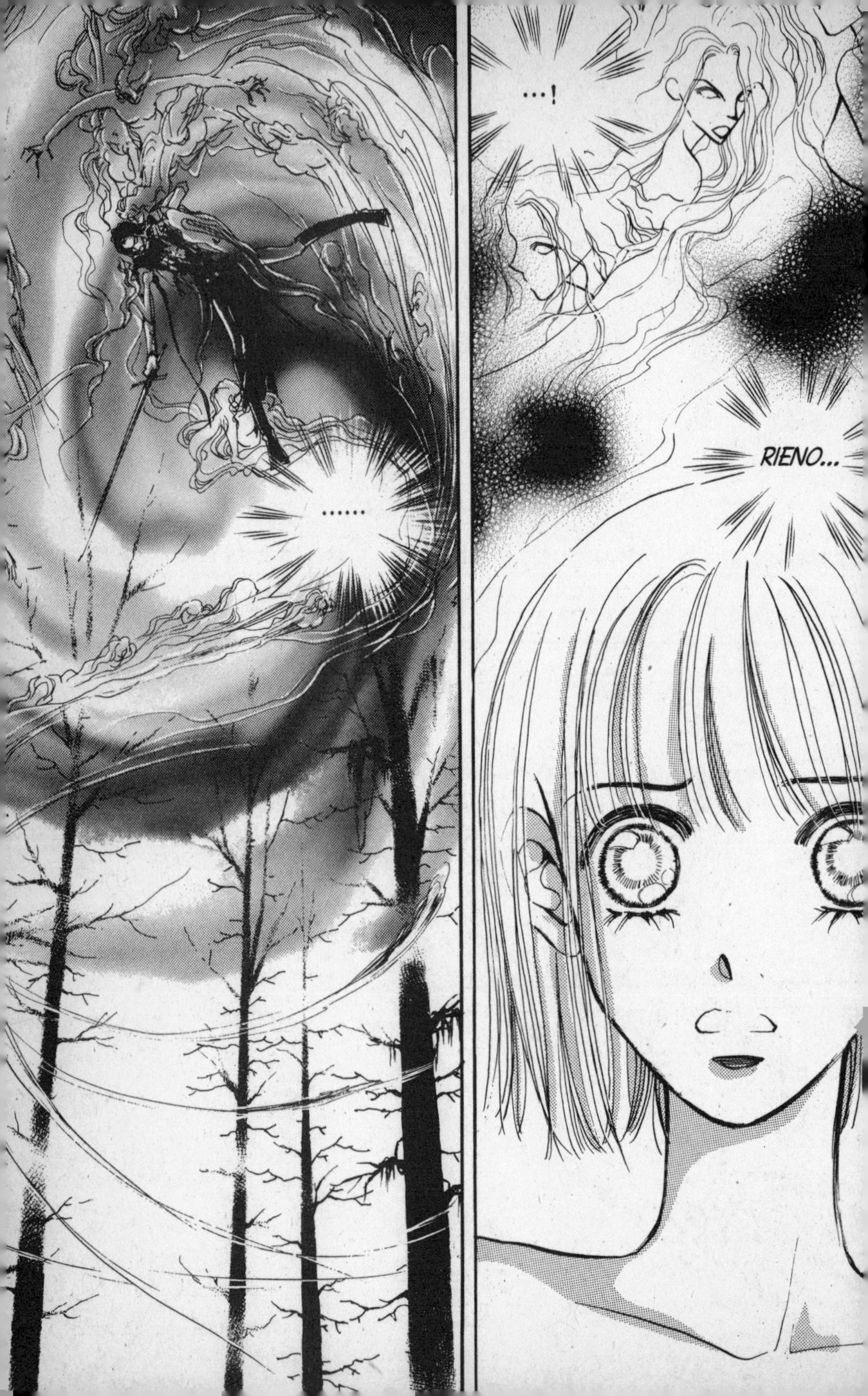
......
...!
RIENO...

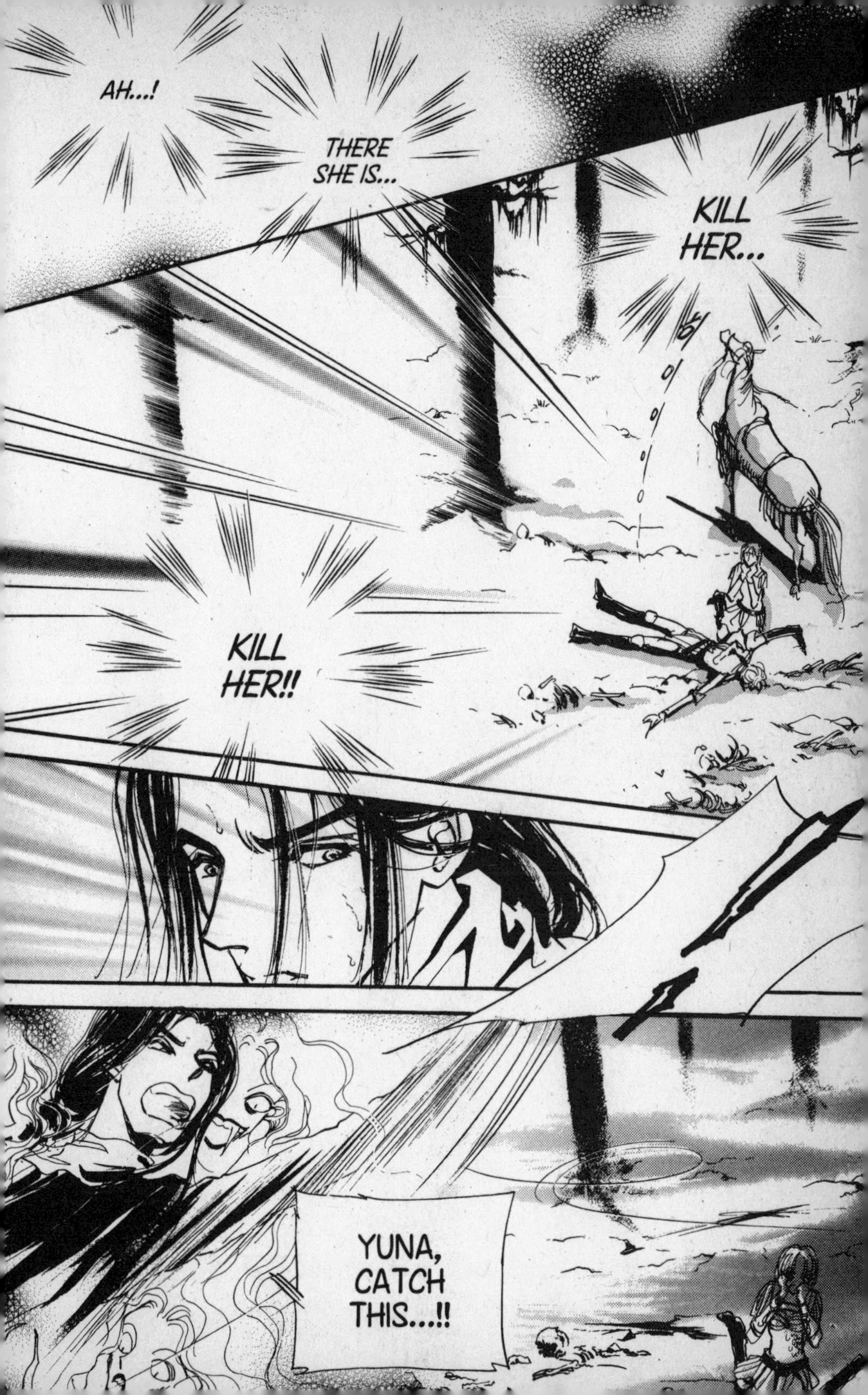
AH...!
THERE SHE IS...
KILL HER...
KILL HER!!
YUNA, CATCH THIS...!!

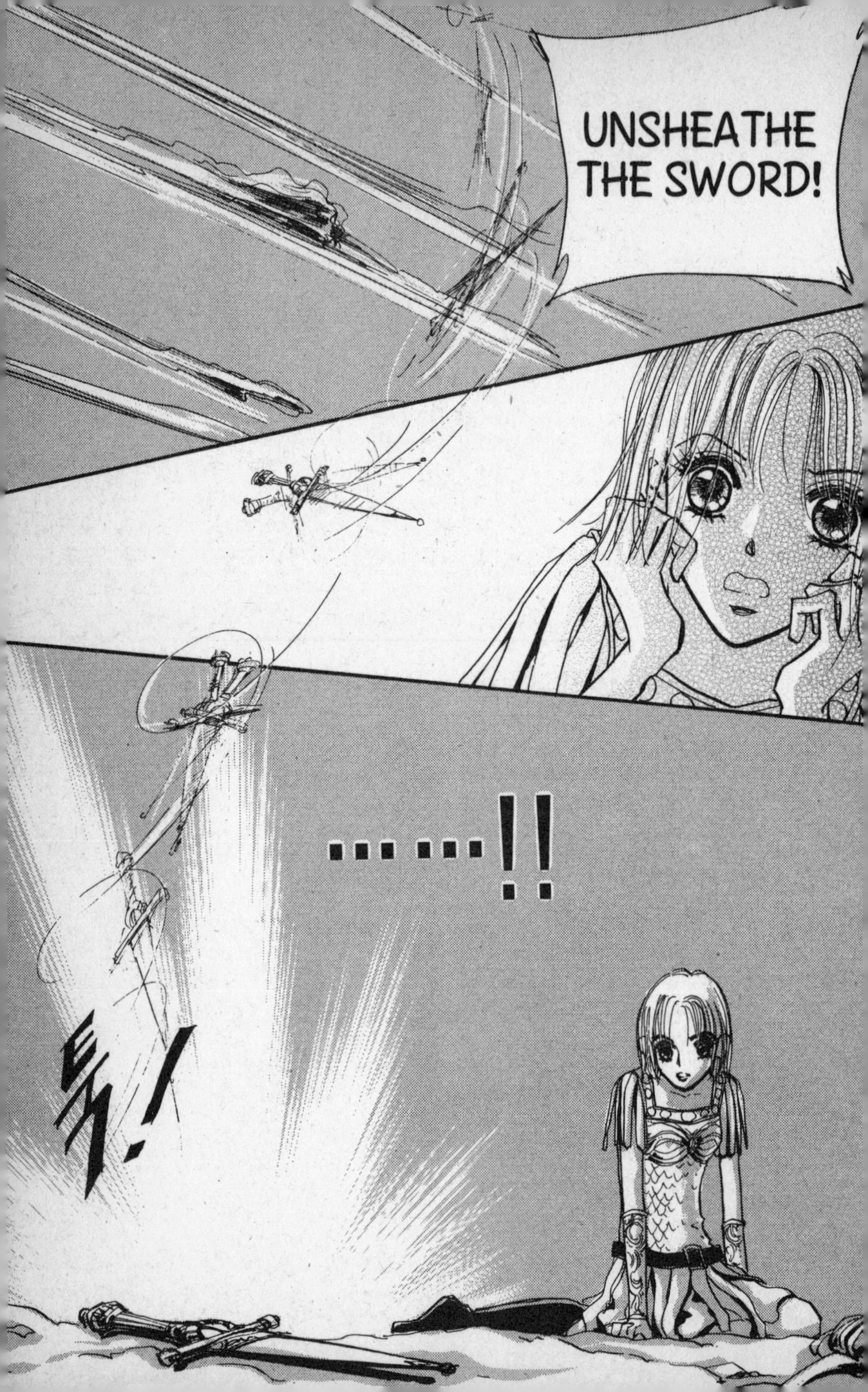
UNSHEATHE THE SWORD!
......!!

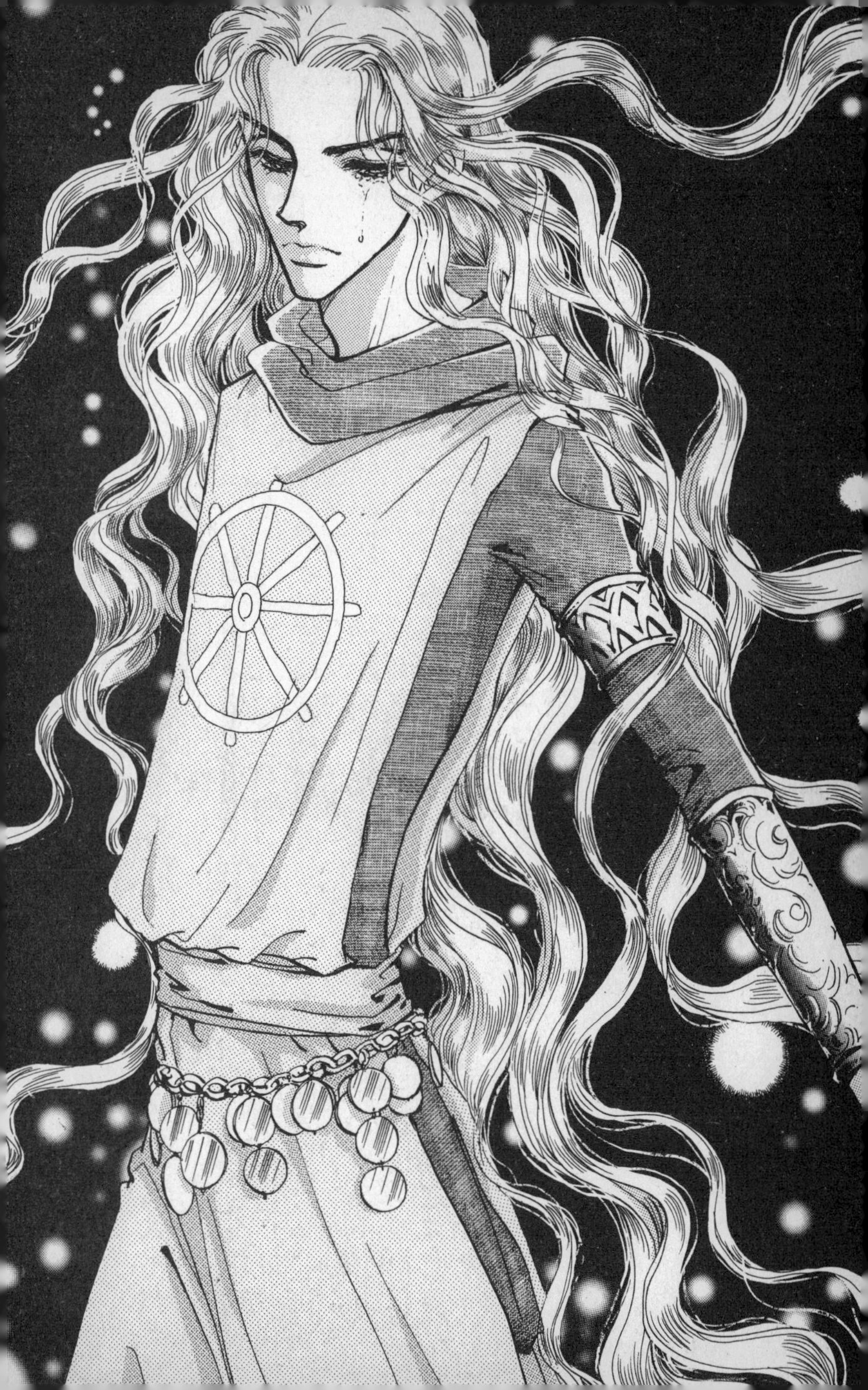

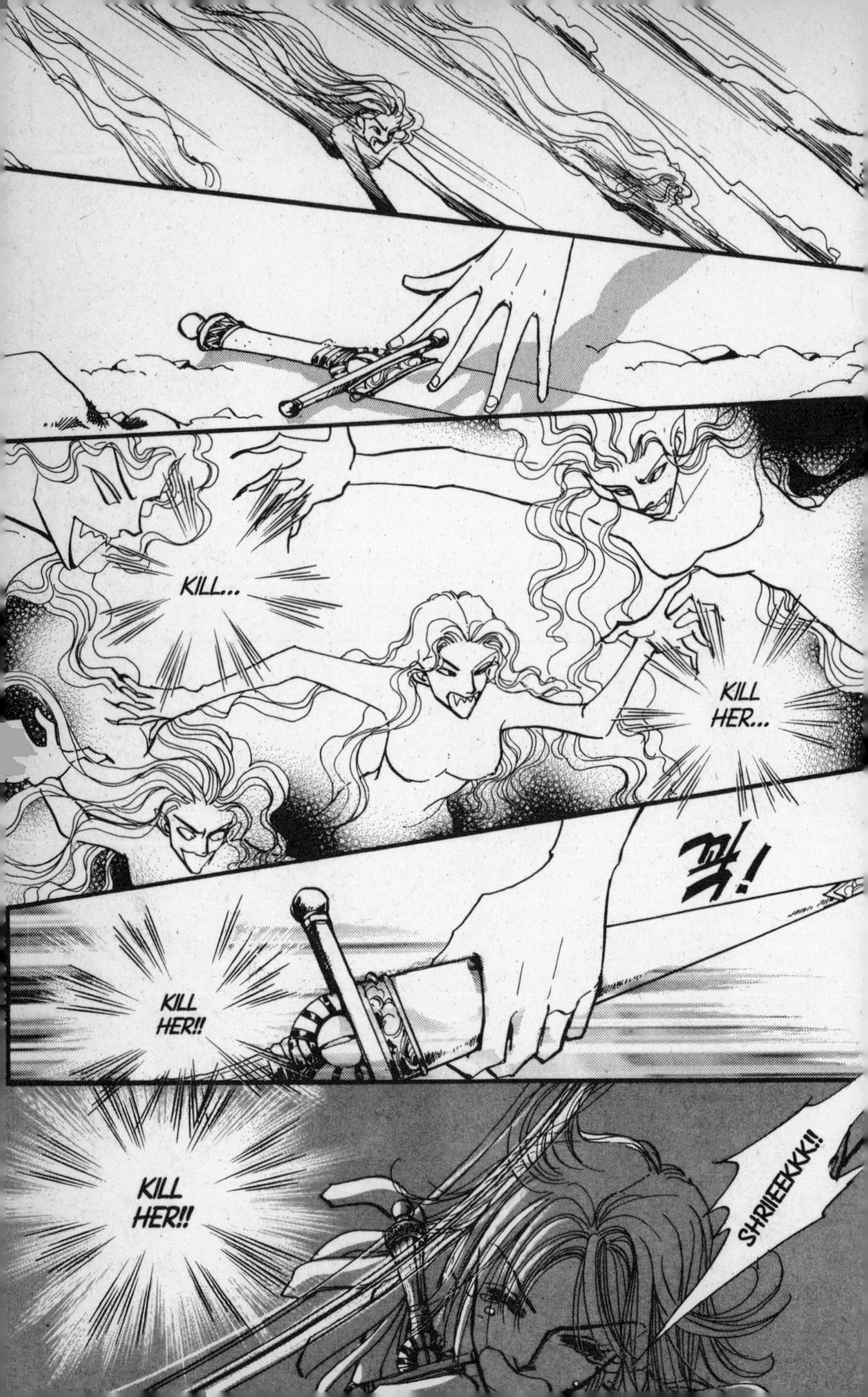
KILL...
KILL HER...
꽉!
KILL HER!!
KILL HER!!
SHRIIEEKKK!!

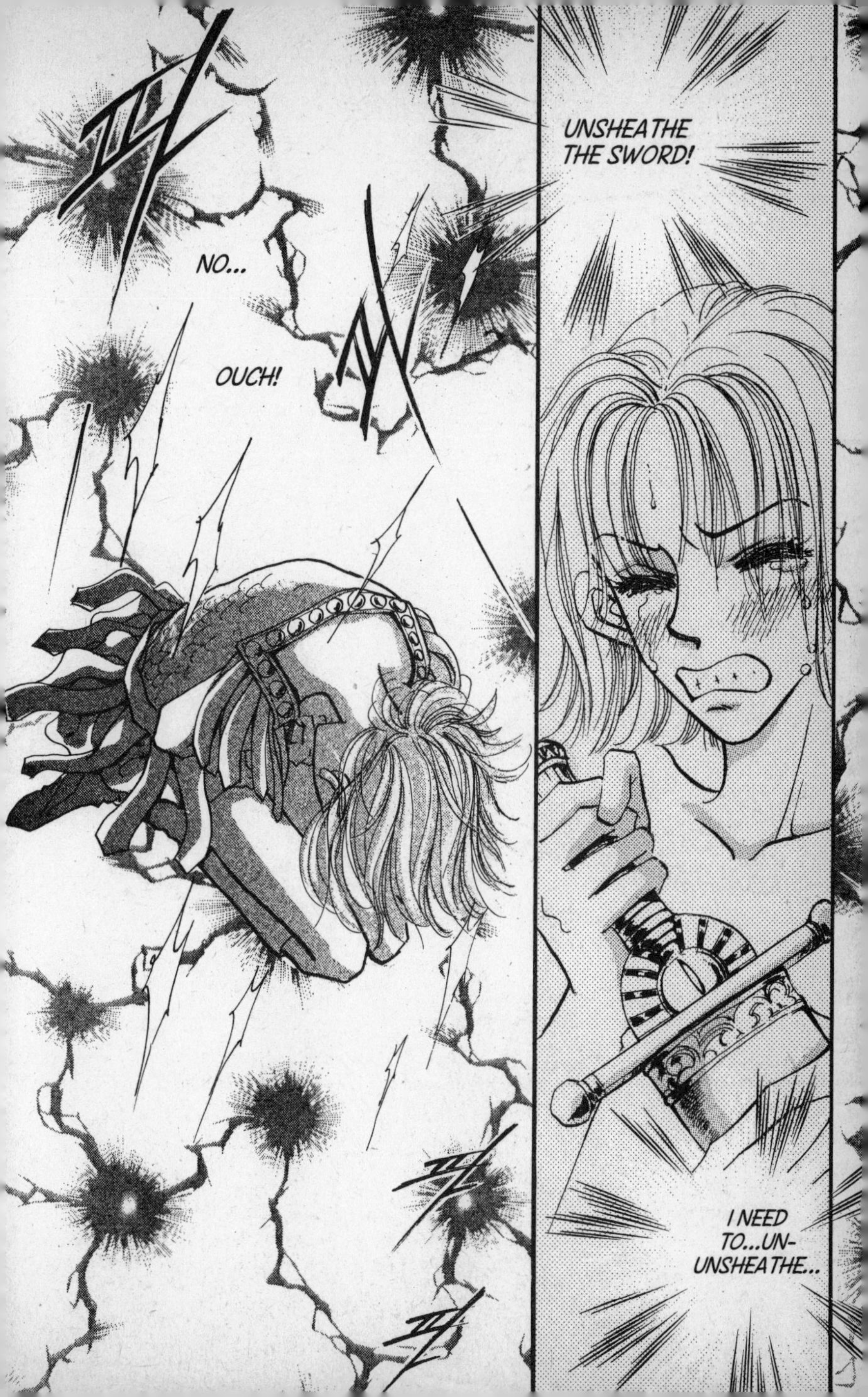
NO...
OUCH!
UNSHEATHE THE SWORD!
I NEED TO...UN-UNSHEATHE...

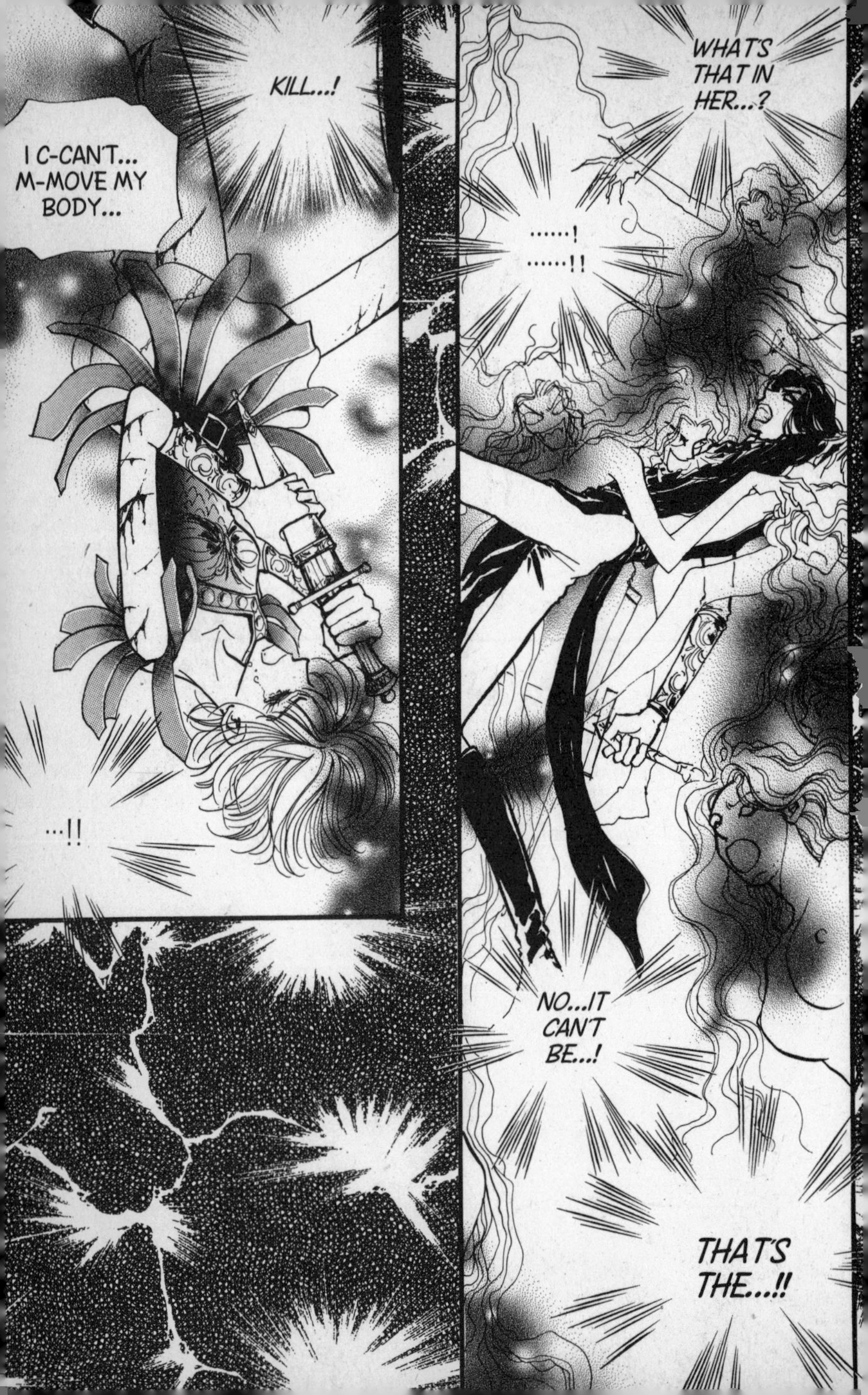
KILL...!
I C-CAN'T... M-MOVE MY BODY...
...!!
WHAT'S THAT IN HER...?
......!
......!!
NO...IT CAN'T BE...!
THAT'S THE...!!

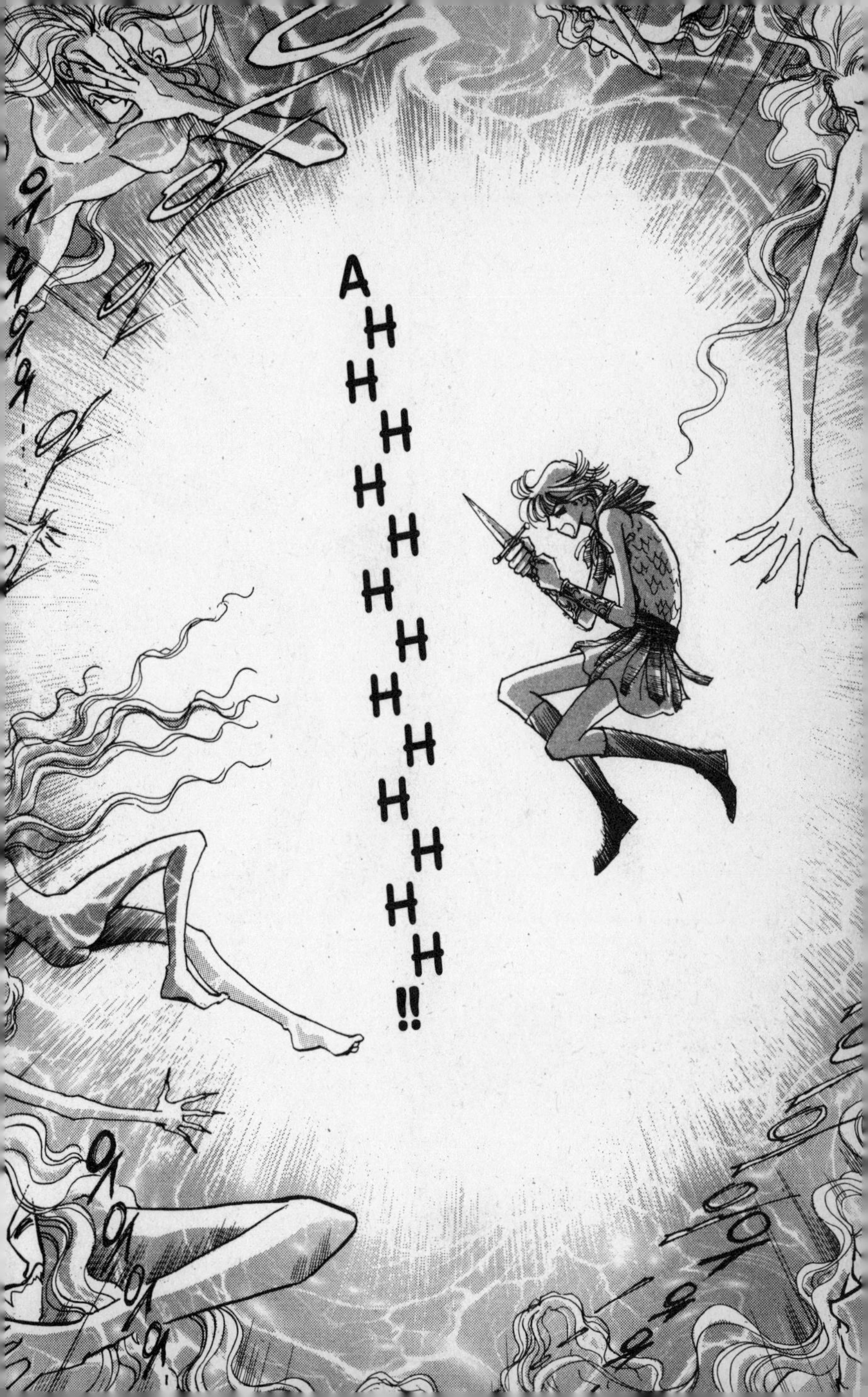
AHHHHHHHHHHHHH!!

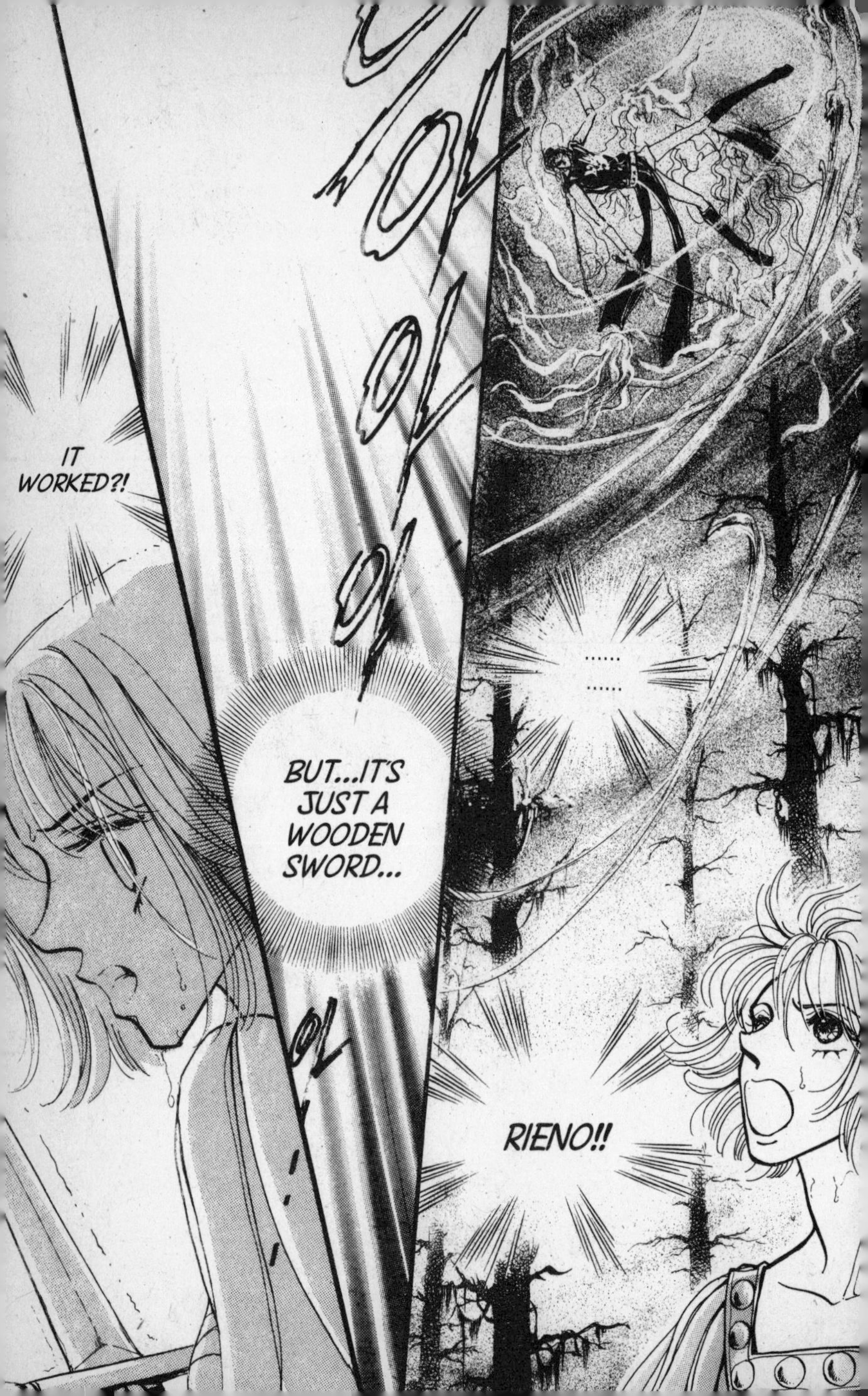
IT WORKED?!
BUT...IT'S JUST A WOODEN SWORD...
......
......
RIENO!!

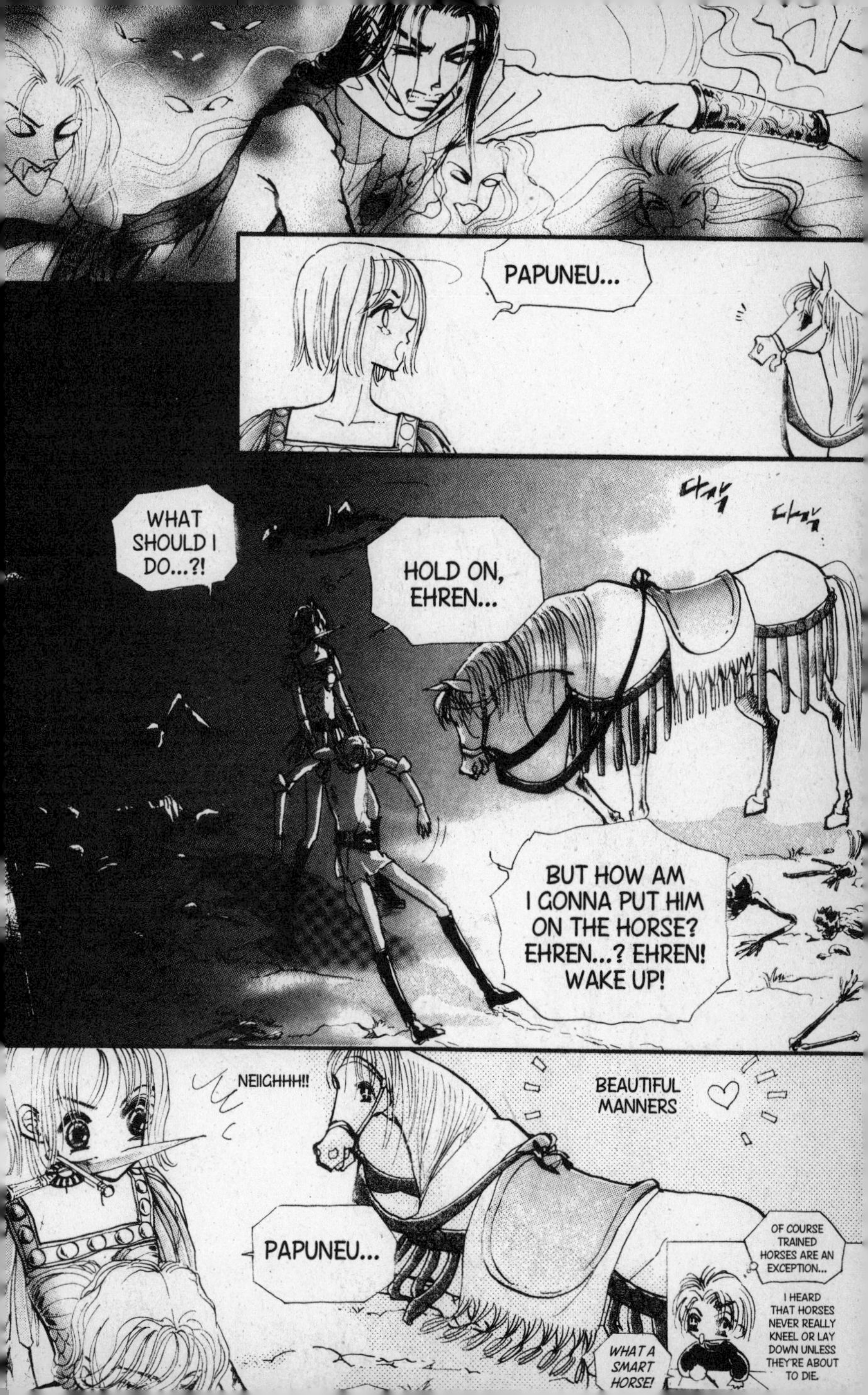
PAPUNEU...
WHAT SHOULD I DO...?!
HOLD ON, EHREN...
다각
다각
BUT HOW AM I GONNA PUT HIM ON THE HORSE? EHREN...? EHREN! WAKE UP!
NEIIGHHH!!
BEAUTIFUL MANNERS
PAPUNEU...
WHAT A SMART HORSE!
I HEARD THAT HORSES NEVER REALLY KNEEL OR LAY DOWN UNLESS THEY'RE ABOUT TO DIE.
OF COURSE TRAINED HORSES ARE AN EXCEPTION...

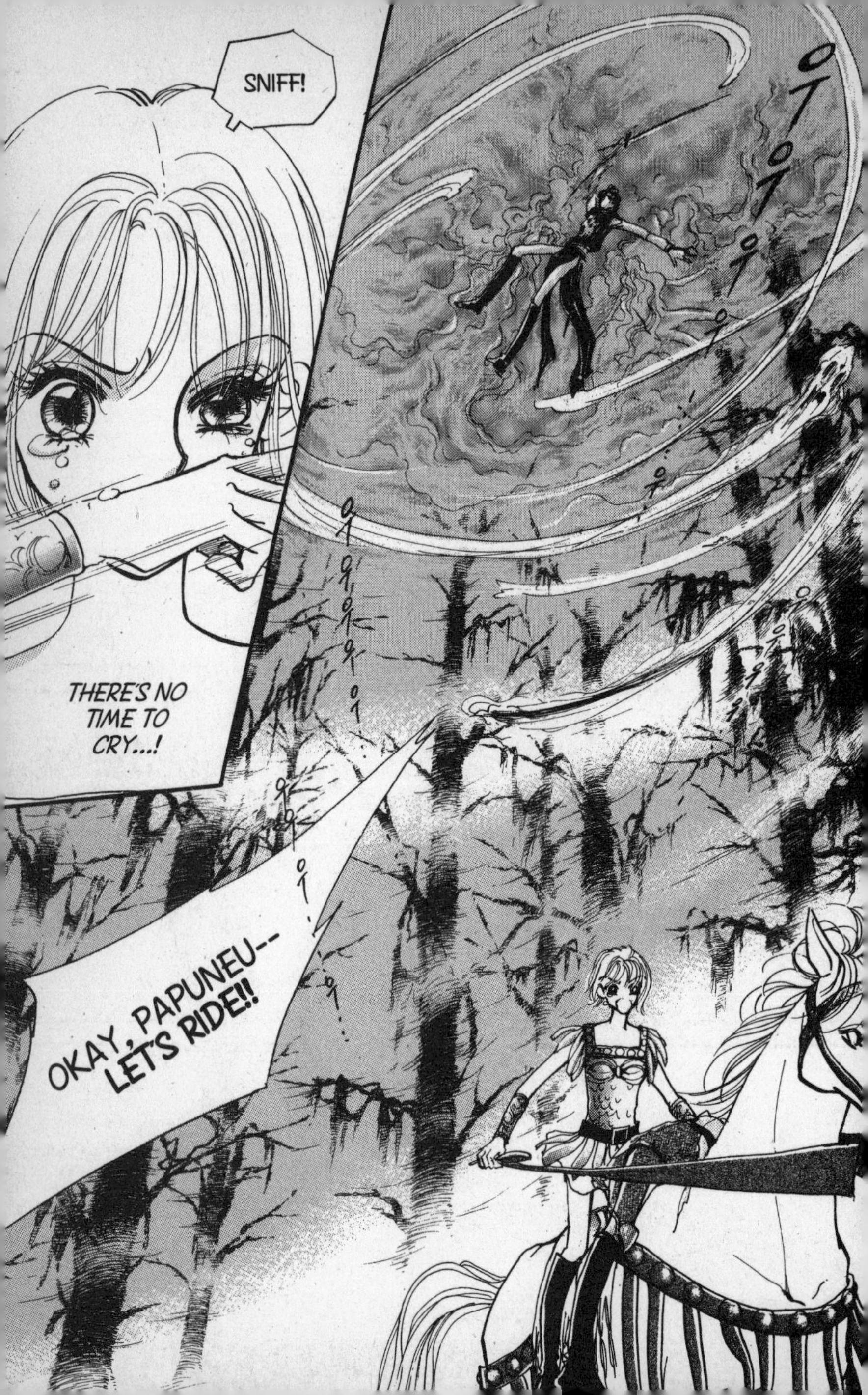
SNIFF!
THERE'S NO TIME TO CRY...!
OKAY, PAPUNEU-- LET'S RIDE!!

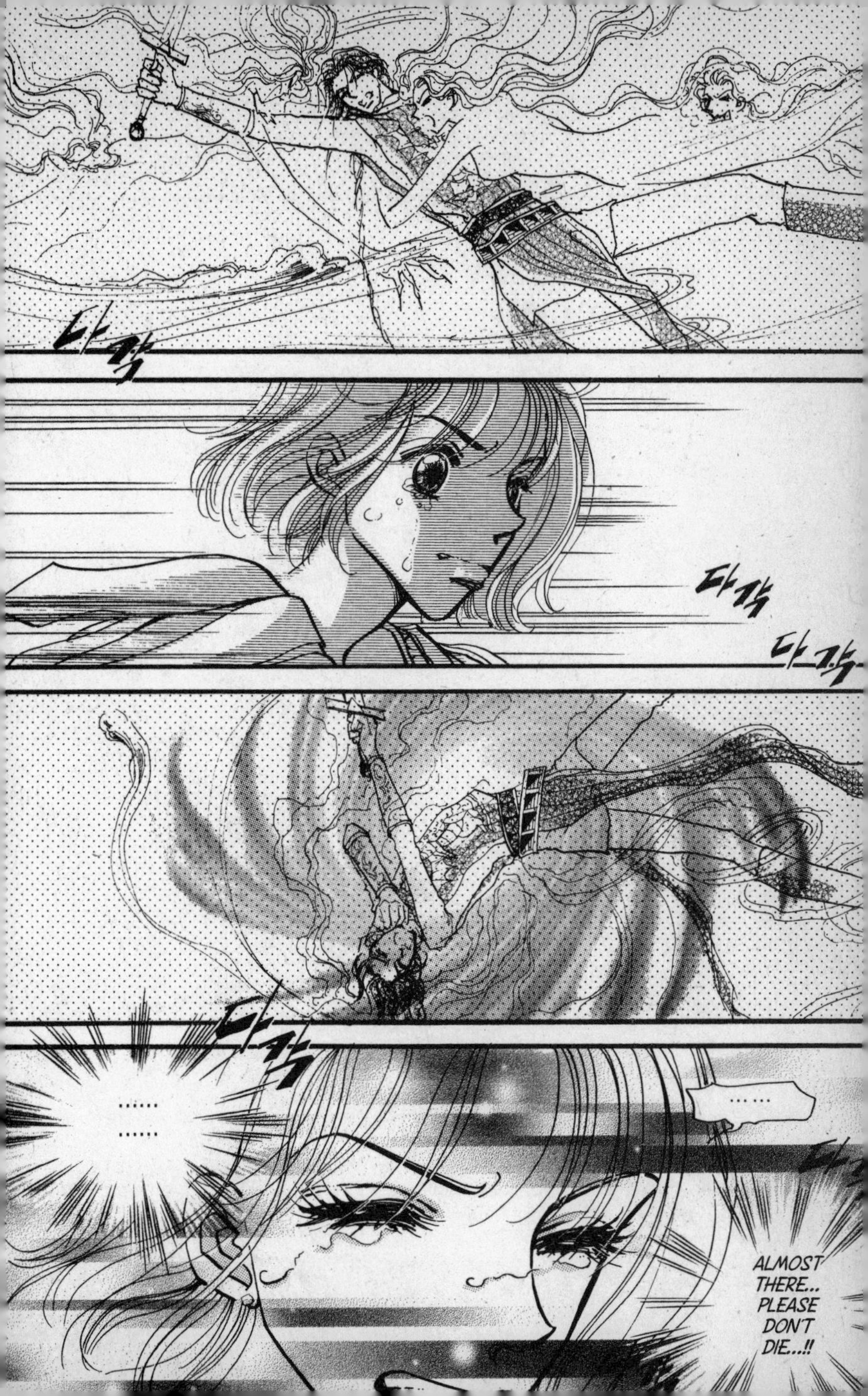
다각
다각
다각
다각
......
......
......
ALMOST THERE... PLEASE DON'T DIE...!!

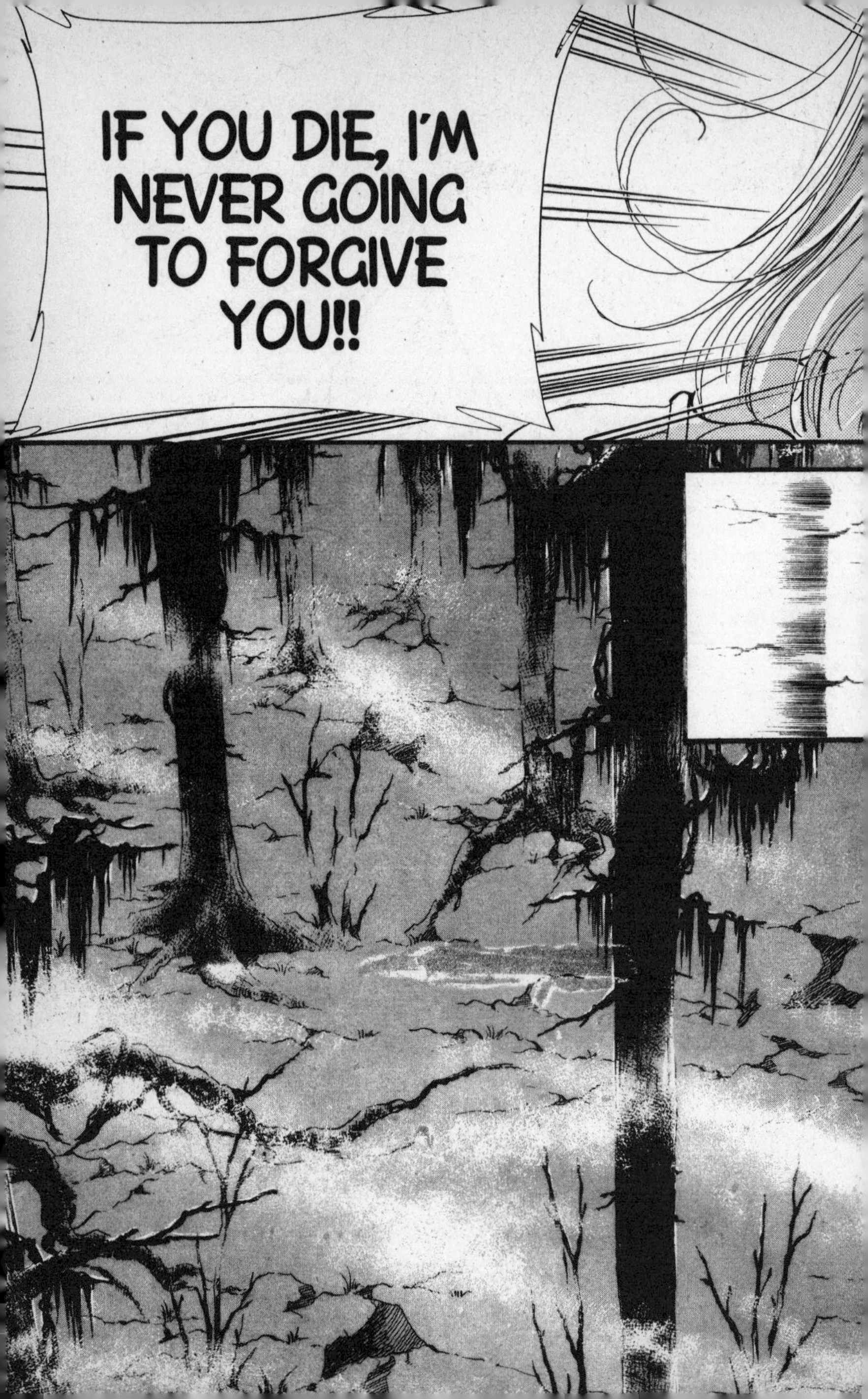
IF YOU DIE, I'M NEVER GOING TO FORGIVE YOU!!

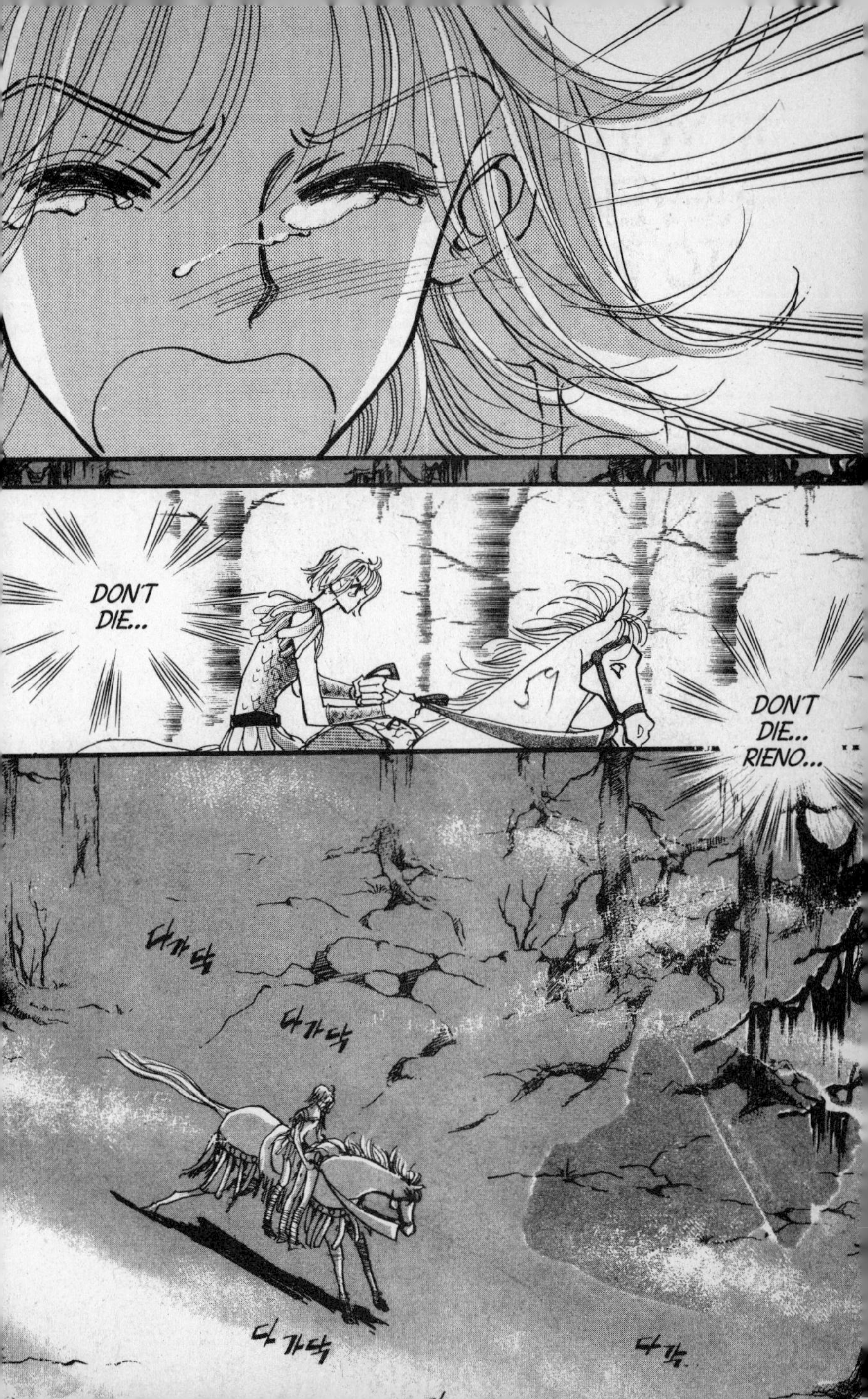
DON'T DIE...
DON'T DIE... RIENO...
다가닥
다가닥
다가닥
다각

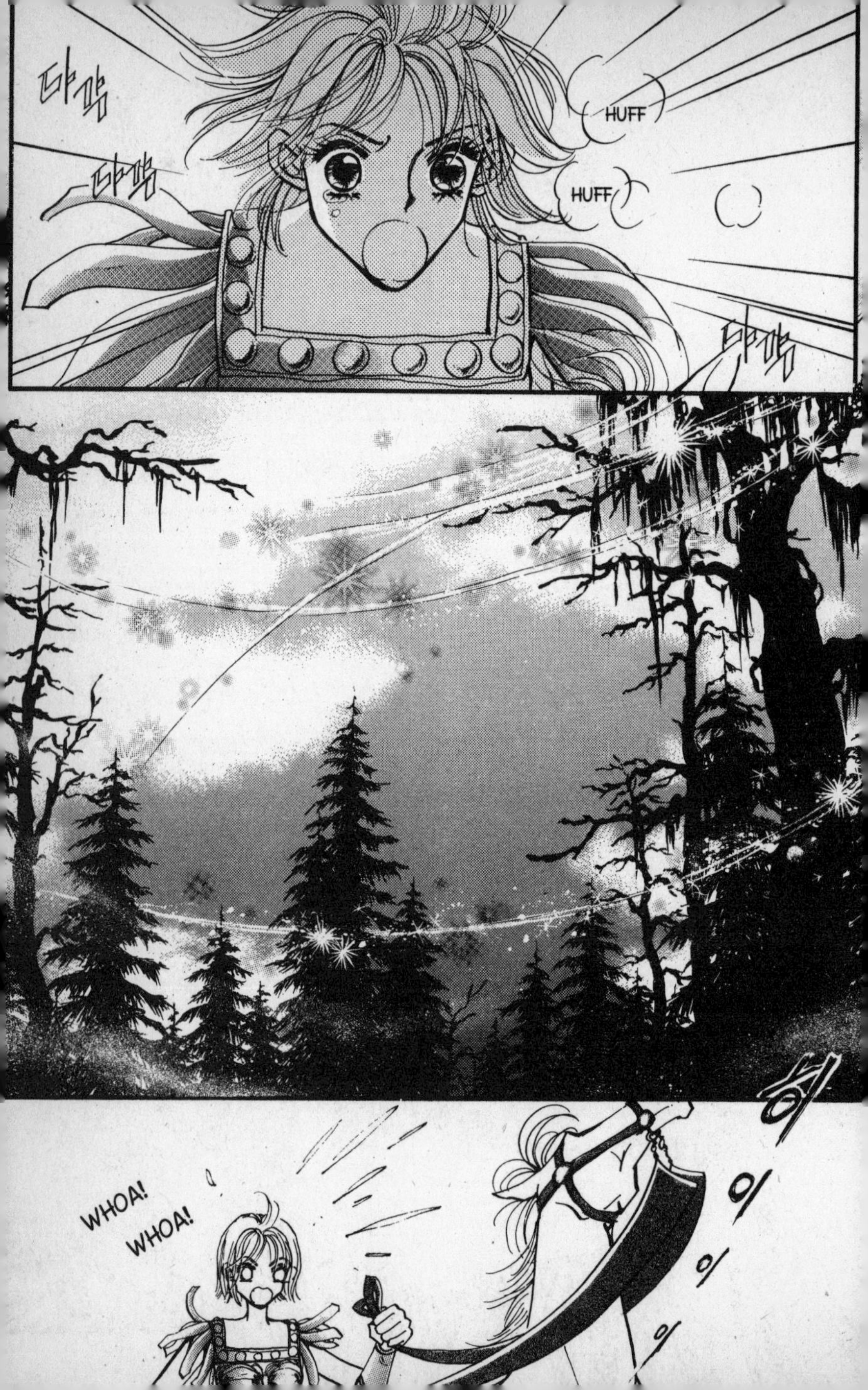
HUFF
HUFF
WHOA!
WHOA!

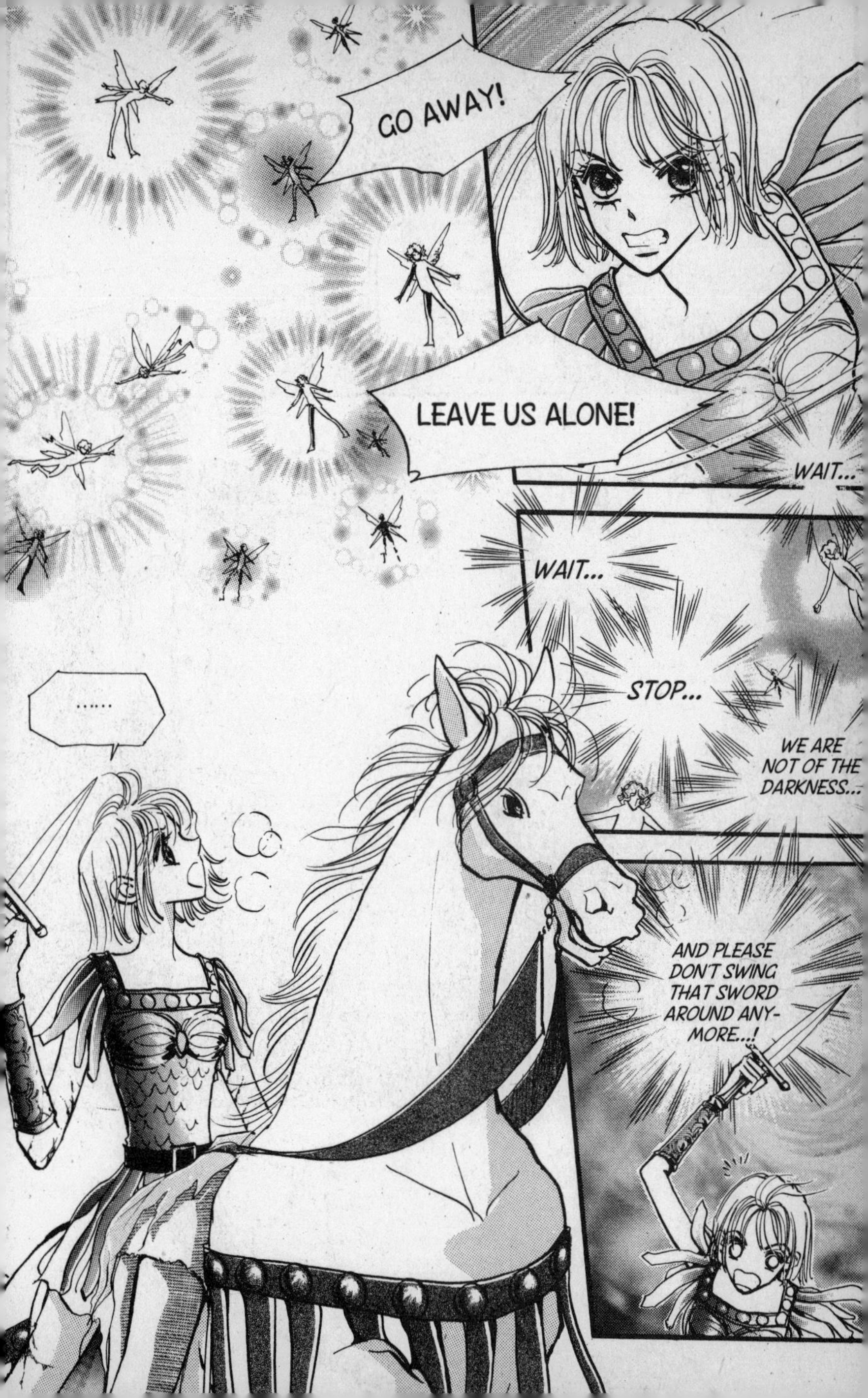
GO AWAY!
LEAVE US ALONE!
WAIT...
WAIT...
......
STOP...
WE ARE NOT OF THE DARKNESS...
AND PLEASE DON'T SWING THAT SWORD AROUND ANY-MORE...!

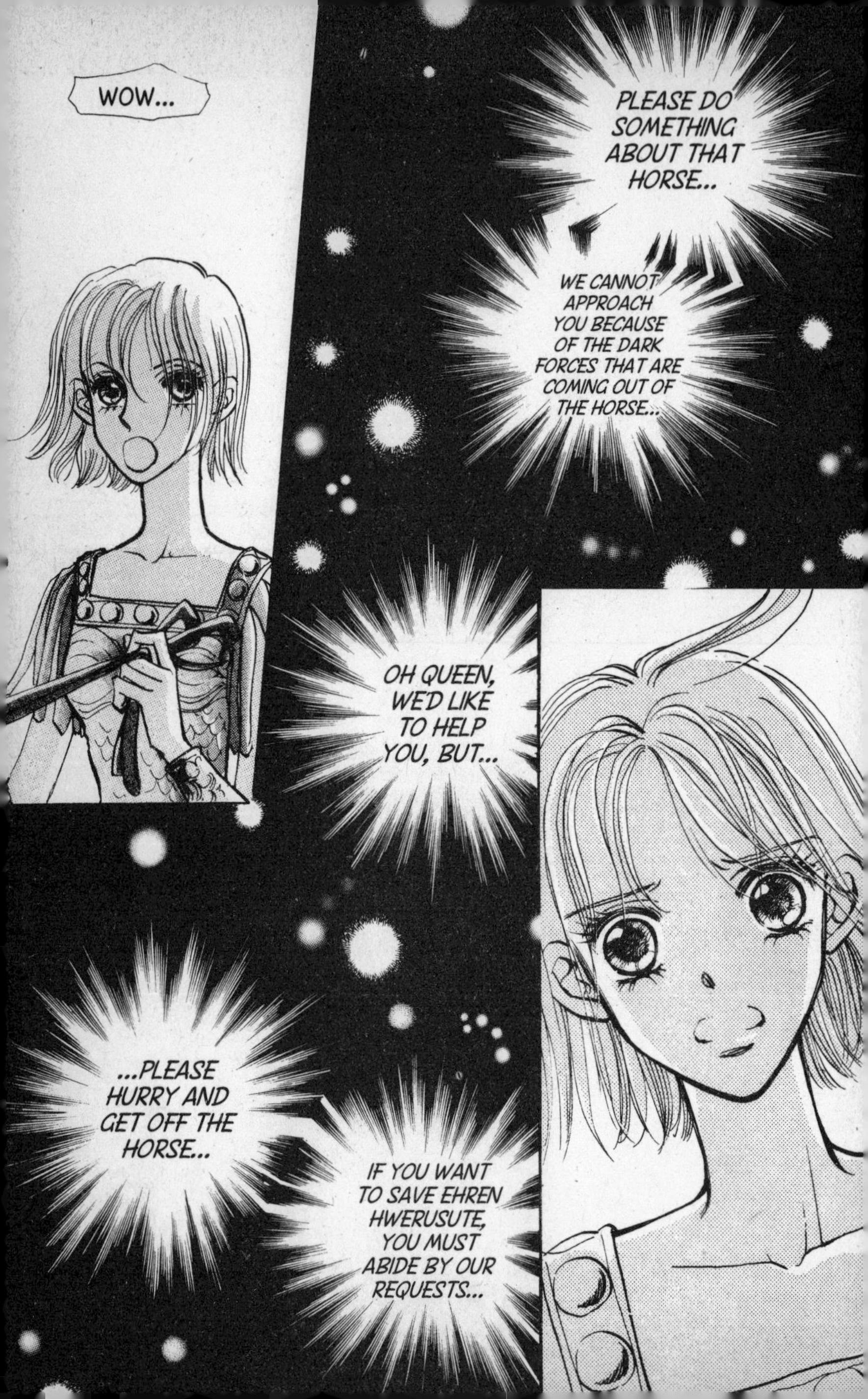
WOW...
PLEASE DO SOMETHING ABOUT THAT HORSE...
WE CANNOT APPROACH YOU BECAUSE OF THE DARK FORCES THAT ARE COMING OUT OF THE HORSE...
OH QUEEN, WE'D LIKE TO HELP YOU, BUT...
...PLEASE HURRY AND GET OFF THE HORSE...
IF YOU WANT TO SAVE EHREN HWERUSUTE, YOU MUST ABIDE BY OUR REQUESTS...

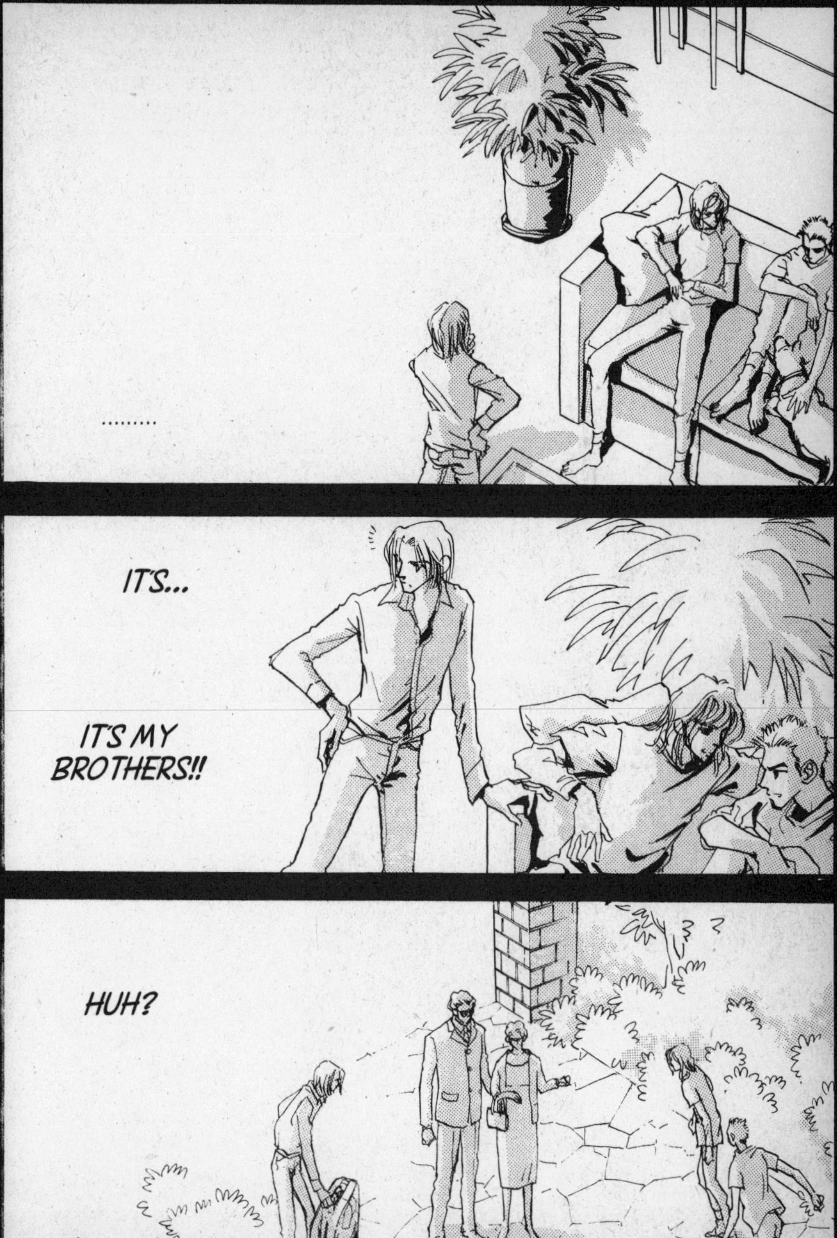
....
IT'S...
IT'S MY BROTHERS!!
HUH?

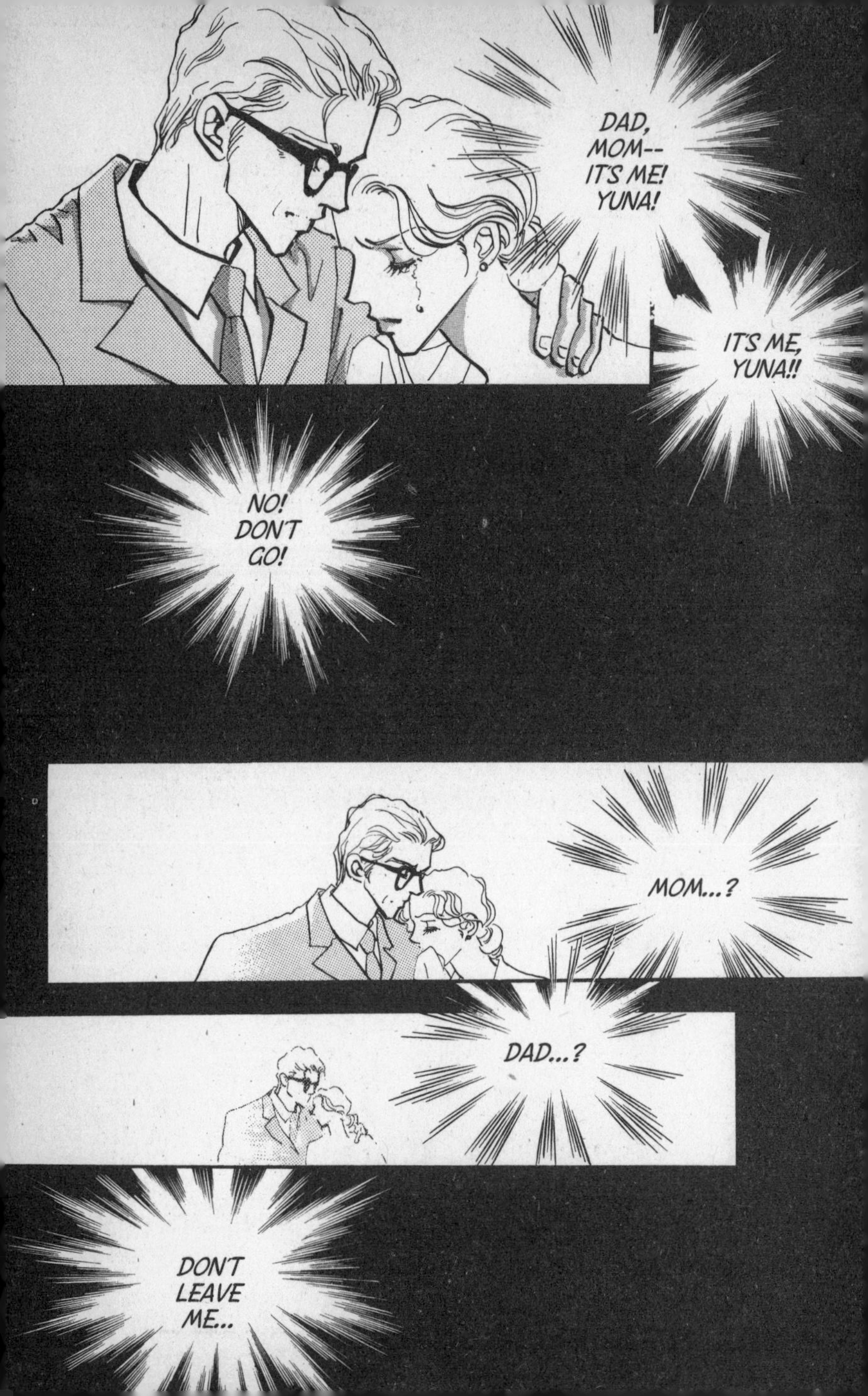
DAD, MOM-- IT'S ME! YUNA!
IT'S ME, YUNA!!
NO! DON'T GO!
MOM...?
DAD...?
DON'T LEAVE ME...

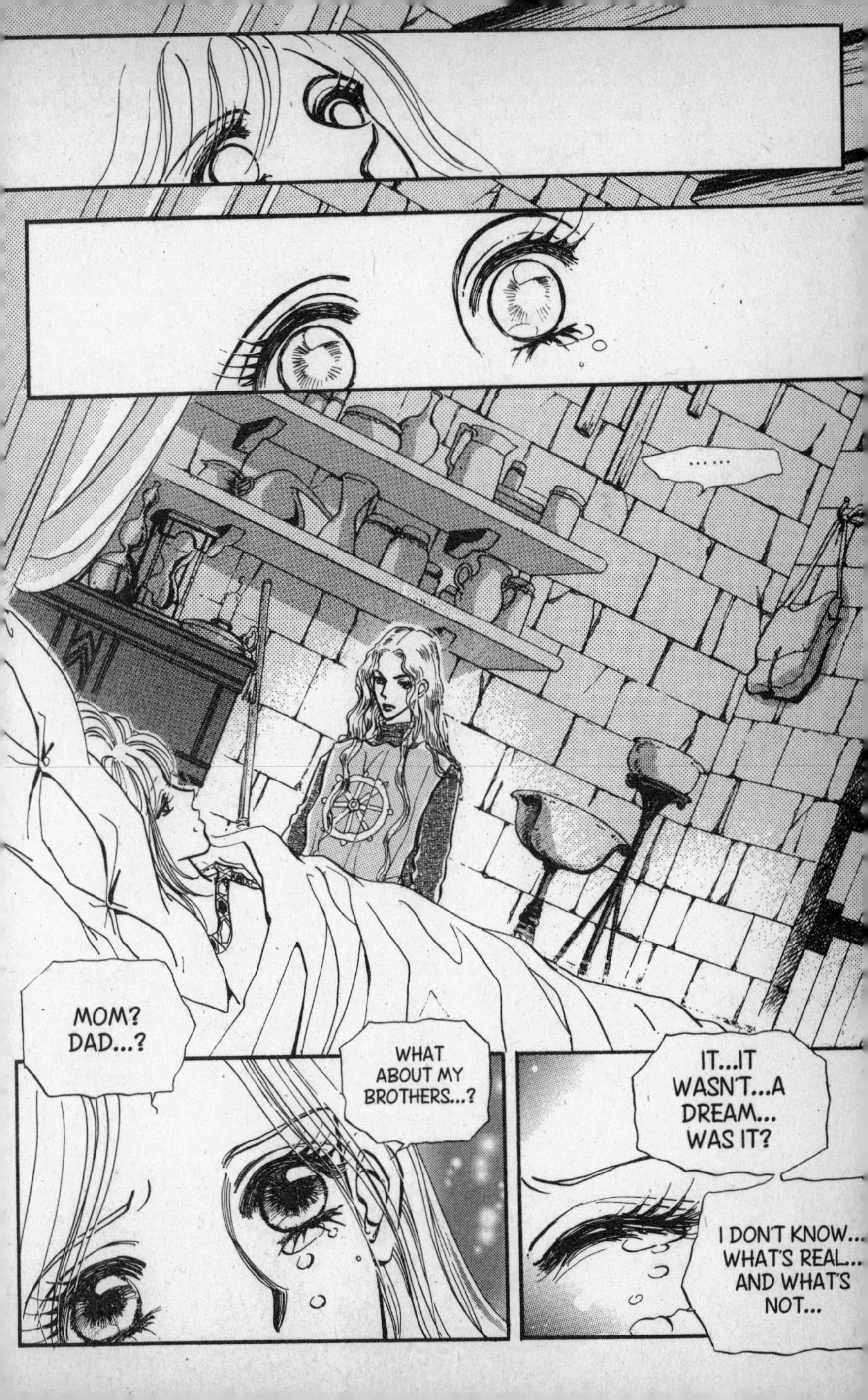
......
MOM? DAD...?
WHAT ABOUT MY BROTHERS...?
IT...IT WASN'T...A DREAM... WAS IT?
I DON'T KNOW... WHAT'S REAL... AND WHAT'S NOT...

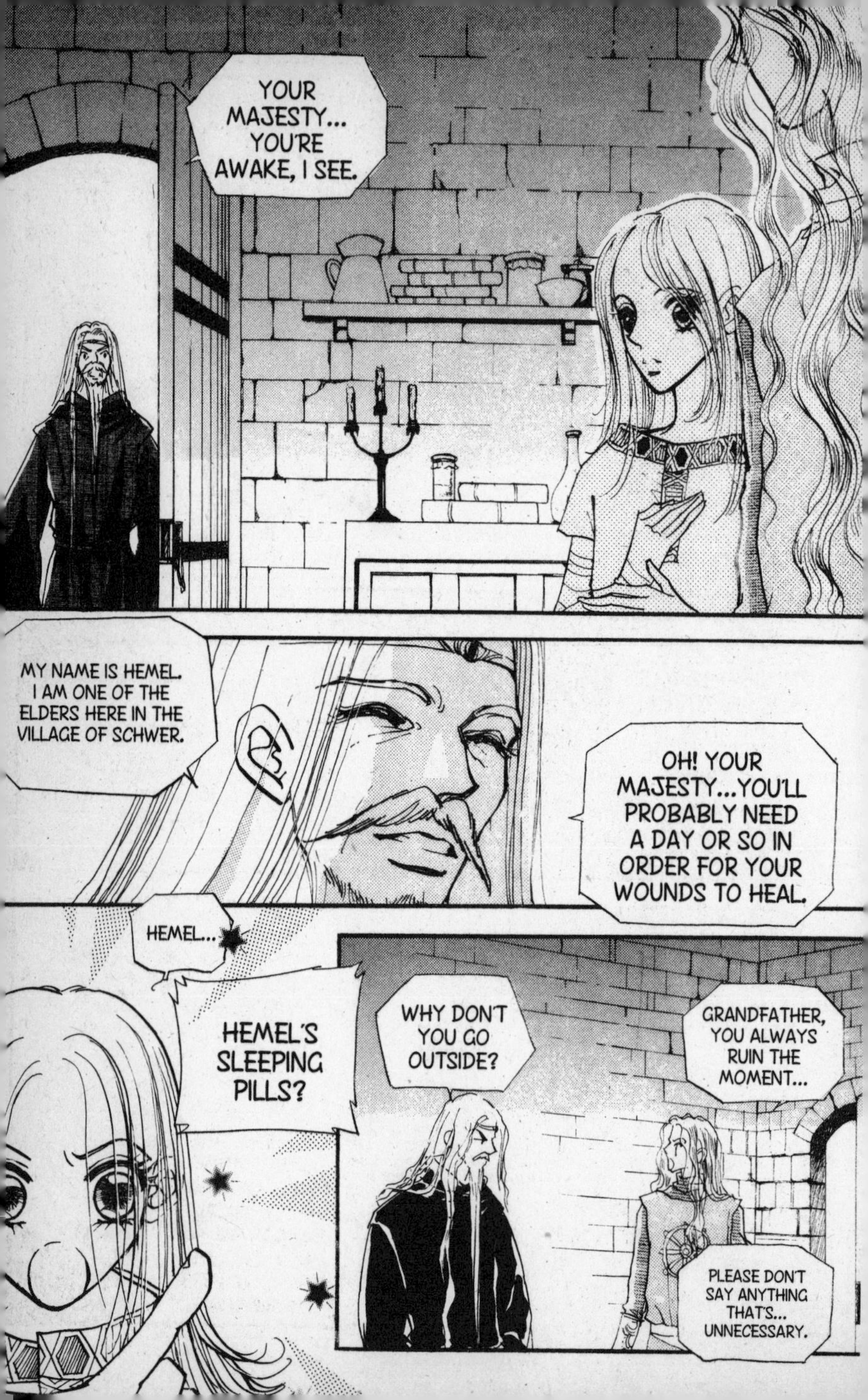
YOUR MAJESTY... YOU'RE AWAKE, I SEE.
MY NAME IS HEMEL. I AM ONE OF THE ELDERS HERE IN THE VILLAGE OF SCHWER.
OH! YOUR MAJESTY...YOU'LL PROBABLY NEED A DAY OR SO IN ORDER FOR YOUR WOUNDS TO HEAL.
HEMEL...
HEMEL'S SLEEPING PILLS?
WHY DON'T YOU GO OUTSIDE?
GRANDFATHER, YOU ALWAYS RUIN THE MOMENT...
PLEASE DON'T SAY ANYTHING THAT'S... UNNECESSARY.

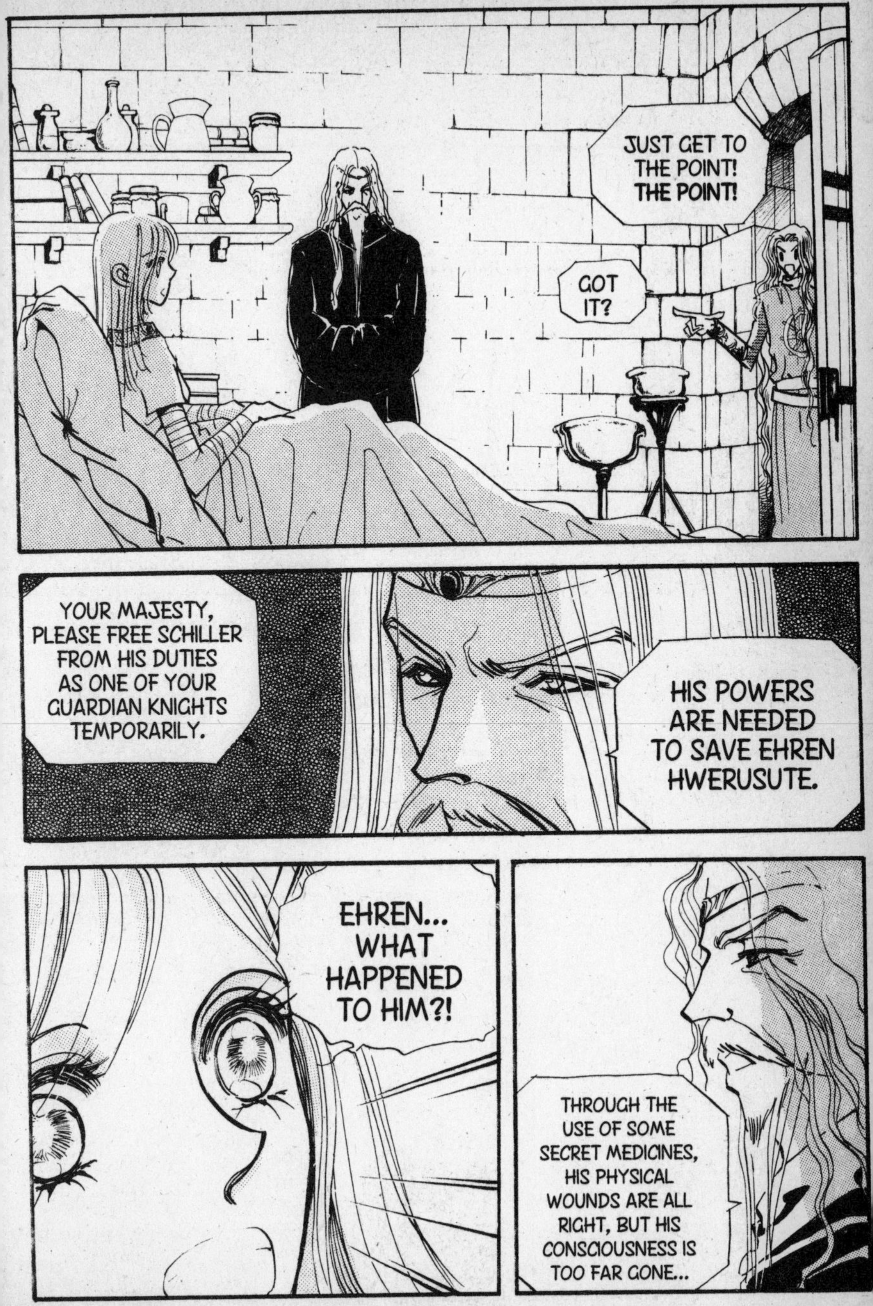
JUST GET TO THE POINT! THE POINT!
GOT IT?
YOUR MAJESTY, PLEASE FREE SCHILLER FROM HIS DUTIES AS ONE OF YOUR GUARDIAN KNIGHTS TEMPORARILY.
HIS POWERS ARE NEEDED TO SAVE EHREN HWERUSUTE.
EHREN... WHAT HAPPENED TO HIM?!
THROUGH THE USE OF SOME SECRET MEDICINES, HIS PHYSICAL WOUNDS ARE ALL RIGHT, BUT HIS CONSCIOUSNESS IS TOO FAR GONE...

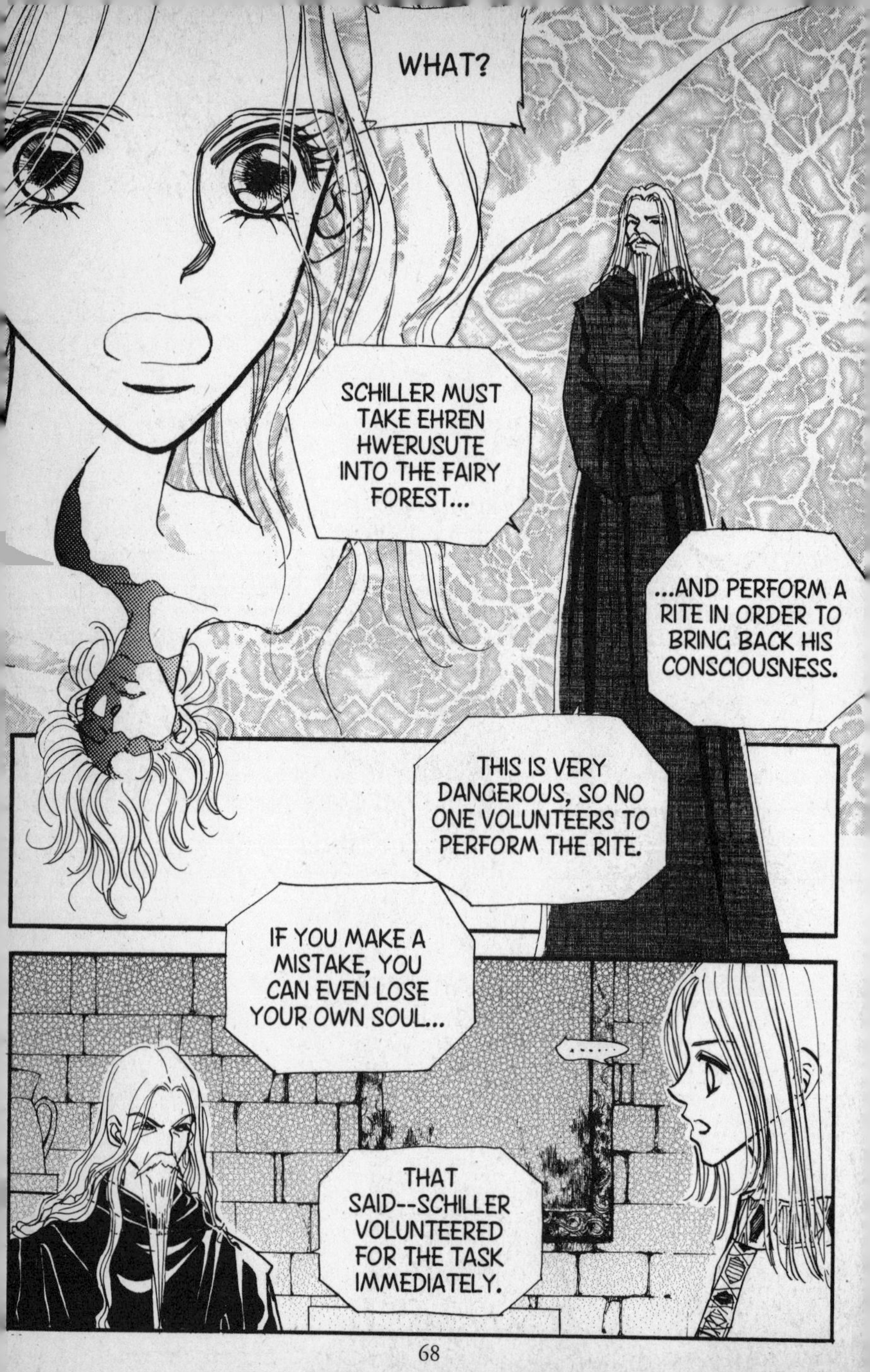
WHAT?
SCHILLER MUST TAKE EHREN HWERUSUTE INTO THE FAIRY FOREST...
...AND PERFORM A RITE IN ORDER TO BRING BACK HIS CONSCIOUSNESS.
THIS IS VERY DANGEROUS, SO NO ONE VOLUNTEERS TO PERFORM THE RITE.
IF YOU MAKE A MISTAKE, YOU CAN EVEN LOSE YOUR OWN SOUL...
......
THAT SAID--SCHILLER VOLUNTEERED FOR THE TASK IMMEDIATELY.

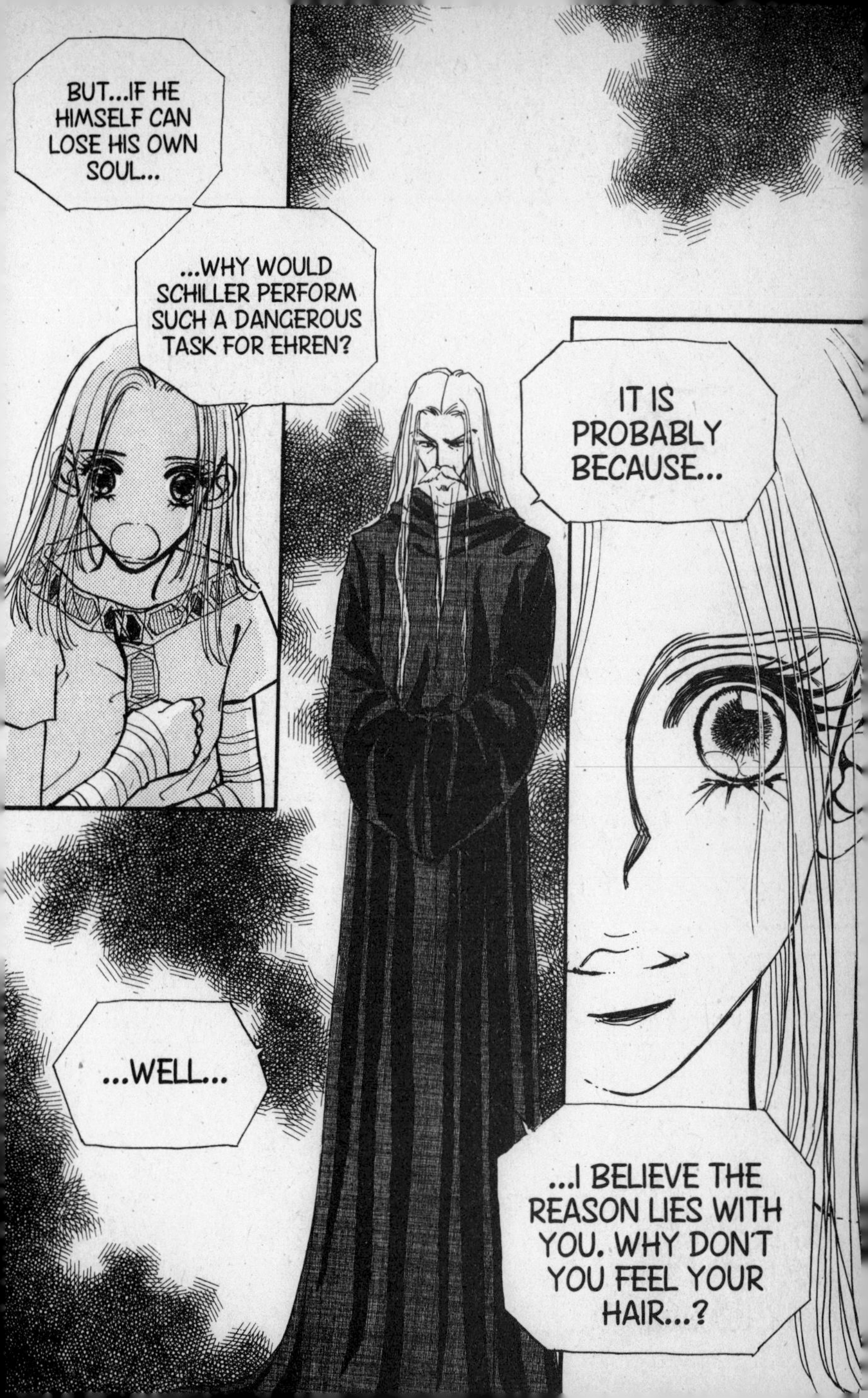
BUT...IF HE HIMSELF CAN LOSE HIS OWN SOUL...
...WHY WOULD SCHILLER PERFORM SUCH A DANGEROUS TASK FOR EHREN?
...WELL...
IT IS PROBABLY BECAUSE...
...I BELIEVE THE REASON LIES WITH YOU. WHY DON'T YOU FEEL YOUR HAIR...?

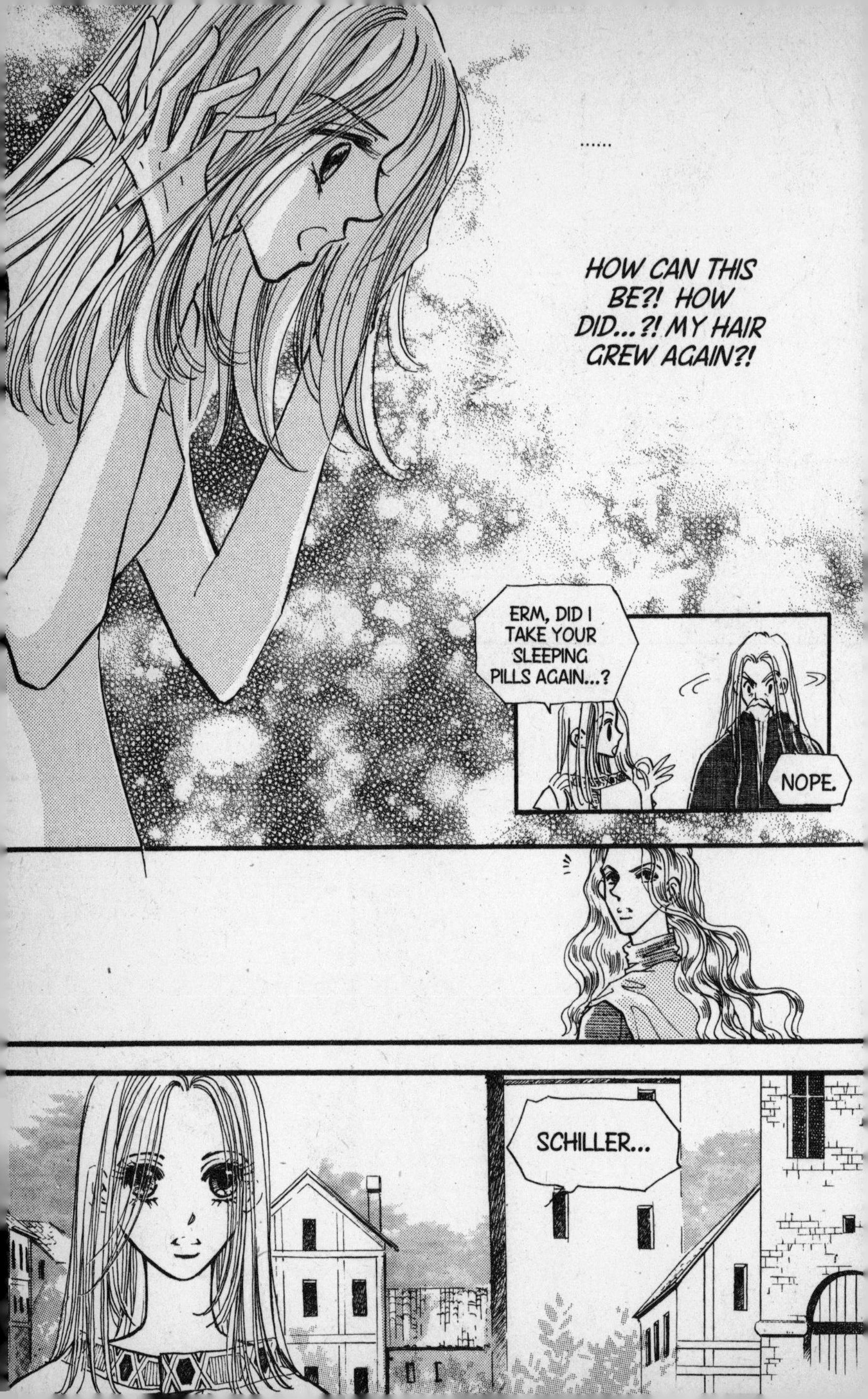
......
HOW CAN THIS BE?! HOW DID...?! MY HAIR GREW AGAIN?!
ERM, DID I TAKE YOUR SLEEPING PILLS AGAIN...?
NOPE.
SCHILLER...

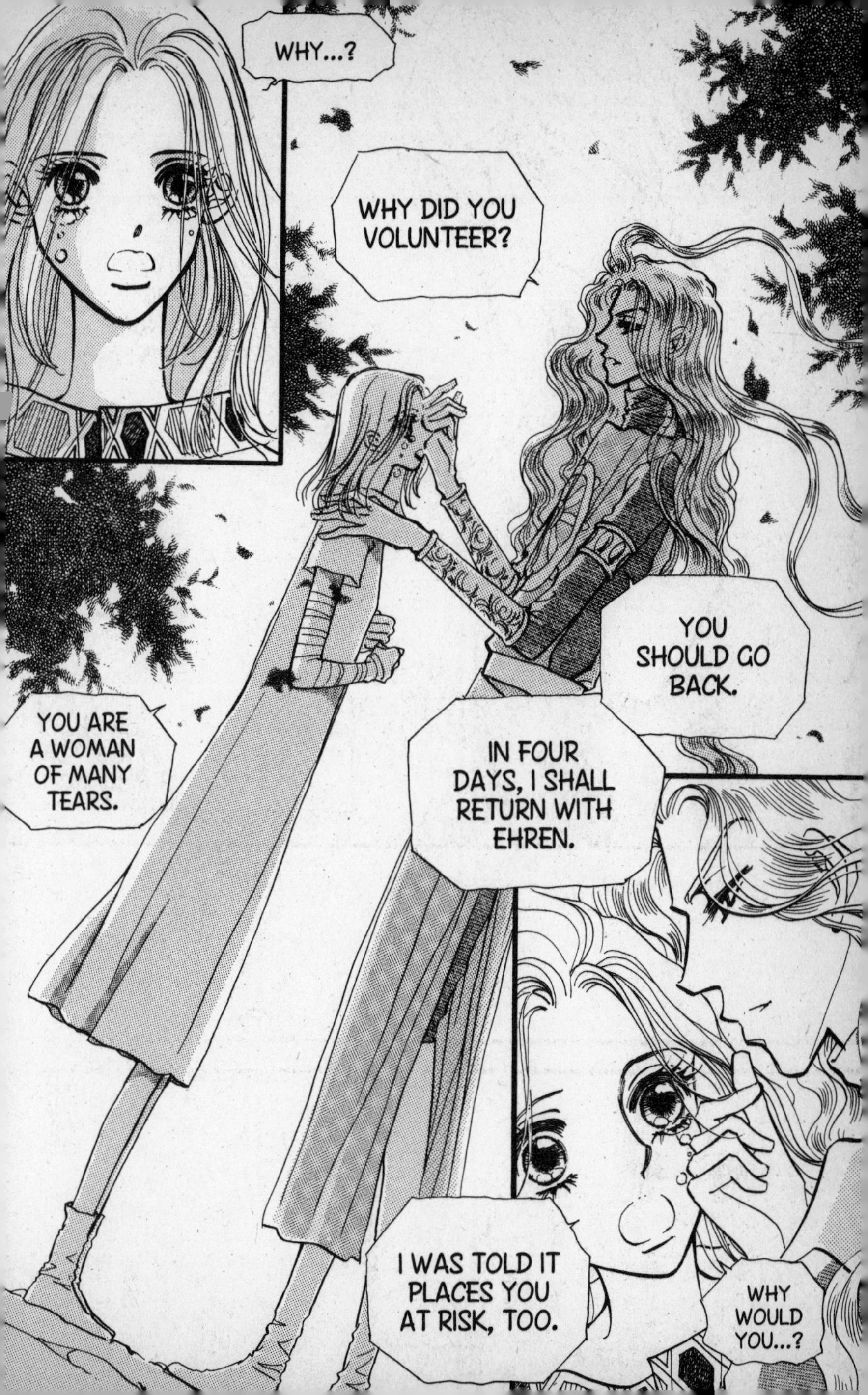
WHY...?
WHY DID YOU VOLUNTEER?
YOU ARE A WOMAN OF MANY TEARS.
YOU SHOULD GO BACK.
IN FOUR DAYS, I SHALL RETURN WITH EHREN.
I WAS TOLD IT PLACES YOU AT RISK, TOO.
WHY WOULD YOU...?

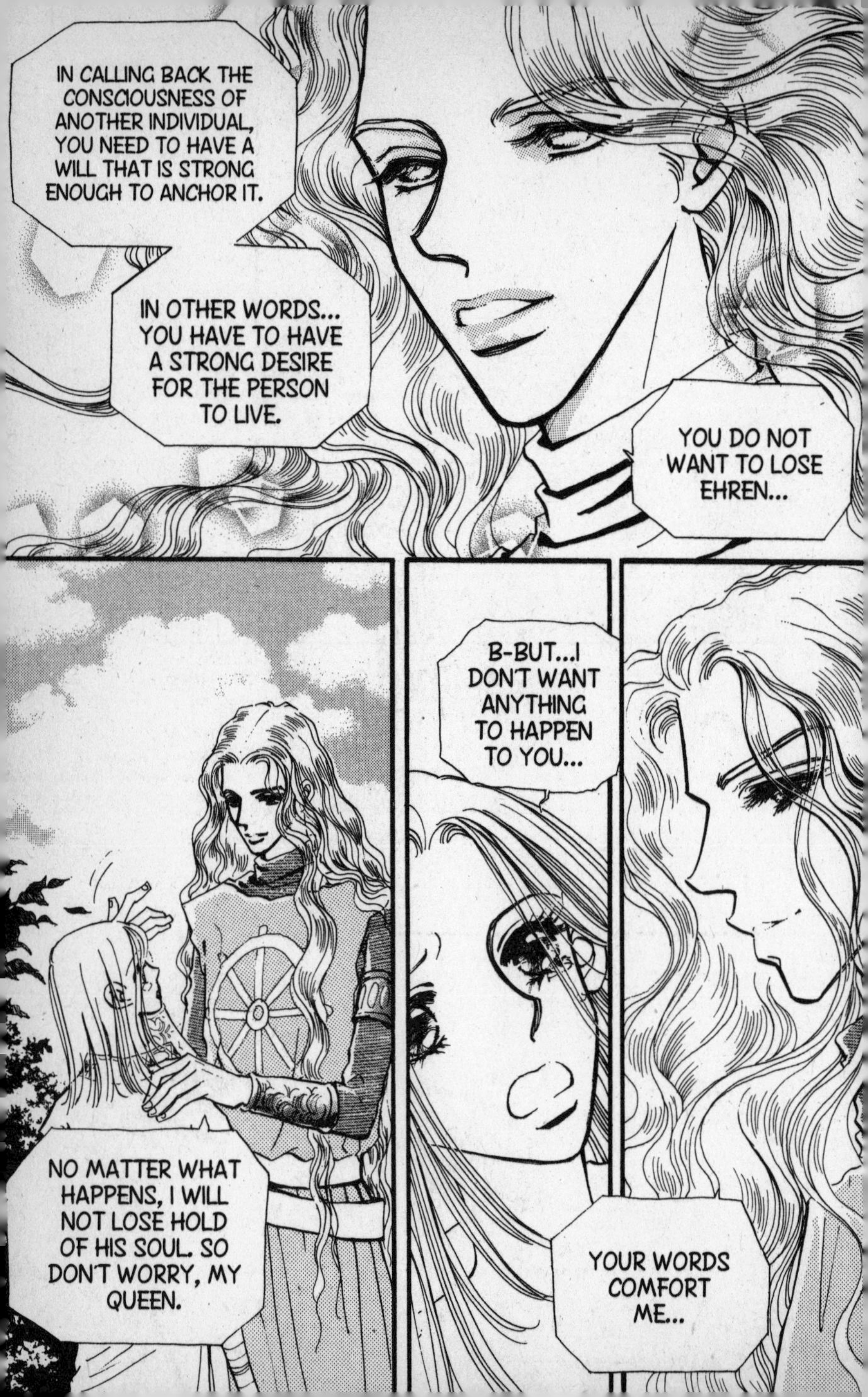
IN CALLING BACK THE CONSCIOUSNESS OF ANOTHER INDIVIDUAL, YOU NEED TO HAVE A WILL THAT IS STRONG ENOUGH TO ANCHOR IT.
IN OTHER WORDS... YOU HAVE TO HAVE A STRONG DESIRE FOR THE PERSON TO LIVE.
YOU DO NOT WANT TO LOSE EHREN...
NO MATTER WHAT HAPPENS, I WILL NOT LOSE HOLD OF HIS SOUL. SO DON'T WORRY, MY QUEEN.
B-BUT...I DON'T WANT ANYTHING TO HAPPEN TO YOU...
YOUR WORDS COMFORT ME...

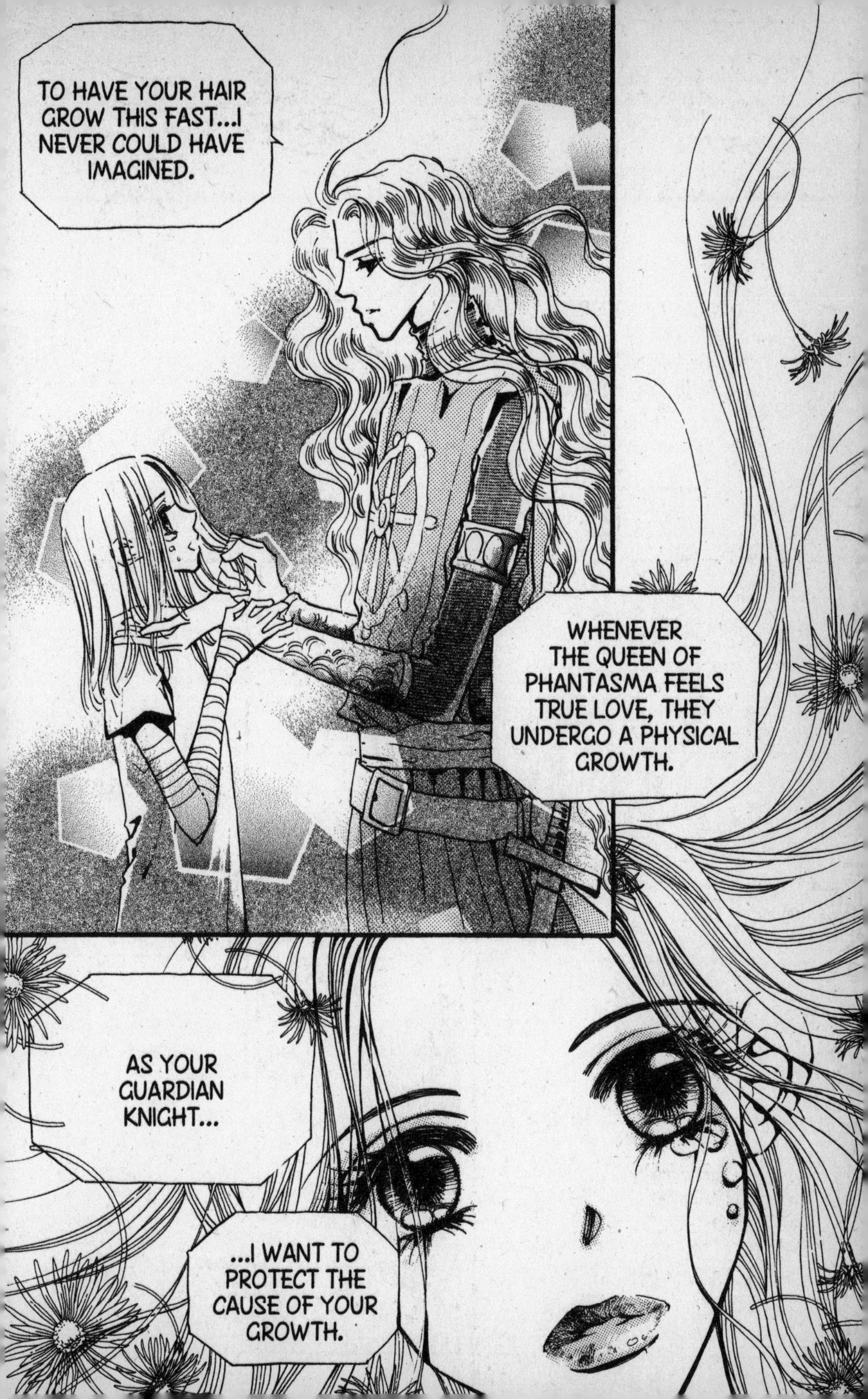
TO HAVE YOUR HAIR GROW THIS FAST...I NEVER COULD HAVE IMAGINED.
WHENEVER THE QUEEN OF PHANTASMA FEELS TRUE LOVE, THEY UNDERGO A PHYSICAL GROWTH.
AS YOUR GUARDIAN KNIGHT...
...I WANT TO PROTECT THE CAUSE OF YOUR GROWTH.

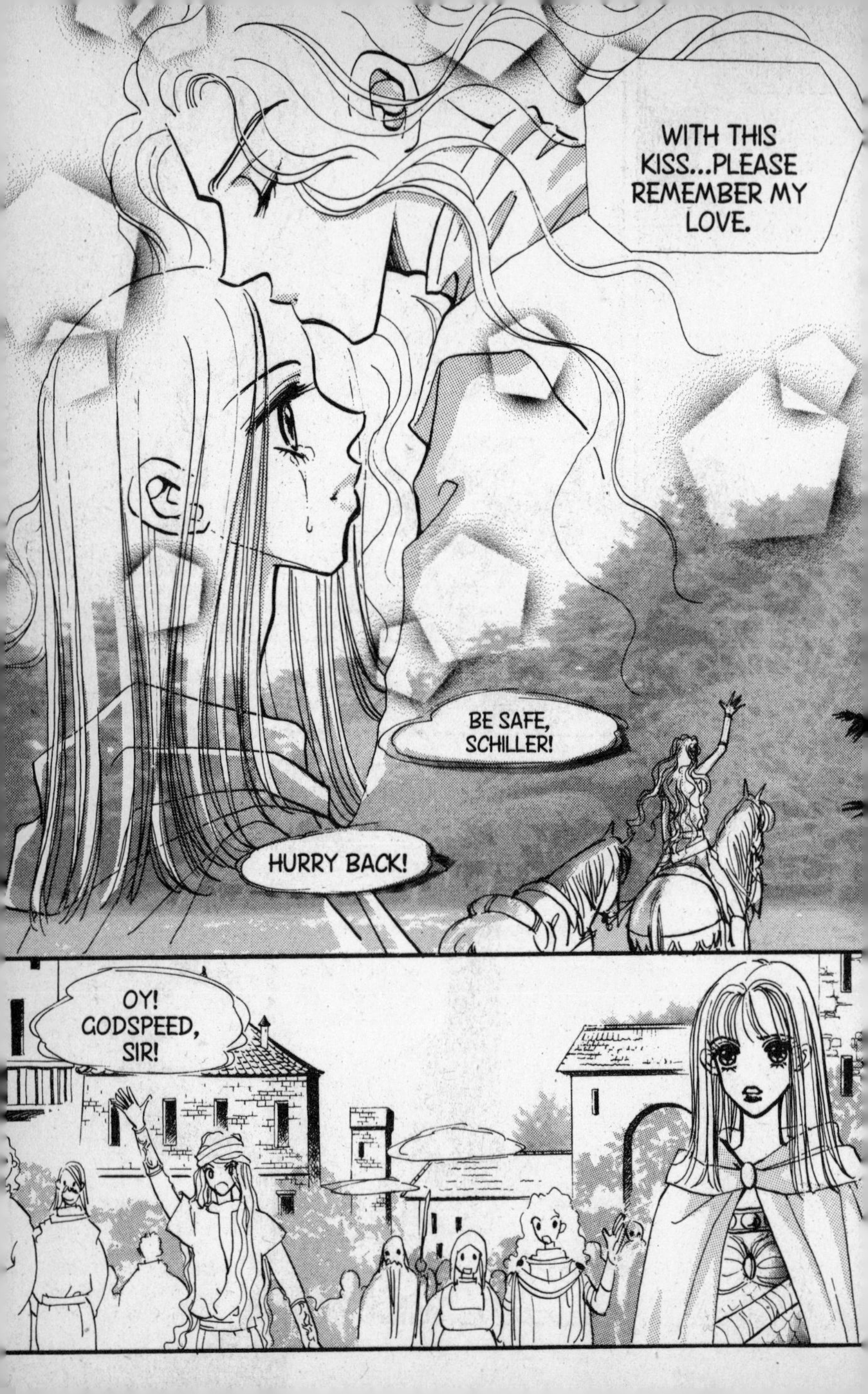
WITH THIS KISS...PLEASE REMEMBER MY LOVE.
BE SAFE, SCHILLER!
HURRY BACK!
OY! GODSPEED, SIR!

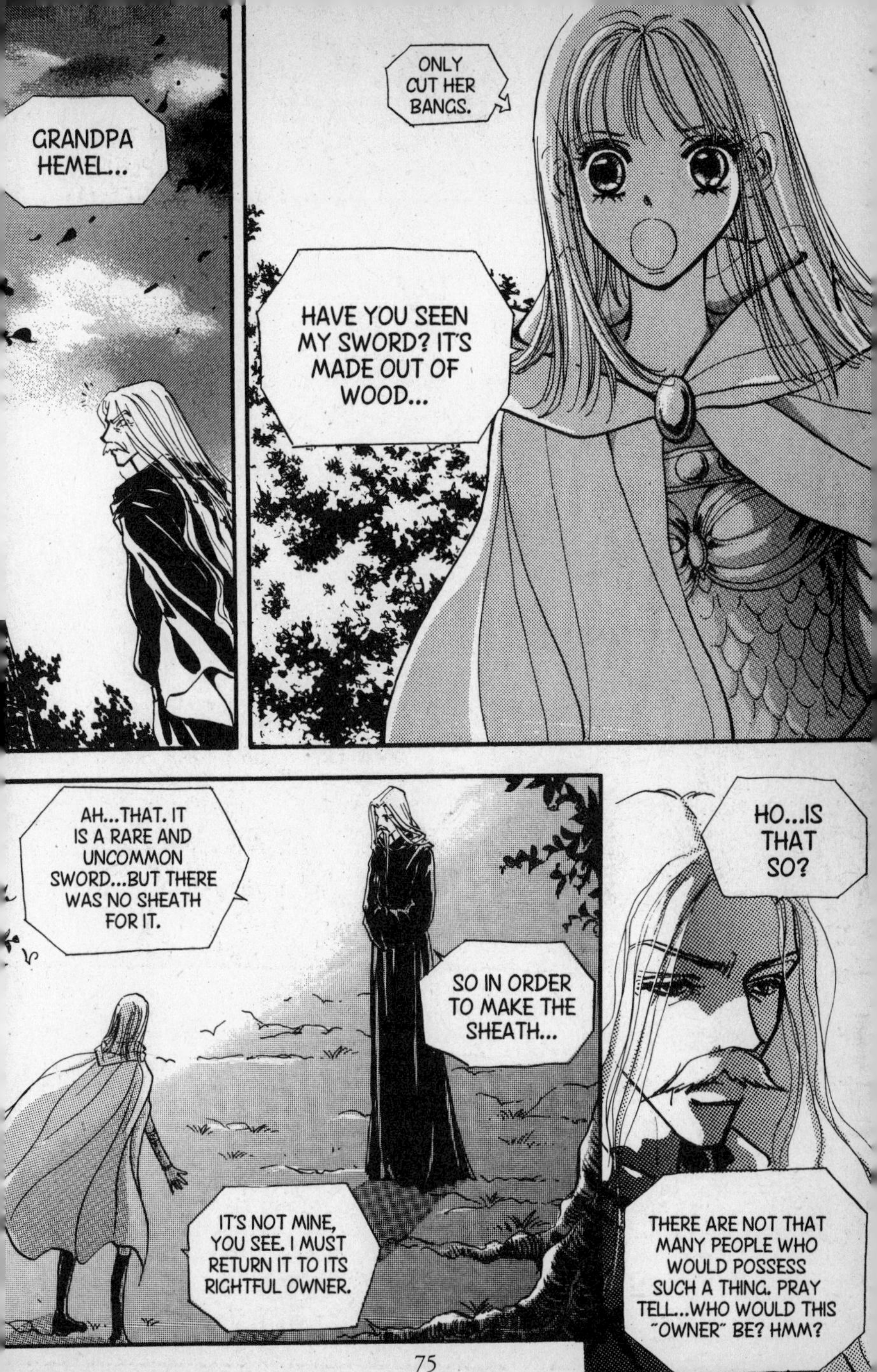
GRANDPA HEMEL...
ONLY CUT HER BANGS.
HAVE YOU SEEN MY SWORD? IT'S MADE OUT OF WOOD...
AH...THAT. IT IS A RARE AND UNCOMMON SWORD...BUT THERE WAS NO SHEATH FOR IT.
SO IN ORDER TO MAKE THE SHEATH...
IT'S NOT MINE, YOU SEE. I MUST RETURN IT TO ITS RIGHTFUL OWNER.
HO...IS THAT SO?
THERE ARE NOT THAT MANY PEOPLE WHO WOULD POSSESS SUCH A THING. PRAY TELL...WHO WOULD THIS "OWNER" BE? HMM?

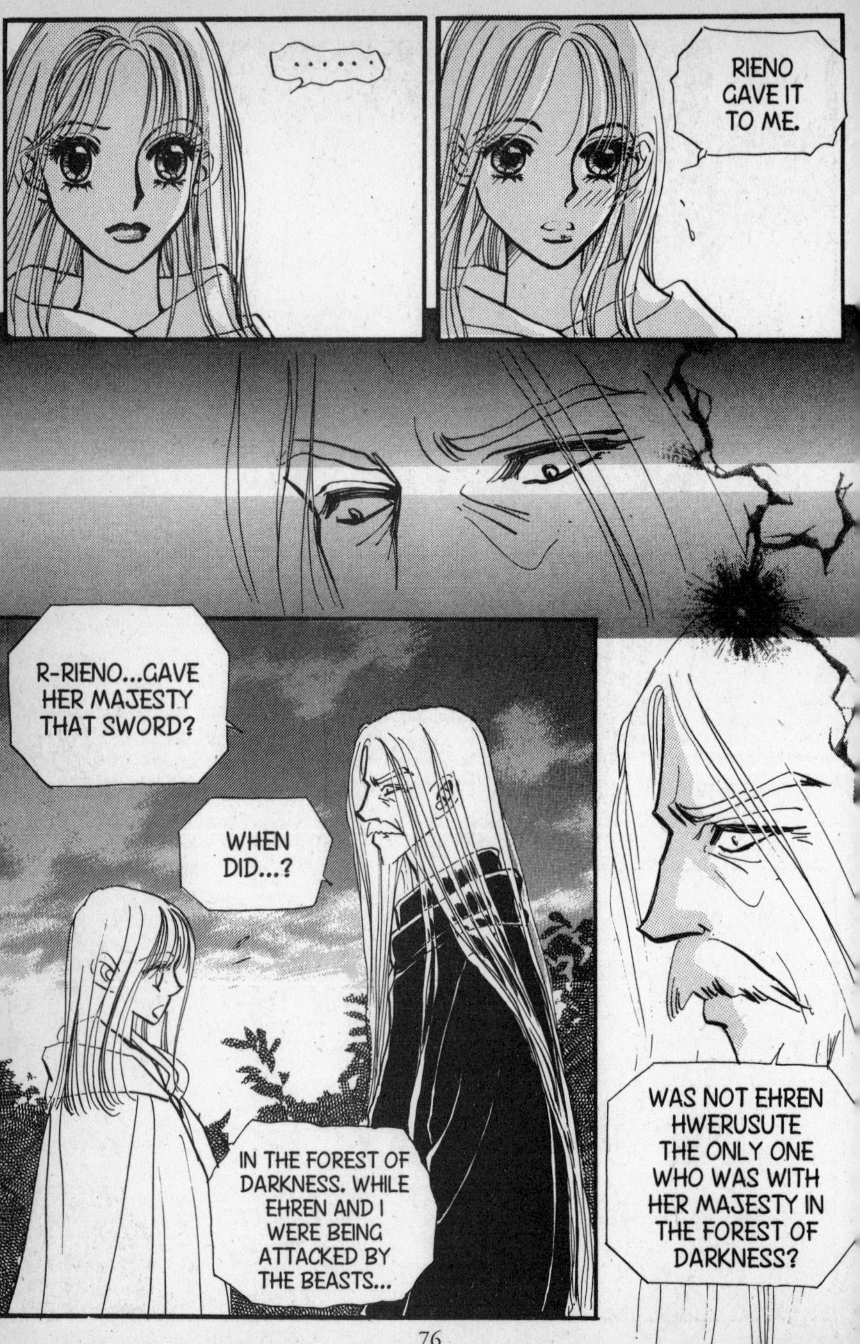
......
RIENO GAVE IT TO ME.
R-RIENO...GAVE HER MAJESTY THAT SWORD?
WHEN DID...?
IN THE FOREST OF DARKNESS. WHILE EHREN AND I WERE BEING ATTACKED BY THE BEASTS...
WAS NOT EHREN HWERUSUTE THE ONLY ONE WHO WAS WITH HER MAJESTY IN THE FOREST OF DARKNESS?

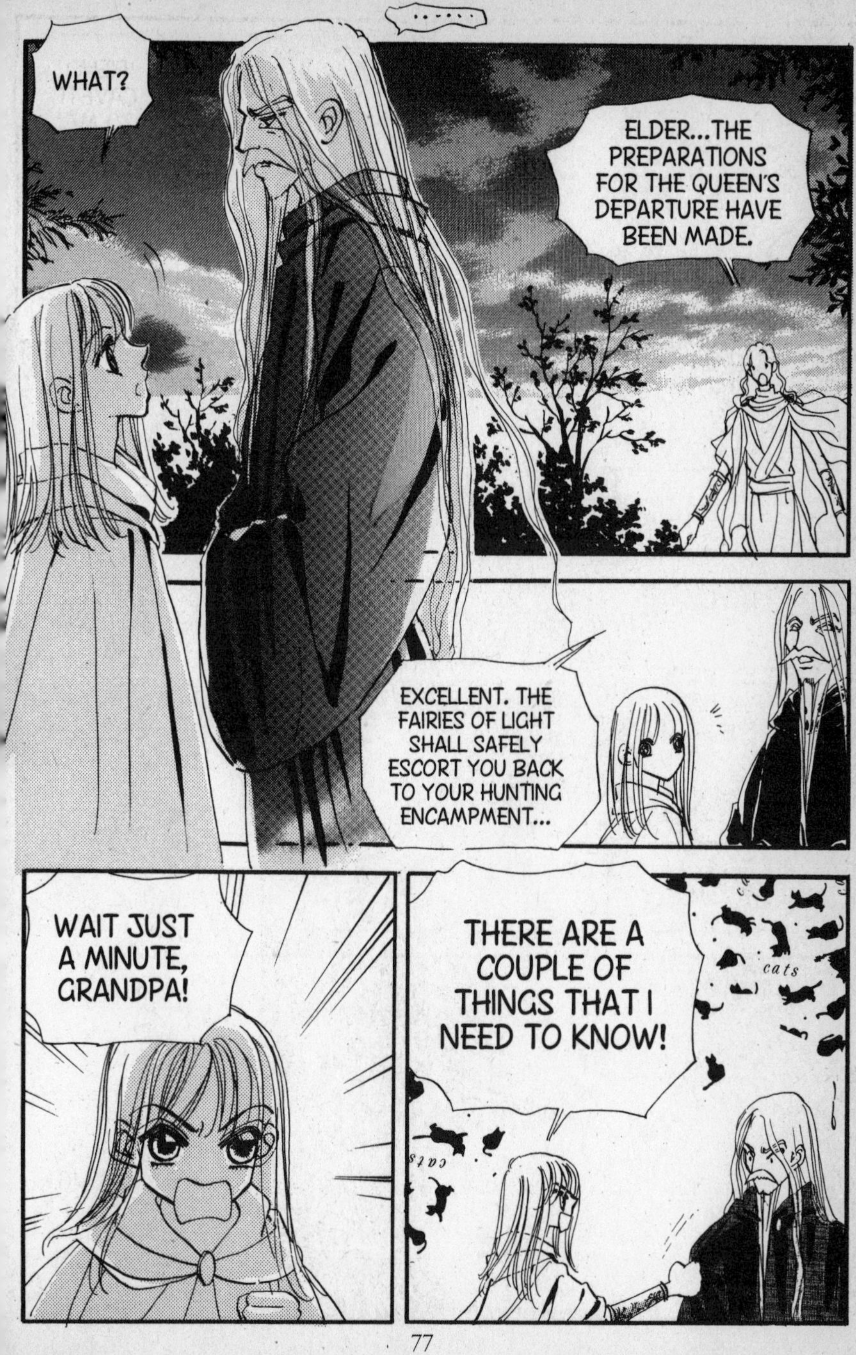

......
WHAT?
ELDER...THE PREPARATIONS FOR THE QUEEN'S DEPARTURE HAVE BEEN MADE.
EXCELLENT. THE FAIRIES OF LIGHT SHALL SAFELY ESCORT YOU BACK TO YOUR HUNTING ENCAMPMENT...
WAIT JUST A MINUTE, GRANDPA!
THERE ARE A COUPLE OF THINGS THAT I NEED TO KNOW!
cats
cats

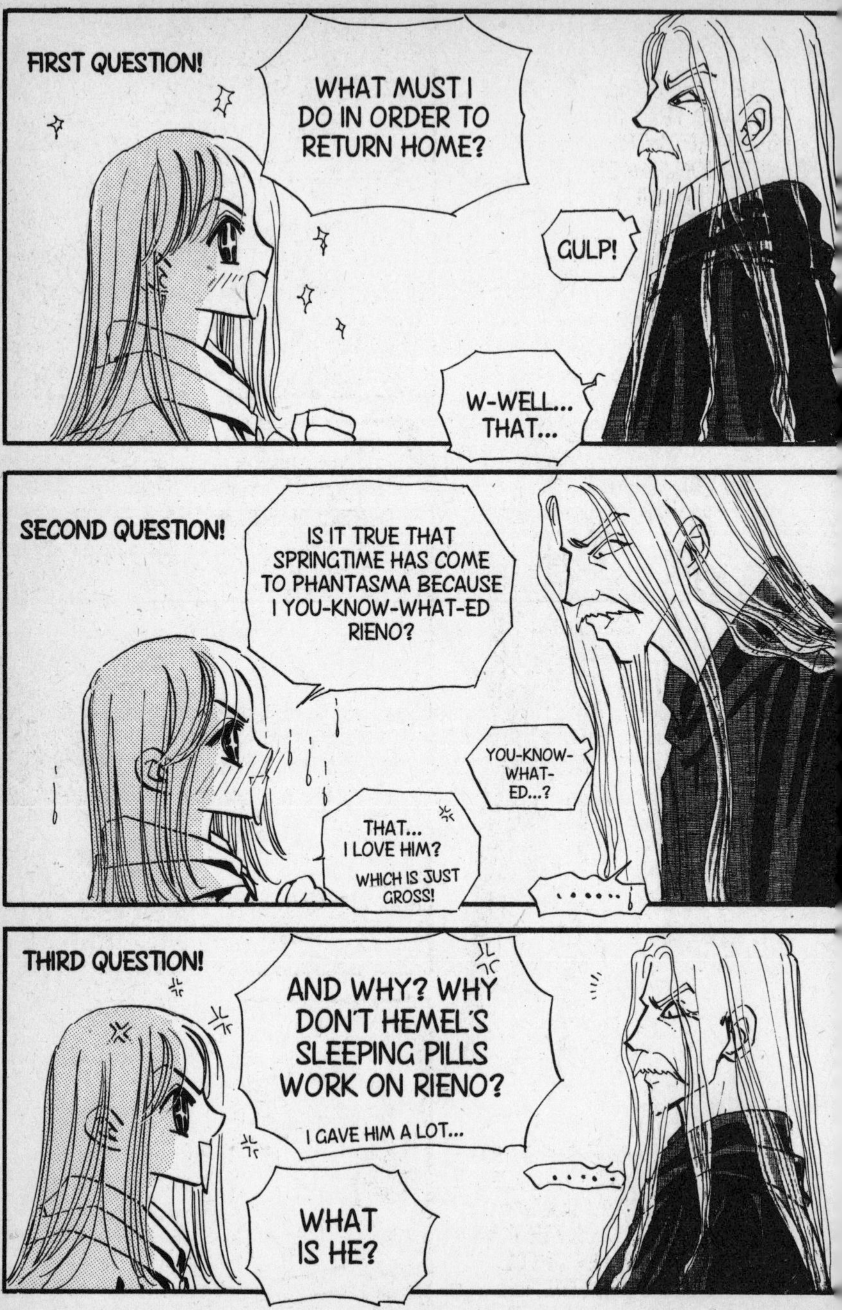
FIRST QUESTION!
WHAT MUST I DO IN ORDER TO RETURN HOME?
GULP!
W-WELL... THAT...
SECOND QUESTION!
IS IT TRUE THAT SPRINGTIME HAS COME TO PHANTASMA BECAUSE I YOU-KNOW-WHAT-ED RIENO?
YOU-KNOW-WHAT-ED...?
THAT... I LOVE HIM?
WHICH IS JUST GROSS!
......
THIRD QUESTION!
AND WHY? WHY DON'T HEMEL'S SLEEPING PILLS WORK ON RIENO?
I GAVE HIM A LOT...
.....
WHAT IS HE?

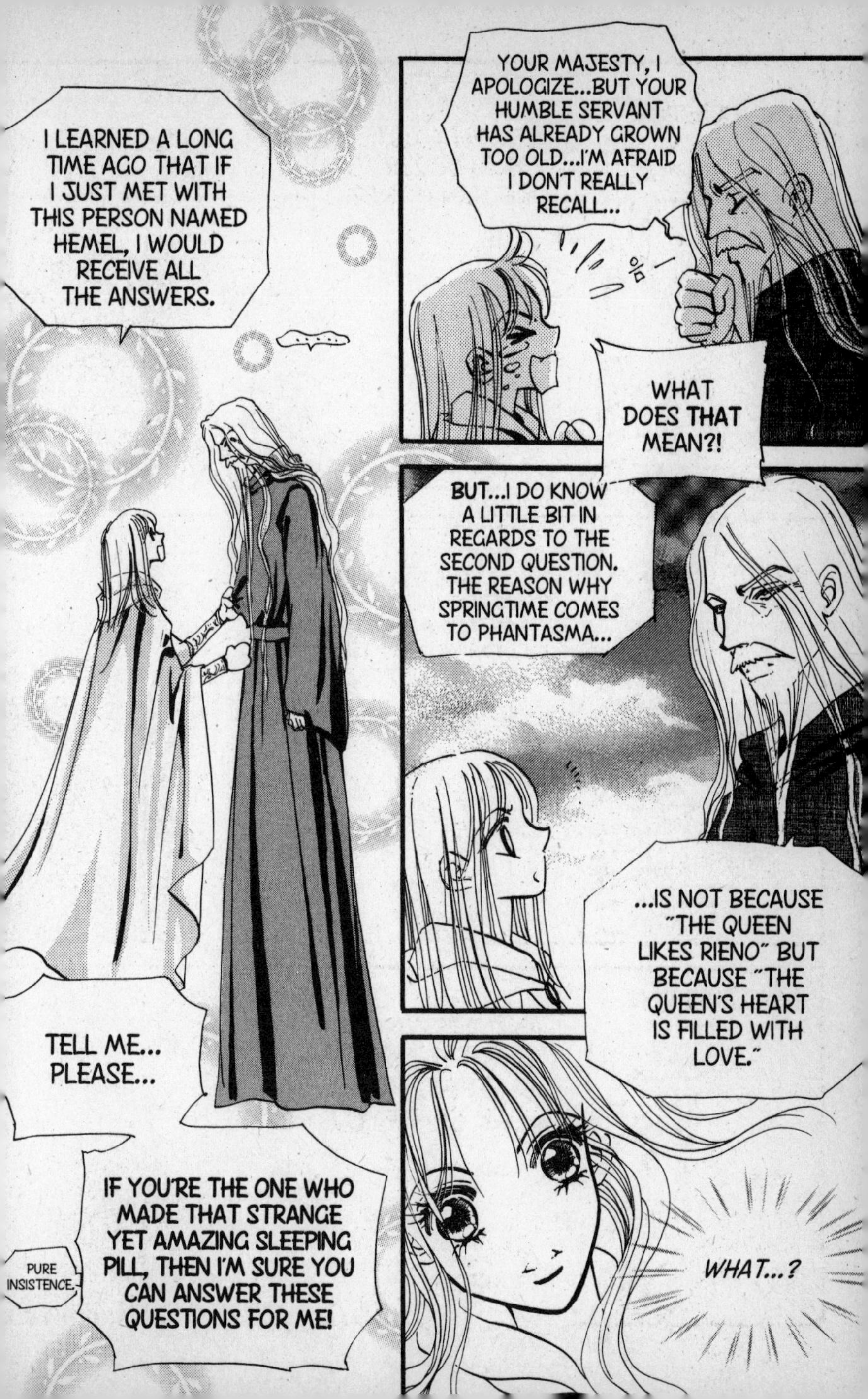
I LEARNED A LONG TIME AGO THAT IF I JUST MET WITH THIS PERSON NAMED HEMEL, I WOULD RECEIVE ALL THE ANSWERS.
...
TELL ME... PLEASE...
IF YOU'RE THE ONE WHO MADE THAT STRANGE YET AMAZING SLEEPING PILL, THEN I'M SURE YOU CAN ANSWER THESE QUESTIONS FOR ME!
PURE INSISTENCE.
YOUR MAJESTY, I APOLOGIZE...BUT YOUR HUMBLE SERVANT HAS ALREADY GROWN TOO OLD...I'M AFRAID I DON'T REALLY RECALL...
WHAT DOES THAT MEAN?!
BUT...I DO KNOW A LITTLE BIT IN REGARDS TO THE SECOND QUESTION. THE REASON WHY SPRINGTIME COMES TO PHANTASMA...
...IS NOT BECAUSE "THE QUEEN LIKES RIENO" BUT BECAUSE "THE QUEEN'S HEART IS FILLED WITH LOVE."
WHAT...?

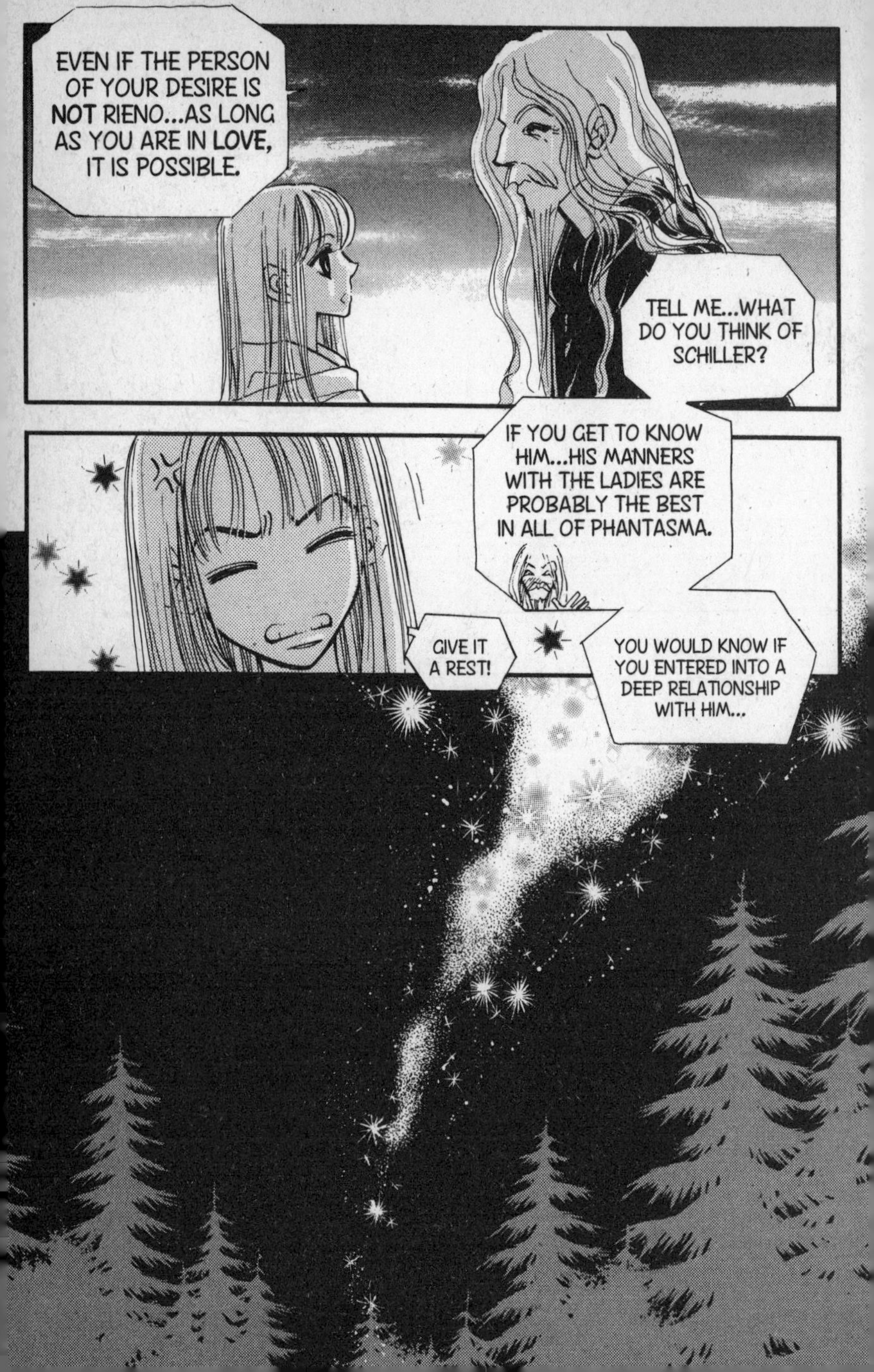
EVEN IF THE PERSON OF YOUR DESIRE IS NOT RIENO...AS LONG AS YOU ARE IN LOVE, IT IS POSSIBLE.
TELL ME...WHAT DO YOU THINK OF SCHILLER?
IF YOU GET TO KNOW HIM...HIS MANNERS WITH THE LADIES ARE PROBABLY THE BEST IN ALL OF PHANTASMA.
GIVE IT A REST!
YOU WOULD KNOW IF YOU ENTERED INTO A DEEP RELATIONSHIP WITH HIM...

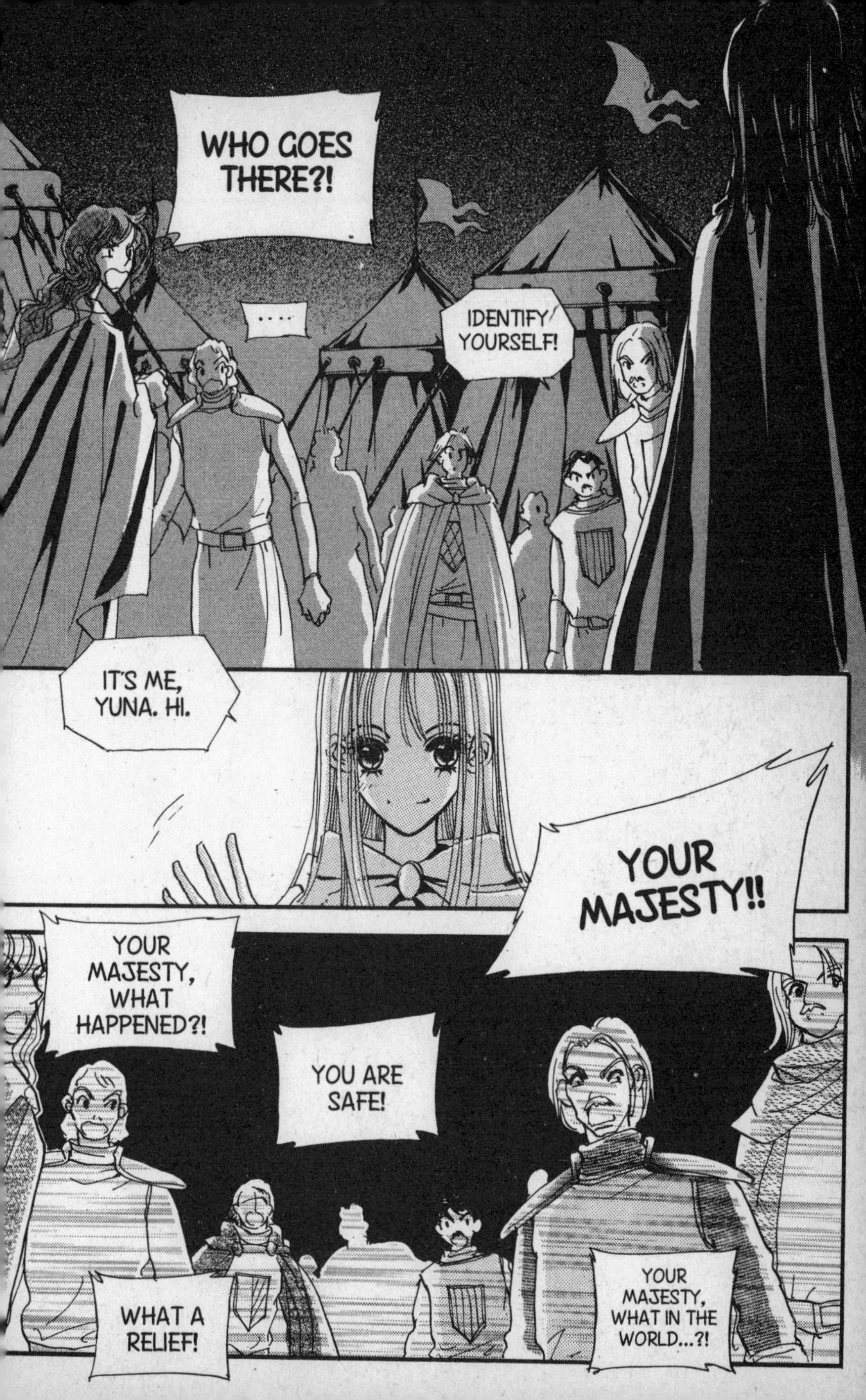
WHO GOES THERE?!
....
IDENTIFY YOURSELF!
IT'S ME, YUNA. HI.
YOUR MAJESTY!!
YOUR MAJESTY, WHAT HAPPENED?!
YOU ARE SAFE!
WHAT A RELIEF!
YOUR MAJESTY, WHAT IN THE WORLD...?!

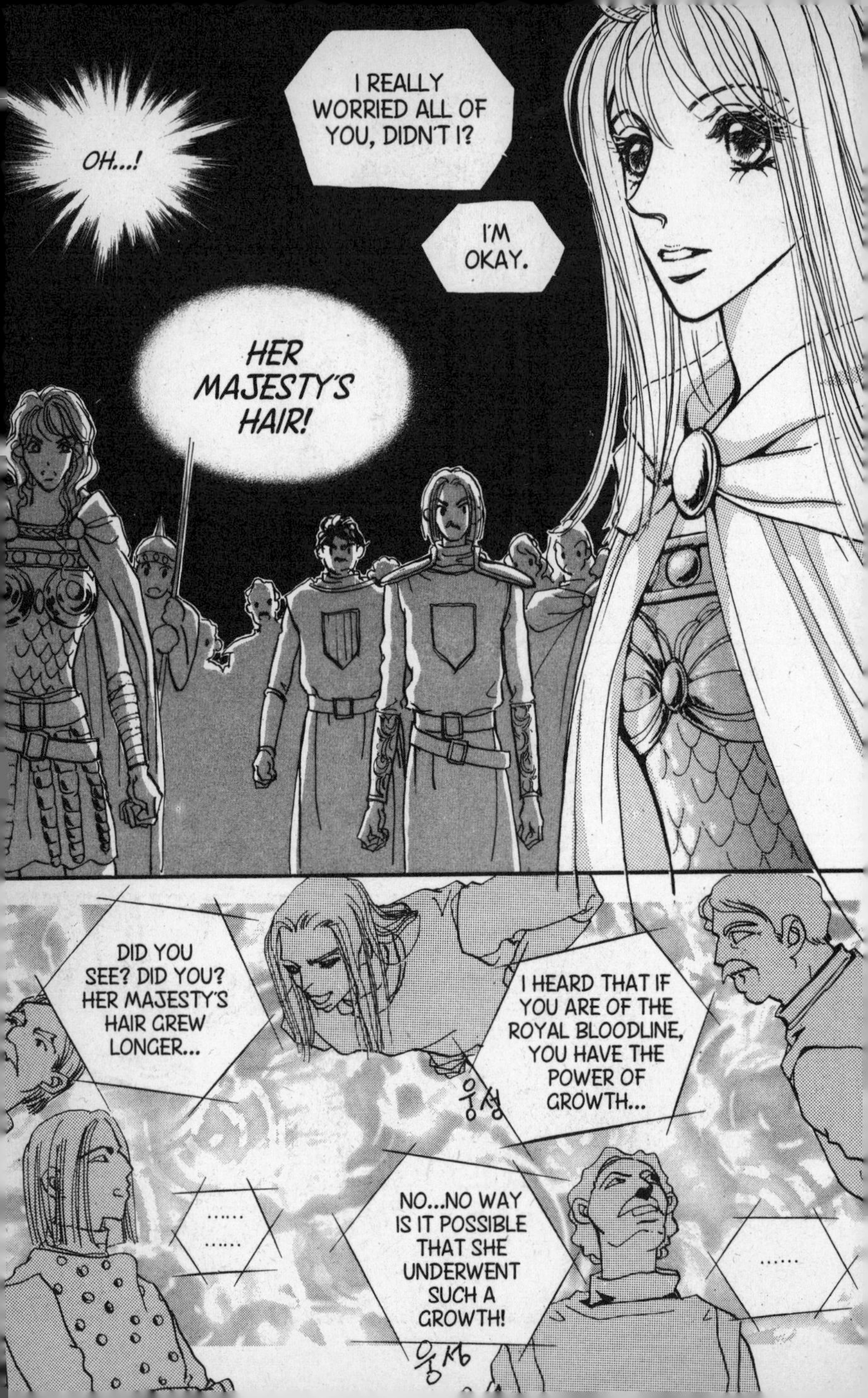
OH...!
I REALLY WORRIED ALL OF YOU, DIDN'T I?
I'M OKAY.
HER MAJESTY'S HAIR!
DID YOU SEE? DID YOU? HER MAJESTY'S HAIR GREW LONGER...
I HEARD THAT IF YOU ARE OF THE ROYAL BLOODLINE, YOU HAVE THE POWER OF GROWTH...
웅성
......
......
NO...NO WAY IS IT POSSIBLE THAT SHE UNDERWENT SUCH A GROWTH!
......
웅성

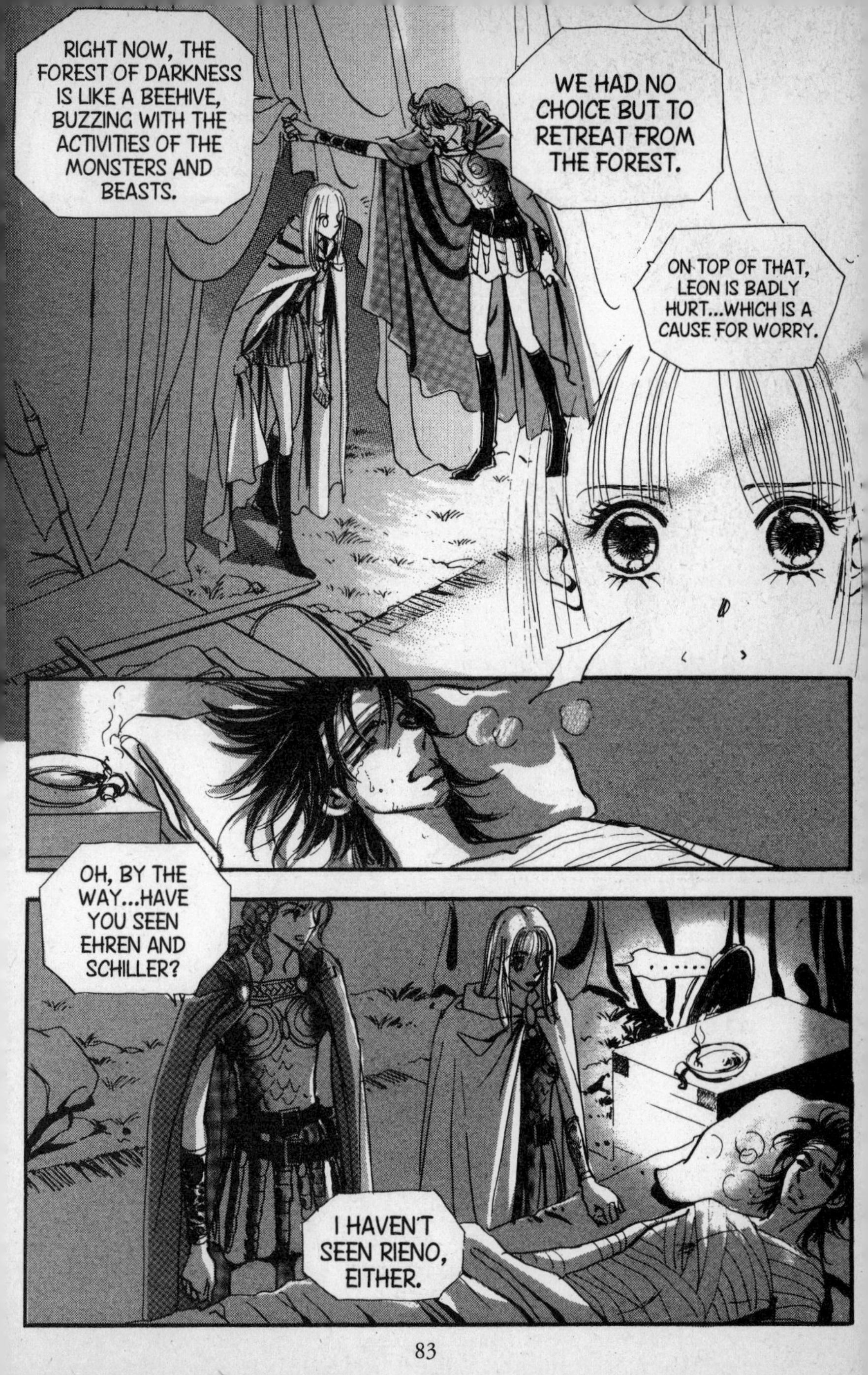
RIGHT NOW, THE FOREST OF DARKNESS IS LIKE A BEEHIVE, BUZZING WITH THE ACTIVITIES OF THE MONSTERS AND BEASTS.
WE HAD NO CHOICE BUT TO RETREAT FROM THE FOREST.
ON TOP OF THAT, LEON IS BADLY HURT...WHICH IS A CAUSE FOR WORRY.
OH, BY THE WAY...HAVE YOU SEEN EHREN AND SCHILLER?
......
I HAVEN'T SEEN RIENO, EITHER.

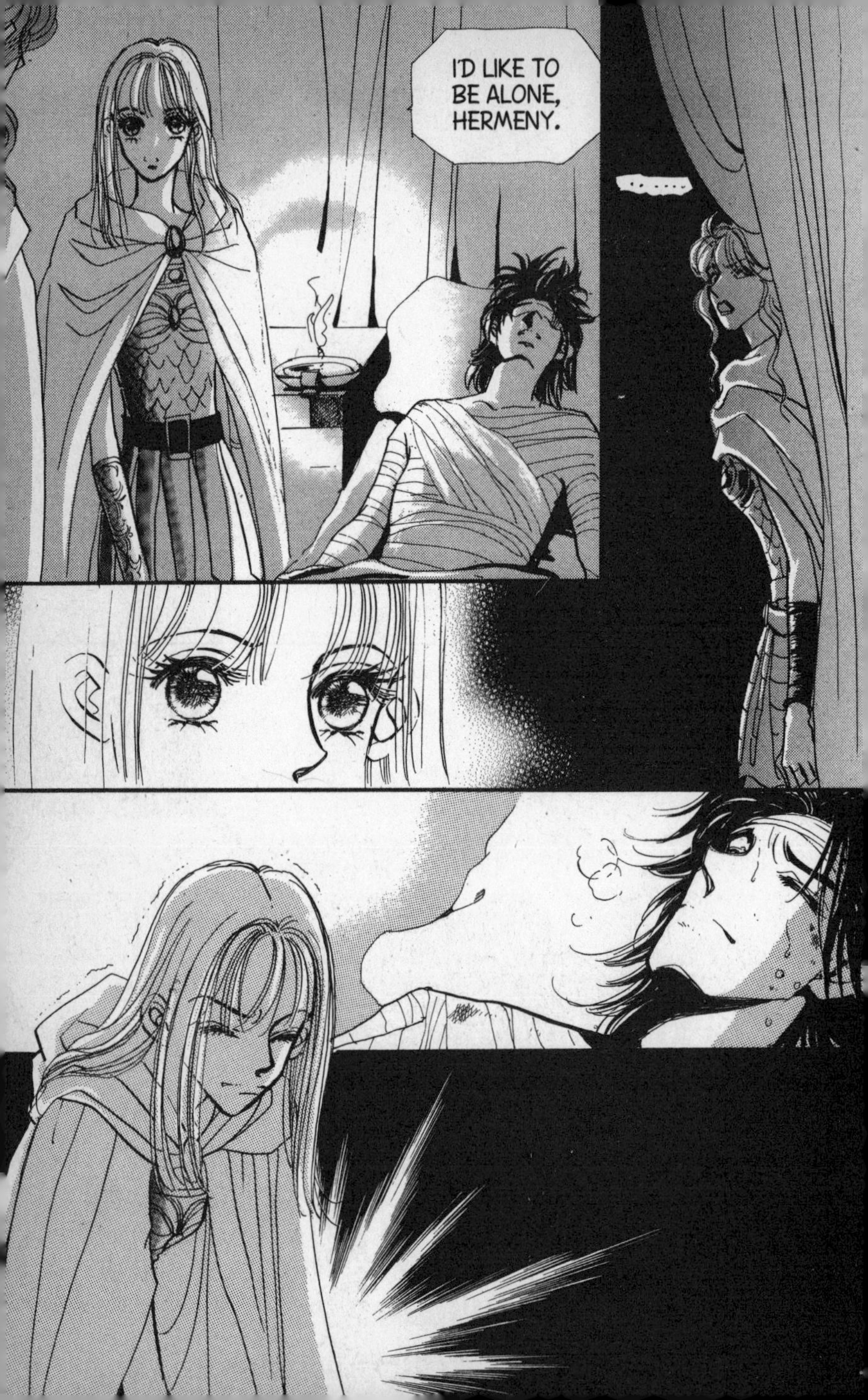
I'D LIKE TO BE ALONE, HERMENY.
......

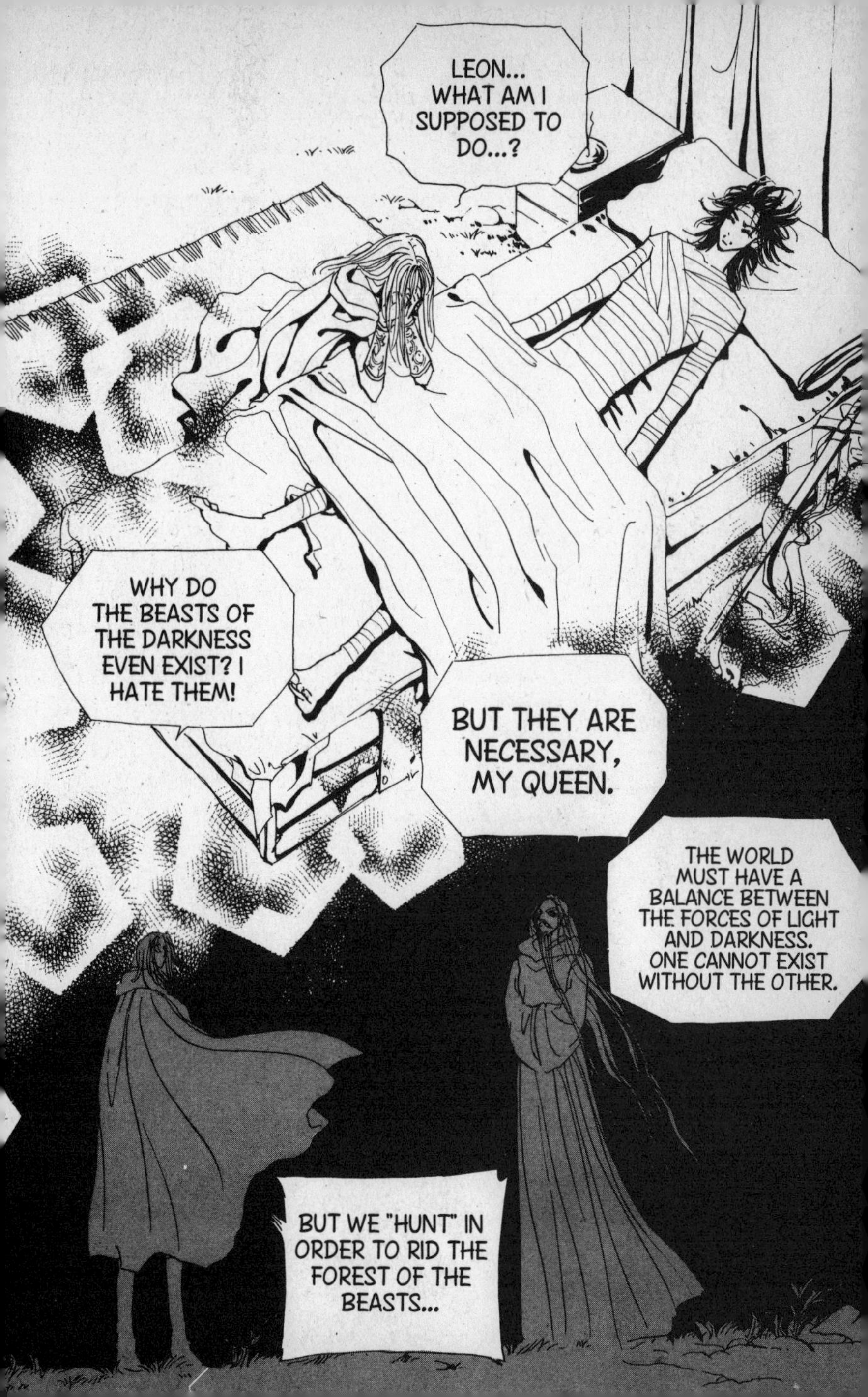
LEON... WHAT AM I SUPPOSED TO DO...?
WHY DO THE BEASTS OF THE DARKNESS EVEN EXIST? I HATE THEM!
BUT THEY ARE NECESSARY, MY QUEEN.
THE WORLD MUST HAVE A BALANCE BETWEEN THE FORCES OF LIGHT AND DARKNESS. ONE CANNOT EXIST WITHOUT THE OTHER.
BUT WE "HUNT" IN ORDER TO RID THE FOREST OF THE BEASTS...

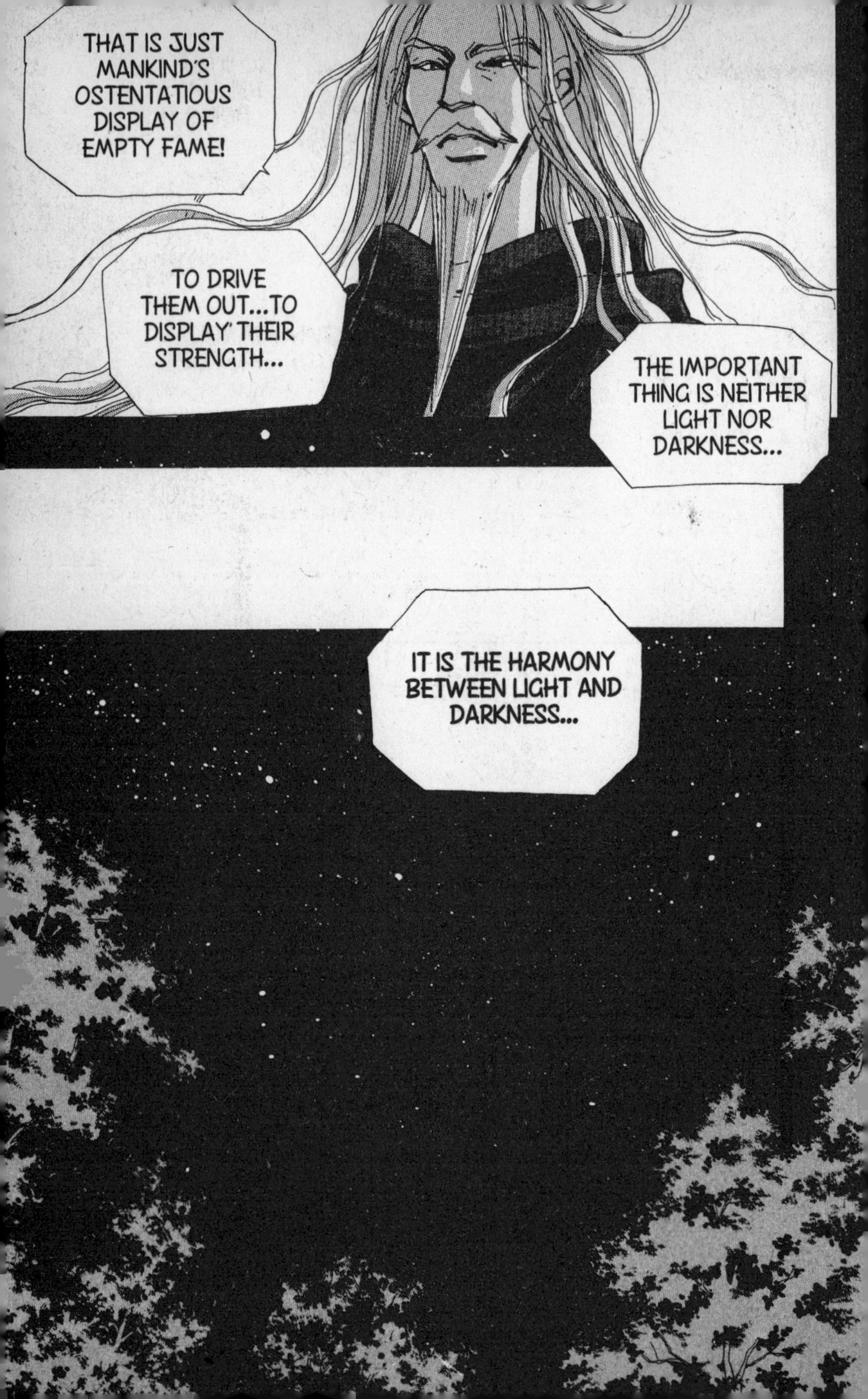
THAT IS JUST MANKIND'S OSTENTATIOUS DISPLAY OF EMPTY FAME!
TO DRIVE THEM OUT...TO DISPLAY THEIR STRENGTH...
THE IMPORTANT THING IS NEITHER LIGHT NOR DARKNESS...
IT IS THE HARMONY BETWEEN LIGHT AND DARKNESS...

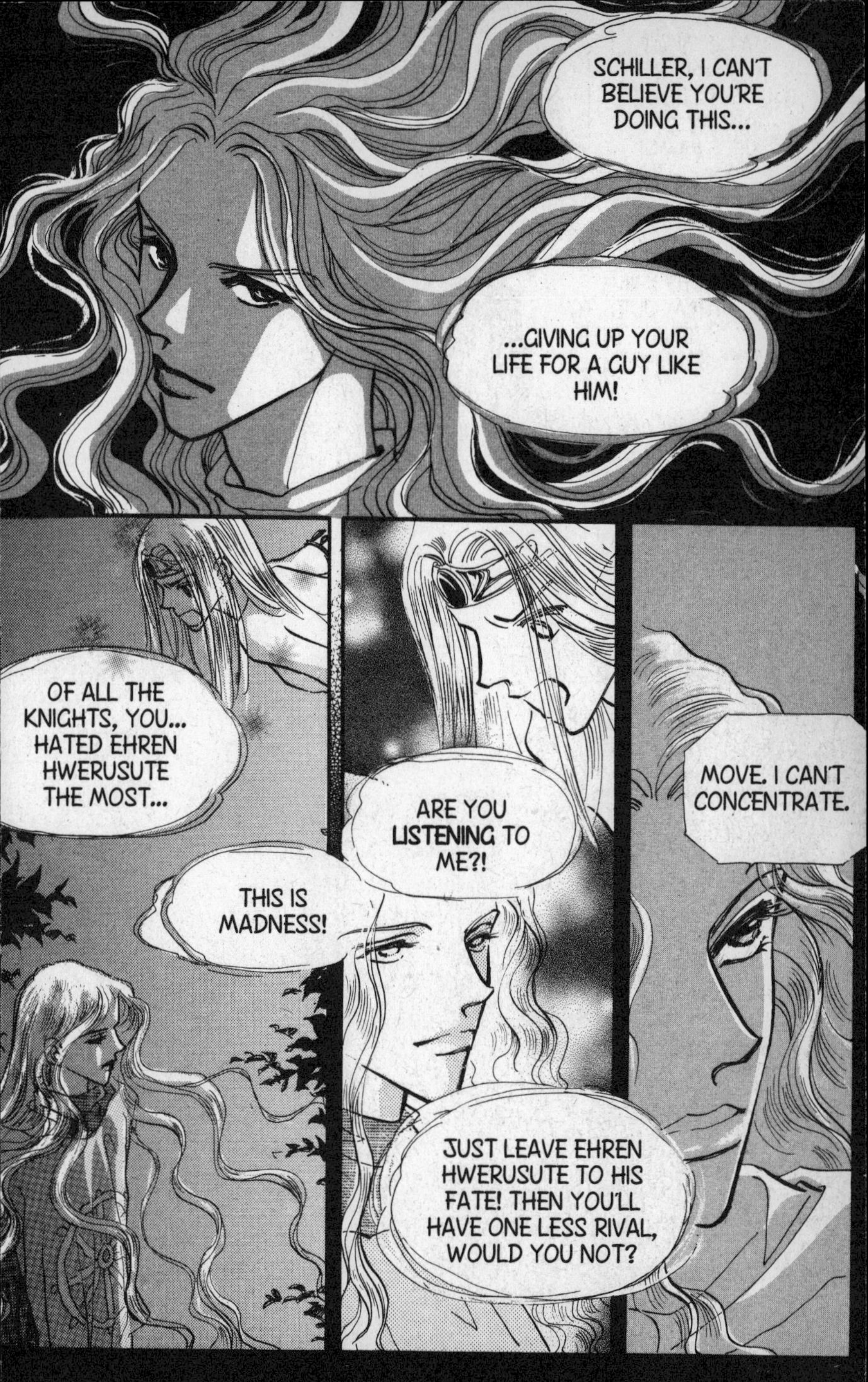
SCHILLER, I CAN'T BELIEVE YOU'RE DOING THIS...
...GIVING UP YOUR LIFE FOR A GUY LIKE HIM!
OF ALL THE KNIGHTS, YOU... HATED EHREN HWERUSUTE THE MOST...
THIS IS MADNESS!
ARE YOU LISTENING TO ME?!
JUST LEAVE EHREN HWERUSUTE TO HIS FATE! THEN YOU'LL HAVE ONE LESS RIVAL, WOULD YOU NOT?
MOVE. I CAN'T CONCENTRATE.

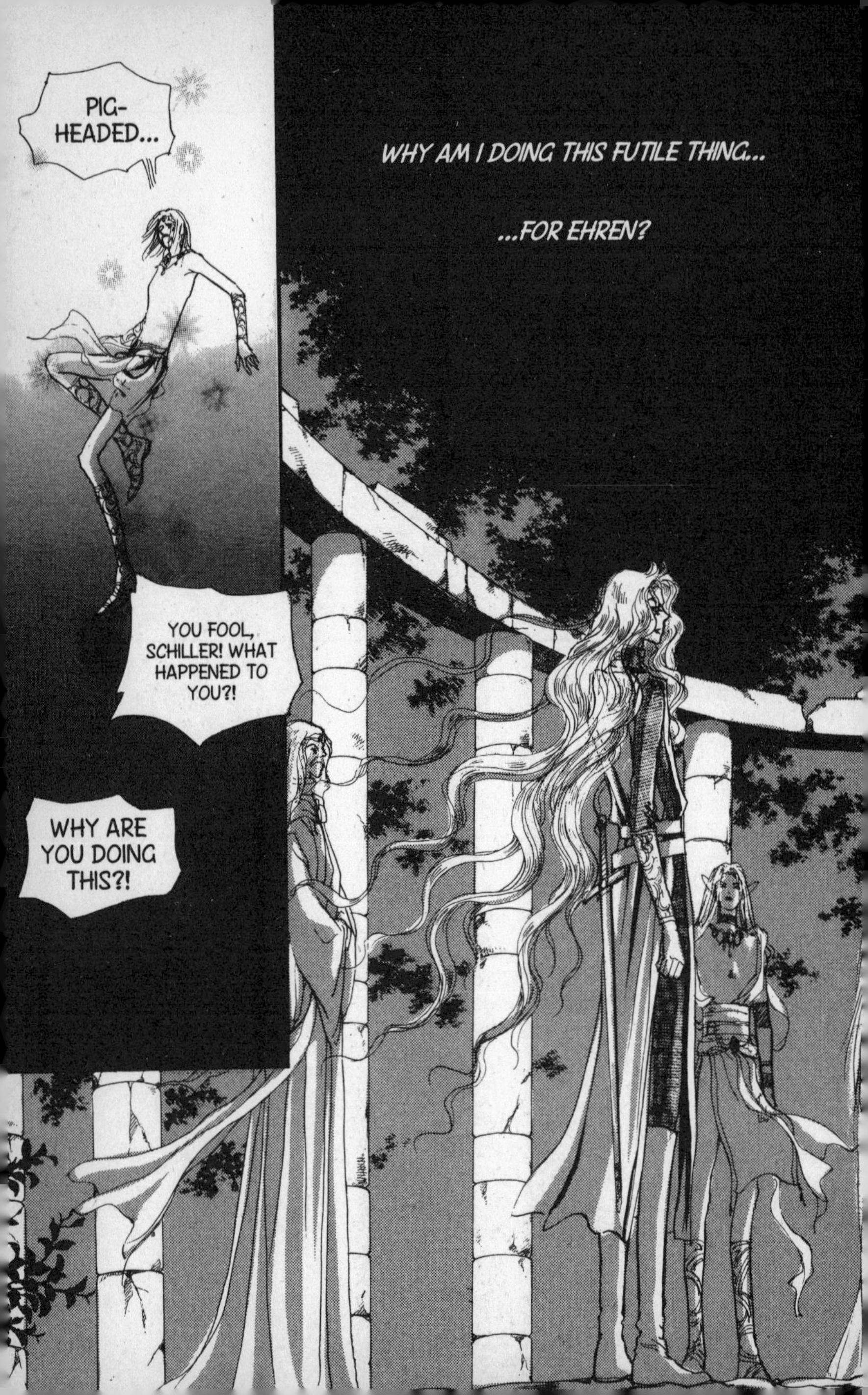
WHY AM I DOING THIS FUTILE THING...
...FOR EHREN?
PIG-HEADED...
YOU FOOL, SCHILLER! WHAT HAPPENED TO YOU?!
WHY ARE YOU DOING THIS?!

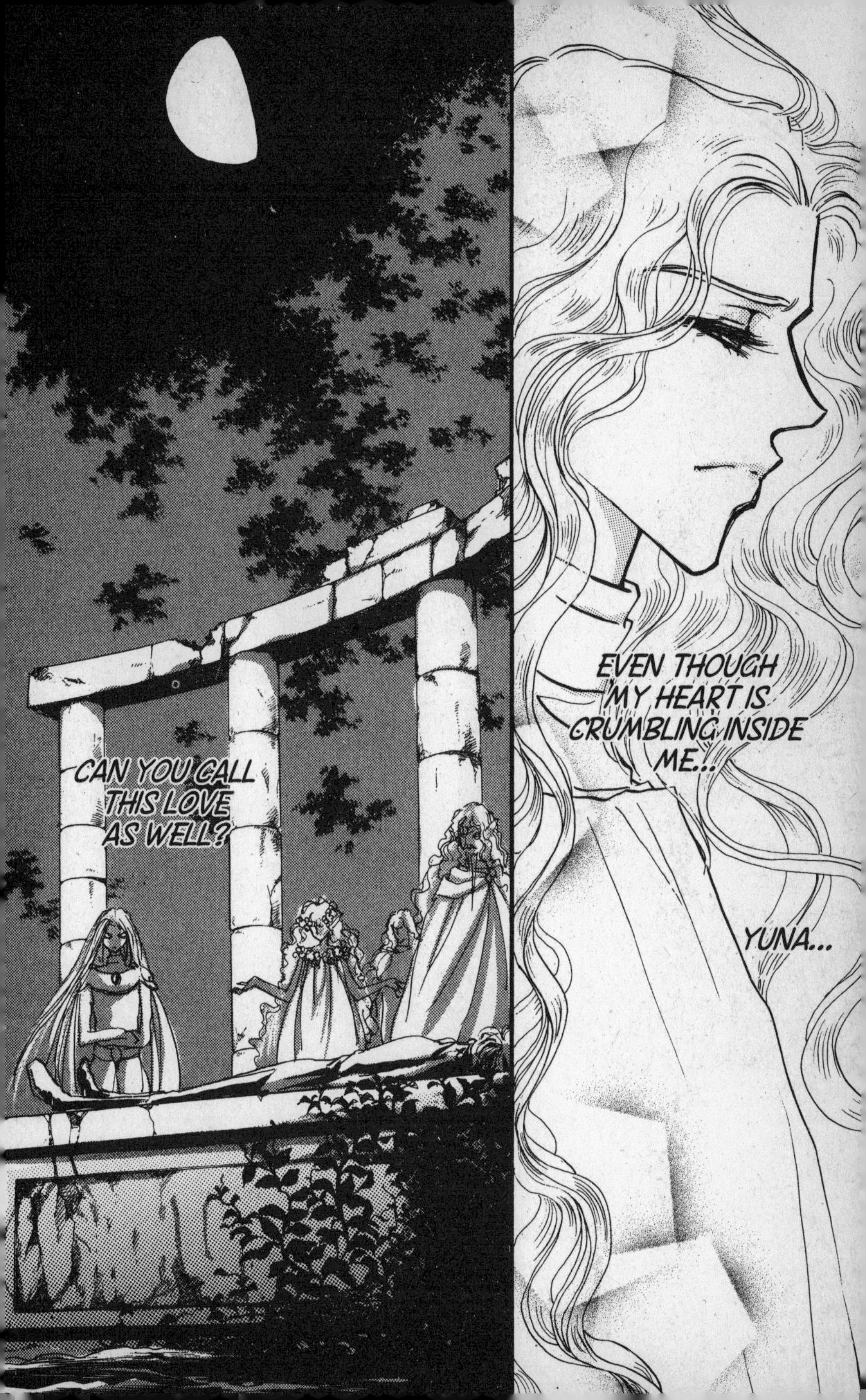
CAN YOU CALL THIS LOVE AS WELL?
EVEN THOUGH MY HEART IS CRUMBLING INSIDE ME...
YUNA...

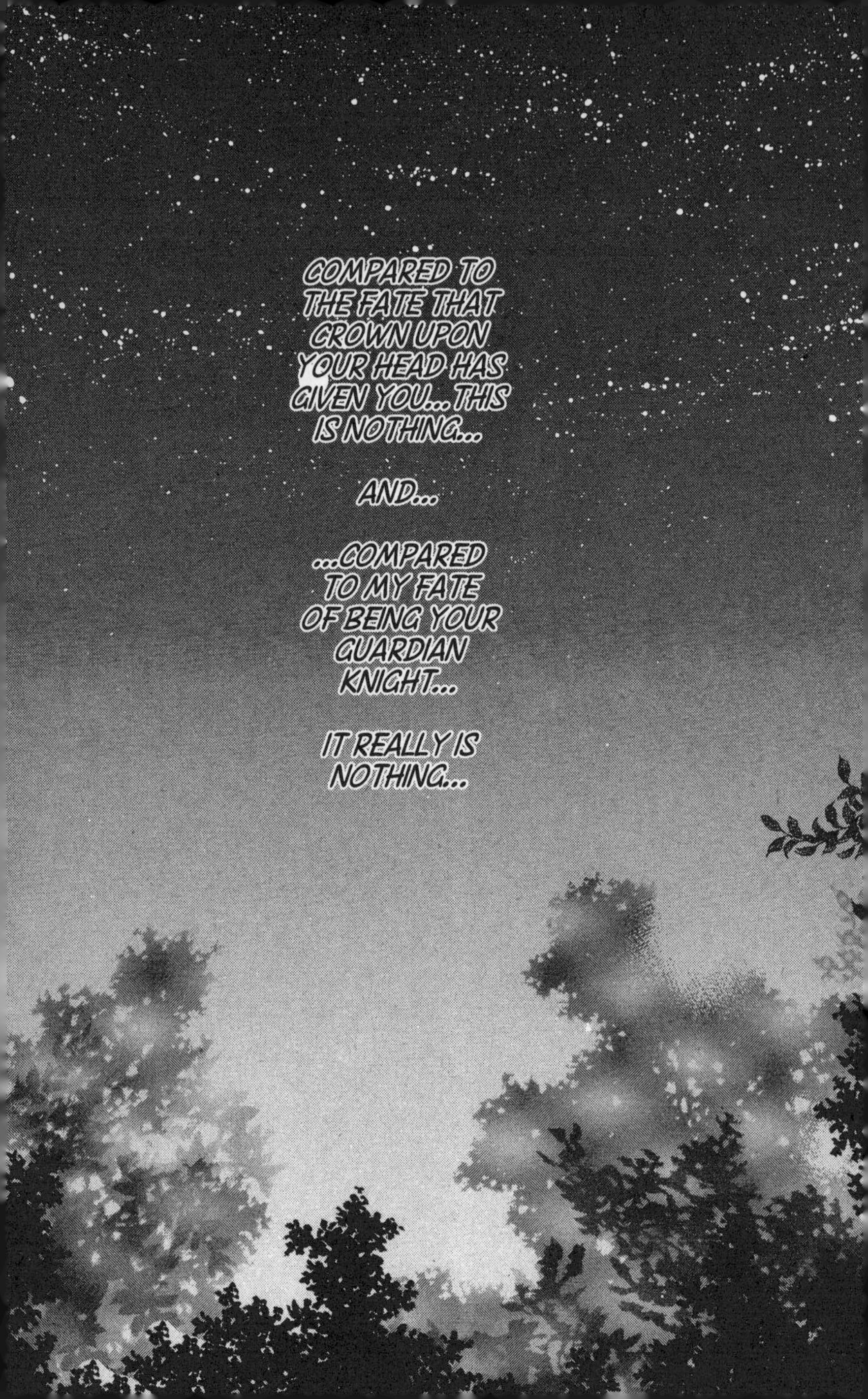
COMPARED TO THE FATE THAT CROWN UPON YOUR HEAD HAS GIVEN YOU...THIS IS NOTHING...
AND...
...COMPARED TO MY FATE OF BEING YOUR GUARDIAN KNIGHT...
IT REALLY IS NOTHING...

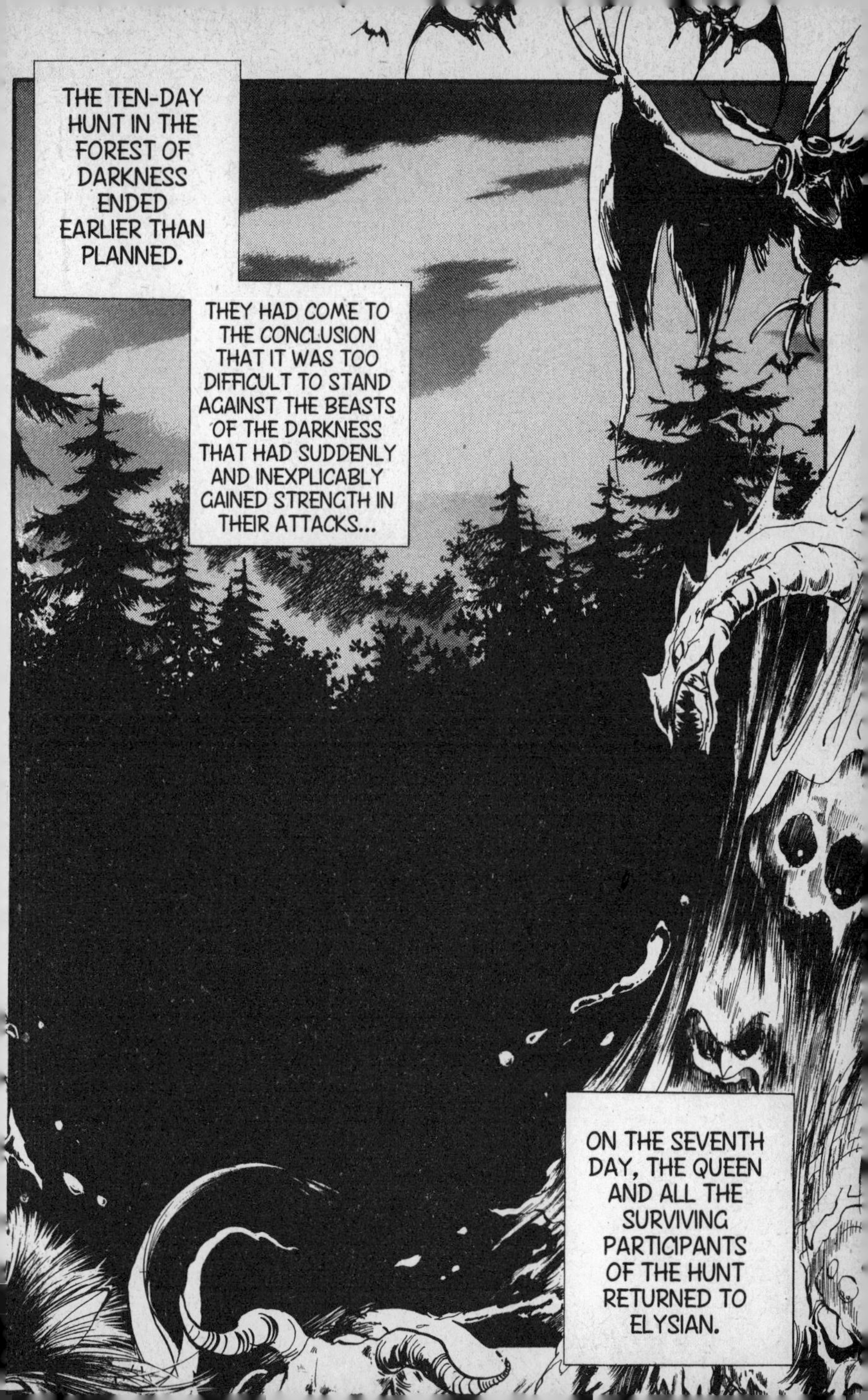
THE TEN-DAY HUNT IN THE FOREST OF DARKNESS ENDED EARLIER THAN PLANNED.
THEY HAD COME TO THE CONCLUSION THAT IT WAS TOO DIFFICULT TO STAND AGAINST THE BEASTS OF THE DARKNESS THAT HAD SUDDENLY AND INEXPLICABLY GAINED STRENGTH IN THEIR ATTACKS...
ON THE SEVENTH DAY, THE QUEEN AND ALL THE SURVIVING PARTICIPANTS OF THE HUNT RETURNED TO ELYSIAN.

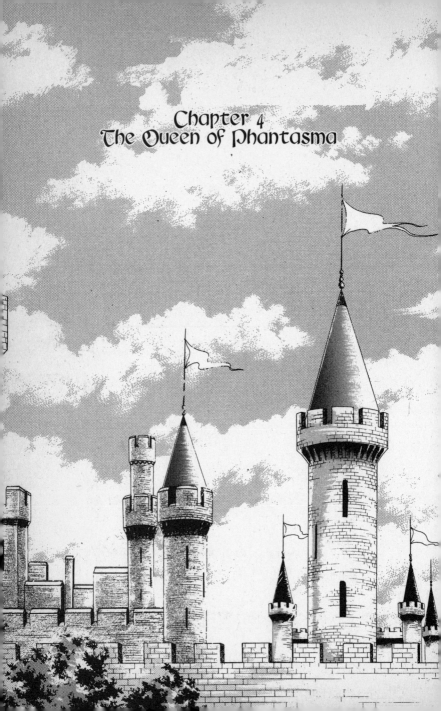

Chapter 4
The Queen of Phantasma

Growth

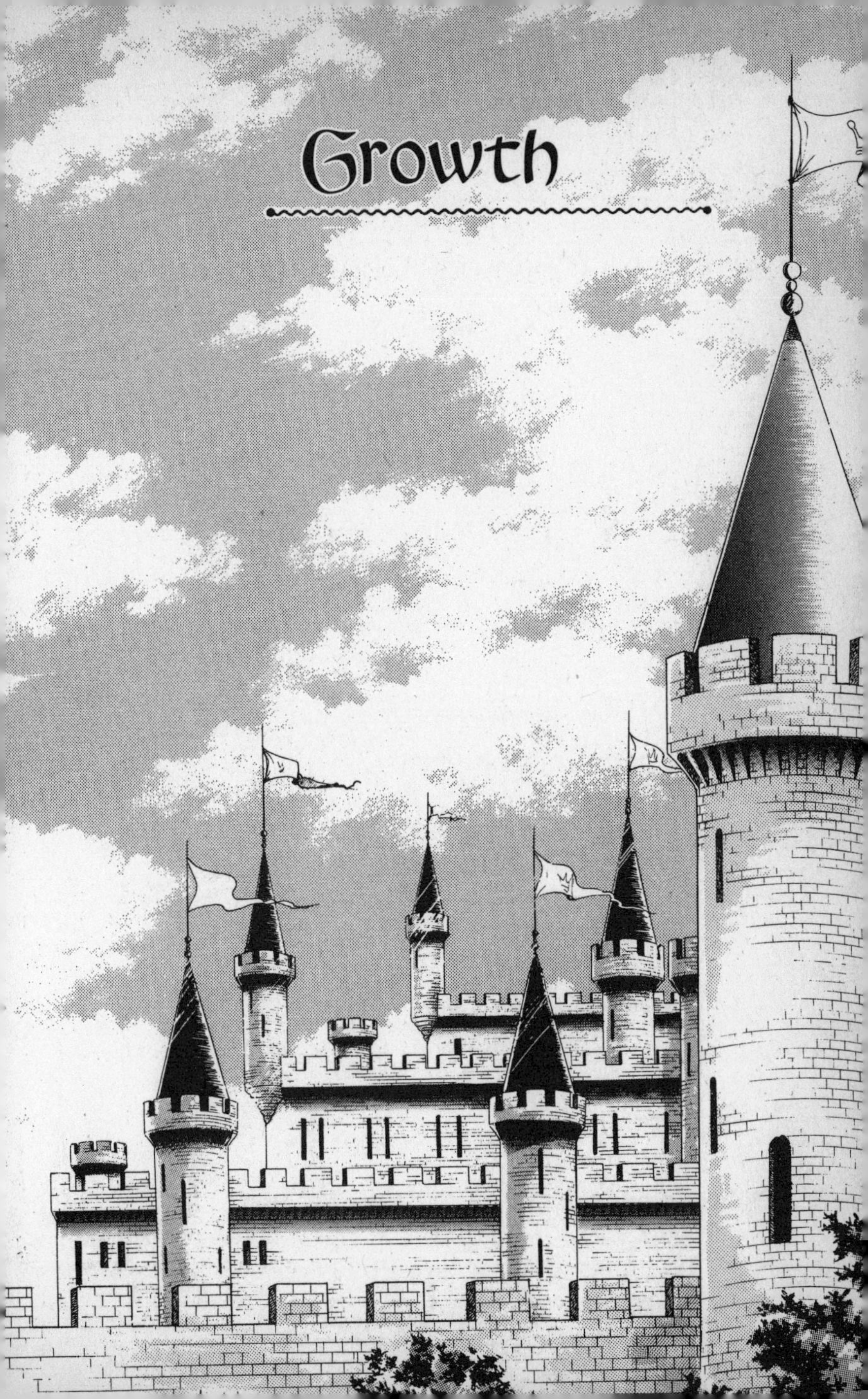

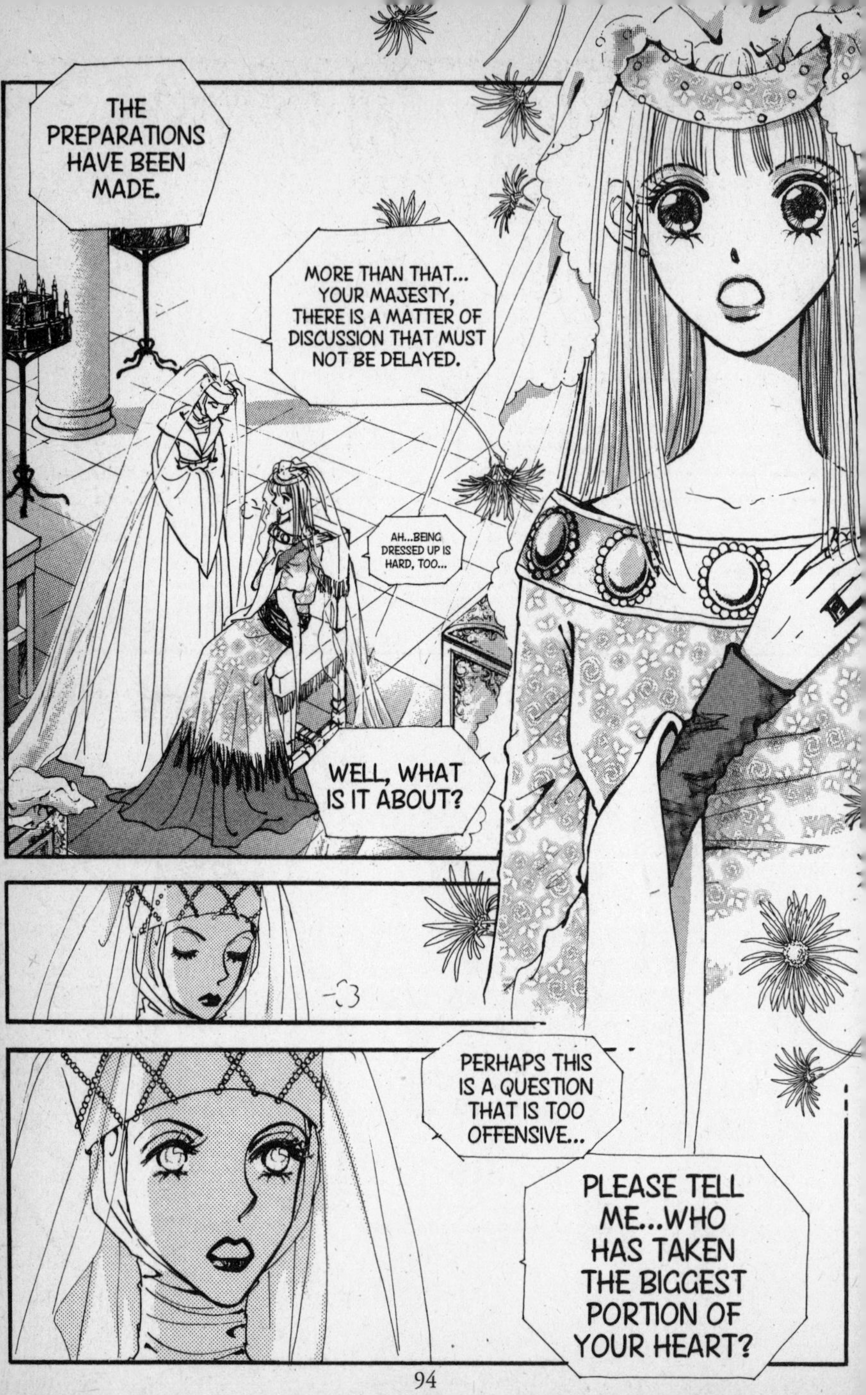
THE PREPARATIONS HAVE BEEN MADE.
MORE THAN THAT... YOUR MAJESTY, THERE IS A MATTER OF DISCUSSION THAT MUST NOT BE DELAYED.
AH...BEING DRESSED UP IS HARD, TOO...
WELL, WHAT IS IT ABOUT?
PERHAPS THIS IS A QUESTION THAT IS TOO OFFENSIVE...
PLEASE TELL ME...WHO HAS TAKEN THE BIGGEST PORTION OF YOUR HEART?

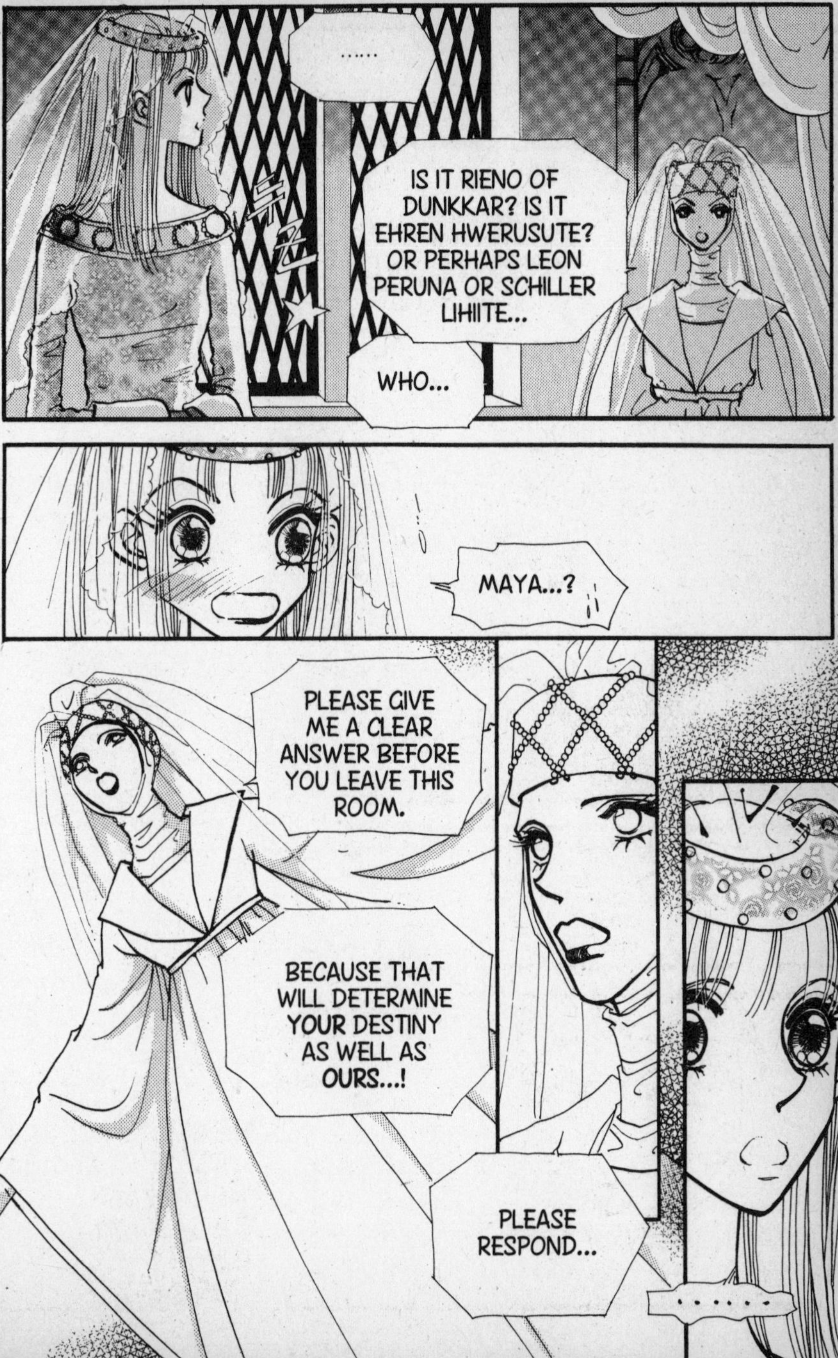
......
IS IT RIENO OF DUNKKAR? IS IT EHREN HWERUSUTE? OR PERHAPS LEON PERUNA OR SCHILLER LIHIITE...
WHO...
MAYA...?
PLEASE GIVE ME A CLEAR ANSWER BEFORE YOU LEAVE THIS ROOM.
BECAUSE THAT WILL DETERMINE YOUR DESTINY AS WELL AS OURS...!
PLEASE RESPOND...
......

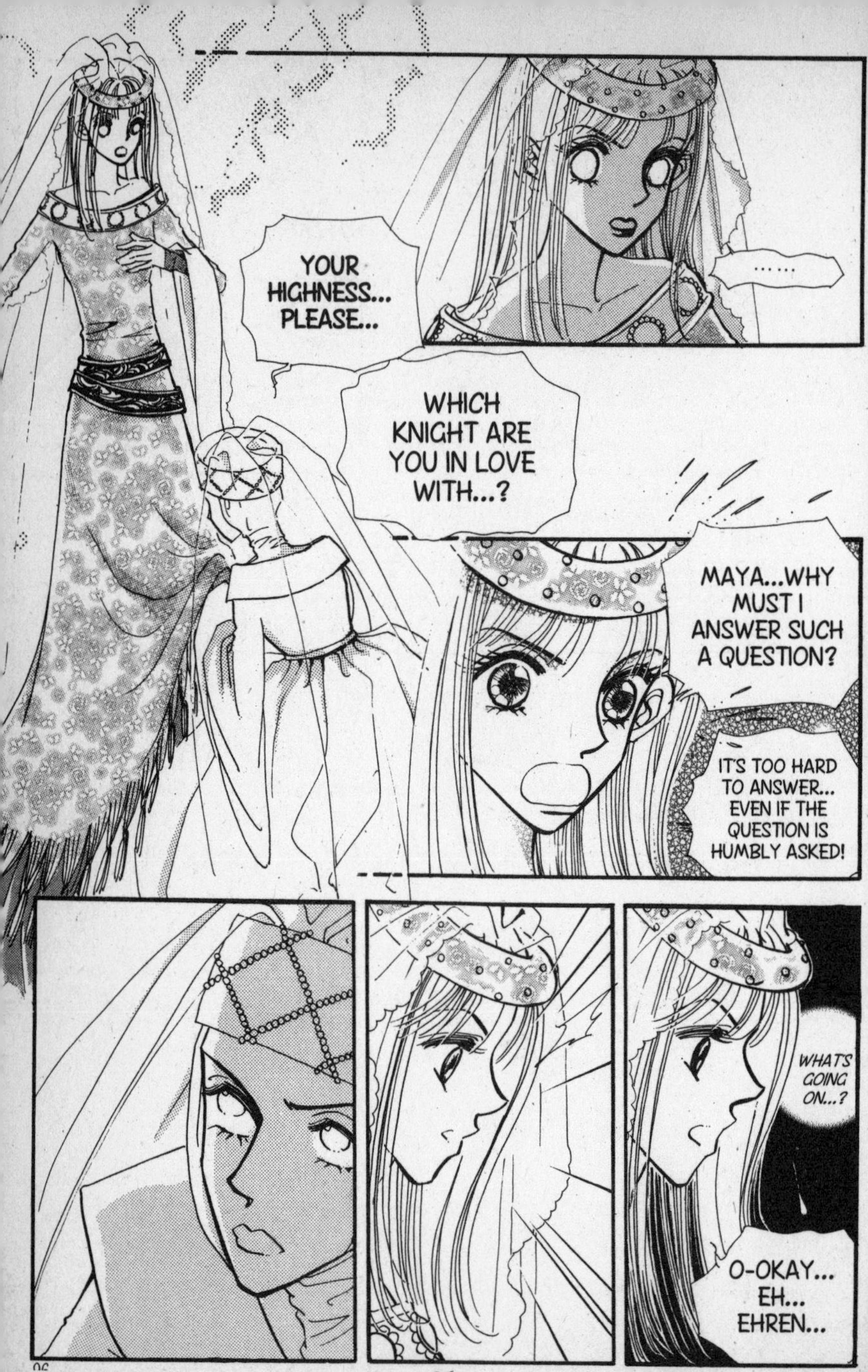
YOUR HIGHNESS... PLEASE...
......
WHICH KNIGHT ARE YOU IN LOVE WITH...?
MAYA...WHY MUST I ANSWER SUCH A QUESTION?
IT'S TOO HARD TO ANSWER... EVEN IF THE QUESTION IS HUMBLY ASKED!
WHAT'S GOING ON...?
O-OKAY... EH... EHREN...

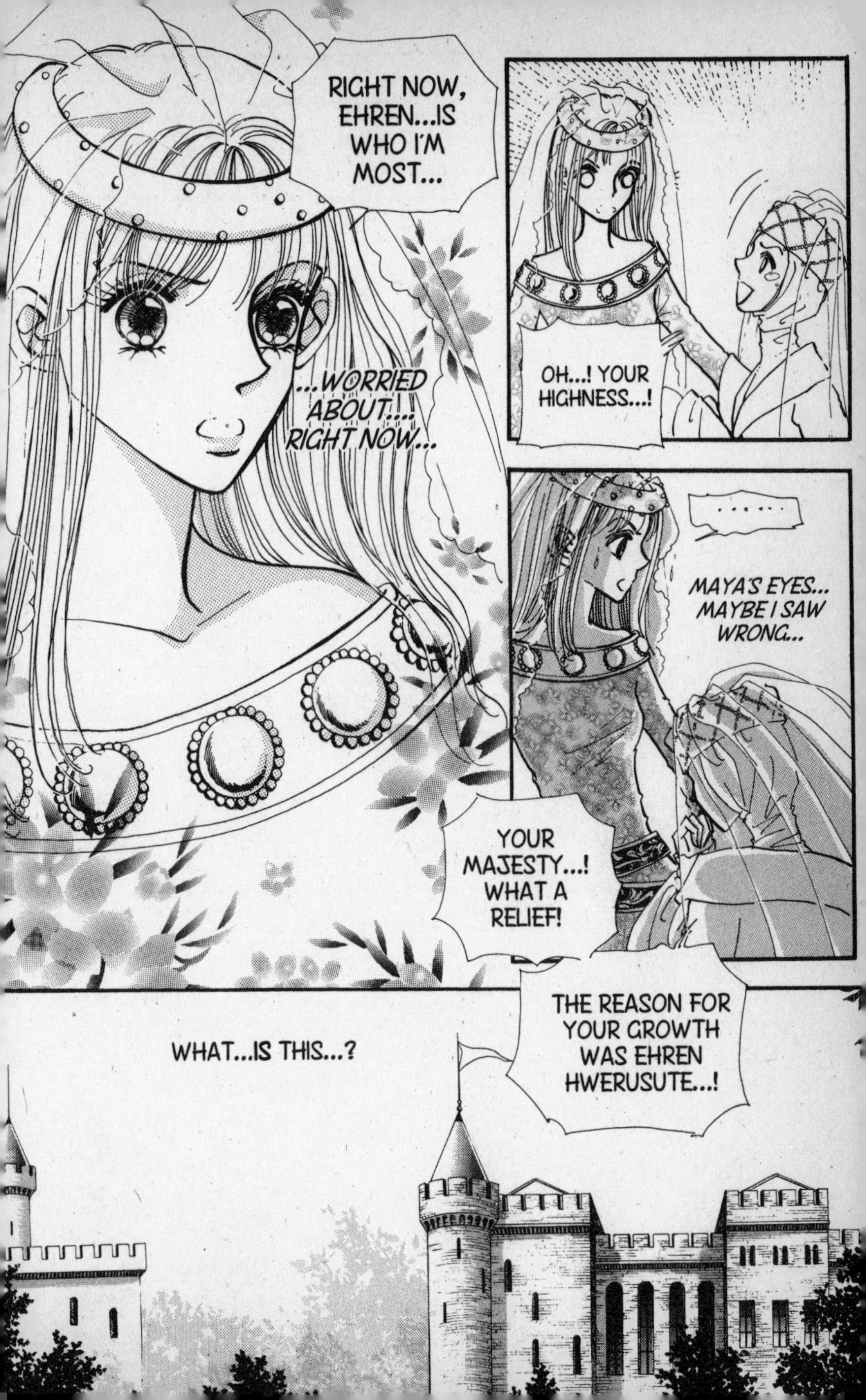
RIGHT NOW, EHREN...IS WHO I'M MOST...
...WORRIED ABOUT.... RIGHT NOW...
OH...! YOUR HIGHNESS...!
......
MAYA'S EYES... MAYBE I SAW WRONG...
YOUR MAJESTY...! WHAT A RELIEF!
WHAT...IS THIS...?
THE REASON FOR YOUR GROWTH WAS EHREN HWERUSUTE...!

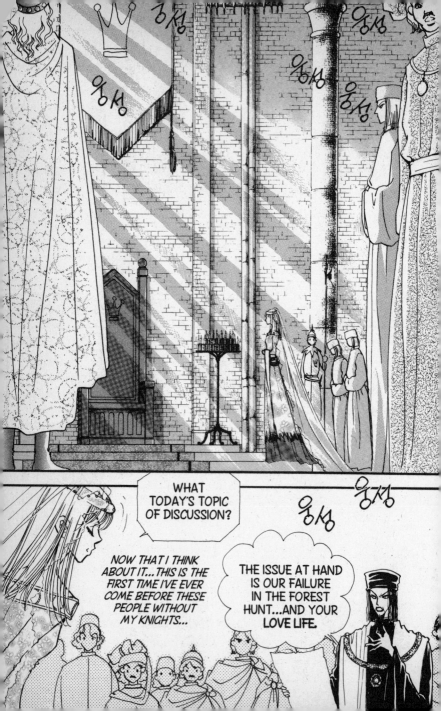

WHAT TODAY'S TOPIC OF DISCUSSION?

NOW THAT I THINK ABOUT IT...THIS IS THE FIRST TIME I'VE EVER COME BEFORE THESE PEOPLE WITHOUT MY KNIGHTS...

THE ISSUE AT HAND IS OUR FAILURE IN THE FOREST HUNT...AND YOUR LOVE LIFE.

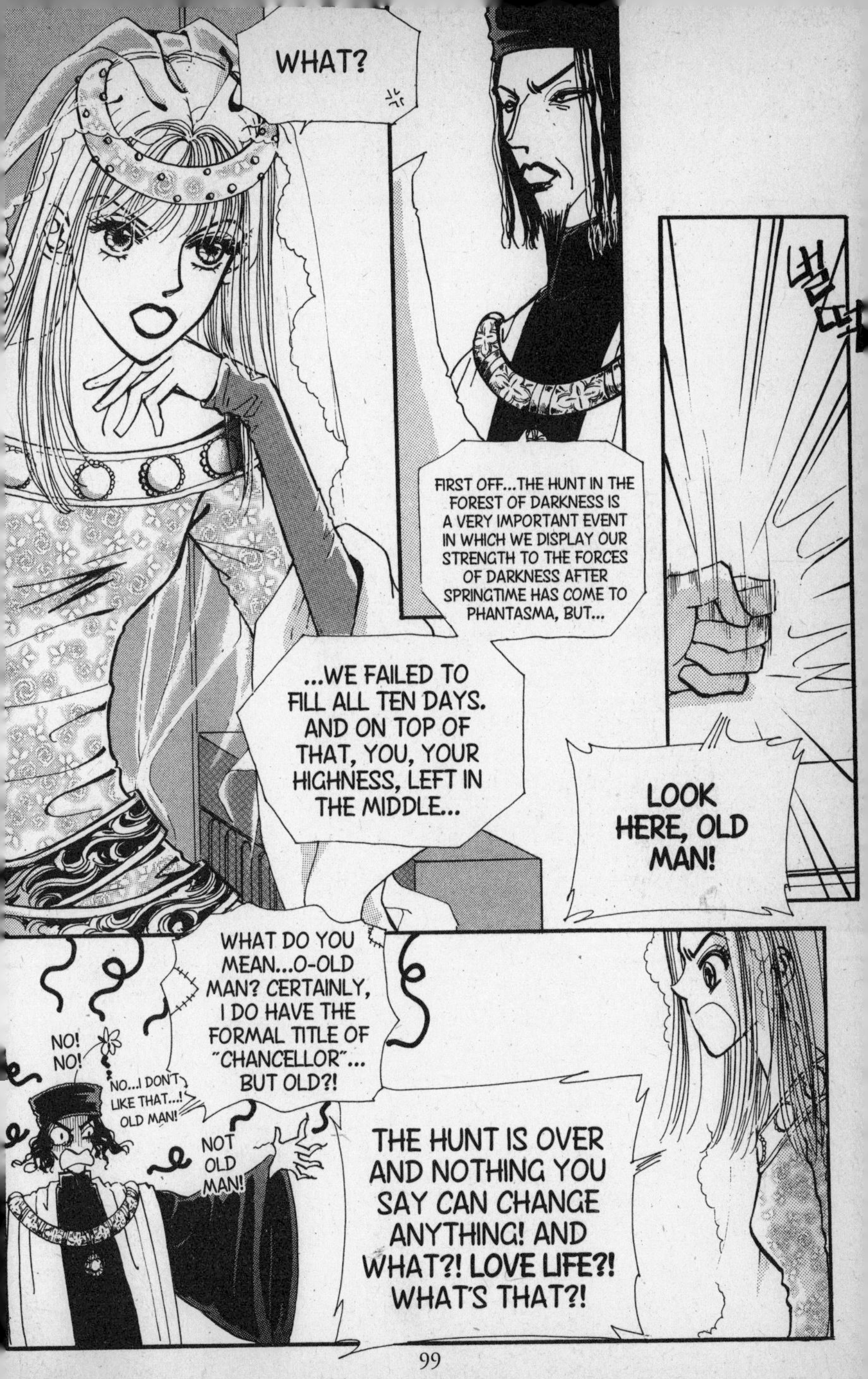
WHAT?
FIRST OFF...THE HUNT IN THE FOREST OF DARKNESS IS A VERY IMPORTANT EVENT IN WHICH WE DISPLAY OUR STRENGTH TO THE FORCES OF DARKNESS AFTER SPRINGTIME HAS COME TO PHANTASMA, BUT...
...WE FAILED TO FILL ALL TEN DAYS. AND ON TOP OF THAT, YOU, YOUR HIGHNESS, LEFT IN THE MIDDLE...
LOOK HERE, OLD MAN!
WHAT DO YOU MEAN...O-OLD MAN? CERTAINLY, I DO HAVE THE FORMAL TITLE OF "CHANCELLOR"... BUT OLD?!
NO! NO!
NO...I DON'T LIKE THAT...! OLD MAN!
NOT OLD MAN!
THE HUNT IS OVER AND NOTHING YOU SAY CAN CHANGE ANYTHING! AND WHAT?! LOVE LIFE?! WHAT'S THAT?!

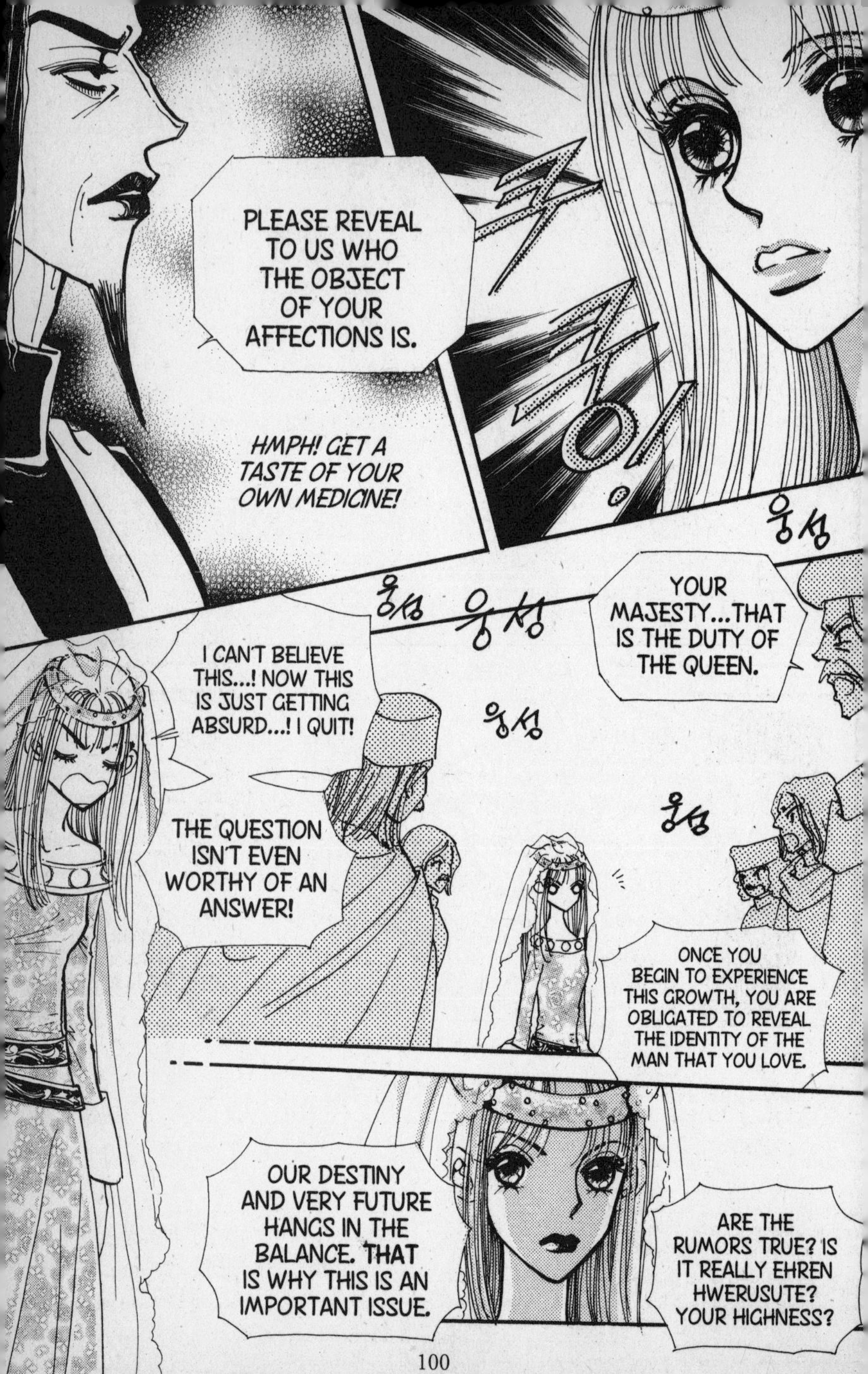
PLEASE REVEAL TO US WHO THE OBJECT OF YOUR AFFECTIONS IS.
HMPH! GET A TASTE OF YOUR OWN MEDICINE!
웅성
I CAN'T BELIEVE THIS...! NOW THIS IS JUST GETTING ABSURD...! I QUIT!
THE QUESTION ISN'T EVEN WORTHY OF AN ANSWER!
웅성 웅성
YOUR MAJESTY...THAT IS THE DUTY OF THE QUEEN.
웅성
웅성
ONCE YOU BEGIN TO EXPERIENCE THIS GROWTH, YOU ARE OBLIGATED TO REVEAL THE IDENTITY OF THE MAN THAT YOU LOVE.
OUR DESTINY AND VERY FUTURE HANGS IN THE BALANCE. THAT IS WHY THIS IS AN IMPORTANT ISSUE.
ARE THE RUMORS TRUE? IS IT REALLY EHREN HWERUSUTE? YOUR HIGHNESS?

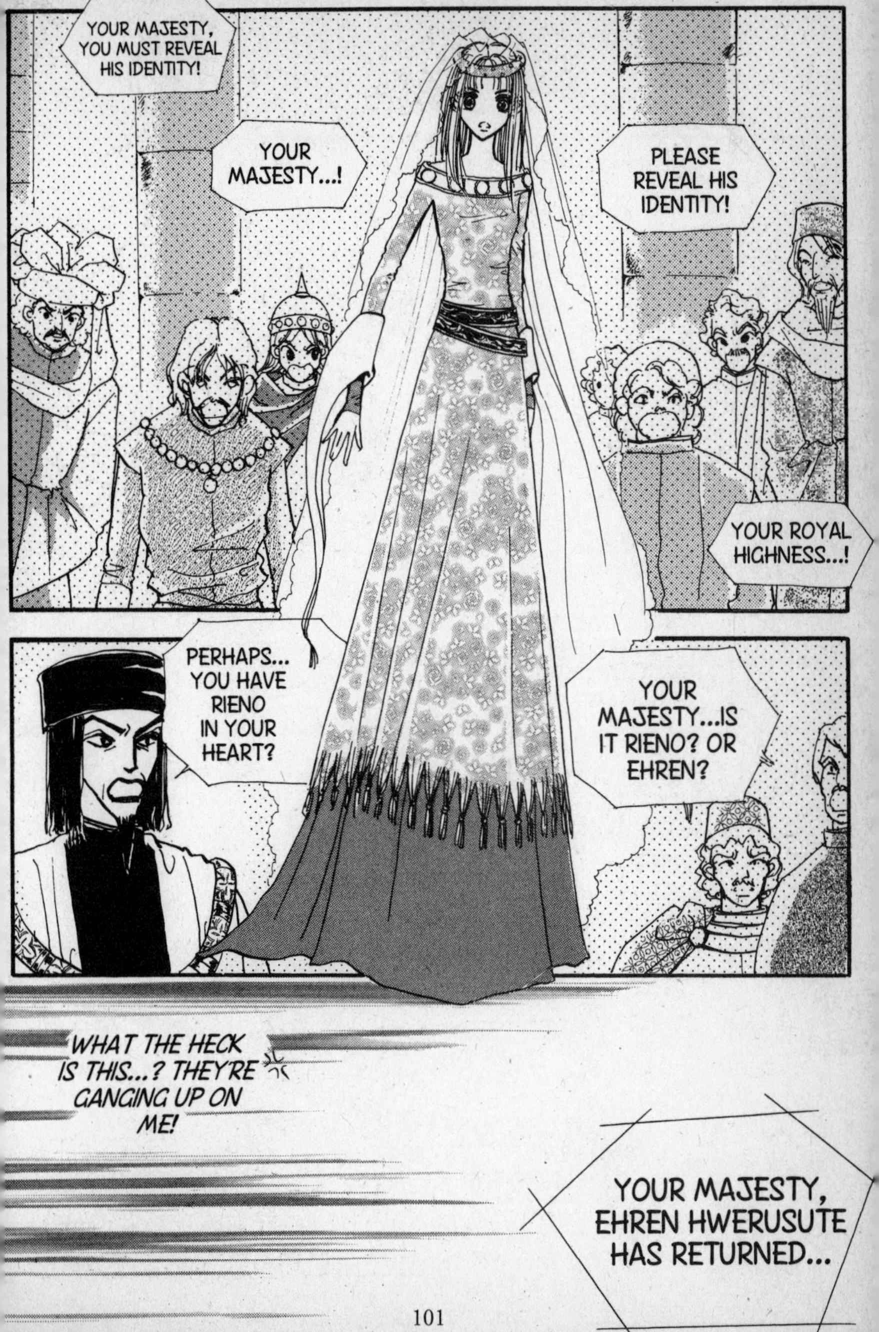
YOUR MAJESTY, YOU MUST REVEAL HIS IDENTITY!
YOUR MAJESTY...!
PLEASE REVEAL HIS IDENTITY!
YOUR ROYAL HIGHNESS...!
PERHAPS... YOU HAVE RIENO IN YOUR HEART?
YOUR MAJESTY...IS IT RIENO? OR EHREN?
WHAT THE HECK IS THIS...? THEY'RE GANGING UP ON ME!
YOUR MAJESTY, EHREN HWERUSUTE HAS RETURNED...

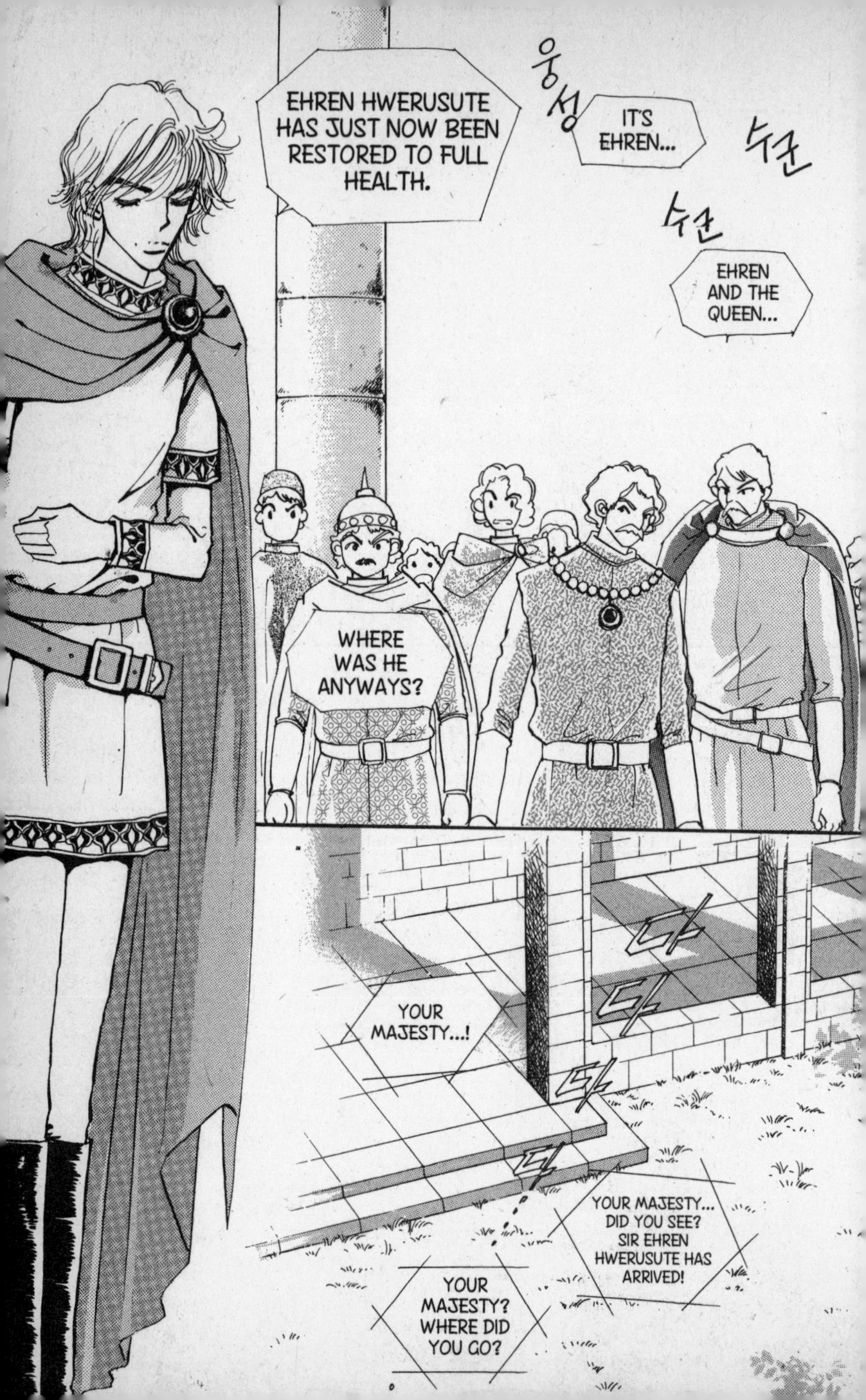
EHREN HWERUSUTE HAS JUST NOW BEEN RESTORED TO FULL HEALTH.
웅성
IT'S EHREN...
수군
수군
EHREN AND THE QUEEN...
WHERE WAS HE ANYWAYS?
다
다
YOUR MAJESTY...!
다
다
YOUR MAJESTY... DID YOU SEE? SIR EHREN HWERUSUTE HAS ARRIVED!
YOUR MAJESTY? WHERE DID YOU GO?

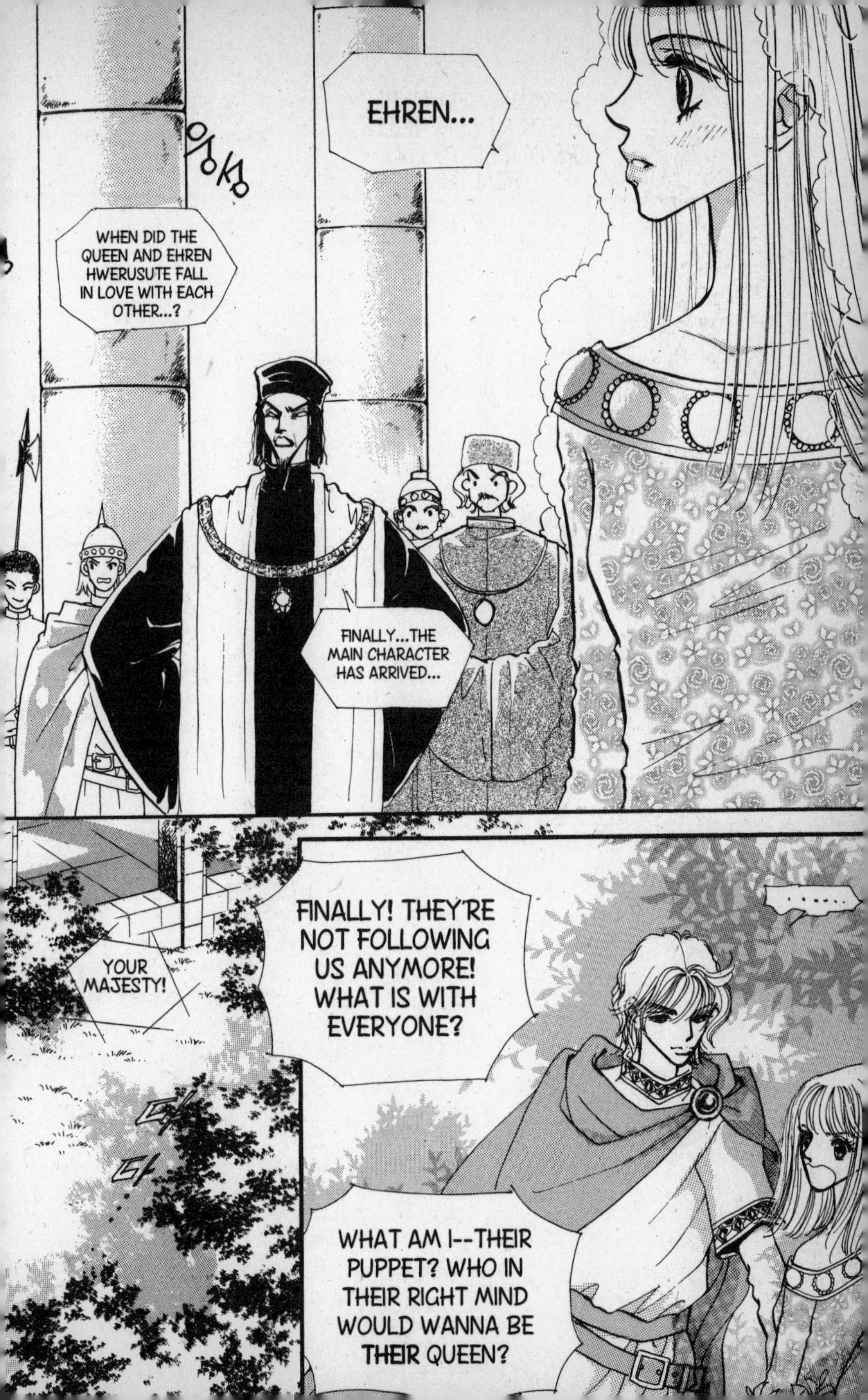
EHREN...
WHEN DID THE QUEEN AND EHREN HWERUSUTE FALL IN LOVE WITH EACH OTHER...?
FINALLY...THE MAIN CHARACTER HAS ARRIVED...
YOUR MAJESTY!
FINALLY! THEY'RE NOT FOLLOWING US ANYMORE! WHAT IS WITH EVERYONE?
......
WHAT AM I--THEIR PUPPET? WHO IN THEIR RIGHT MIND WOULD WANNA BE THEIR QUEEN?

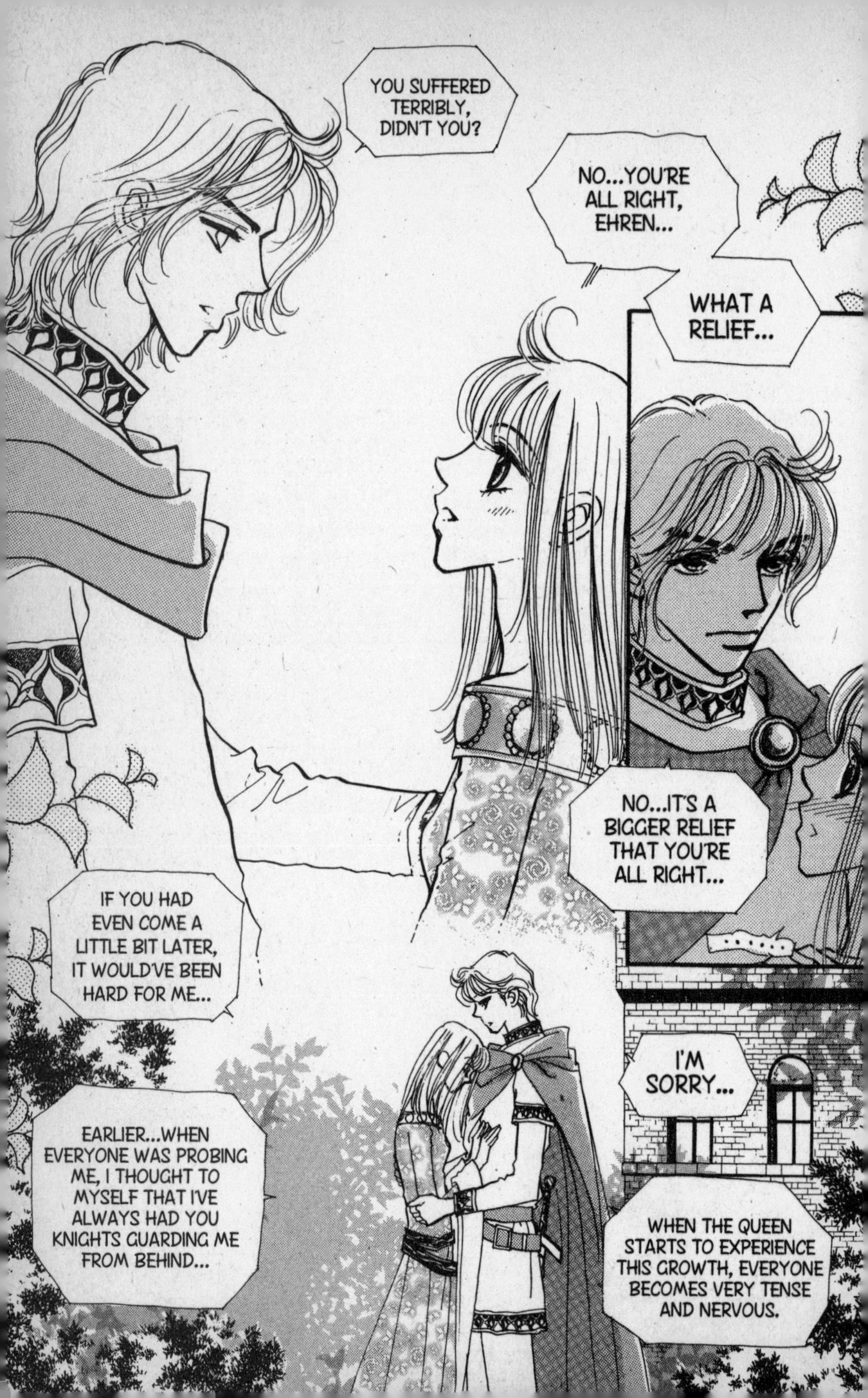
YOU SUFFERED TERRIBLY, DIDN'T YOU?
NO...YOU'RE ALL RIGHT, EHREN...
WHAT A RELIEF...
NO...IT'S A BIGGER RELIEF THAT YOU'RE ALL RIGHT...
IF YOU HAD EVEN COME A LITTLE BIT LATER, IT WOULD'VE BEEN HARD FOR ME...
I'M SORRY...
EARLIER...WHEN EVERYONE WAS PROBING ME, I THOUGHT TO MYSELF THAT I'VE ALWAYS HAD YOU KNIGHTS GUARDING ME FROM BEHIND...
WHEN THE QUEEN STARTS TO EXPERIENCE THIS GROWTH, EVERYONE BECOMES VERY TENSE AND NERVOUS.

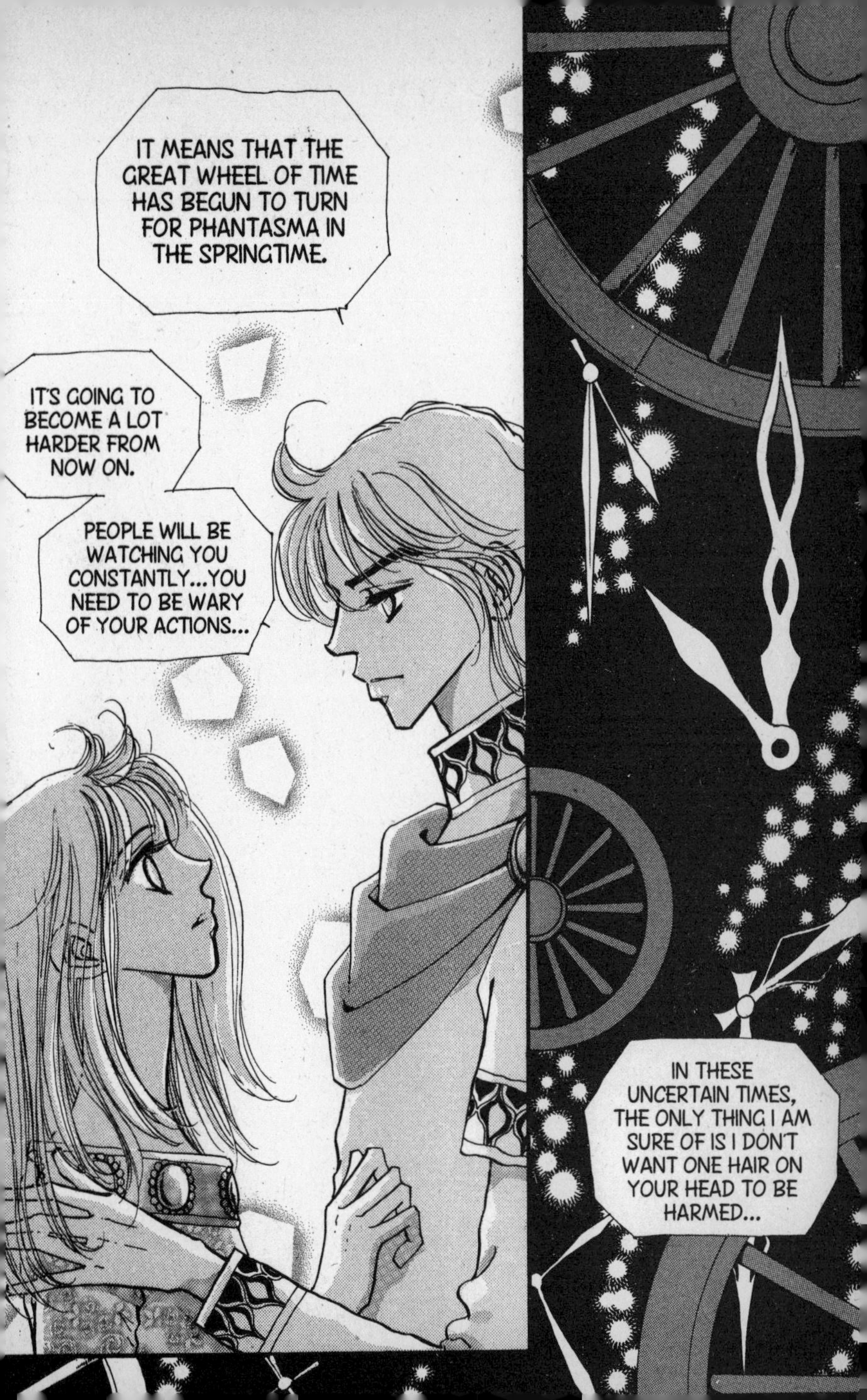
IT MEANS THAT THE GREAT WHEEL OF TIME HAS BEGUN TO TURN FOR PHANTASMA IN THE SPRINGTIME.
IT'S GOING TO BECOME A LOT HARDER FROM NOW ON.
PEOPLE WILL BE WATCHING YOU CONSTANTLY...YOU NEED TO BE WARY OF YOUR ACTIONS...
IN THESE UNCERTAIN TIMES, THE ONLY THING I AM SURE OF IS I DON'T WANT ONE HAIR ON YOUR HEAD TO BE HARMED...

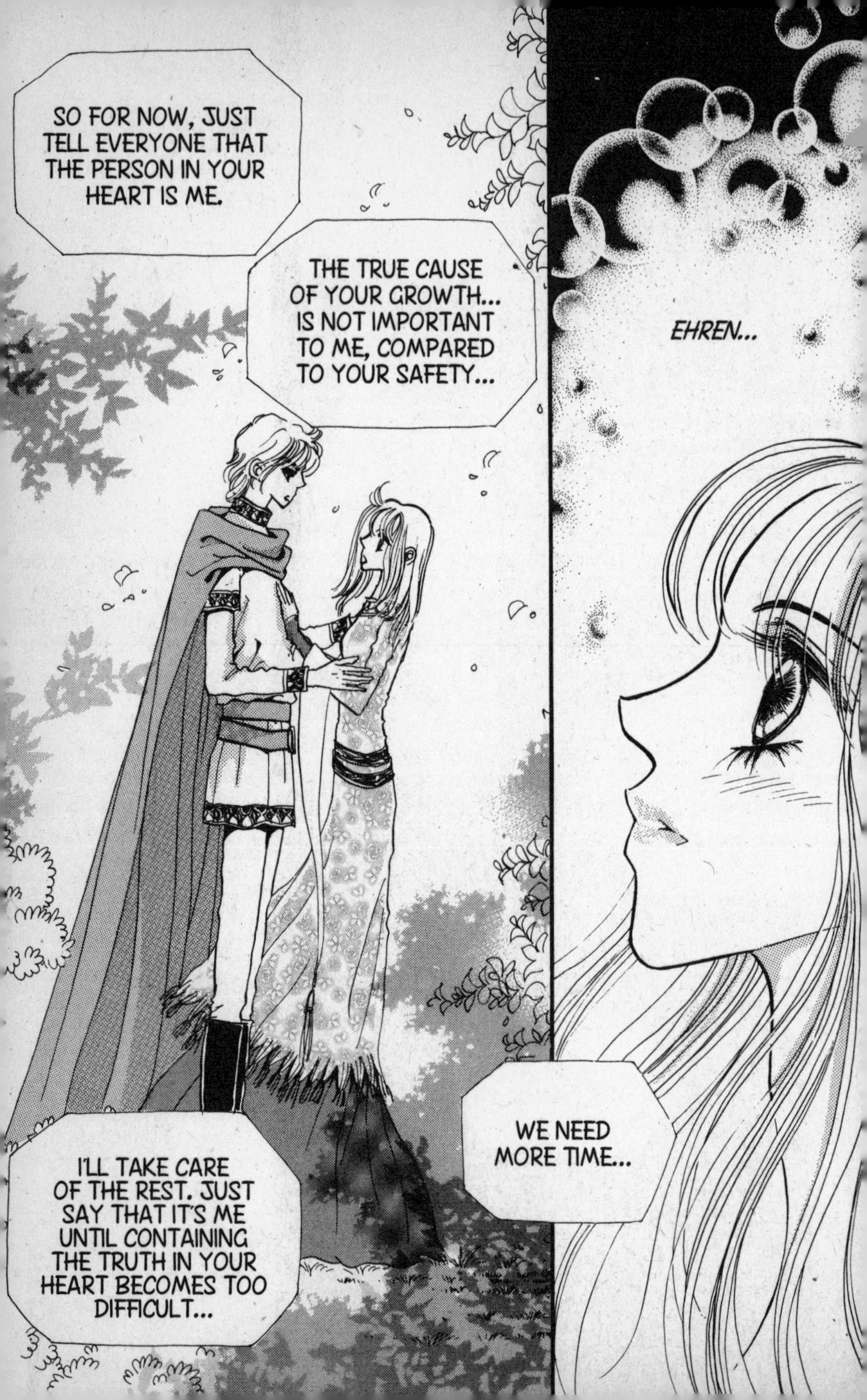
SO FOR NOW, JUST TELL EVERYONE THAT THE PERSON IN YOUR HEART IS ME.
THE TRUE CAUSE OF YOUR GROWTH... IS NOT IMPORTANT TO ME, COMPARED TO YOUR SAFETY...
I'LL TAKE CARE OF THE REST. JUST SAY THAT IT'S ME UNTIL CONTAINING THE TRUTH IN YOUR HEART BECOMES TOO DIFFICULT...
EHREN...
WE NEED MORE TIME...

WILL YOU PROMISE ME, TOO? TO ALWAYS BE BY MY SIDE...
THEN...I'LL BE ABLE TO DO WHAT NEEDS TO BE DONE.
BUT MORE THAN ANYTHING...I'M SO GLAD YOU'RE OKAY...EHREN...
...IN ORDER TO RIGHT THE WHEEL AND RID PHANTASMA OF THIS CURSE.
SO HELP ME...YUNA...

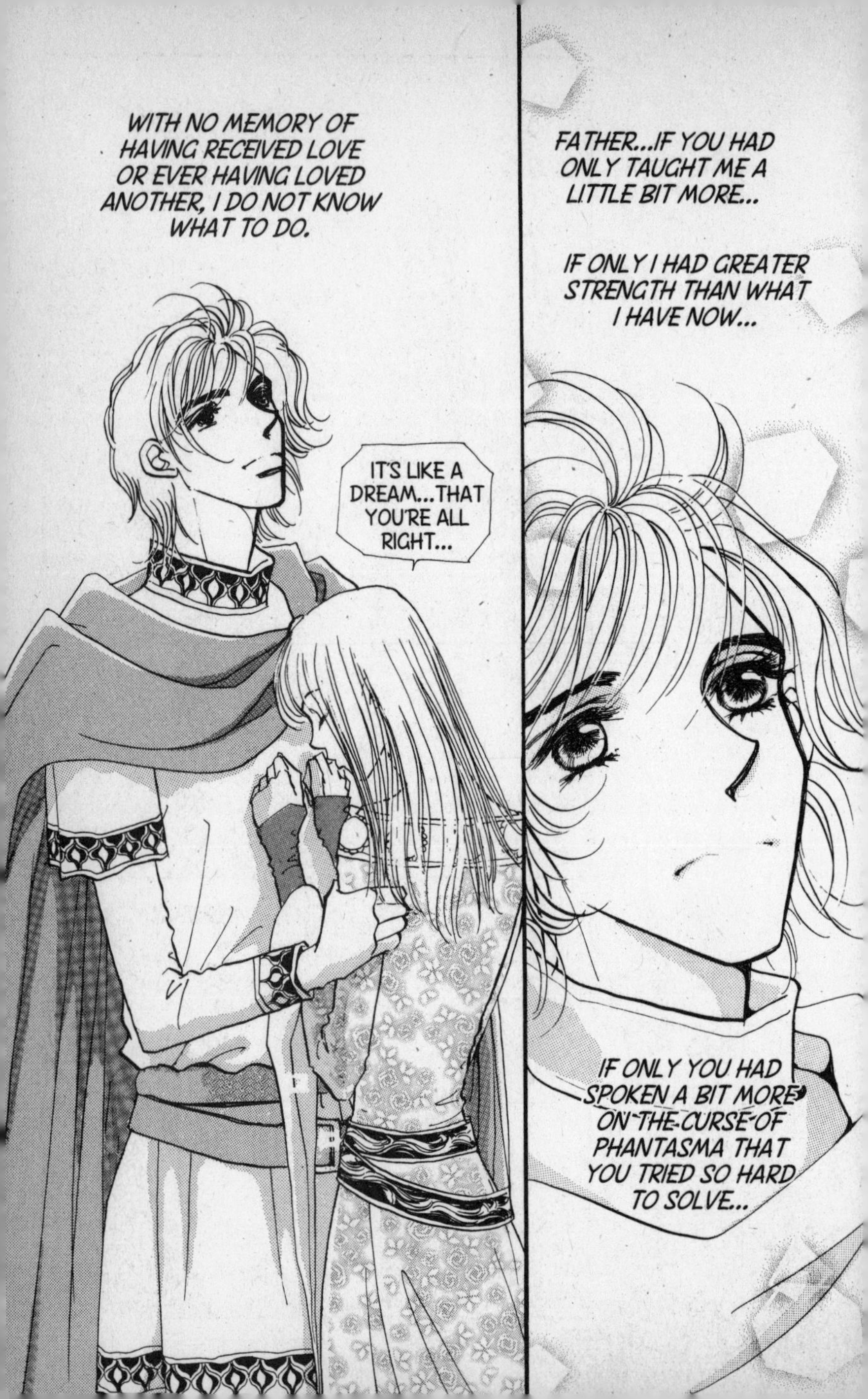
WITH NO MEMORY OF HAVING RECEIVED LOVE OR EVER HAVING LOVED ANOTHER, I DO NOT KNOW WHAT TO DO.
IT'S LIKE A DREAM...THAT YOU'RE ALL RIGHT...
FATHER...IF YOU HAD ONLY TAUGHT ME A LITTLE BIT MORE...
IF ONLY I HAD GREATER STRENGTH THAN WHAT I HAVE NOW...
IF ONLY YOU HAD SPOKEN A BIT MORE ON THE CURSE OF PHANTASMA THAT YOU TRIED SO HARD TO SOLVE...

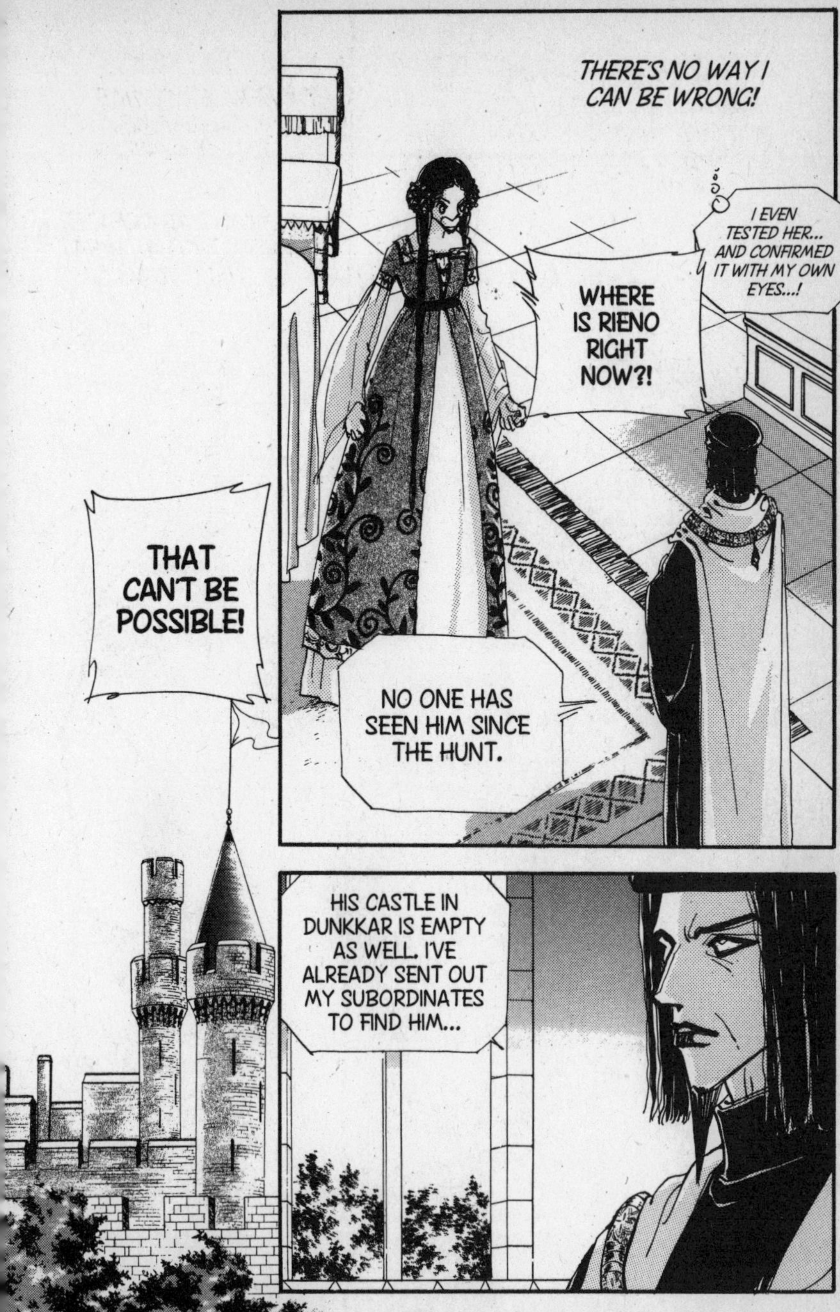
THAT CAN'T BE POSSIBLE!
THERE'S NO WAY I CAN BE WRONG!
I EVEN TESTED HER... AND CONFIRMED IT WITH MY OWN EYES...!
WHERE IS RIENO RIGHT NOW?!
NO ONE HAS SEEN HIM SINCE THE HUNT.
HIS CASTLE IN DUNKKAR IS EMPTY AS WELL. I'VE ALREADY SENT OUT MY SUBORDINATES TO FIND HIM...

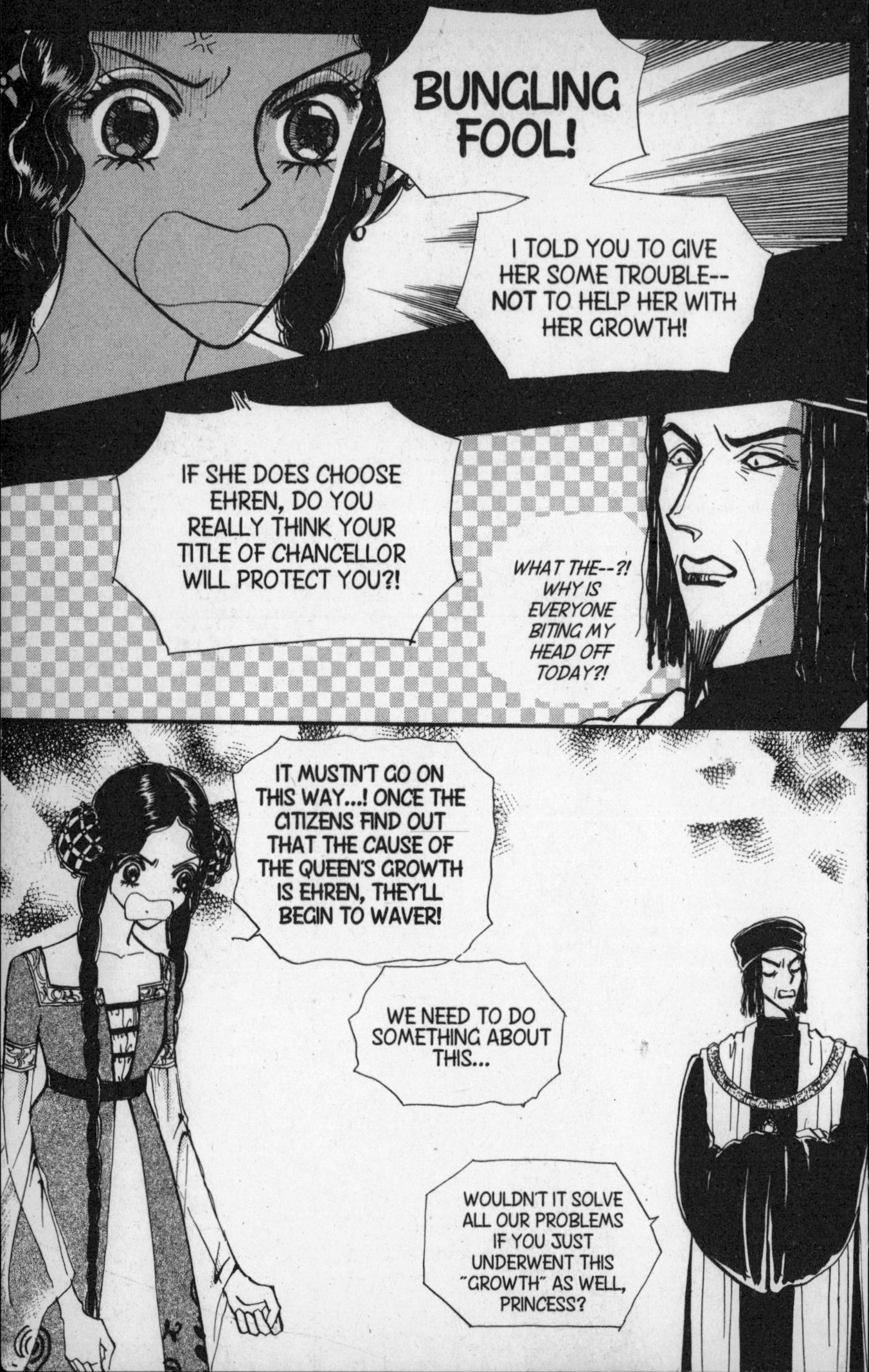
BUNGLING FOOL!
I TOLD YOU TO GIVE HER SOME TROUBLE-- NOT TO HELP HER WITH HER GROWTH!
IF SHE DOES CHOOSE EHREN, DO YOU REALLY THINK YOUR TITLE OF CHANCELLOR WILL PROTECT YOU?!
WHAT THE--?! WHY IS EVERYONE BITING MY HEAD OFF TODAY?!
IT MUSTN'T GO ON THIS WAY...! ONCE THE CITIZENS FIND OUT THAT THE CAUSE OF THE QUEEN'S GROWTH IS EHREN, THEY'LL BEGIN TO WAVER!
WE NEED TO DO SOMETHING ABOUT THIS...
WOULDN'T IT SOLVE ALL OUR PROBLEMS IF YOU JUST UNDERWENT THIS "GROWTH" AS WELL, PRINCESS?

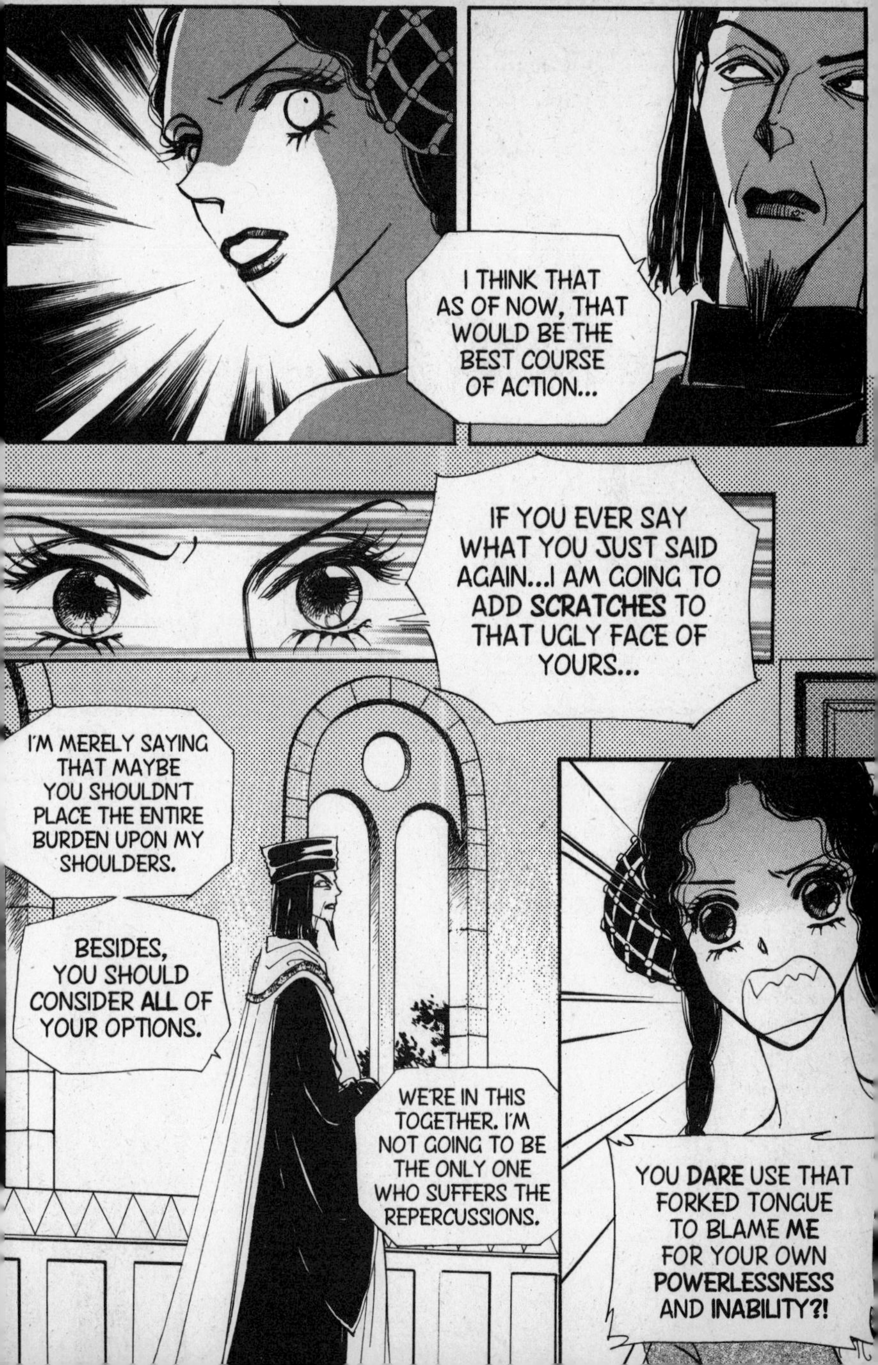
I THINK THAT AS OF NOW, THAT WOULD BE THE BEST COURSE OF ACTION...
IF YOU EVER SAY WHAT YOU JUST SAID AGAIN...I AM GOING TO ADD SCRATCHES TO THAT UGLY FACE OF YOURS...
I'M MERELY SAYING THAT MAYBE YOU SHOULDN'T PLACE THE ENTIRE BURDEN UPON MY SHOULDERS.
BESIDES, YOU SHOULD CONSIDER ALL OF YOUR OPTIONS.
WE'RE IN THIS TOGETHER. I'M NOT GOING TO BE THE ONLY ONE WHO SUFFERS THE REPERCUSSIONS.
YOU DARE USE THAT FORKED TONGUE TO BLAME ME FOR YOUR OWN POWERLESSNESS AND INABILITY?!

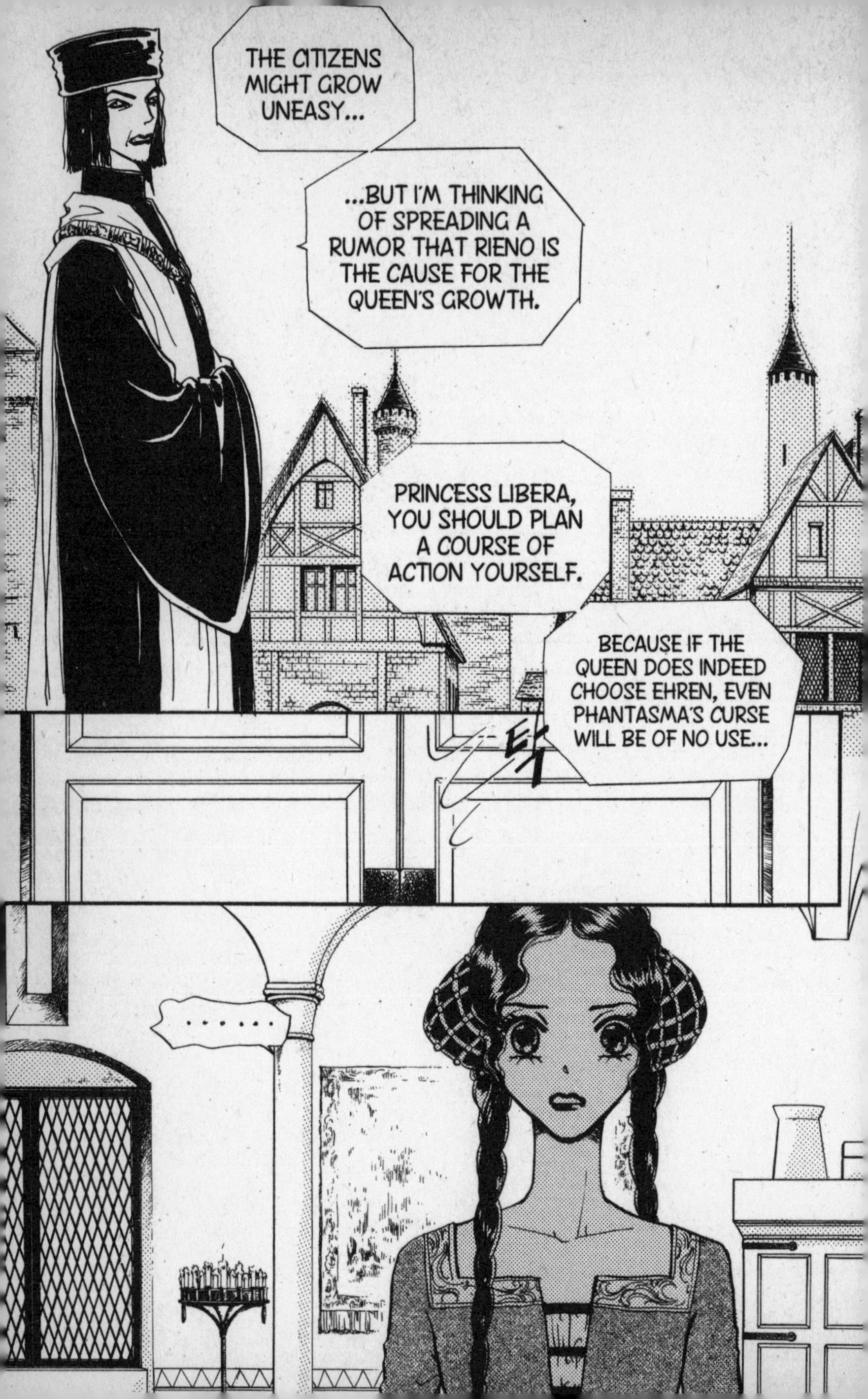
THE CITIZENS MIGHT GROW UNEASY...
...BUT I'M THINKING OF SPREADING A RUMOR THAT RIENO IS THE CAUSE FOR THE QUEEN'S GROWTH.
PRINCESS LIBERA, YOU SHOULD PLAN A COURSE OF ACTION YOURSELF.
BECAUSE IF THE QUEEN DOES INDEED CHOOSE EHREN, EVEN PHANTASMA'S CURSE WILL BE OF NO USE...
......

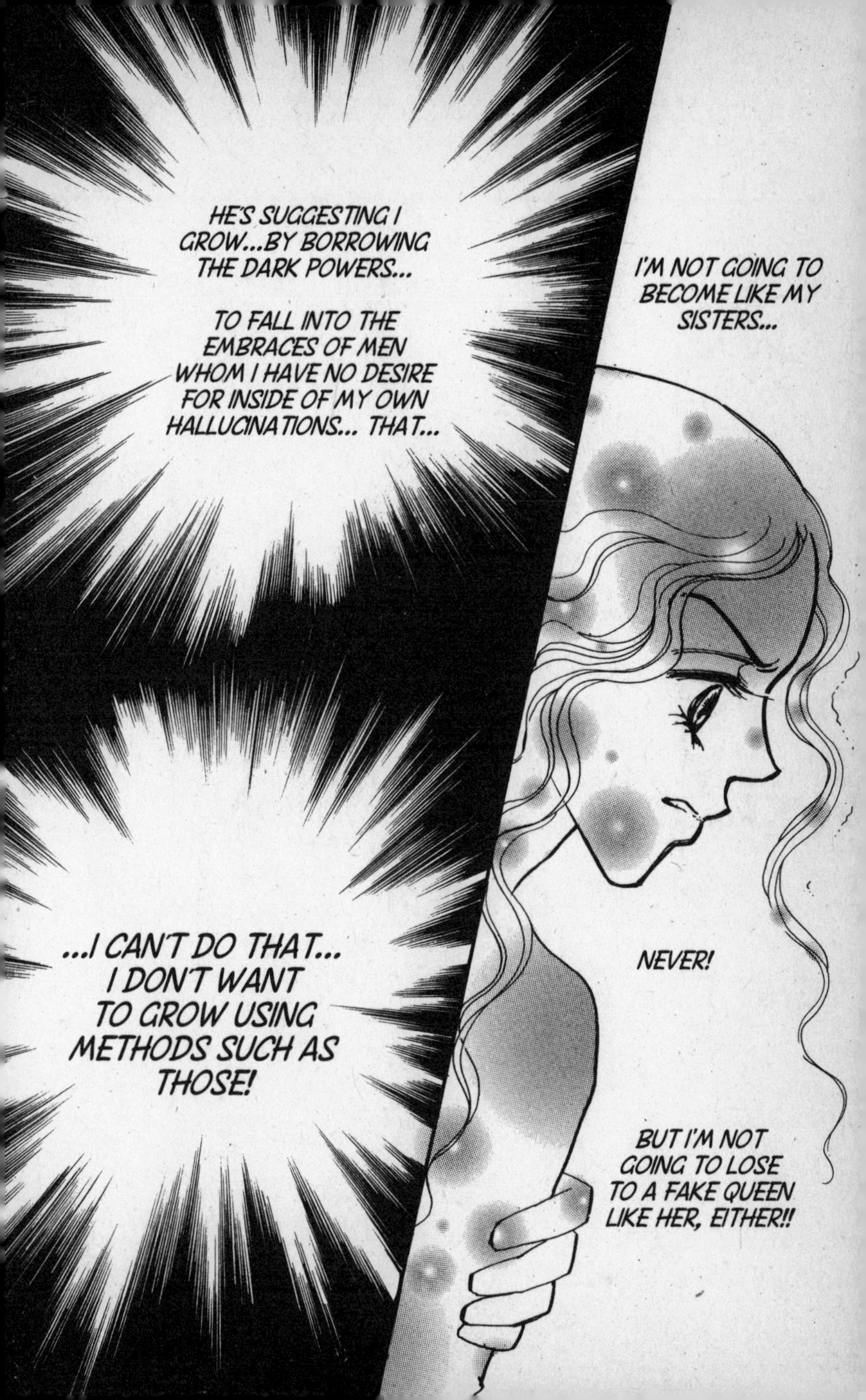
HE'S SUGGESTING I GROW...BY BORROWING THE DARK POWERS...
TO FALL INTO THE EMBRACES OF MEN WHOM I HAVE NO DESIRE FOR INSIDE OF MY OWN HALLUCINATIONS... THAT...
...I CAN'T DO THAT... I DON'T WANT TO GROW USING METHODS SUCH AS THOSE!
I'M NOT GOING TO BECOME LIKE MY SISTERS...
NEVER!
BUT I'M NOT GOING TO LOSE TO A FAKE QUEEN LIKE HER, EITHER!!

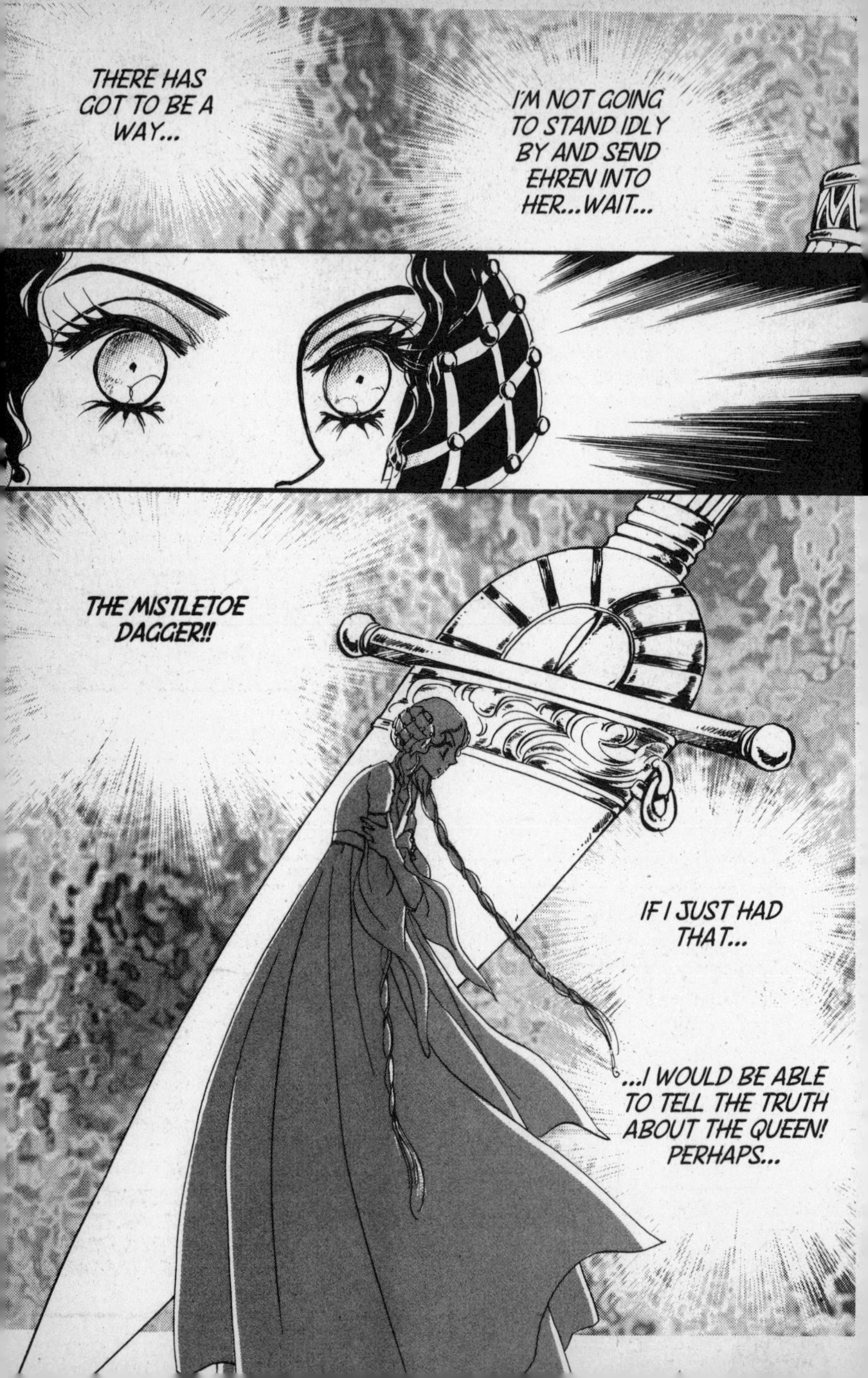
I'M NOT GOING TO STAND IDLY BY AND SEND EHREN INTO HER...WAIT...
THERE HAS GOT TO BE A WAY...
THE MISTLETOE DAGGER!!
IF I JUST HAD THAT...
...I WOULD BE ABLE TO TELL THE TRUTH ABOUT THE QUEEN! PERHAPS...

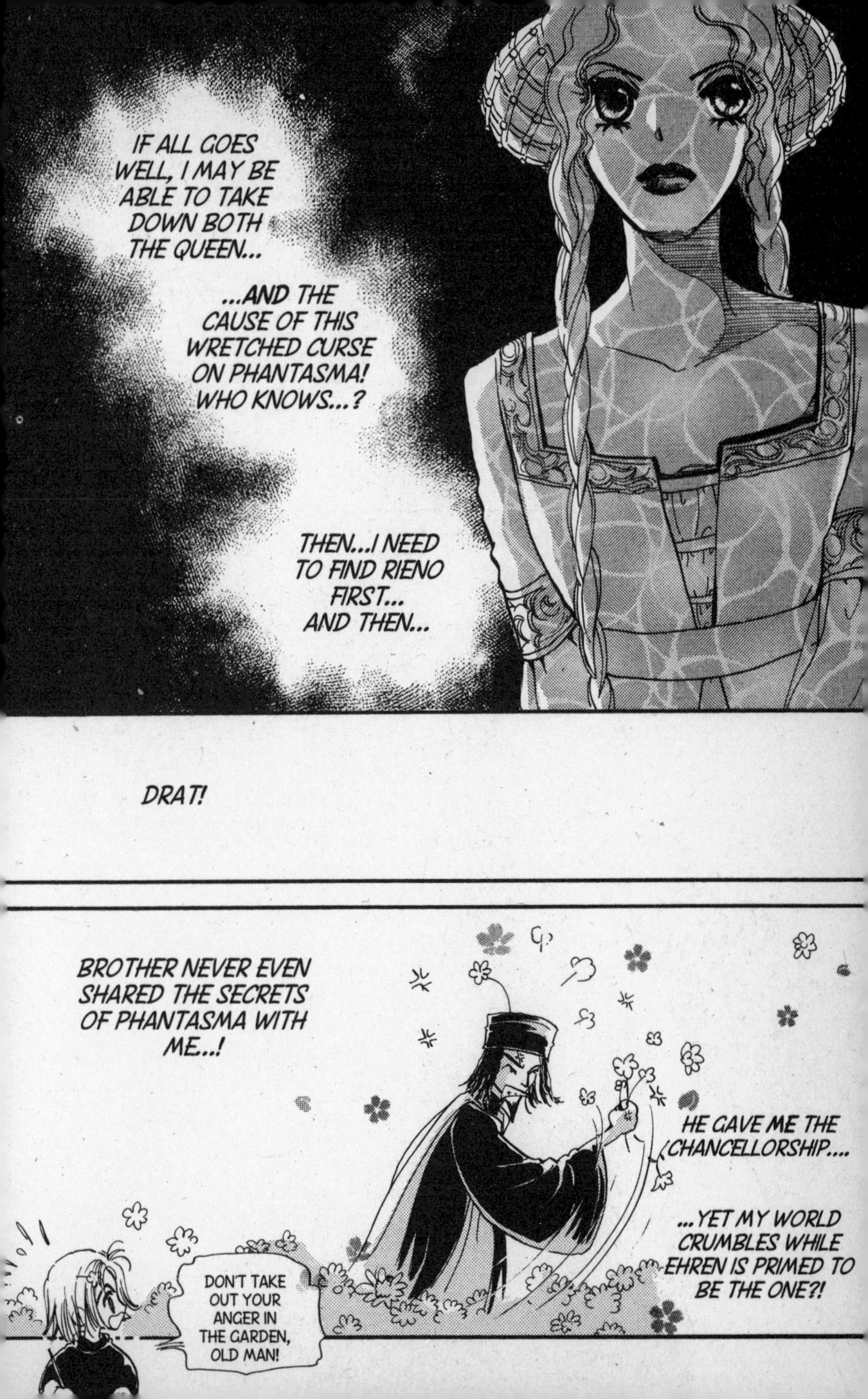
IF ALL GOES WELL, I MAY BE ABLE TO TAKE DOWN BOTH THE QUEEN...
...AND THE CAUSE OF THIS WRETCHED CURSE ON PHANTASMA! WHO KNOWS...?
THEN...I NEED TO FIND RIENO FIRST... AND THEN...
DRAT!
BROTHER NEVER EVEN SHARED THE SECRETS OF PHANTASMA WITH ME...!
HE GAVE ME THE CHANCELLORSHIP....
...YET MY WORLD CRUMBLES WHILE EHREN IS PRIMED TO BE THE ONE?!
DON'T TAKE OUT YOUR ANGER IN THE GARDEN, OLD MAN!

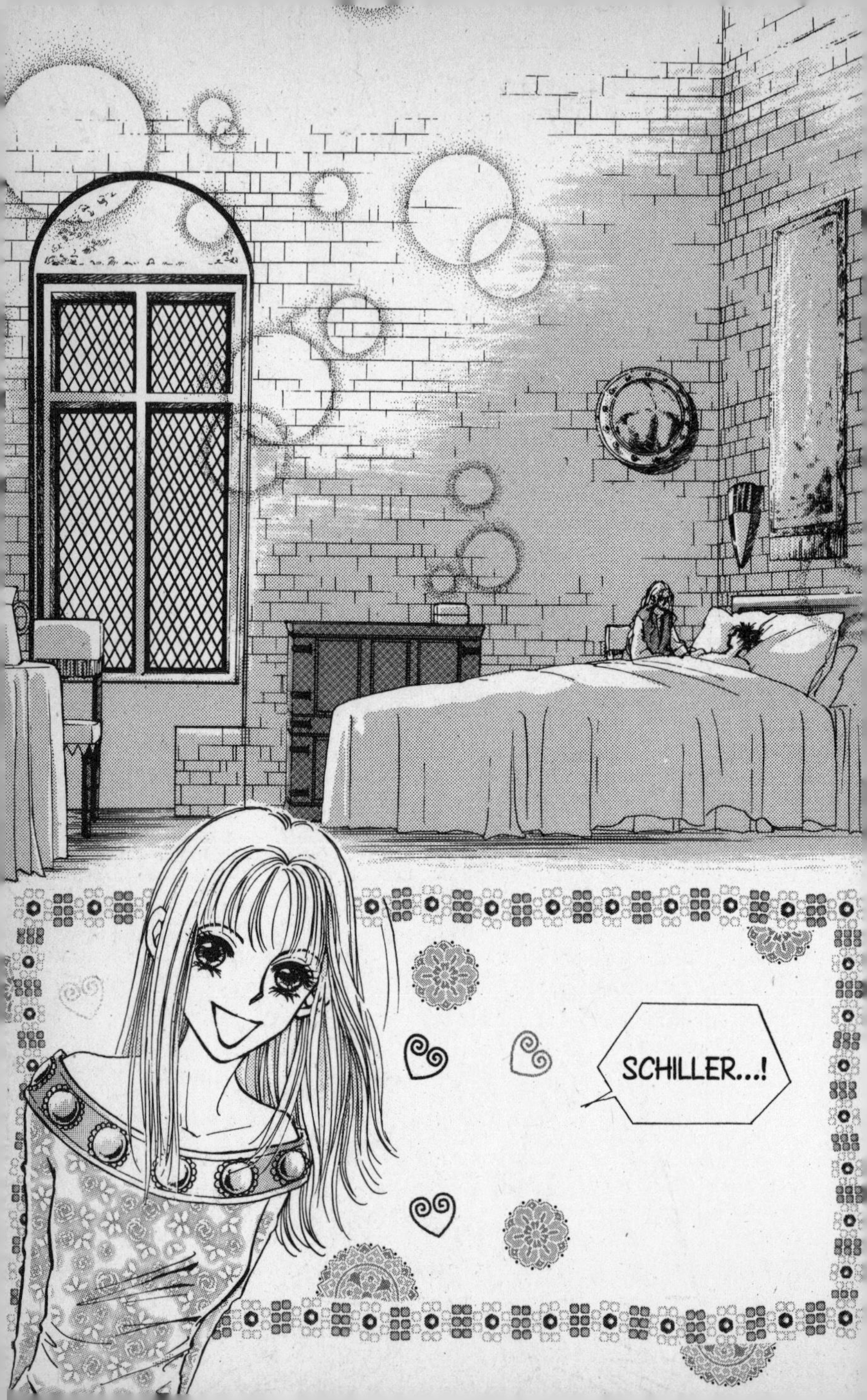
SCHILLER...!

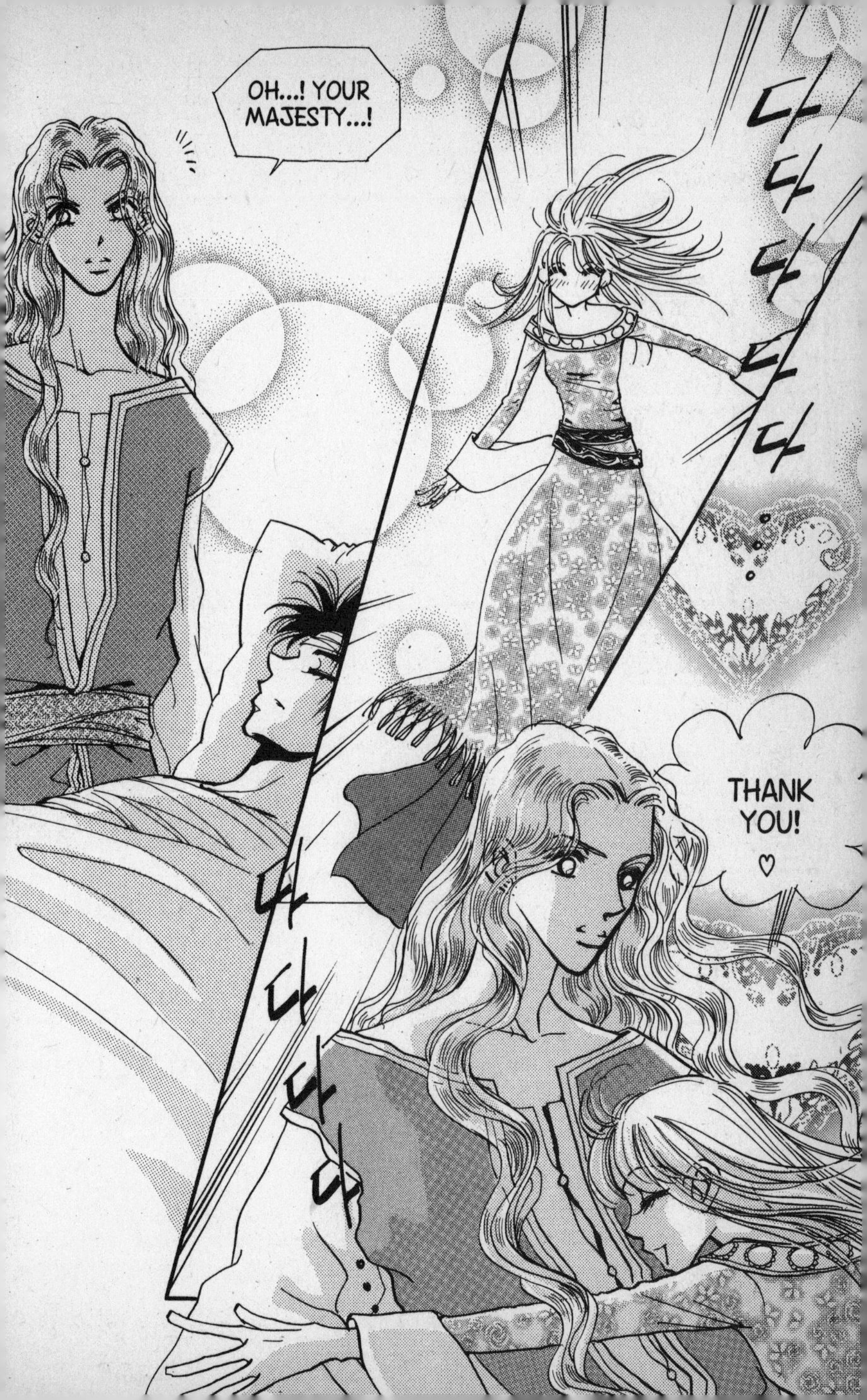
OH...! YOUR MAJESTY...!
다다다다다다
다다다다
THANK YOU! ♡

I'M SO GLAD THAT YOU CAME BACK SAFE AND SOUND!

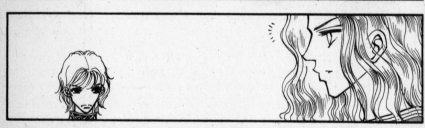

ARE REALLY YOU **THAT** HAPPY THAT I'M SAFE...?

OR...THAT EHREN IS SAFE...?

HA HA! I'M JOKING, OF COURSE! THOUGH IF YOU ARE **THAT** HAPPY, I'D LIKE TO RECEIVE A GIFT FROM YOU...

YOUR MAJESTY...I DON'T LIKE FREEBIES...

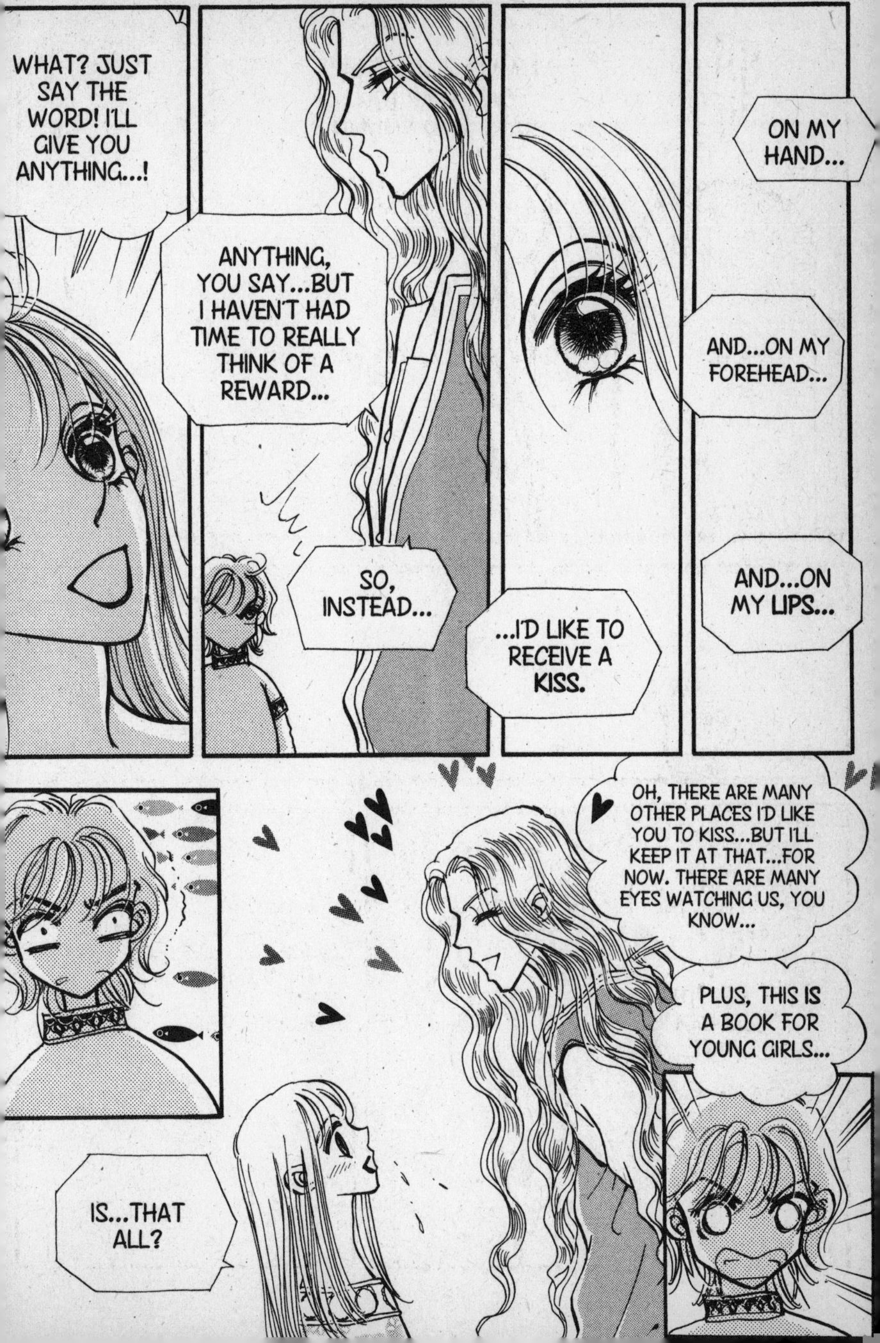
WHAT? JUST SAY THE WORD! I'LL GIVE YOU ANYTHING...!
ANYTHING, YOU SAY...BUT I HAVEN'T HAD TIME TO REALLY THINK OF A REWARD...
SO, INSTEAD...
...I'D LIKE TO RECEIVE A KISS.
ON MY HAND...
AND...ON MY FOREHEAD...
AND...ON MY LIPS...
IS...THAT ALL?
OH, THERE ARE MANY OTHER PLACES I'D LIKE YOU TO KISS...BUT I'LL KEEP IT AT THAT...FOR NOW. THERE ARE MANY EYES WATCHING US, YOU KNOW...
PLUS, THIS IS A BOOK FOR YOUNG GIRLS...

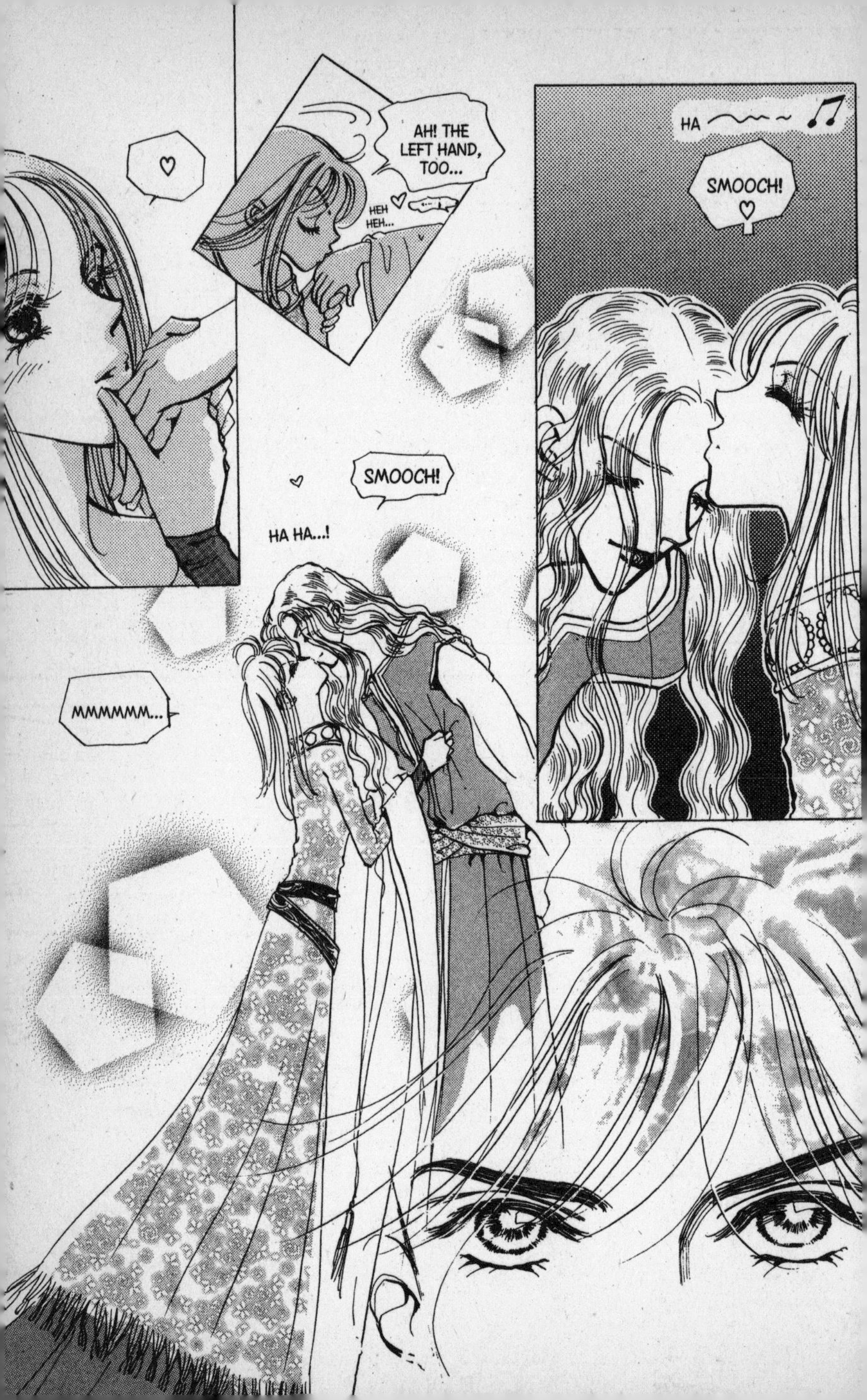
♡
AH! THE LEFT HAND, TOO...
HEH HEH... ♡
...
HA ~~~ ♪
SMOOCH! ♡
♡ SMOOCH!
HA HA...!
MMMMMM...

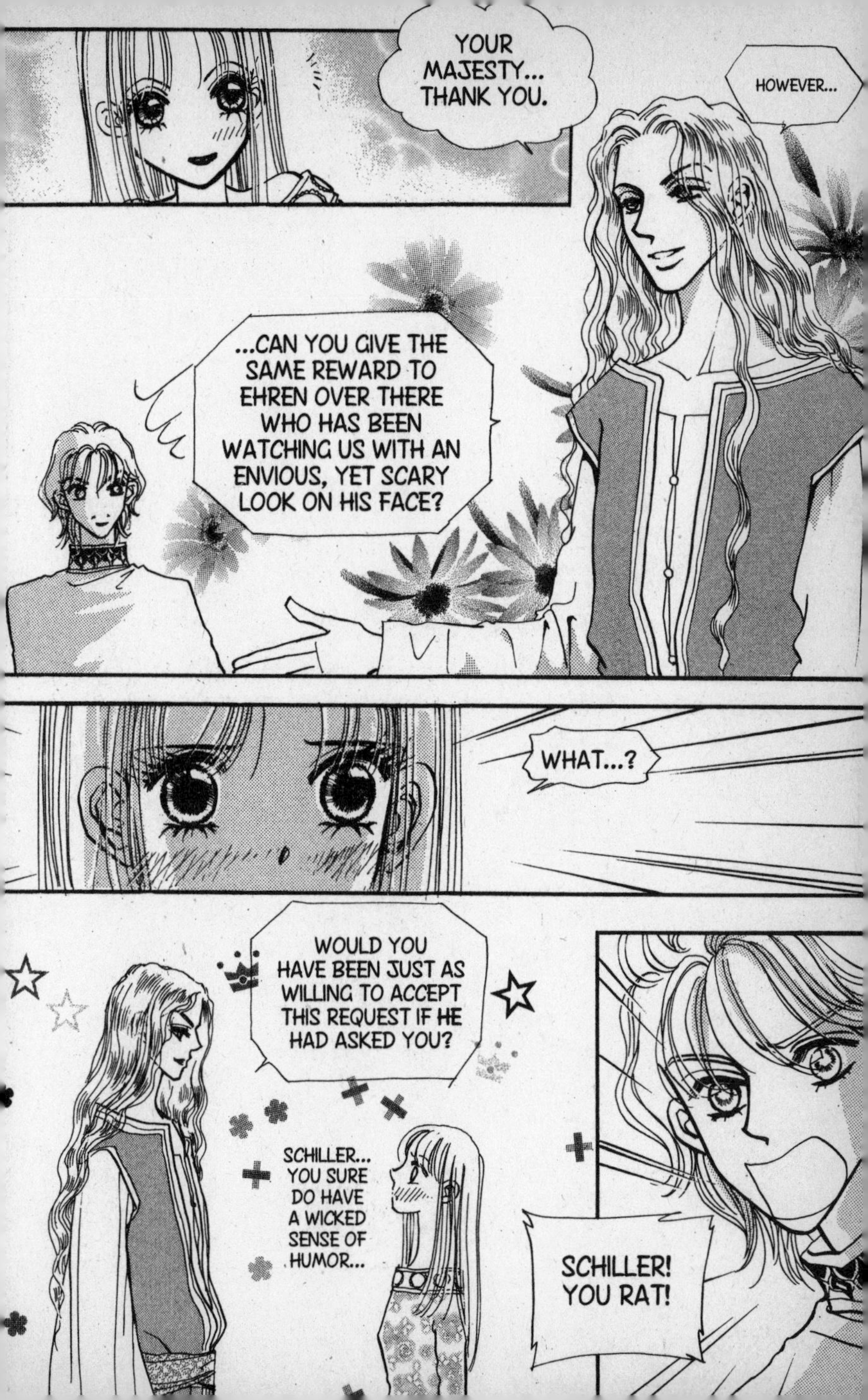
YOUR MAJESTY... THANK YOU.
HOWEVER...
...CAN YOU GIVE THE SAME REWARD TO EHREN OVER THERE WHO HAS BEEN WATCHING US WITH AN ENVIOUS, YET SCARY LOOK ON HIS FACE?
WHAT...?
WOULD YOU HAVE BEEN JUST AS WILLING TO ACCEPT THIS REQUEST IF HE HAD ASKED YOU?
SCHILLER... YOU SURE DO HAVE A WICKED SENSE OF HUMOR...
SCHILLER! YOU RAT!

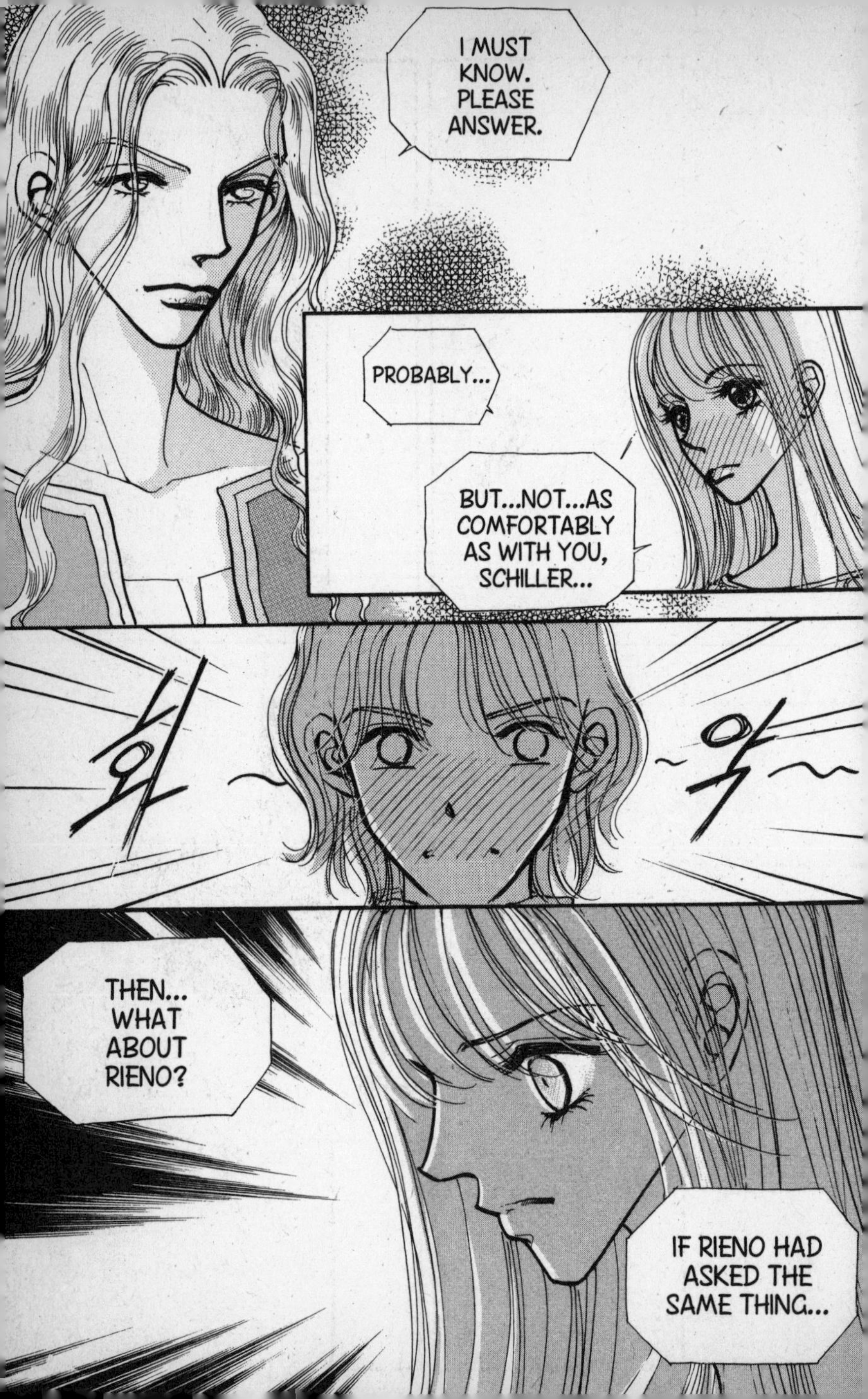
I MUST KNOW. PLEASE ANSWER.
PROBABLY...
BUT...NOT...AS COMFORTABLY AS WITH YOU, SCHILLER...
THEN... WHAT ABOUT RIENO?
IF RIENO HAD ASKED THE SAME THING...

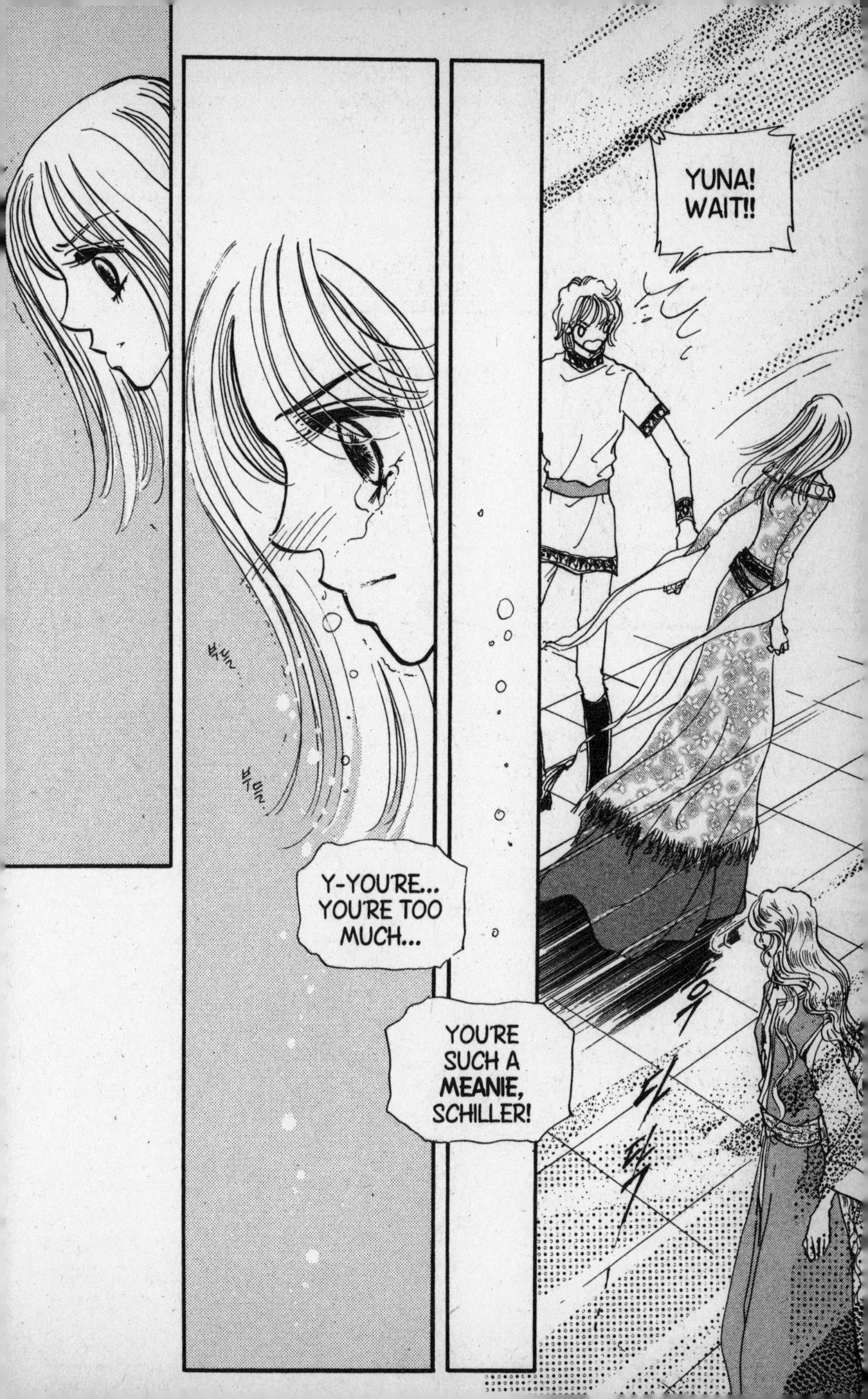
Y-YOU'RE... YOU'RE TOO MUCH...
YOU'RE SUCH A MEANIE, SCHILLER!
YUNA! WAIT!!

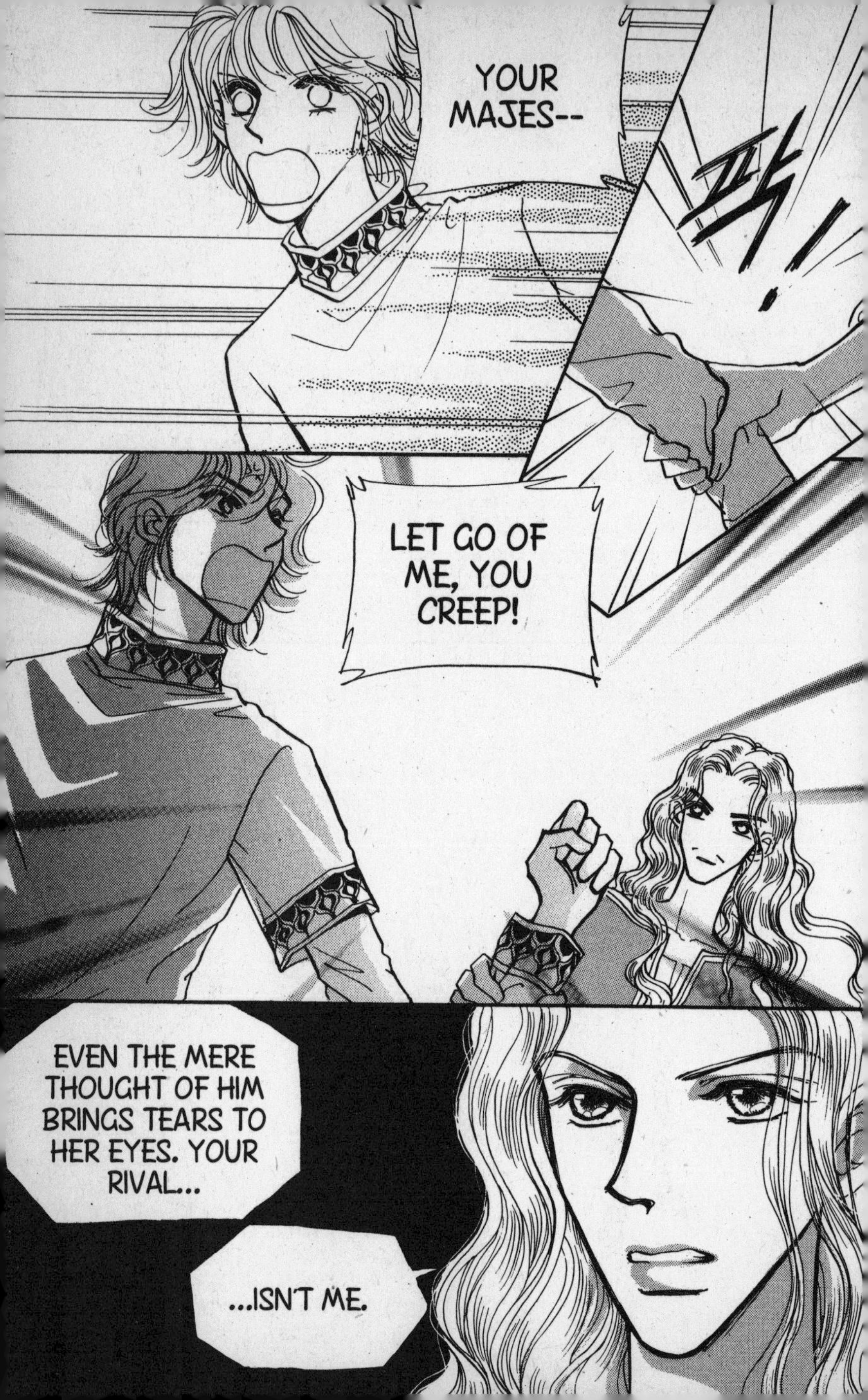
YOUR MAJES--
LET GO OF ME, YOU CREEP!
EVEN THE MERE THOUGHT OF HIM BRINGS TEARS TO HER EYES. YOUR RIVAL...
...ISN'T ME.

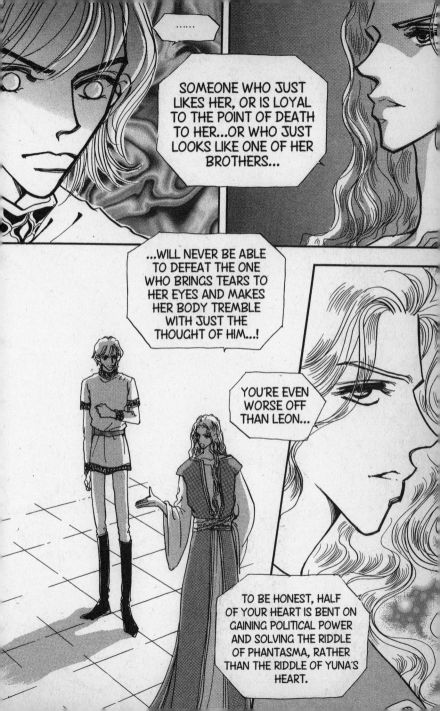

......

SOMEONE WHO JUST LIKES HER, OR IS LOYAL TO THE POINT OF DEATH TO HER...OR WHO JUST LOOKS LIKE ONE OF HER BROTHERS...

...WILL NEVER BE ABLE TO DEFEAT THE ONE WHO BRINGS TEARS TO HER EYES AND MAKES HER BODY TREMBLE WITH JUST THE THOUGHT OF HIM...!

YOU'RE EVEN WORSE OFF THAN LEON...

TO BE HONEST, HALF OF YOUR HEART IS BENT ON GAINING POLITICAL POWER AND SOLVING THE RIDDLE OF PHANTASMA, RATHER THAN THE RIDDLE OF YUNA'S HEART.

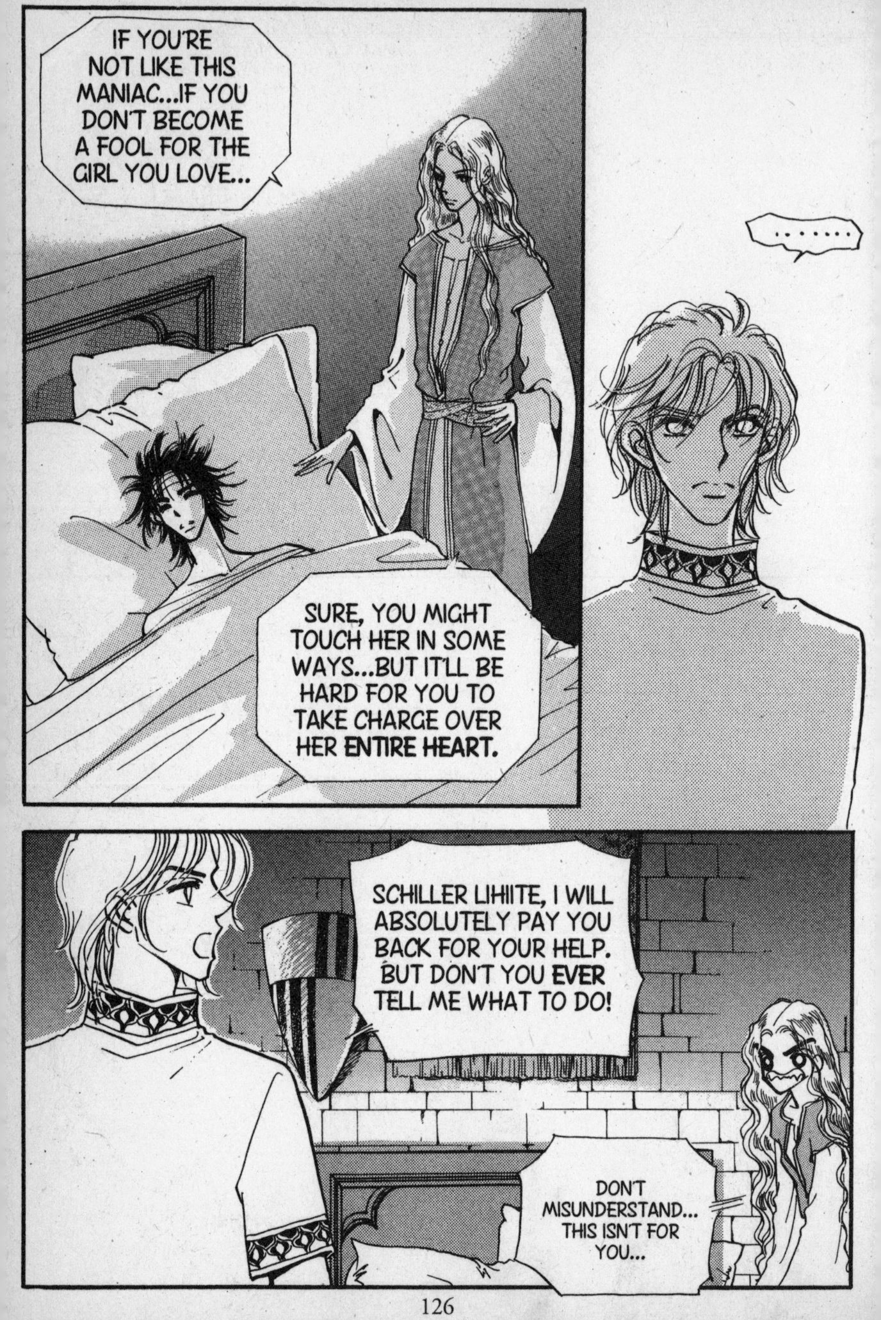

IF YOU'RE NOT LIKE THIS MANIAC...IF YOU DON'T BECOME A FOOL FOR THE GIRL YOU LOVE...
....
SURE, YOU MIGHT TOUCH HER IN SOME WAYS...BUT IT'LL BE HARD FOR YOU TO TAKE CHARGE OVER HER ENTIRE HEART.
SCHILLER LIHIITE, I WILL ABSOLUTELY PAY YOU BACK FOR YOUR HELP. BUT DON'T YOU EVER TELL ME WHAT TO DO!
DON'T MISUNDERSTAND... THIS ISN'T FOR YOU...

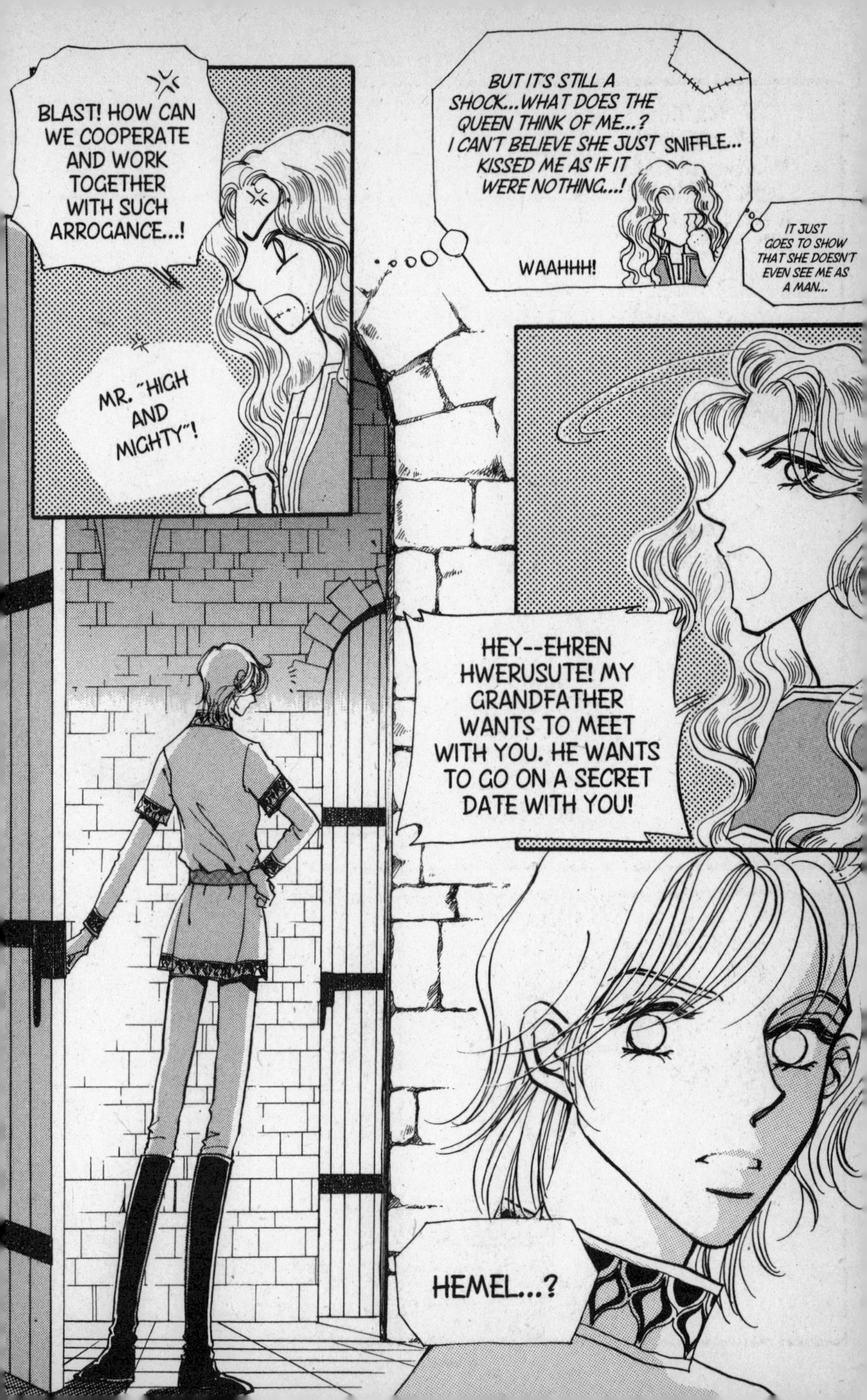
BLAST! HOW CAN WE COOPERATE AND WORK TOGETHER WITH SUCH ARROGANCE...!
MR. "HIGH AND MIGHTY"!
BUT IT'S STILL A SHOCK...WHAT DOES THE QUEEN THINK OF ME...? I CAN'T BELIEVE SHE JUST KISSED ME AS IF IT WERE NOTHING...!
SNIFFLE...
WAAHHH!
IT JUST GOES TO SHOW THAT SHE DOESN'T EVEN SEE ME AS A MAN...
HEY--EHREN HWERUSUTE! MY GRANDFATHER WANTS TO MEET WITH YOU. HE WANTS TO GO ON A SECRET DATE WITH YOU!
HEMEL...?

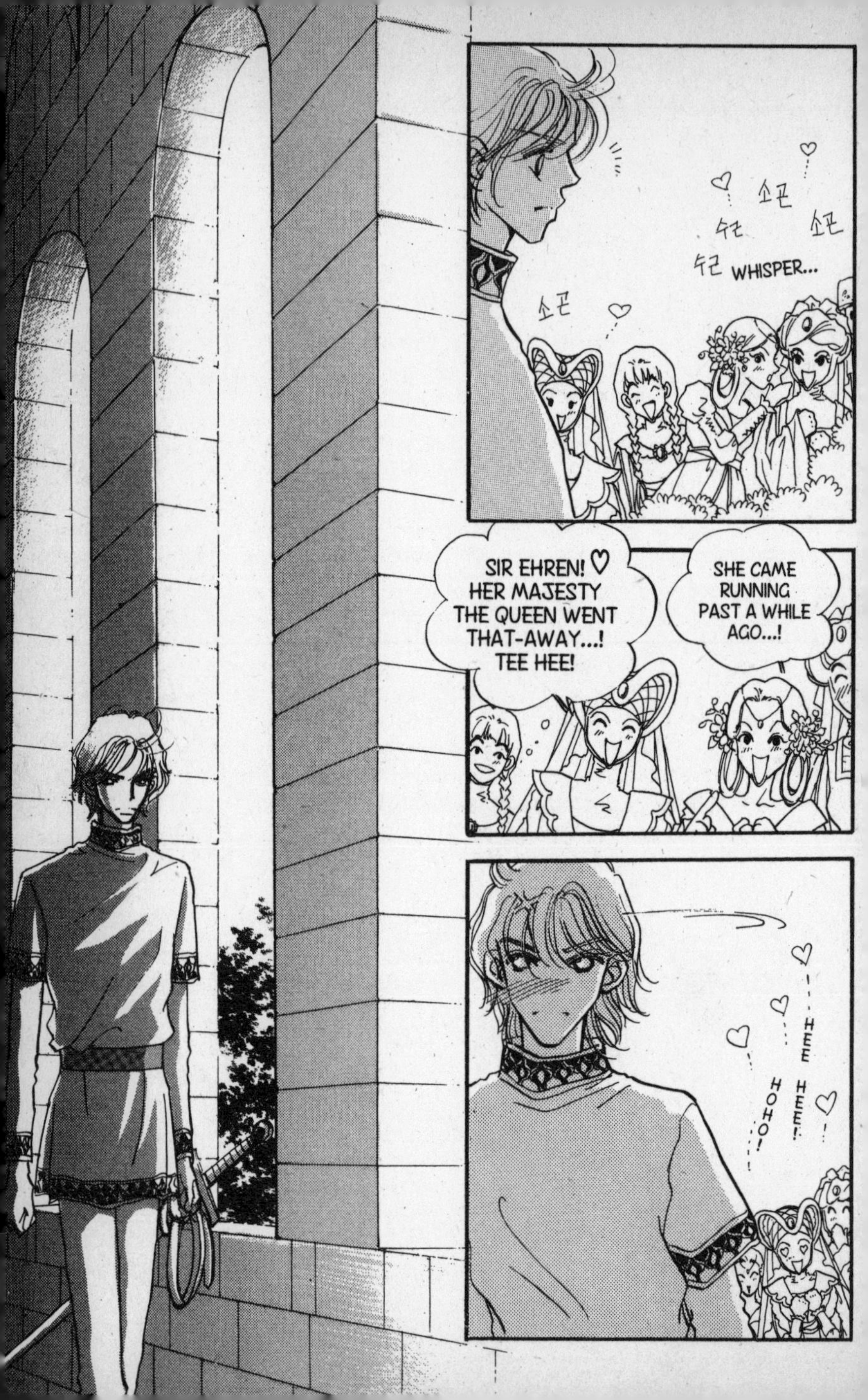
소곤
수군
소곤
수군
WHISPER...
소곤
SIR EHREN! ♡ HER MAJESTY THE QUEEN WENT THAT-AWAY...! TEE HEE!
SHE CAME RUNNING PAST A WHILE AGO...!
HEE HEE!
HOHO!

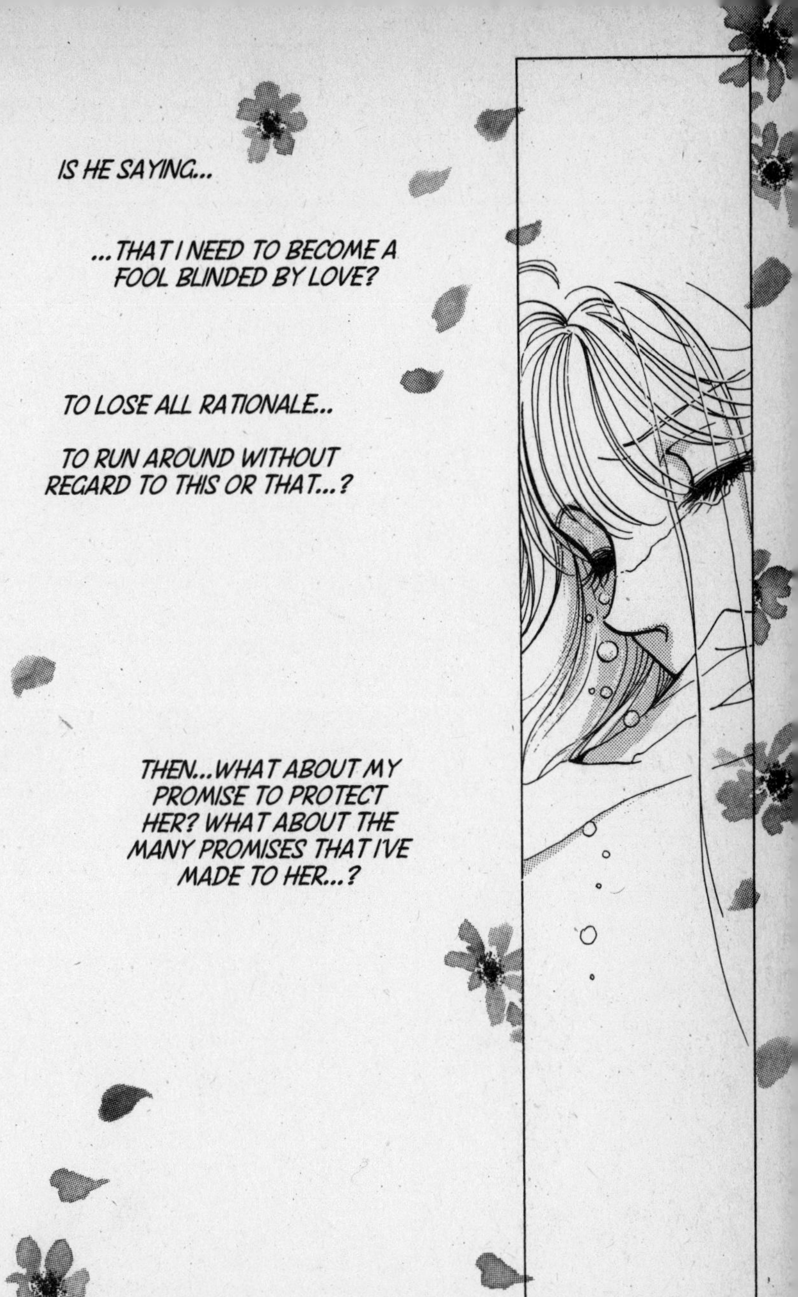
IS HE SAYING...
...THAT I NEED TO BECOME A FOOL BLINDED BY LOVE?
TO LOSE ALL RATIONALE...
TO RUN AROUND WITHOUT REGARD TO THIS OR THAT...?
THEN...WHAT ABOUT MY PROMISE TO PROTECT HER? WHAT ABOUT THE MANY PROMISES THAT I'VE MADE TO HER...?

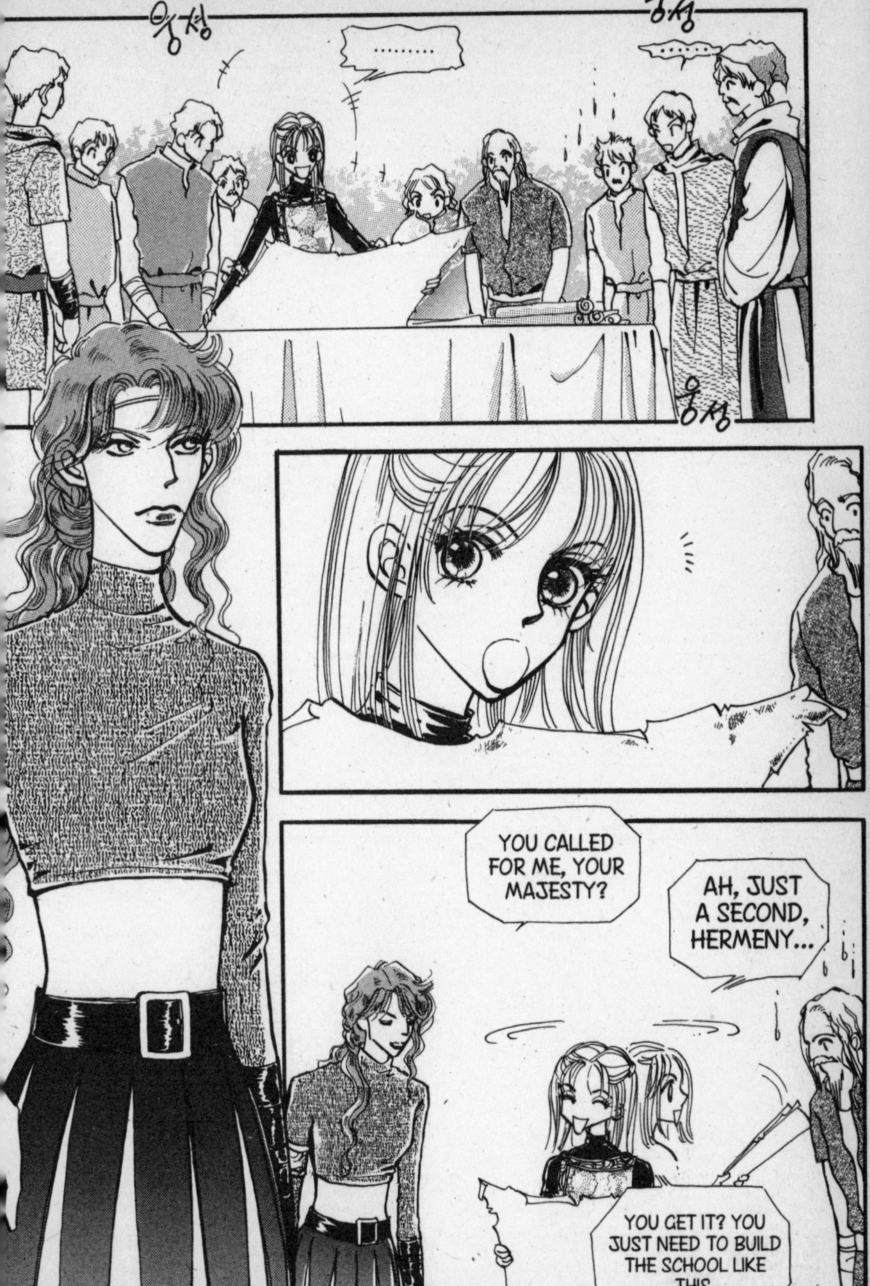

웅성
....
웅성
......
웅성
YOU CALLED FOR ME, YOUR MAJESTY?
AH, JUST A SECOND, HERMENY...
YOU GET IT? YOU JUST NEED TO BUILD THE SCHOOL LIKE THIS.

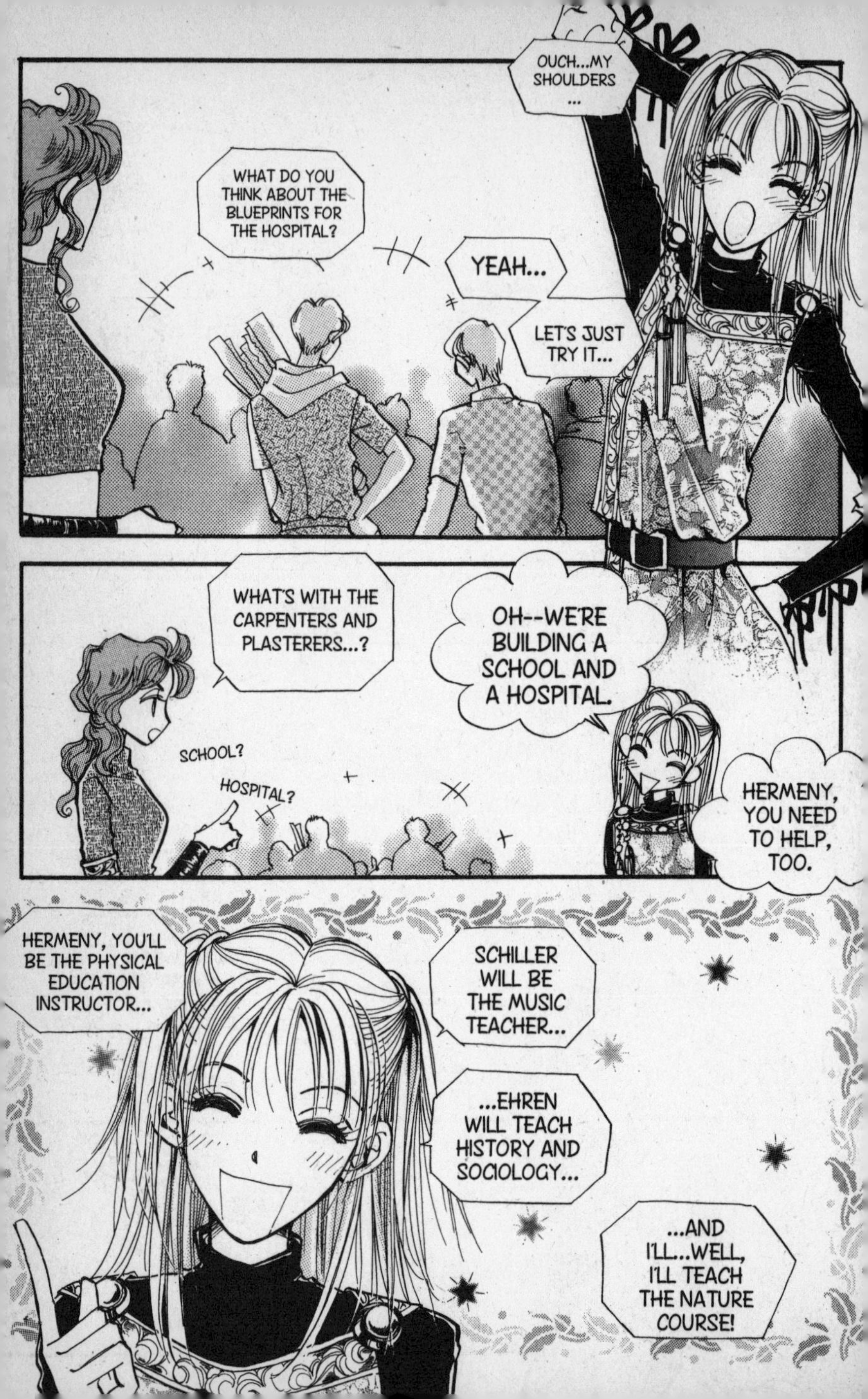
WHAT DO YOU THINK ABOUT THE BLUEPRINTS FOR THE HOSPITAL?
YEAH...
LET'S JUST TRY IT...
OUCH...MY SHOULDERS ...
WHAT'S WITH THE CARPENTERS AND PLASTERERS...?
SCHOOL?
HOSPITAL?
OH--WE'RE BUILDING A SCHOOL AND A HOSPITAL.
HERMENY, YOU NEED TO HELP, TOO.
HERMENY, YOU'LL BE THE PHYSICAL EDUCATION INSTRUCTOR...
SCHILLER WILL BE THE MUSIC TEACHER...
...EHREN WILL TEACH HISTORY AND SOCIOLOGY...
...AND I'LL...WELL, I'LL TEACH THE NATURE COURSE!

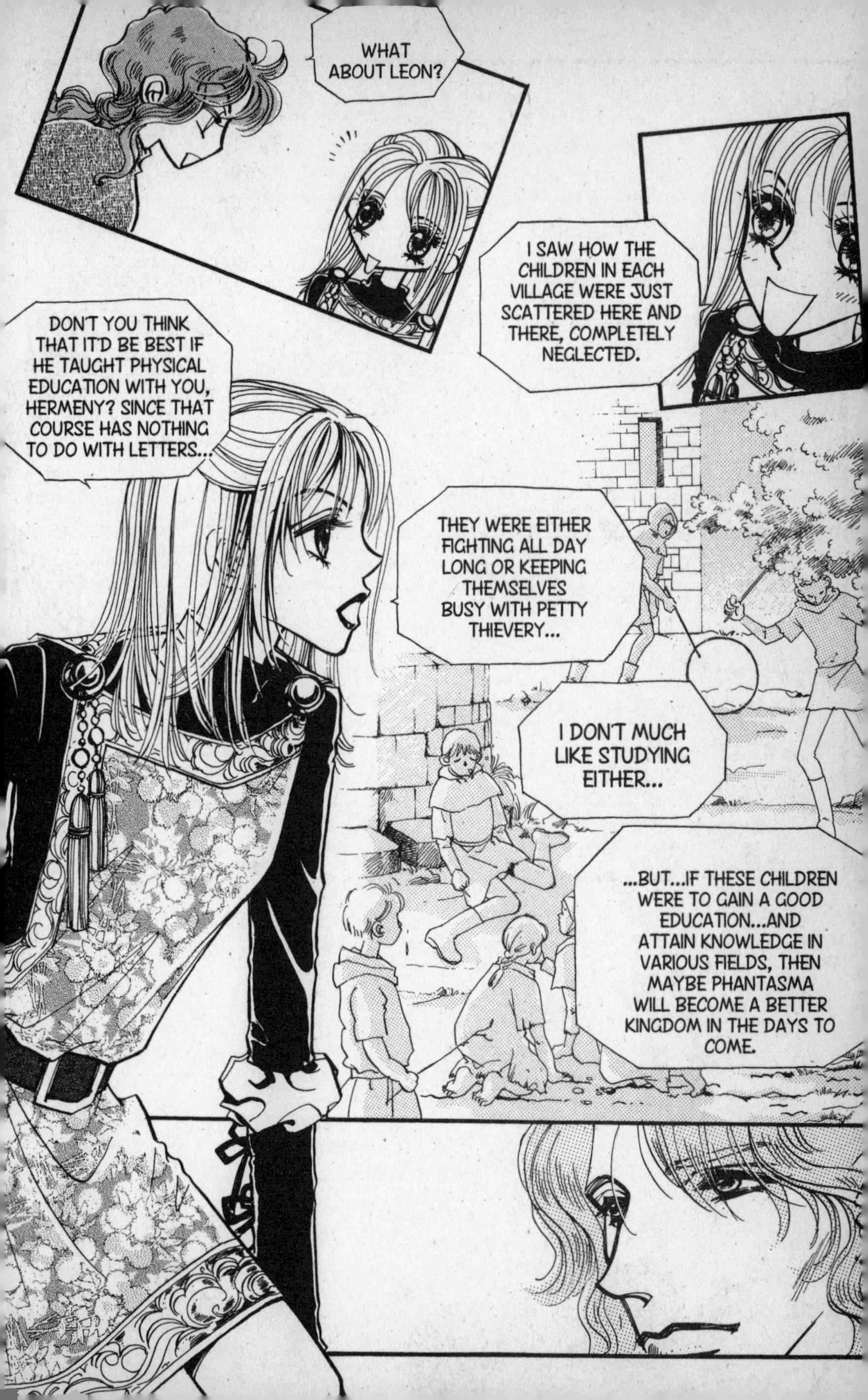
WHAT ABOUT LEON?
DON'T YOU THINK THAT IT'D BE BEST IF HE TAUGHT PHYSICAL EDUCATION WITH YOU, HERMENY? SINCE THAT COURSE HAS NOTHING TO DO WITH LETTERS...
I SAW HOW THE CHILDREN IN EACH VILLAGE WERE JUST SCATTERED HERE AND THERE, COMPLETELY NEGLECTED.
THEY WERE EITHER FIGHTING ALL DAY LONG OR KEEPING THEMSELVES BUSY WITH PETTY THIEVERY...
I DON'T MUCH LIKE STUDYING EITHER...
...BUT...IF THESE CHILDREN WERE TO GAIN A GOOD EDUCATION...AND ATTAIN KNOWLEDGE IN VARIOUS FIELDS, THEN MAYBE PHANTASMA WILL BECOME A BETTER KINGDOM IN THE DAYS TO COME.

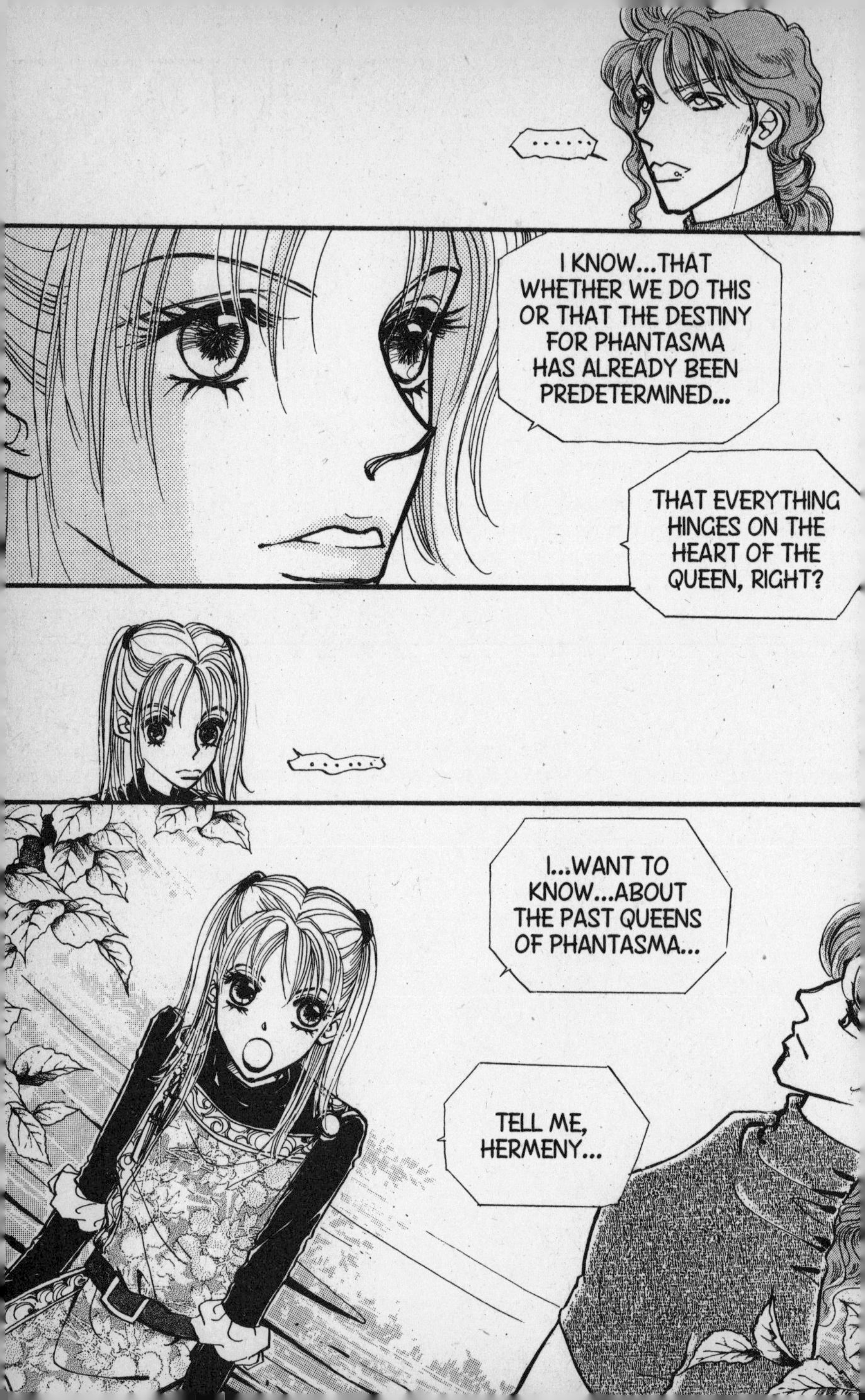
......
I KNOW...THAT WHETHER WE DO THIS OR THAT THE DESTINY FOR PHANTASMA HAS ALREADY BEEN PREDETERMINED...
THAT EVERYTHING HINGES ON THE HEART OF THE QUEEN, RIGHT?
......
I...WANT TO KNOW...ABOUT THE PAST QUEENS OF PHANTASMA...
TELL ME, HERMENY...

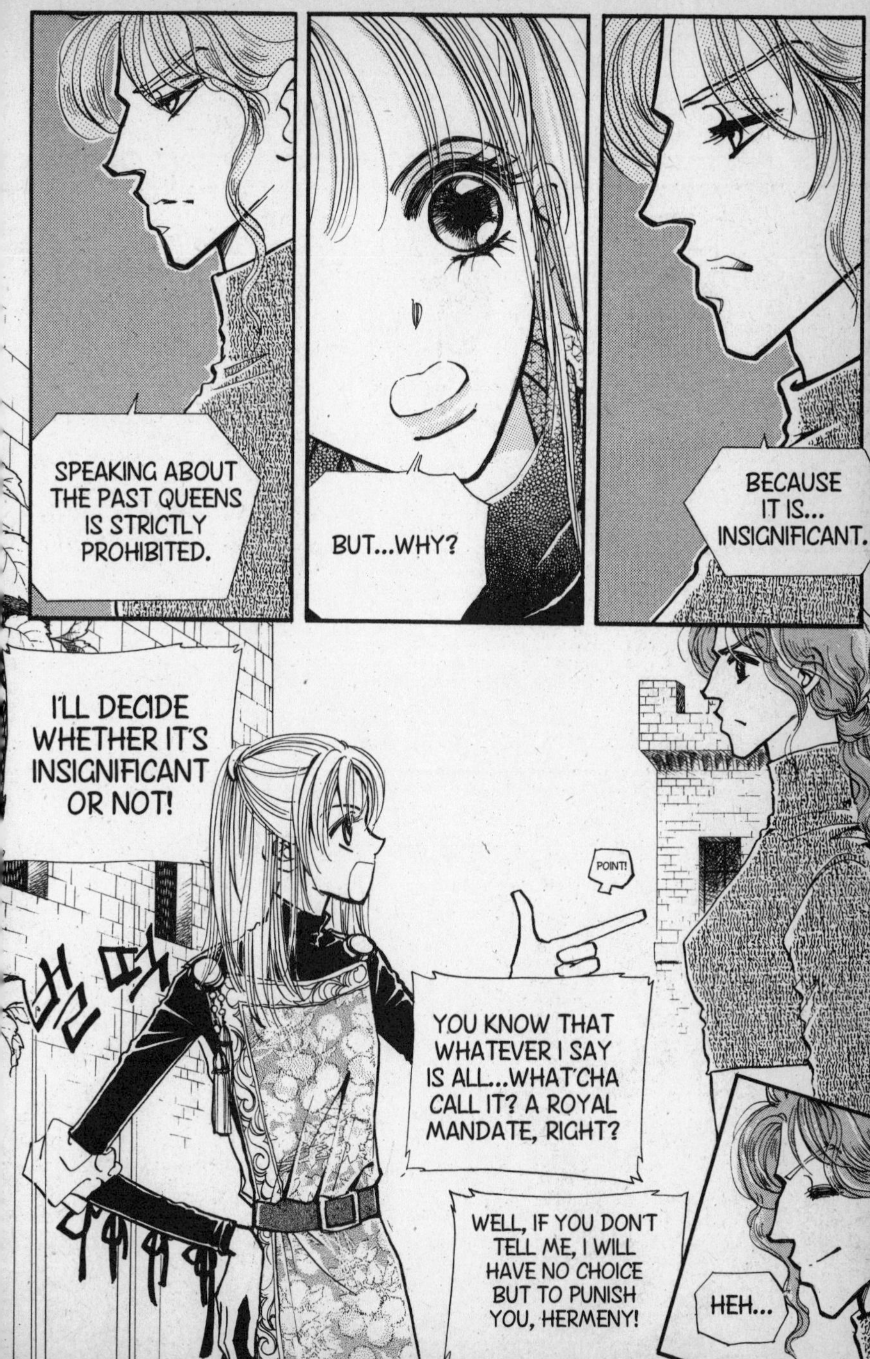
SPEAKING ABOUT THE PAST QUEENS IS STRICTLY PROHIBITED.
BUT...WHY?
BECAUSE IT IS... INSIGNIFICANT.
I'LL DECIDE WHETHER IT'S INSIGNIFICANT OR NOT!
POINT!
YOU KNOW THAT WHATEVER I SAY IS ALL...WHAT'CHA CALL IT? A ROYAL MANDATE, RIGHT?
WELL, IF YOU DON'T TELL ME, I WILL HAVE NO CHOICE BUT TO PUNISH YOU, HERMENY!
HEH...

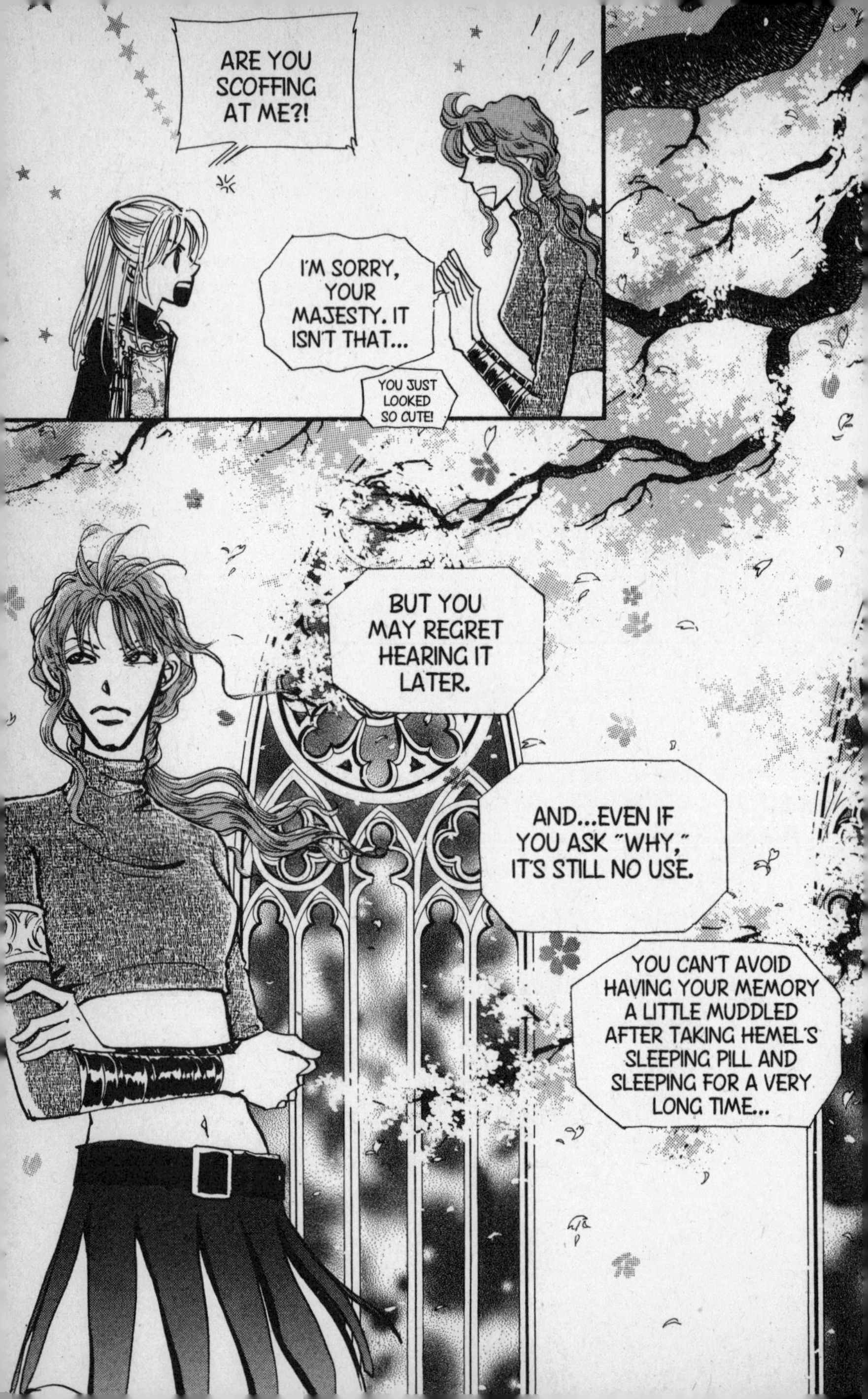
ARE YOU SCOFFING AT ME?!
I'M SORRY, YOUR MAJESTY. IT ISN'T THAT...
YOU JUST LOOKED SO CUTE!
BUT YOU MAY REGRET HEARING IT LATER.
AND...EVEN IF YOU ASK "WHY," IT'S STILL NO USE.
YOU CAN'T AVOID HAVING YOUR MEMORY A LITTLE MUDDLED AFTER TAKING HEMEL'S SLEEPING PILL AND SLEEPING FOR A VERY LONG TIME...

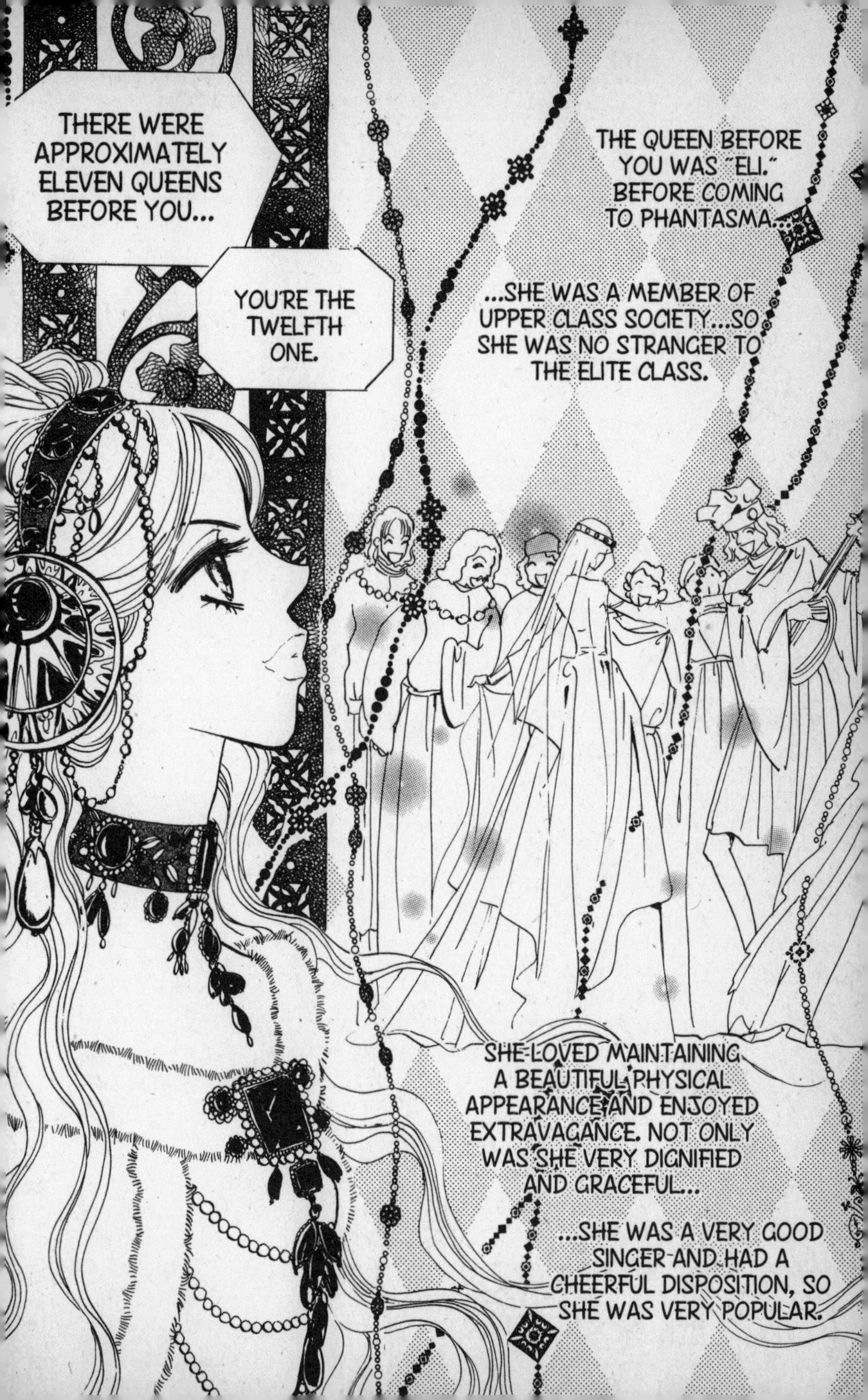
THERE WERE APPROXIMATELY ELEVEN QUEENS BEFORE YOU...
YOU'RE THE TWELFTH ONE.
THE QUEEN BEFORE YOU WAS "ELI." BEFORE COMING TO PHANTASMA...
...SHE WAS A MEMBER OF UPPER CLASS SOCIETY...SO SHE WAS NO STRANGER TO THE ELITE CLASS.
SHE LOVED MAINTAINING A BEAUTIFUL PHYSICAL APPEARANCE AND ENJOYED EXTRAVAGANCE. NOT ONLY WAS SHE VERY DIGNIFIED AND GRACEFUL...
...SHE WAS A VERY GOOD SINGER AND HAD A CHEERFUL DISPOSITION, SO SHE WAS VERY POPULAR.

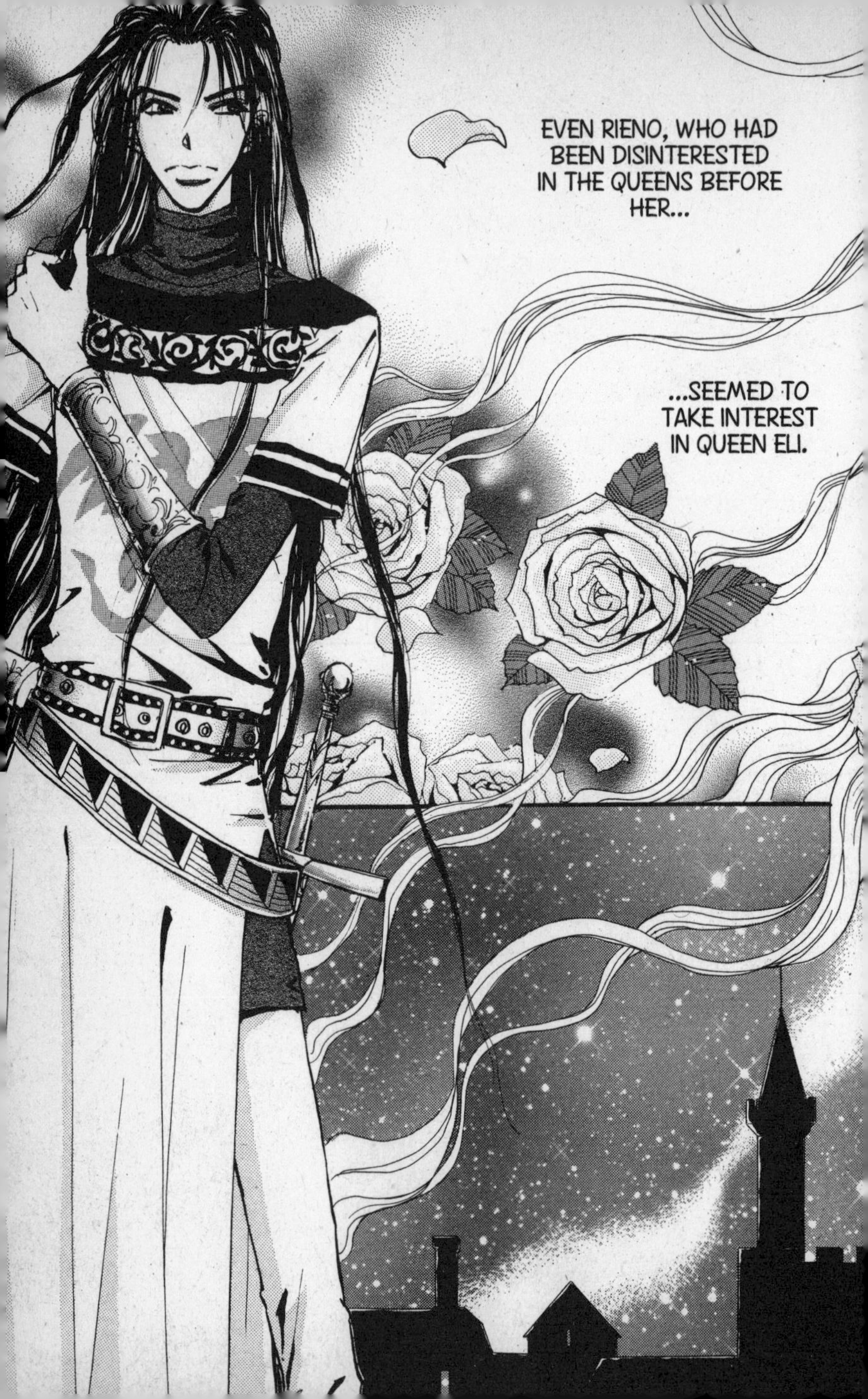
EVEN RIENO, WHO HAD BEEN DISINTERESTED IN THE QUEENS BEFORE HER...
...SEEMED TO TAKE INTEREST IN QUEEN ELI.

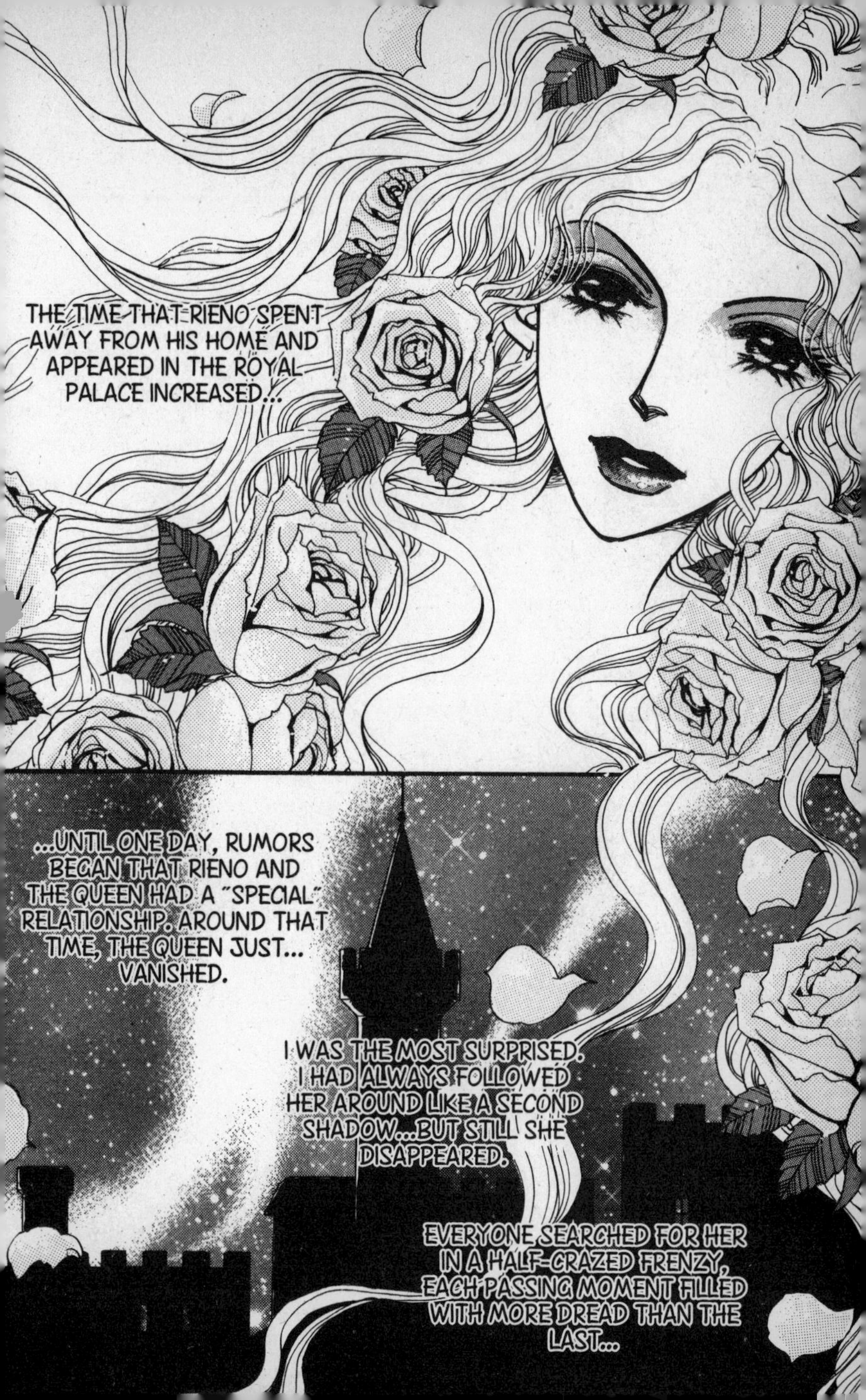
THE TIME THAT RIENO SPENT AWAY FROM HIS HOME AND APPEARED IN THE ROYAL PALACE INCREASED...
...UNTIL ONE DAY, RUMORS BEGAN THAT RIENO AND THE QUEEN HAD A "SPECIAL" RELATIONSHIP. AROUND THAT TIME, THE QUEEN JUST... VANISHED.
I WAS THE MOST SURPRISED. I HAD ALWAYS FOLLOWED HER AROUND LIKE A SECOND SHADOW...BUT STILL SHE DISAPPEARED.
EVERYONE SEARCHED FOR HER IN A HALF-CRAZED FRENZY, EACH PASSING MOMENT FILLED WITH MORE DREAD THAN THE LAST...

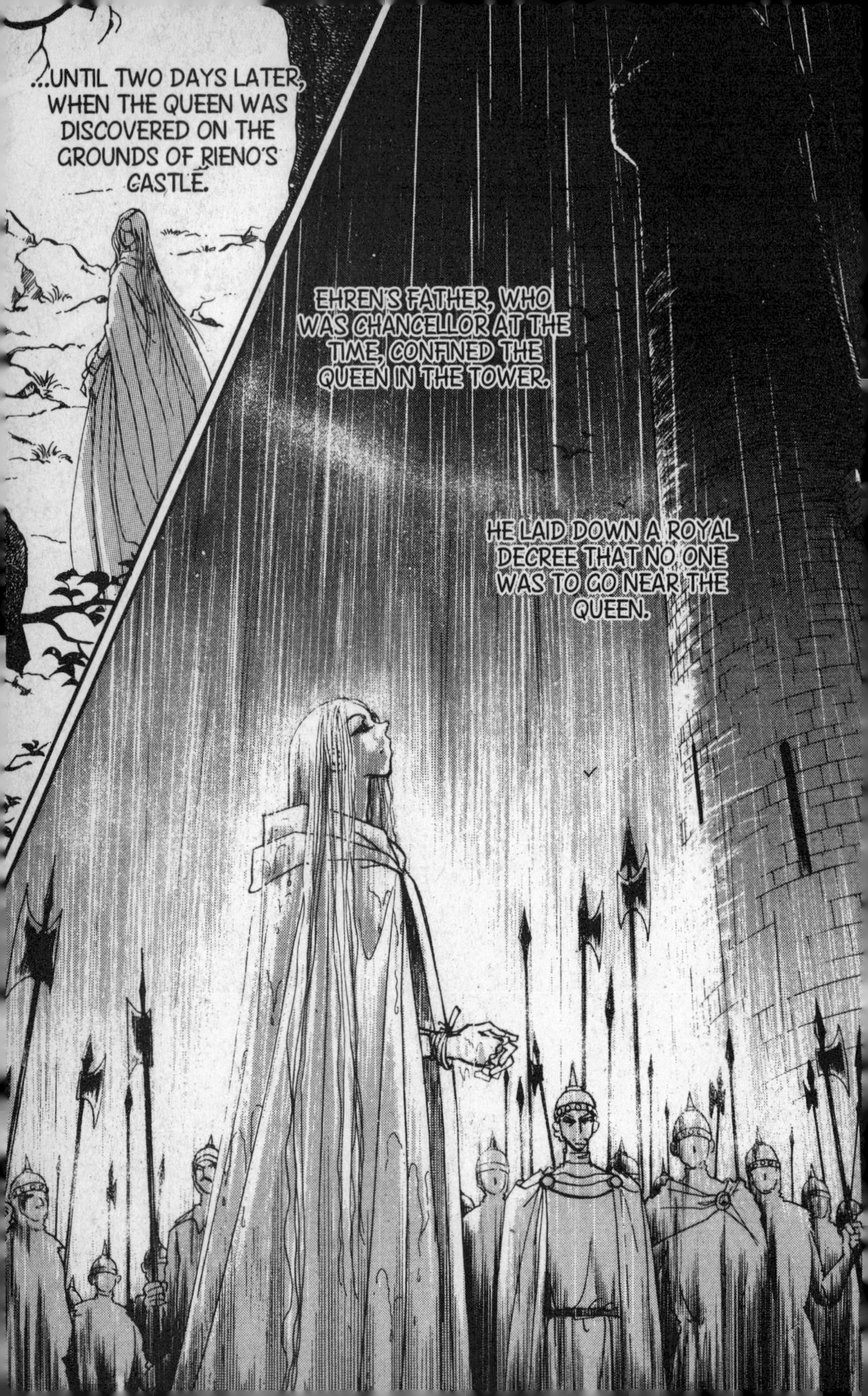
...UNTIL TWO DAYS LATER, WHEN THE QUEEN WAS DISCOVERED ON THE GROUNDS OF RIENO'S CASTLE.
EHREN'S FATHER, WHO WAS CHANCELLOR AT THE TIME, CONFINED THE QUEEN IN THE TOWER.
HE LAID DOWN A ROYAL DECREE THAT NO ONE WAS TO GO NEAR THE QUEEN.

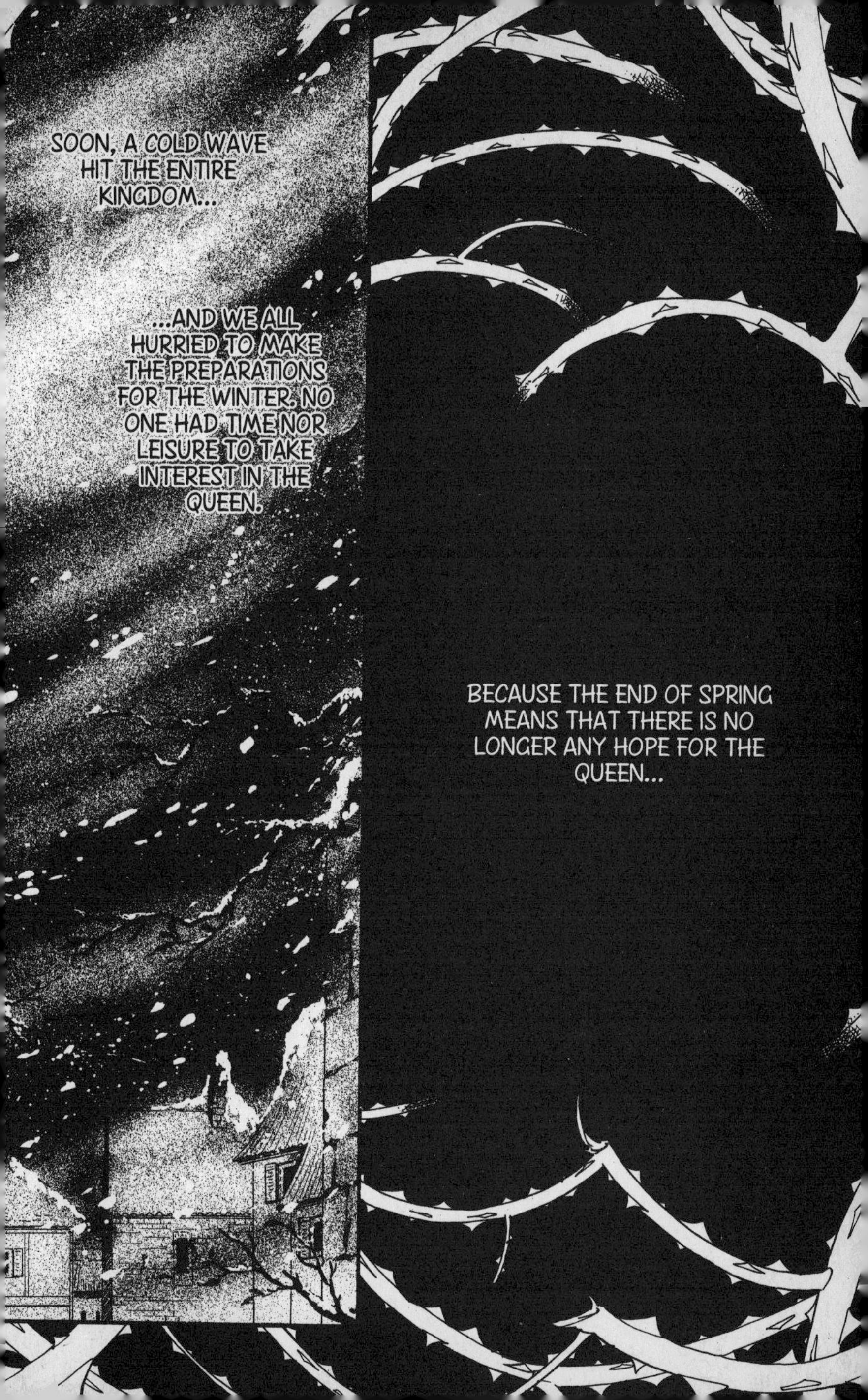
SOON, A COLD WAVE HIT THE ENTIRE KINGDOM...
...AND WE ALL HURRIED TO MAKE THE PREPARATIONS FOR THE WINTER. NO ONE HAD TIME NOR LEISURE TO TAKE INTEREST IN THE QUEEN.
BECAUSE THE END OF SPRING MEANS THAT THERE IS NO LONGER ANY HOPE FOR THE QUEEN...

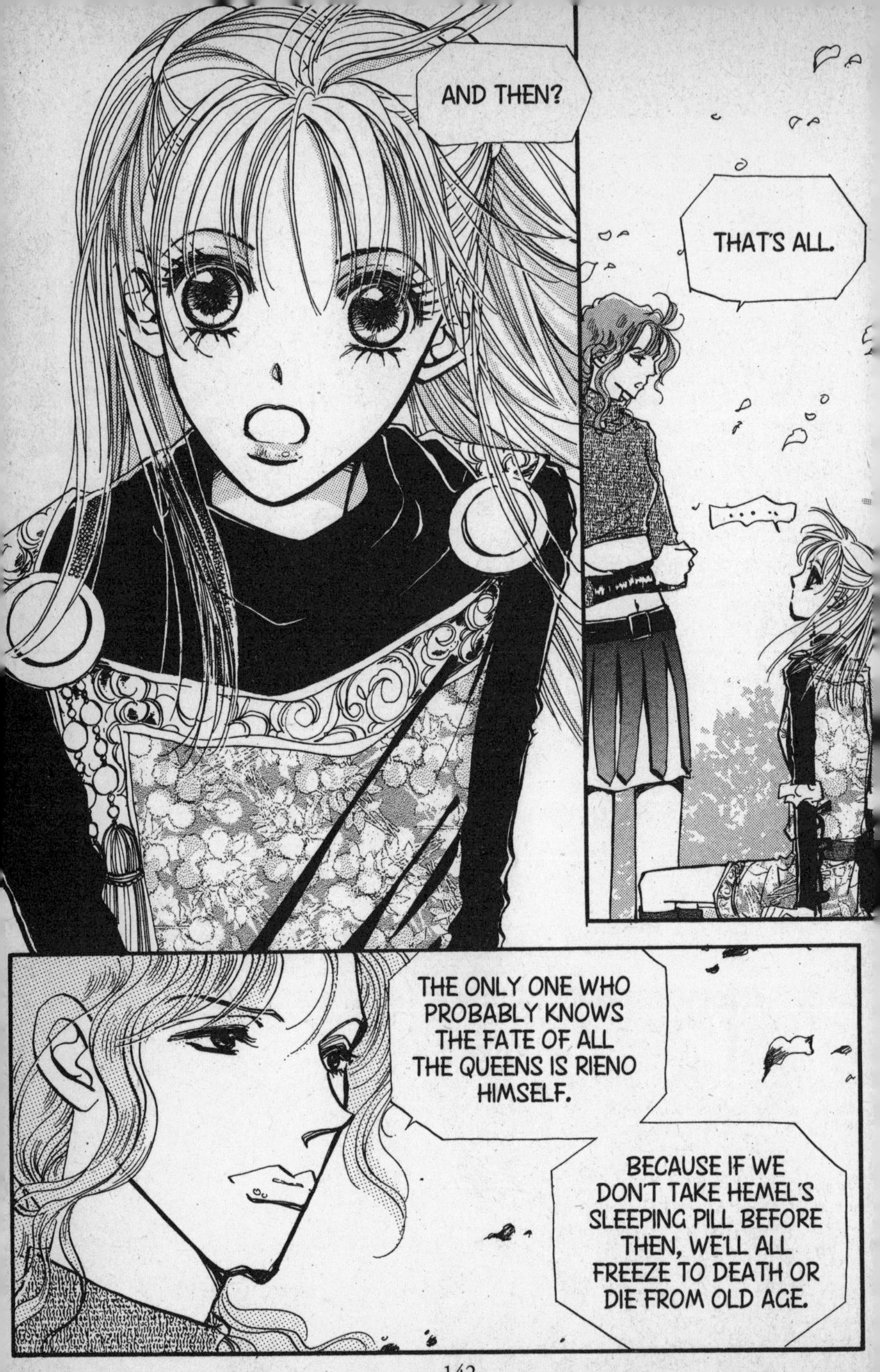
AND THEN?
THAT'S ALL.
...
THE ONLY ONE WHO PROBABLY KNOWS THE FATE OF ALL THE QUEENS IS RIENO HIMSELF.
BECAUSE IF WE DON'T TAKE HEMEL'S SLEEPING PILL BEFORE THEN, WE'LL ALL FREEZE TO DEATH OR DIE FROM OLD AGE.

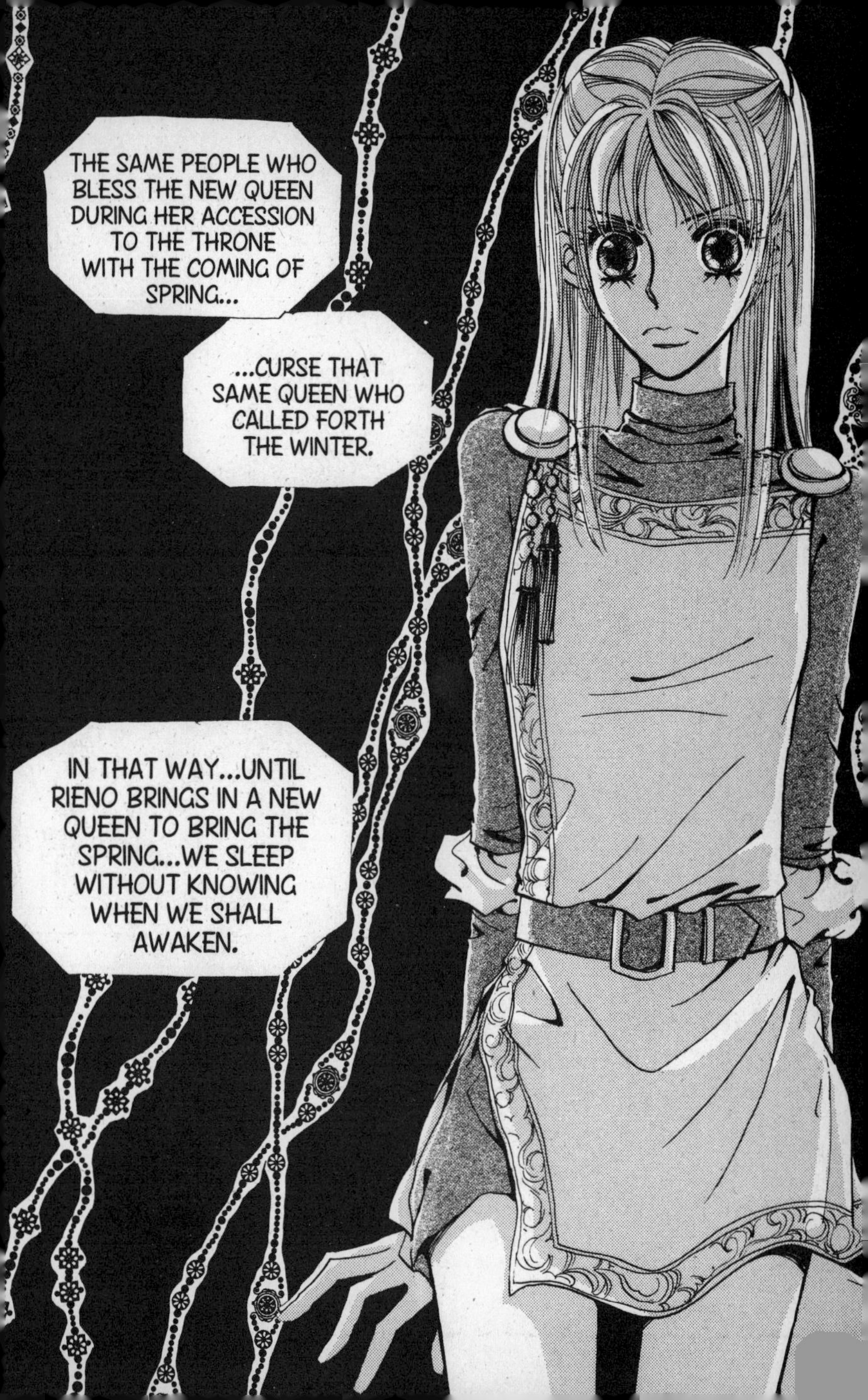
THE SAME PEOPLE WHO BLESS THE NEW QUEEN DURING HER ACCESSION TO THE THRONE WITH THE COMING OF SPRING...
...CURSE THAT SAME QUEEN WHO CALLED FORTH THE WINTER.
IN THAT WAY...UNTIL RIENO BRINGS IN A NEW QUEEN TO BRING THE SPRING...WE SLEEP WITHOUT KNOWING WHEN WE SHALL AWAKEN.

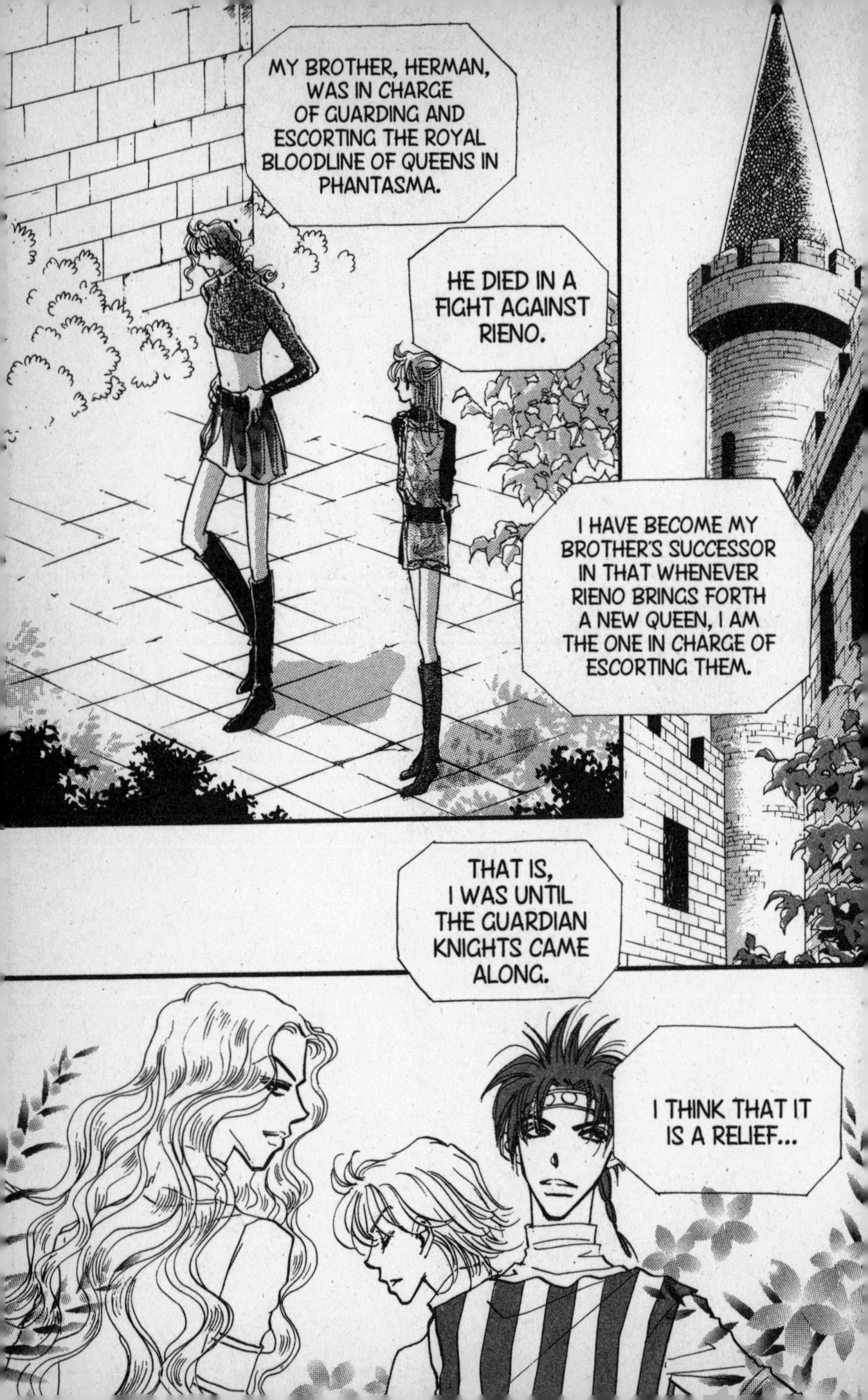
MY BROTHER, HERMAN, WAS IN CHARGE OF GUARDING AND ESCORTING THE ROYAL BLOODLINE OF QUEENS IN PHANTASMA.
HE DIED IN A FIGHT AGAINST RIENO.
I HAVE BECOME MY BROTHER'S SUCCESSOR IN THAT WHENEVER RIENO BRINGS FORTH A NEW QUEEN, I AM THE ONE IN CHARGE OF ESCORTING THEM.
THAT IS, I WAS UNTIL THE GUARDIAN KNIGHTS CAME ALONG.
I THINK THAT IT IS A RELIEF...

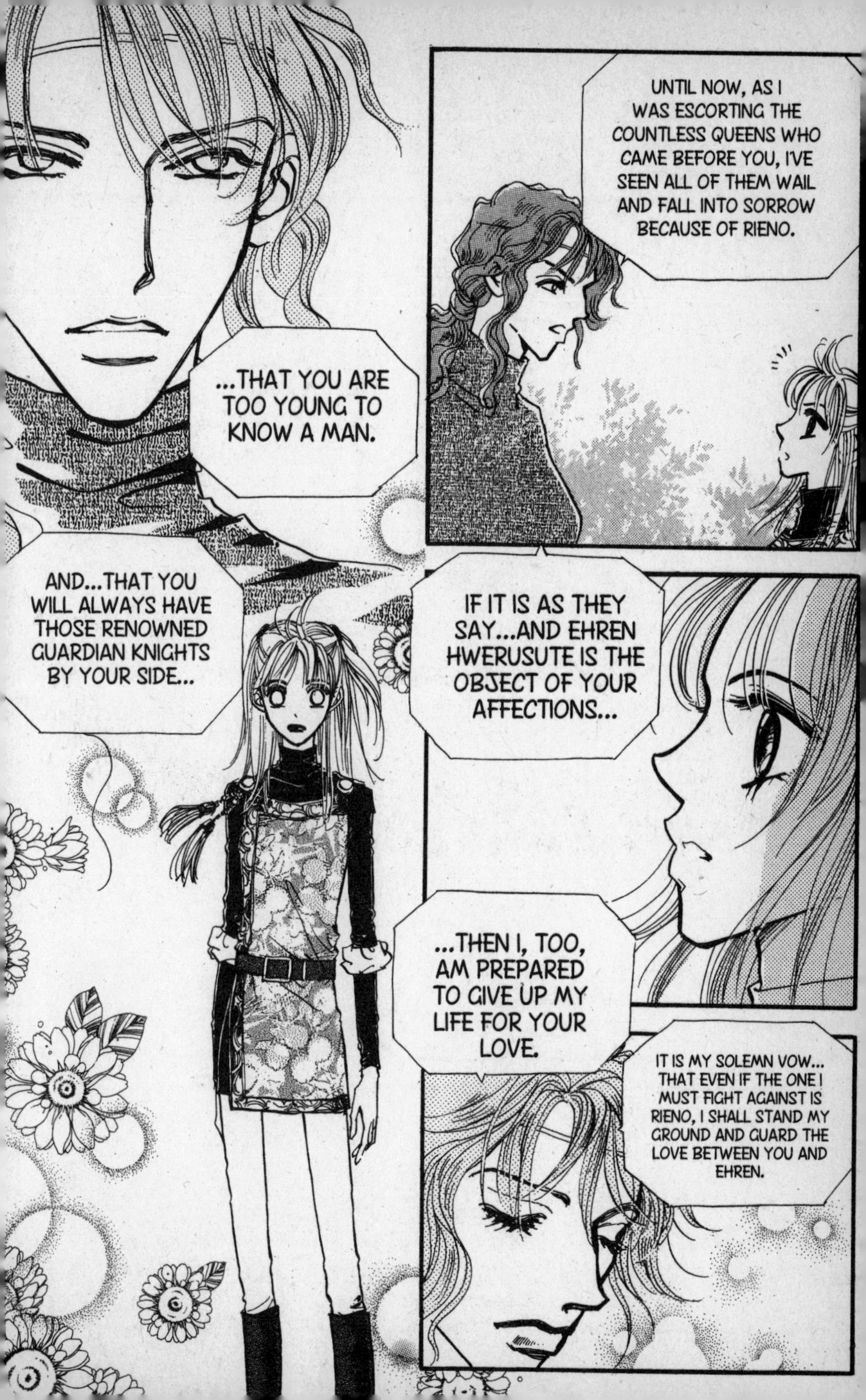
...THAT YOU ARE TOO YOUNG TO KNOW A MAN.
AND...THAT YOU WILL ALWAYS HAVE THOSE RENOWNED GUARDIAN KNIGHTS BY YOUR SIDE...
UNTIL NOW, AS I WAS ESCORTING THE COUNTLESS QUEENS WHO CAME BEFORE YOU, I'VE SEEN ALL OF THEM WAIL AND FALL INTO SORROW BECAUSE OF RIENO.
IF IT IS AS THEY SAY...AND EHREN HWERUSUTE IS THE OBJECT OF YOUR AFFECTIONS...
...THEN I, TOO, AM PREPARED TO GIVE UP MY LIFE FOR YOUR LOVE.
IT IS MY SOLEMN VOW... THAT EVEN IF THE ONE I MUST FIGHT AGAINST IS RIENO, I SHALL STAND MY GROUND AND GUARD THE LOVE BETWEEN YOU AND EHREN.

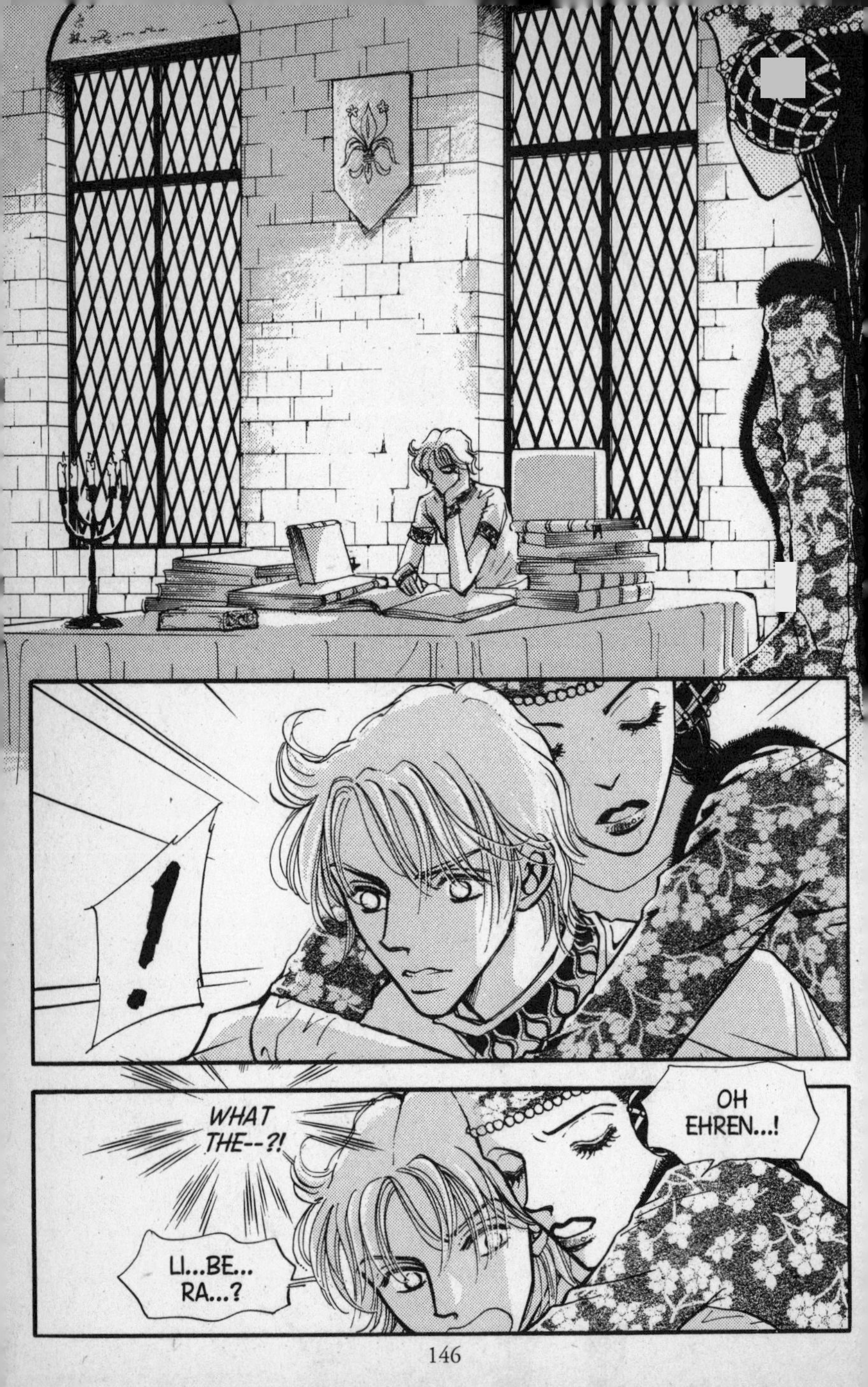
!
WHAT THE--?!
OH EHREN...!
LI...BE... RA...?

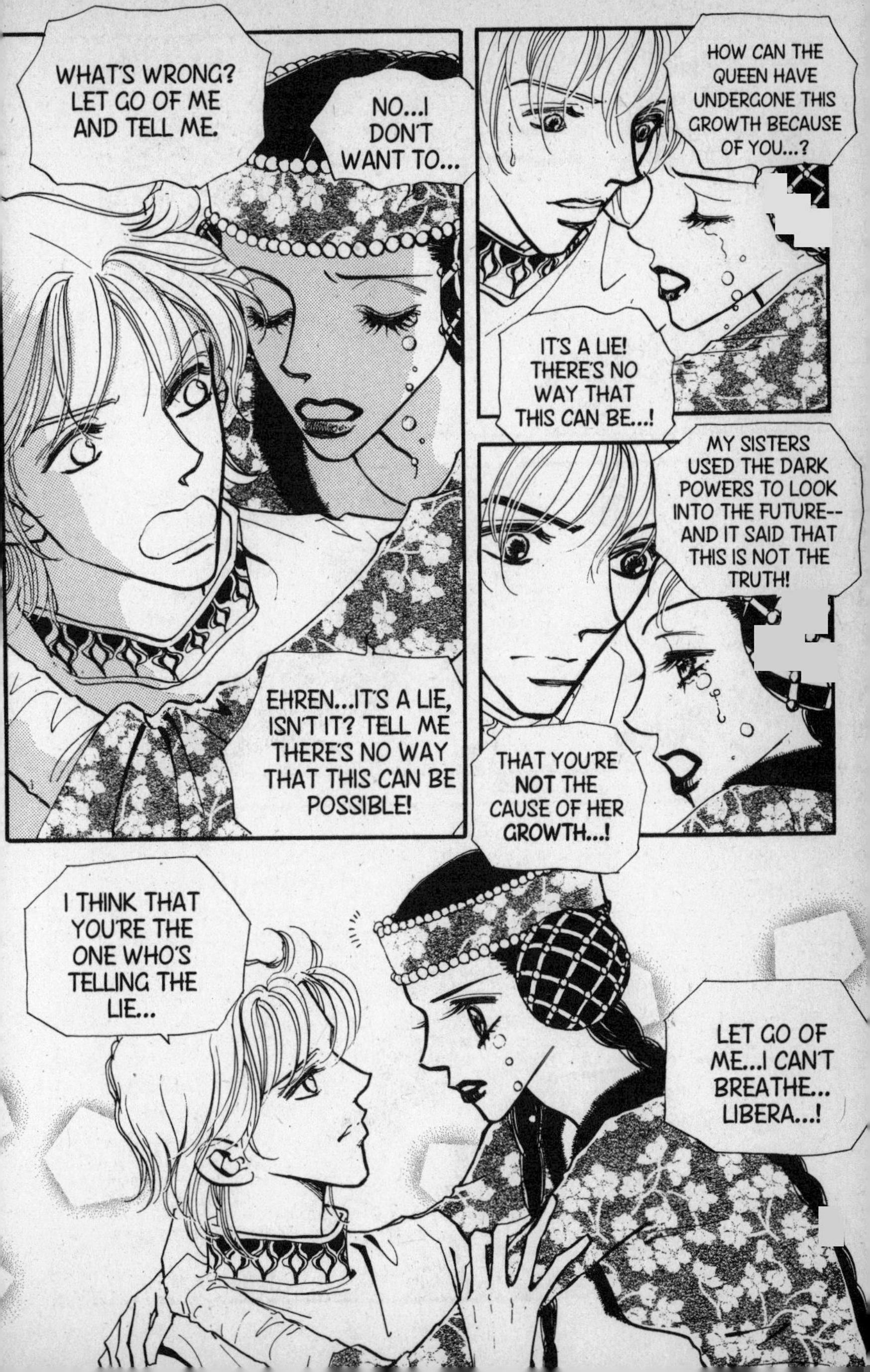
WHAT'S WRONG? LET GO OF ME AND TELL ME.
NO...I DON'T WANT TO...
EHREN...IT'S A LIE, ISN'T IT? TELL ME THERE'S NO WAY THAT THIS CAN BE POSSIBLE!
HOW CAN THE QUEEN HAVE UNDERGONE THIS GROWTH BECAUSE OF YOU...?
IT'S A LIE! THERE'S NO WAY THAT THIS CAN BE...!
MY SISTERS USED THE DARK POWERS TO LOOK INTO THE FUTURE--AND IT SAID THAT THIS IS NOT THE TRUTH!
THAT YOU'RE NOT THE CAUSE OF HER GROWTH...!
I THINK THAT YOU'RE THE ONE WHO'S TELLING THE LIE...
LET GO OF ME...I CAN'T BREATHE... LIBERA...!

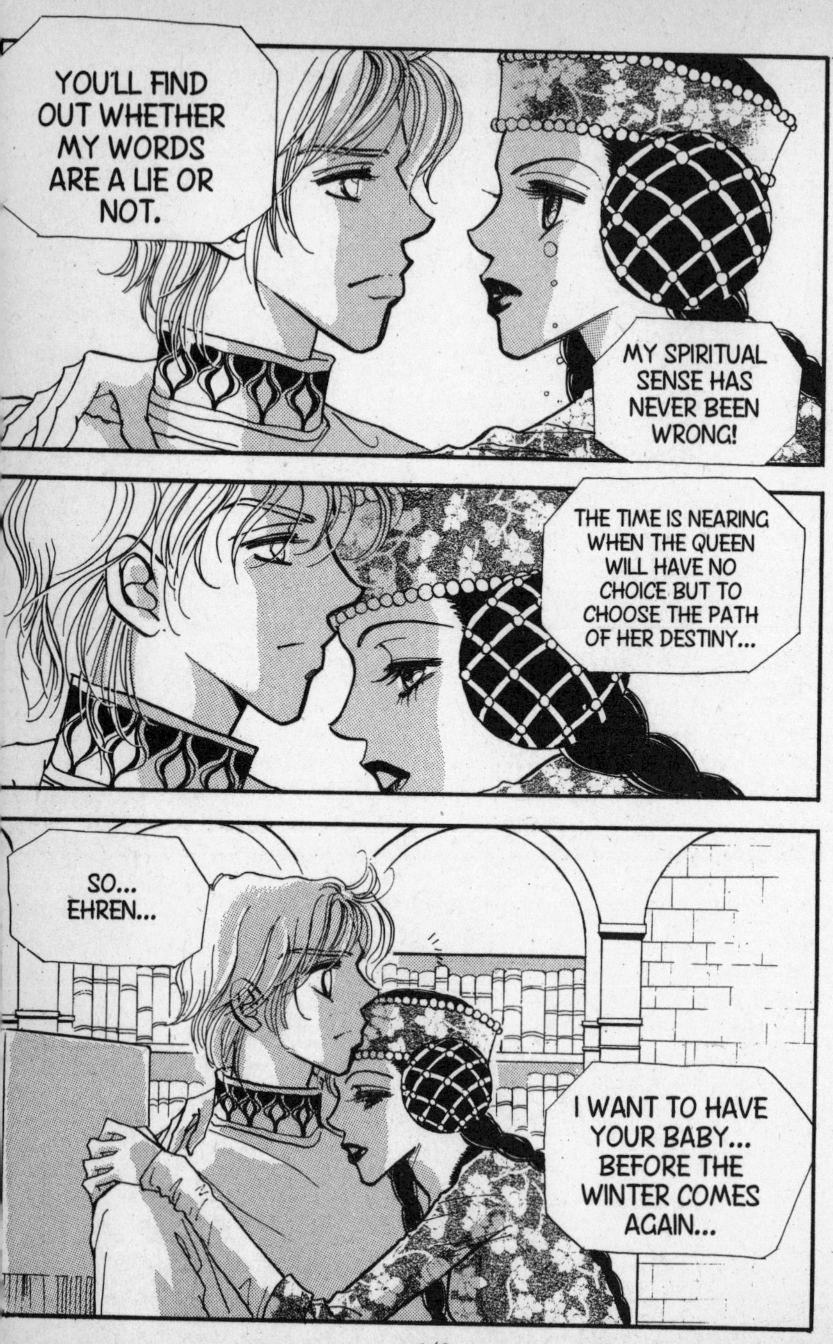
YOU'LL FIND OUT WHETHER MY WORDS ARE A LIE OR NOT.
MY SPIRITUAL SENSE HAS NEVER BEEN WRONG!
THE TIME IS NEARING WHEN THE QUEEN WILL HAVE NO CHOICE BUT TO CHOOSE THE PATH OF HER DESTINY...
SO... EHREN...
I WANT TO HAVE YOUR BABY... BEFORE THE WINTER COMES AGAIN...

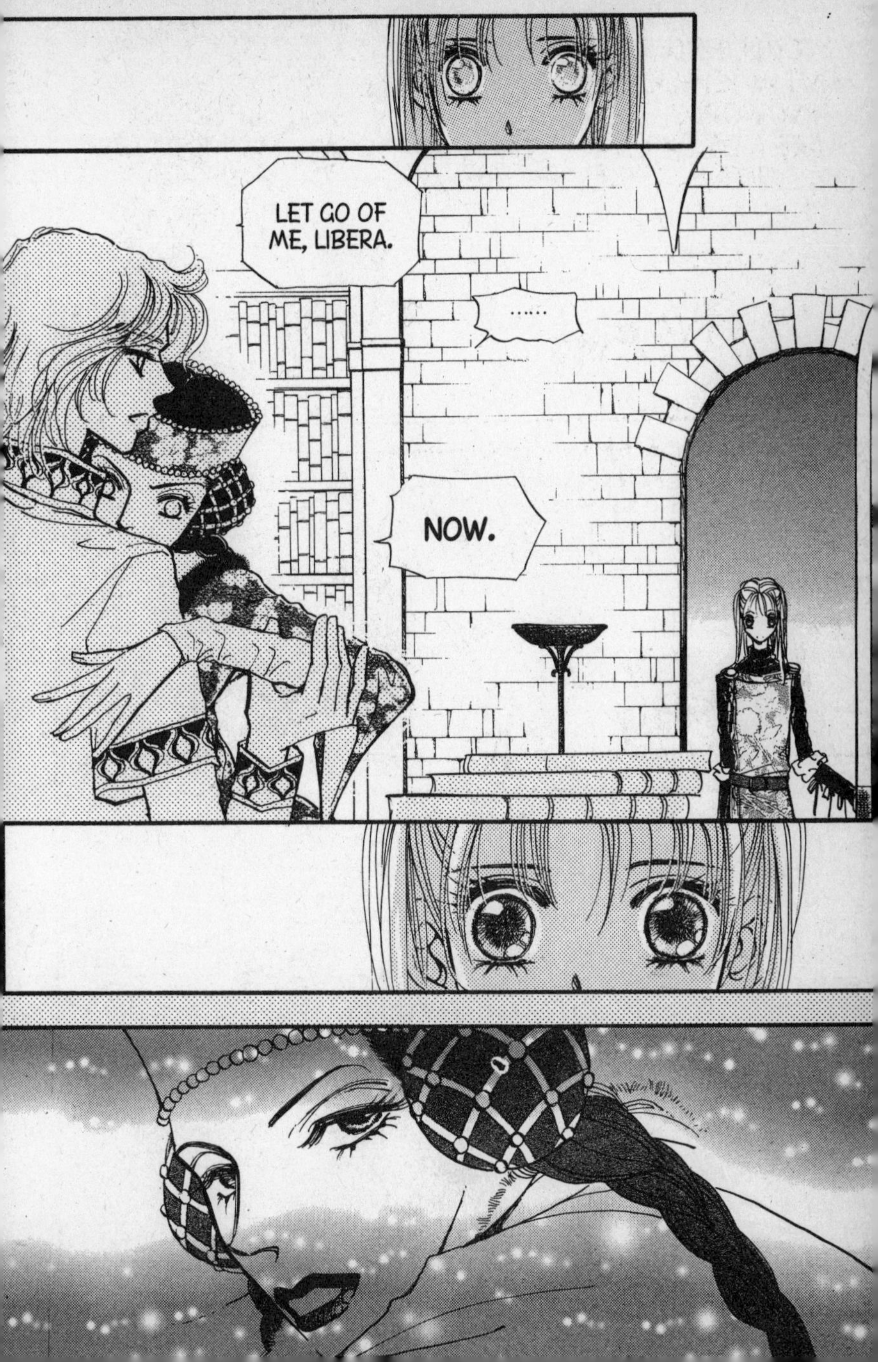
LET GO OF ME, LIBERA.
......
NOW.

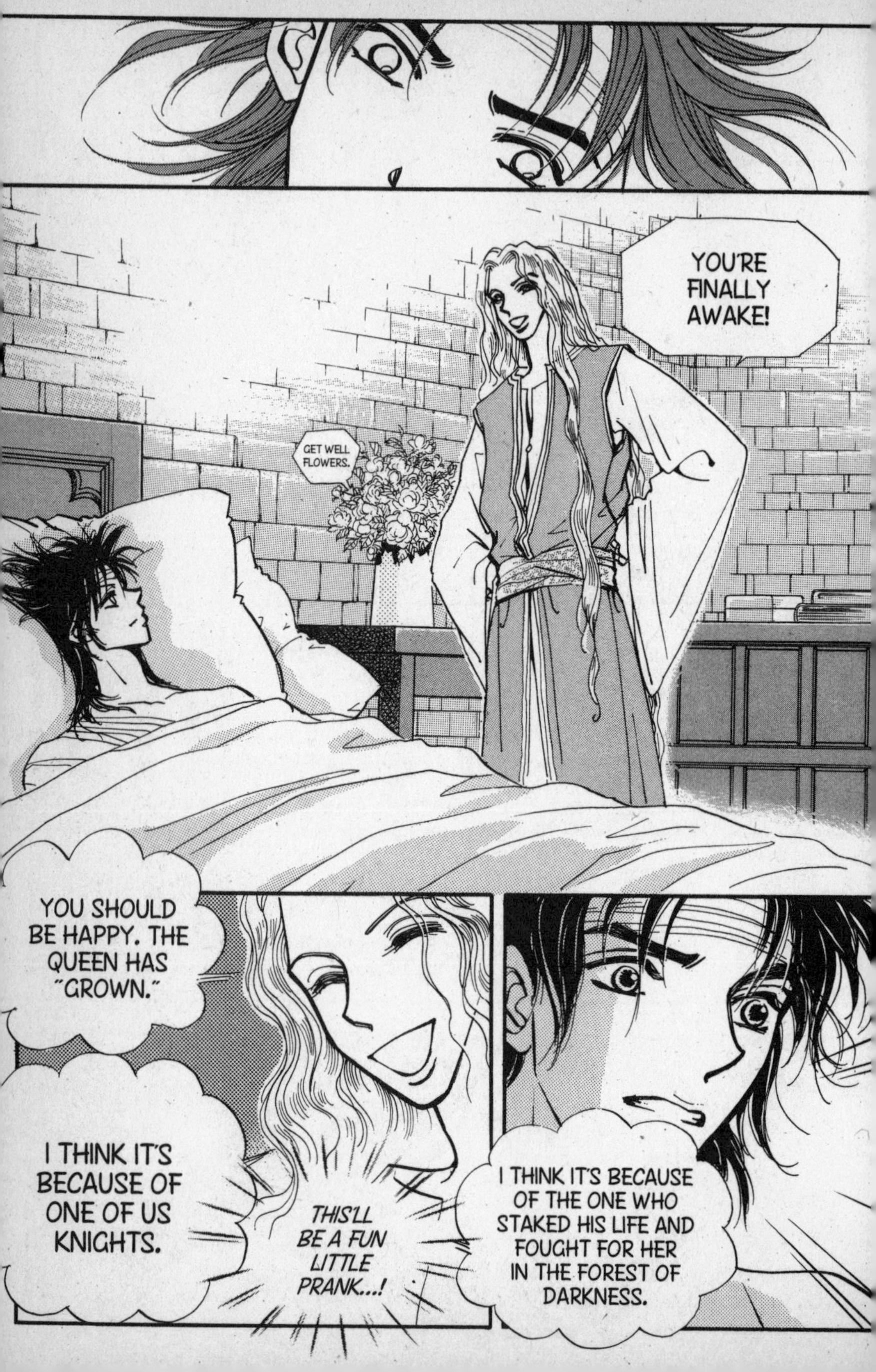
YOU'RE FINALLY AWAKE!
GET WELL FLOWERS.
YOU SHOULD BE HAPPY. THE QUEEN HAS "GROWN."
I THINK IT'S BECAUSE OF ONE OF US KNIGHTS.
THIS'LL BE A FUN LITTLE PRANK...!
I THINK IT'S BECAUSE OF THE ONE WHO STAKED HIS LIFE AND FOUGHT FOR HER IN THE FOREST OF DARKNESS.

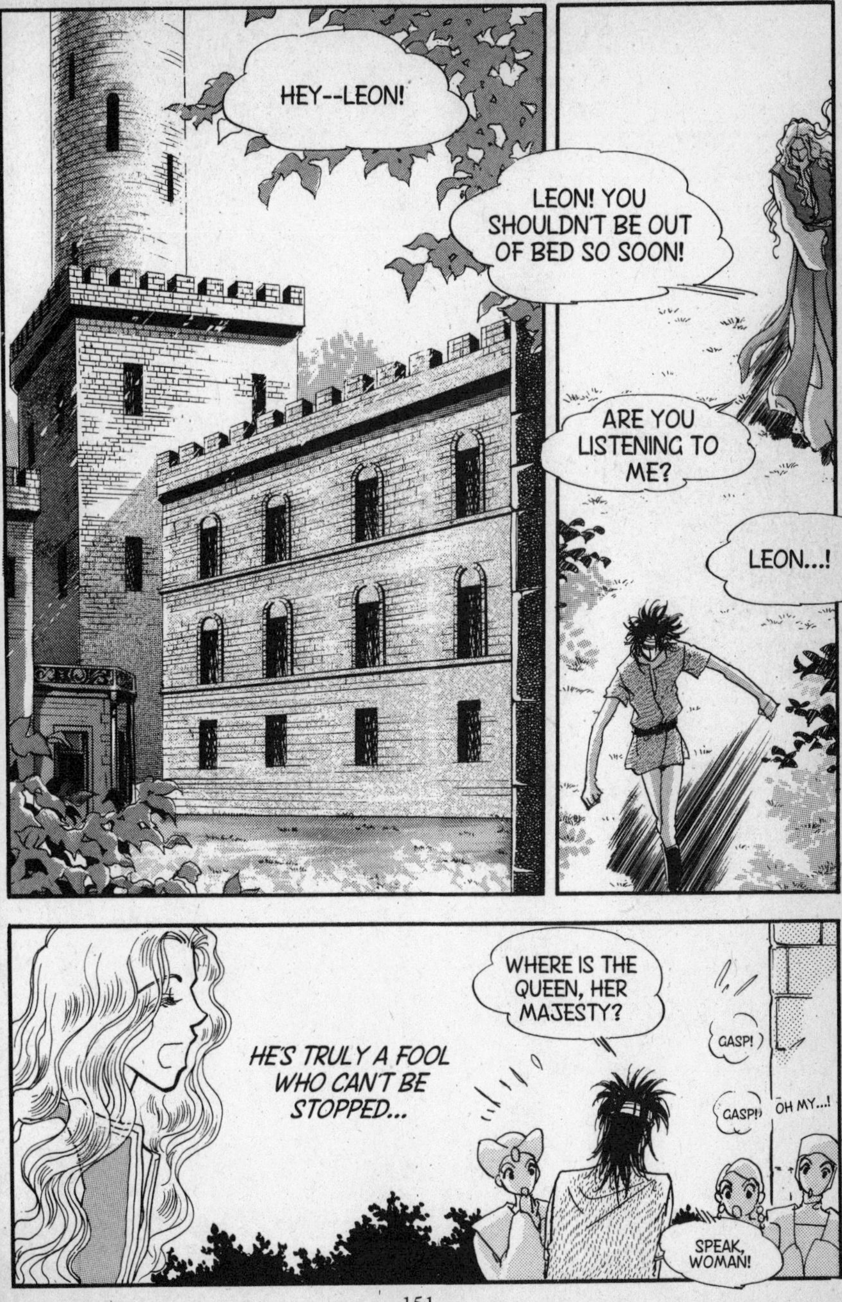
HEY--LEON!
LEON! YOU SHOULDN'T BE OUT OF BED SO SOON!
ARE YOU LISTENING TO ME?
LEON...!
HE'S TRULY A FOOL WHO CAN'T BE STOPPED...
WHERE IS THE QUEEN, HER MAJESTY?
GASP!
GASP!
OH MY...!
SPEAK, WOMAN!

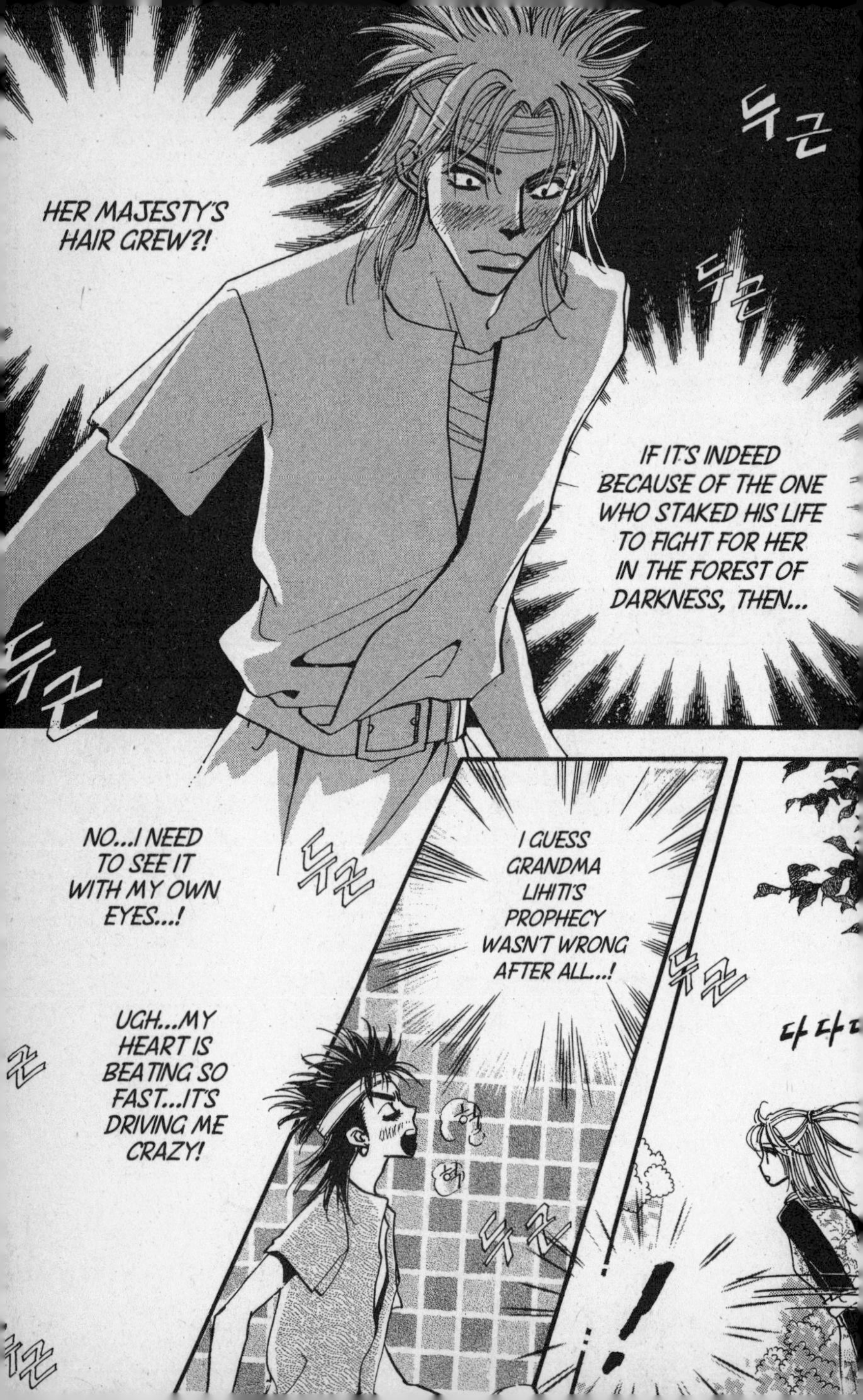
HER MAJESTY'S HAIR GREW?!
두근
두근
IF IT'S INDEED BECAUSE OF THE ONE WHO STAKED HIS LIFE TO FIGHT FOR HER IN THE FOREST OF DARKNESS, THEN...
두근
NO...I NEED TO SEE IT WITH MY OWN EYES...!
두근
UGH...MY HEART IS BEATING SO FAST...IT'S DRIVING ME CRAZY!
I GUESS GRANDMA LIHITI'S PROPHECY WASN'T WRONG AFTER ALL...!
두근
두근
!
다다

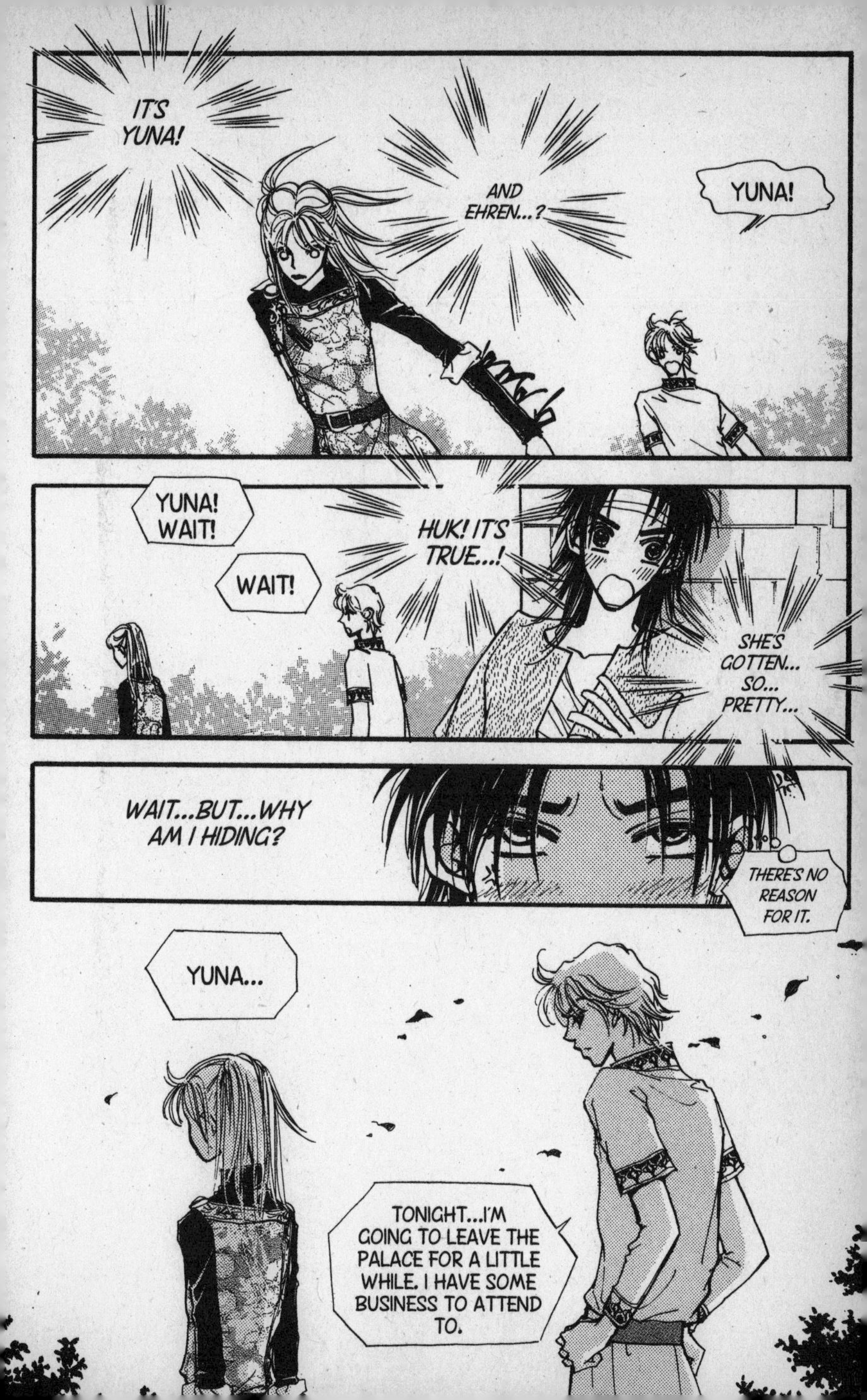

IT'S YUNA!
AND EHREN...?
YUNA!
YUNA! WAIT!
WAIT!
HUK! IT'S TRUE...!
SHE'S GOTTEN... SO... PRETTY...
WAIT...BUT...WHY AM I HIDING?
THERE'S NO REASON FOR IT.
YUNA...
TONIGHT...I'M GOING TO LEAVE THE PALACE FOR A LITTLE WHILE. I HAVE SOME BUSINESS TO ATTEND TO.

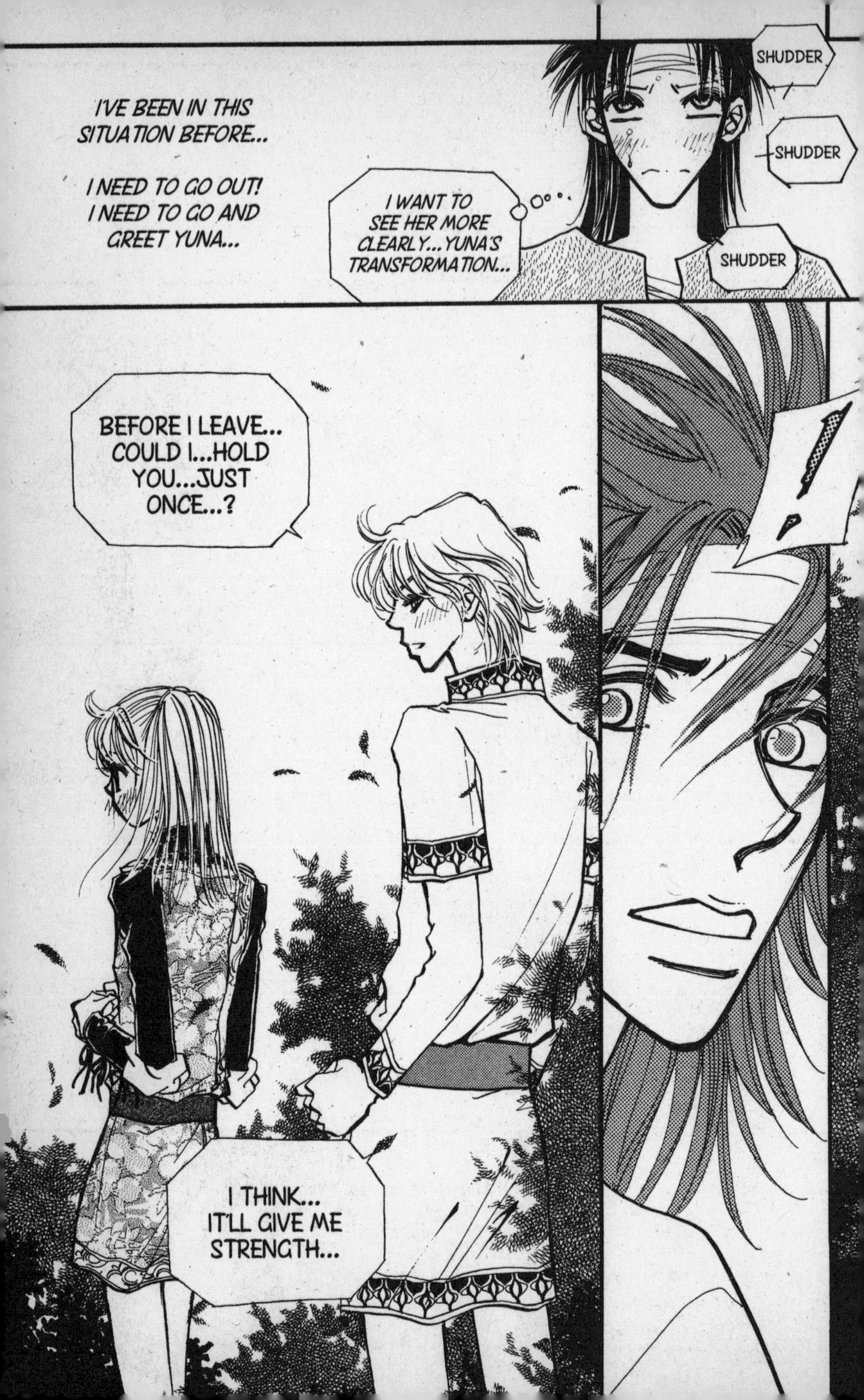
I'VE BEEN IN THIS SITUATION BEFORE...
I NEED TO GO OUT! I NEED TO GO AND GREET YUNA...
I WANT TO SEE HER MORE CLEARLY...YUNA'S TRANSFORMATION...
SHUDDER
SHUDDER
SHUDDER
BEFORE I LEAVE... COULD I...HOLD YOU...JUST ONCE...?
I THINK... IT'LL GIVE ME STRENGTH...
!

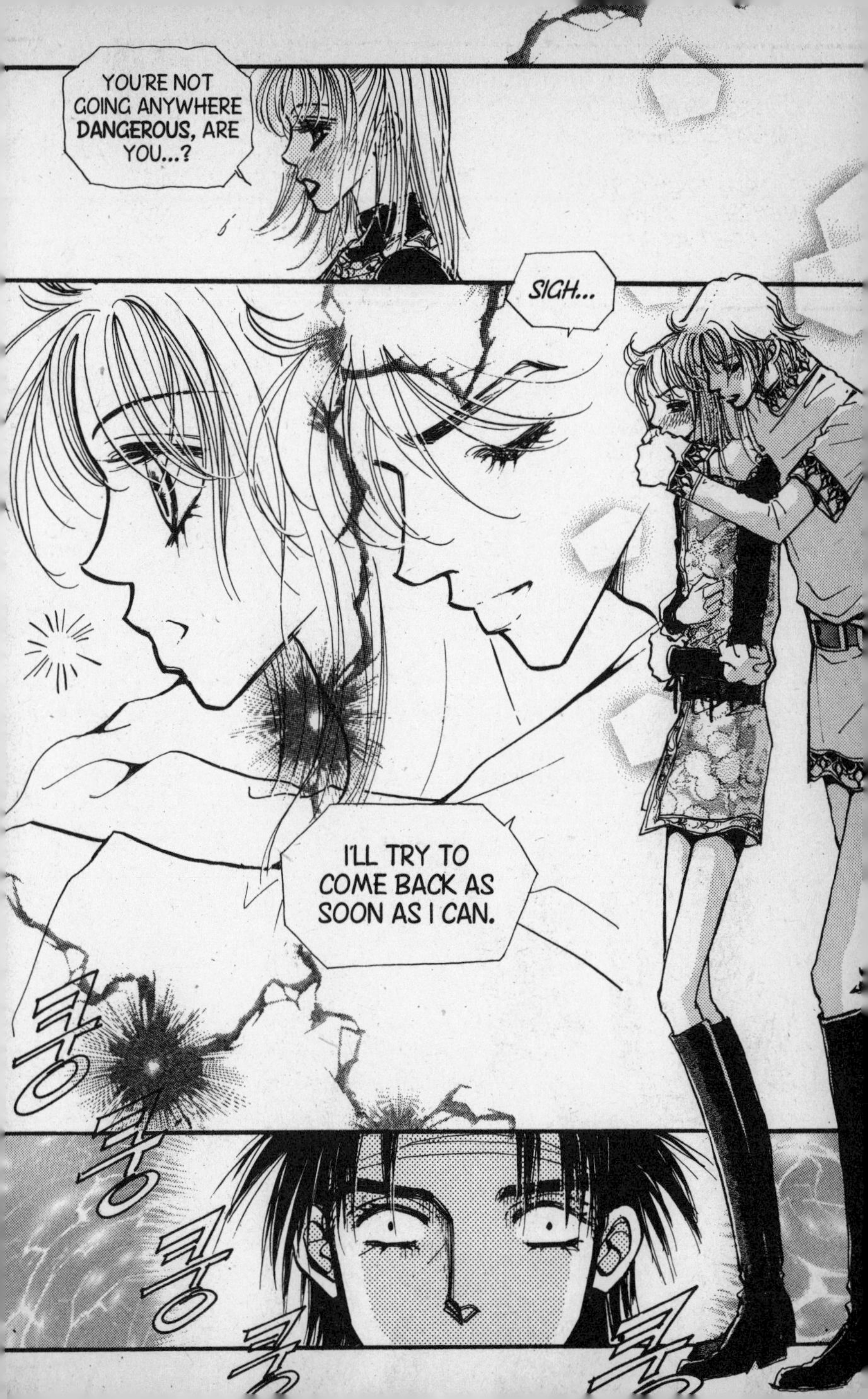
YOU'RE NOT GOING ANYWHERE DANGEROUS, ARE YOU...?
SIGH...
I'LL TRY TO COME BACK AS SOON AS I CAN.

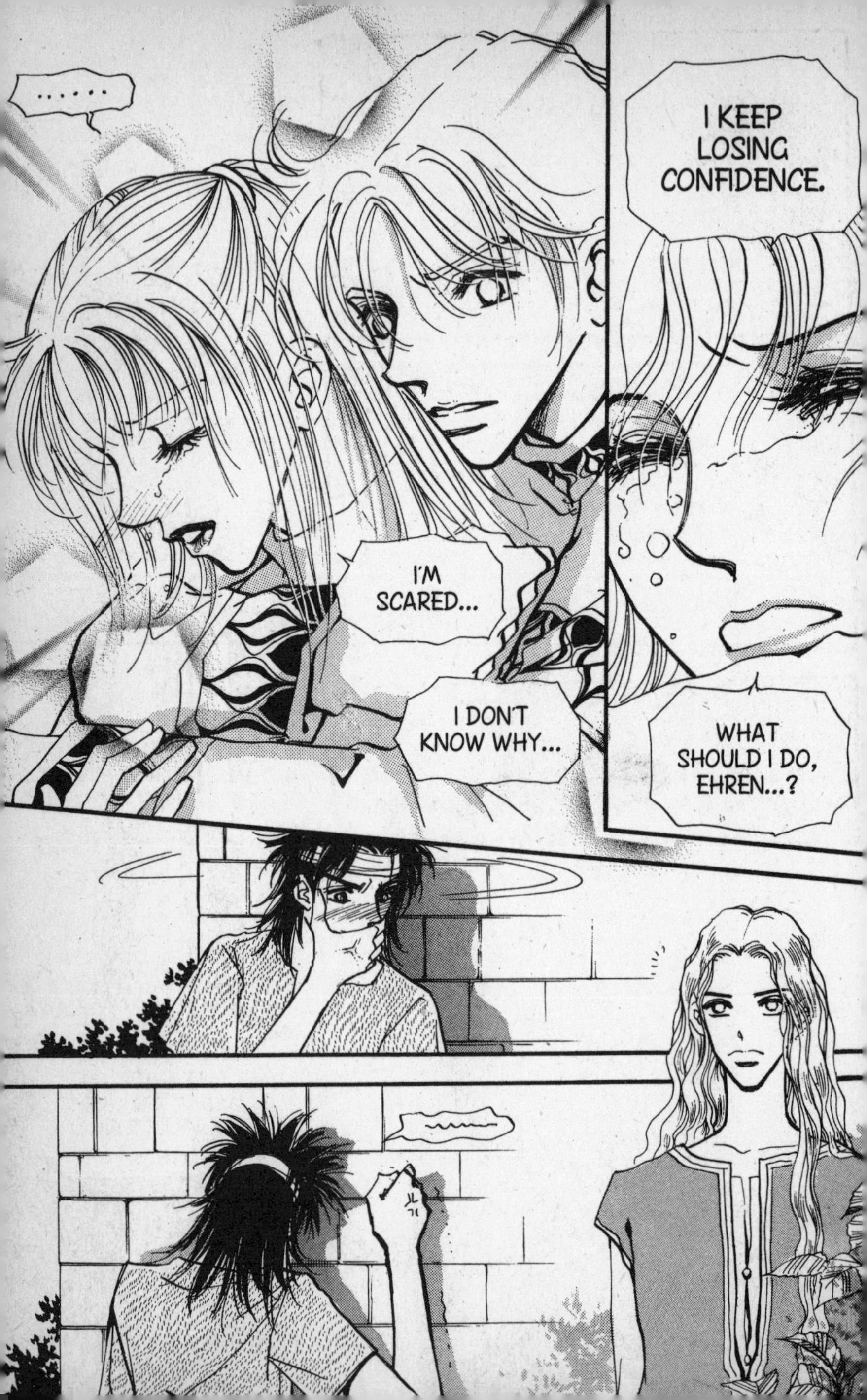
......
I'M SCARED...
I DON'T KNOW WHY...
I KEEP LOSING CONFIDENCE.
WHAT SHOULD I DO, EHREN...?

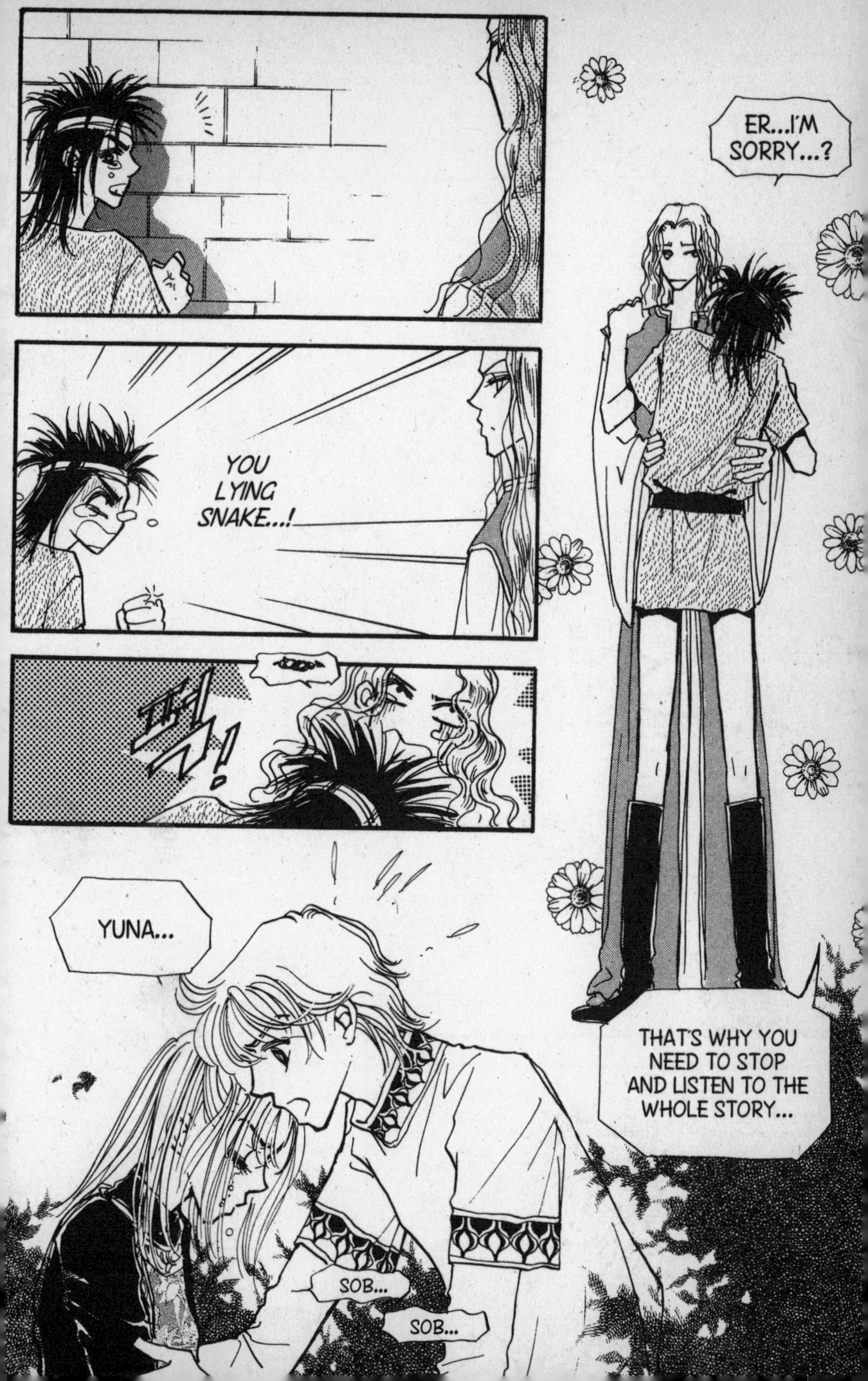
YOU LYING SNAKE...!
ER...I'M SORRY...?
THAT'S WHY YOU NEED TO STOP AND LISTEN TO THE WHOLE STORY...
YUNA...
SOB...
SOB...

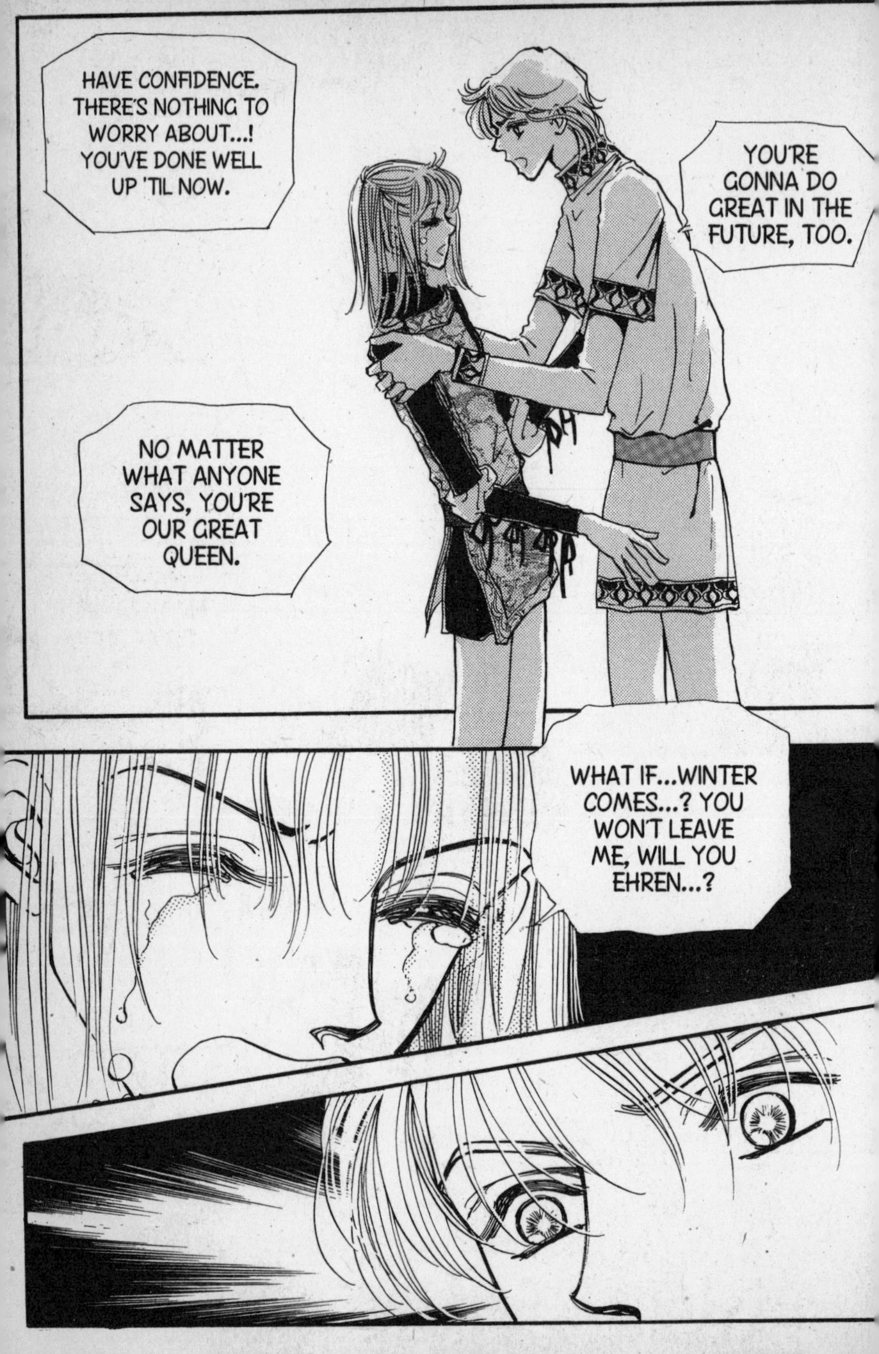
HAVE CONFIDENCE. THERE'S NOTHING TO WORRY ABOUT...! YOU'VE DONE WELL UP 'TIL NOW.
YOU'RE GONNA DO GREAT IN THE FUTURE, TOO.
NO MATTER WHAT ANYONE SAYS, YOU'RE OUR GREAT QUEEN.
WHAT IF...WINTER COMES...? YOU WON'T LEAVE ME, WILL YOU EHREN...?

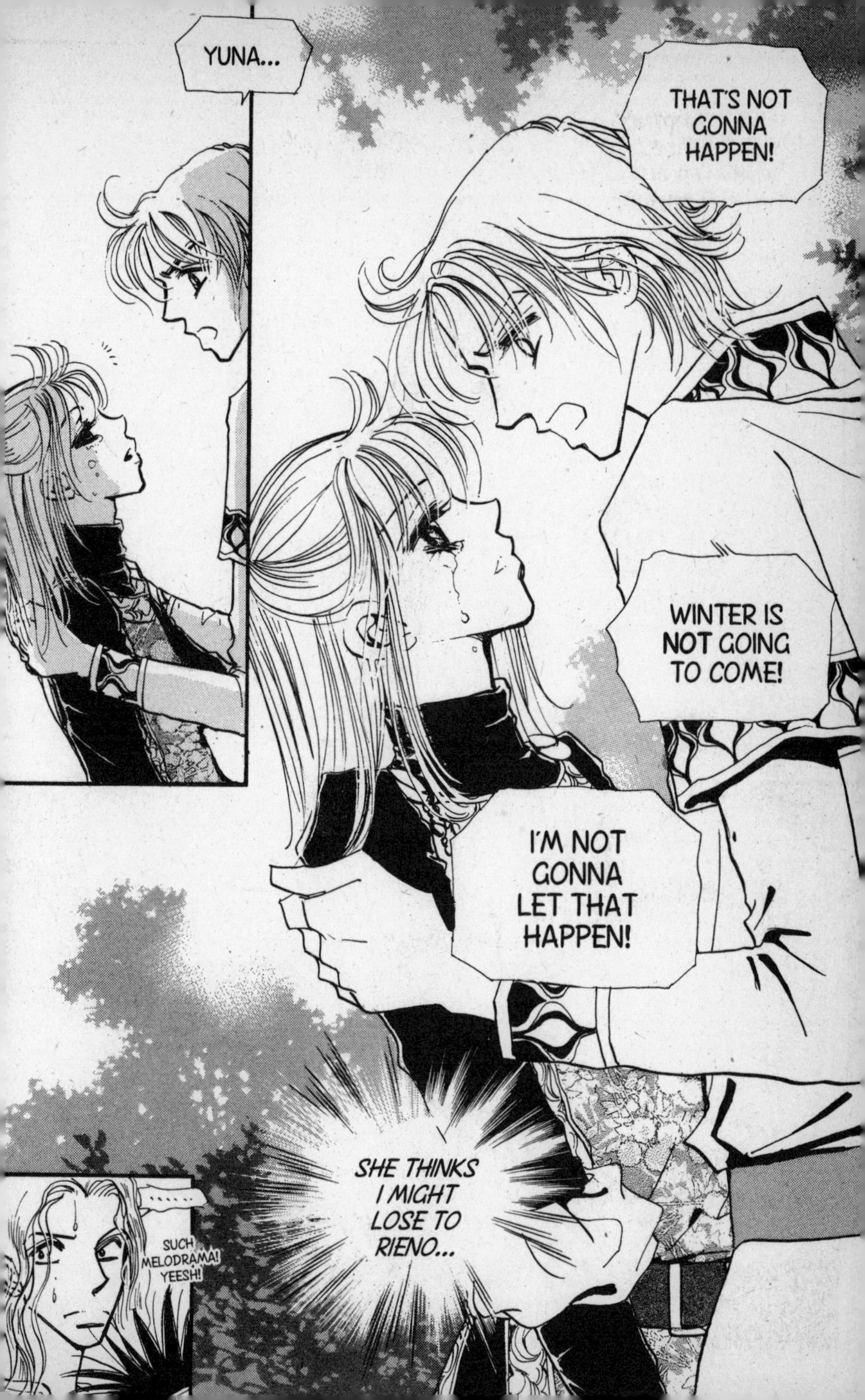
YUNA...
THAT'S NOT GONNA HAPPEN!
WINTER IS NOT GOING TO COME!
I'M NOT GONNA LET THAT HAPPEN!
......
SUCH MELODRAMA! YEESH!
SHE THINKS I MIGHT LOSE TO RIENO...

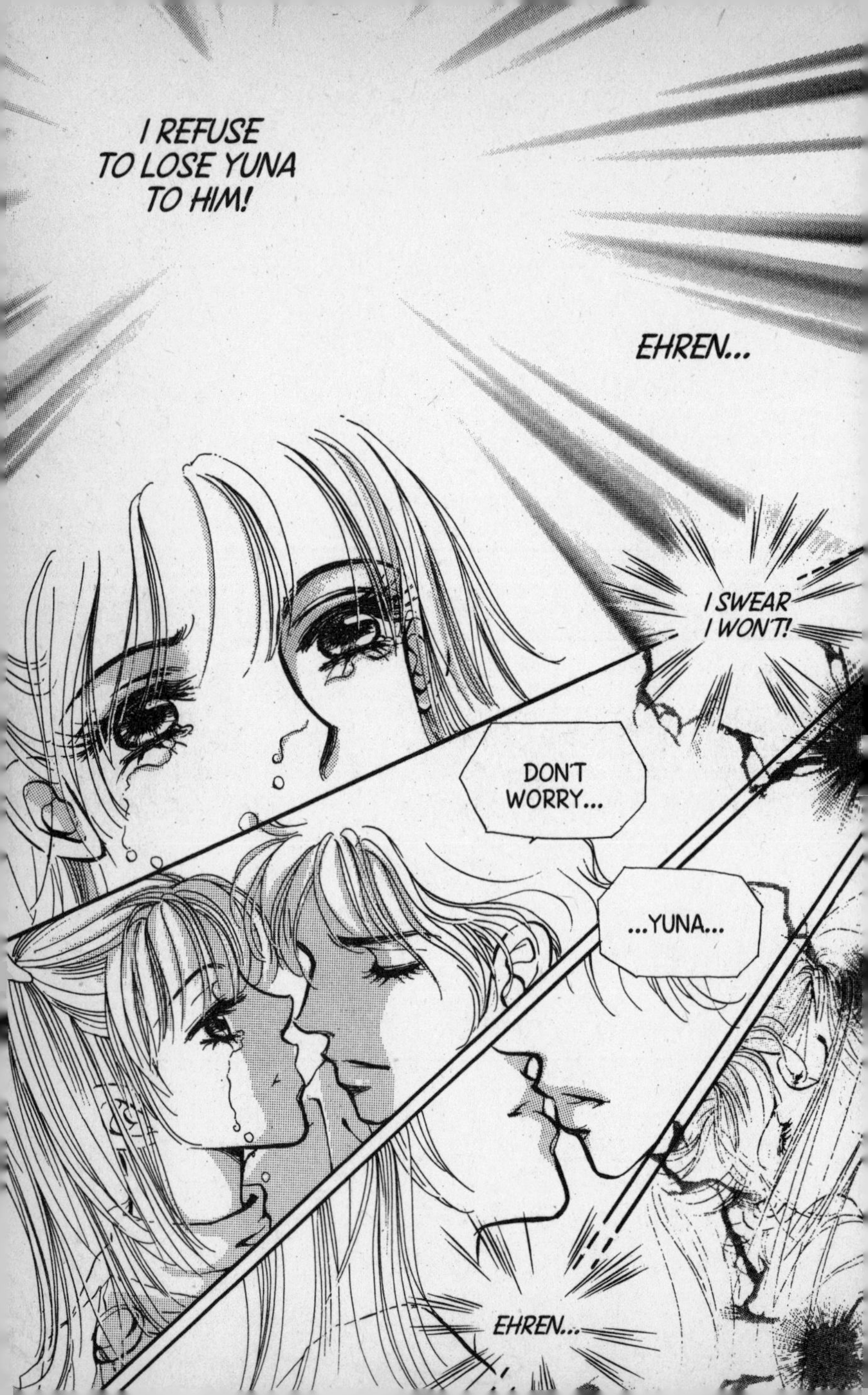
I REFUSE TO LOSE YUNA TO HIM!
EHREN...
I SWEAR I WON'T!
DON'T WORRY...
...YUNA...
EHREN...

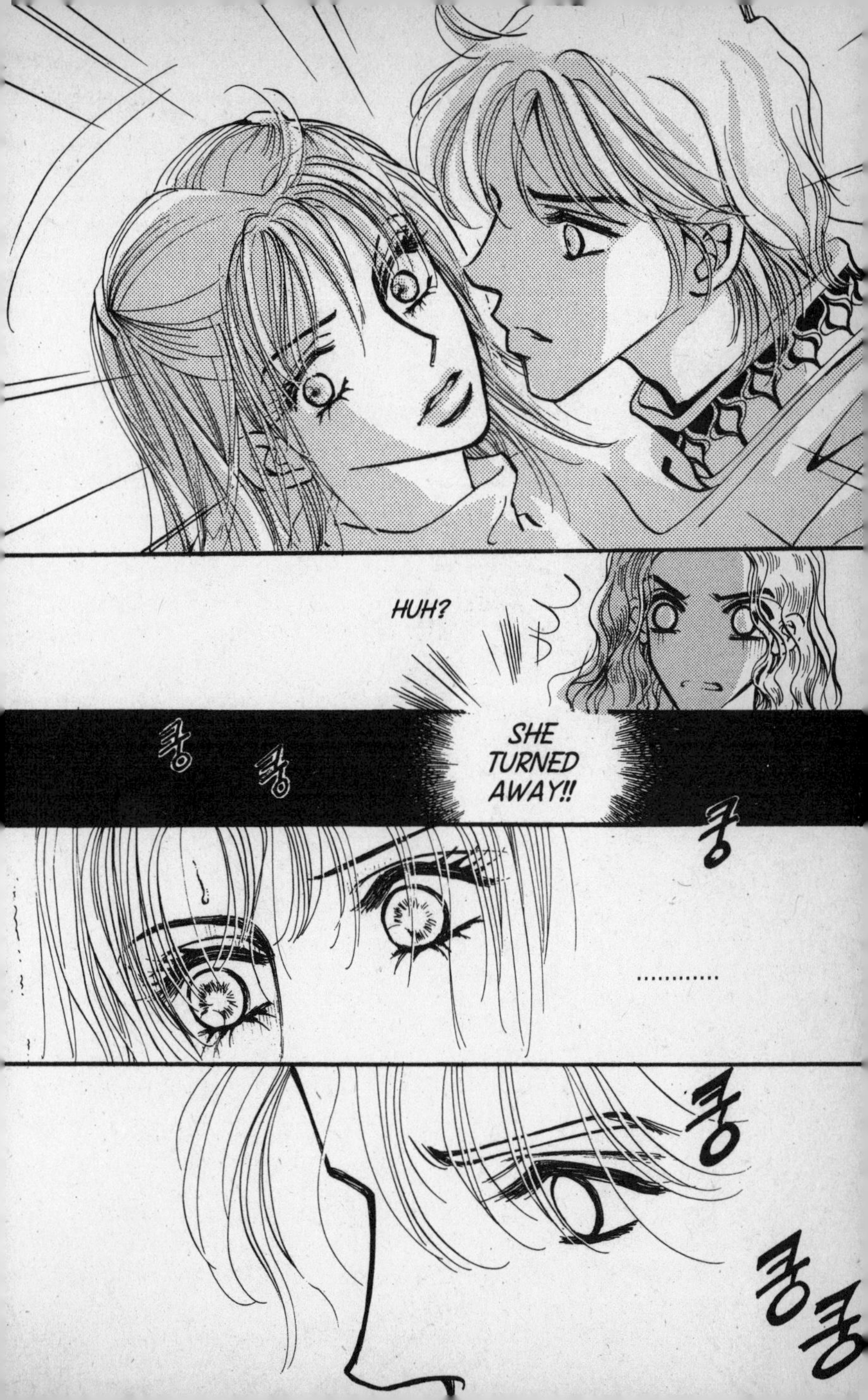
HUH?
쿵
쿵
SHE TURNED AWAY!!
쿵
....
쿵
쿵쿵

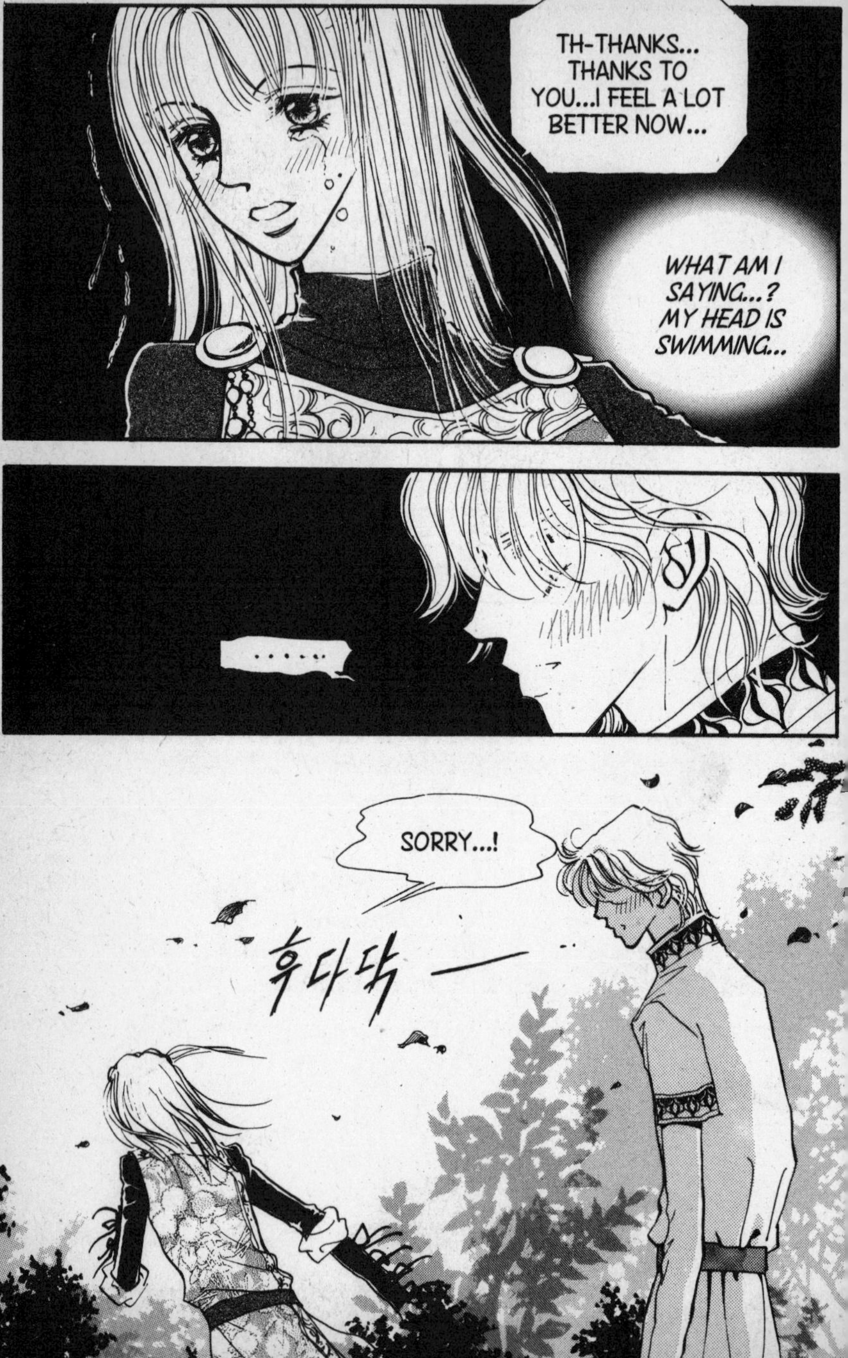

TH-THANKS... THANKS TO YOU...I FEEL A LOT BETTER NOW...
WHAT AM I SAYING...? MY HEAD IS SWIMMING...
......
SORRY...!
후다닥

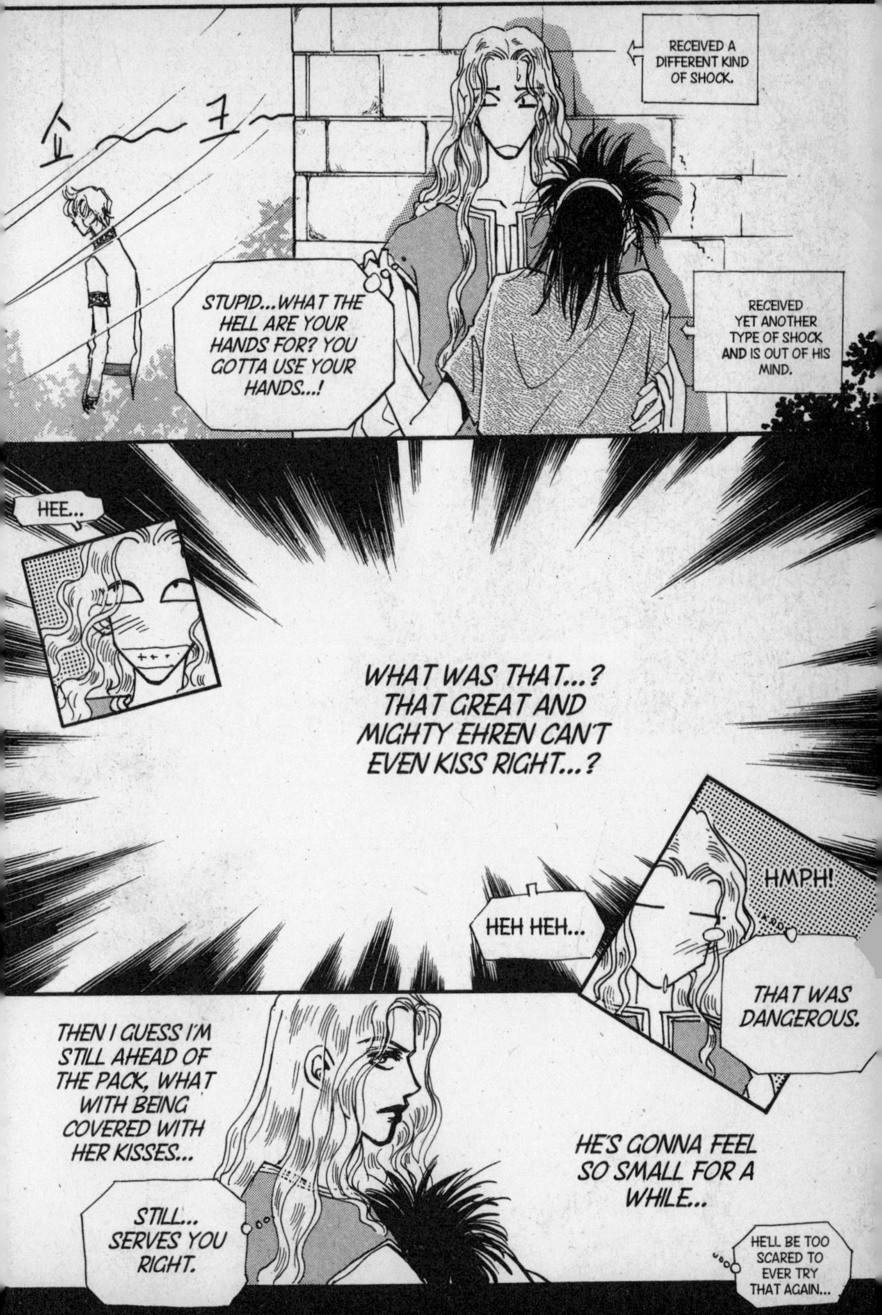
STUPID...WHAT THE HELL ARE YOUR HANDS FOR? YOU GOTTA USE YOUR HANDS...!
RECEIVED A DIFFERENT KIND OF SHOCK.
RECEIVED YET ANOTHER TYPE OF SHOCK AND IS OUT OF HIS MIND.
HEE...
WHAT WAS THAT...? THAT GREAT AND MIGHTY EHREN CAN'T EVEN KISS RIGHT...?
HEH HEH...
HMPH!
THAT WAS DANGEROUS.
THEN I GUESS I'M STILL AHEAD OF THE PACK, WHAT WITH BEING COVERED WITH HER KISSES...
STILL... SERVES YOU RIGHT.
HE'S GONNA FEEL SO SMALL FOR A WHILE...
HE'LL BE TOO SCARED TO EVER TRY THAT AGAIN...

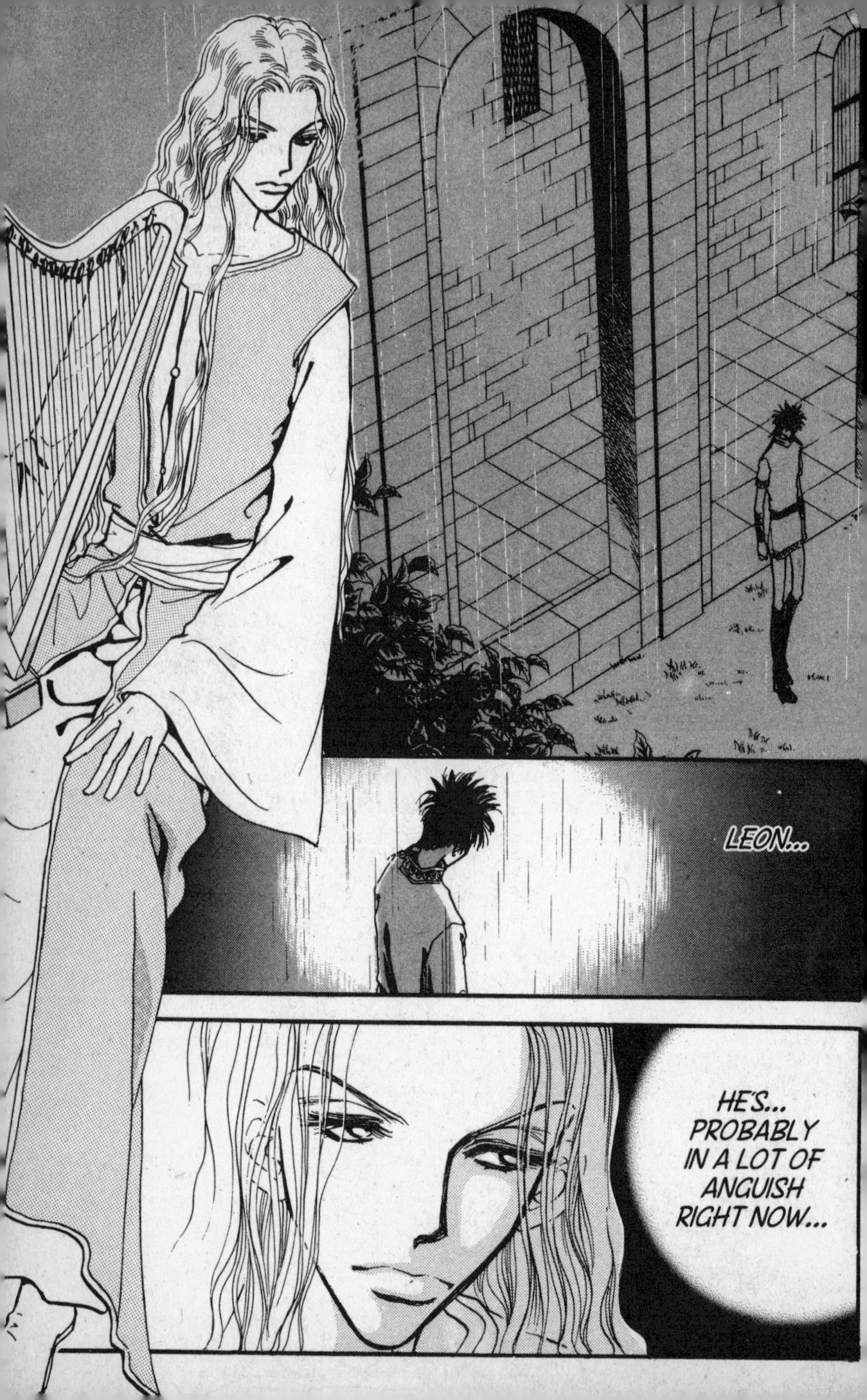
LEON...
HE'S... PROBABLY IN A LOT OF ANGUISH RIGHT NOW...

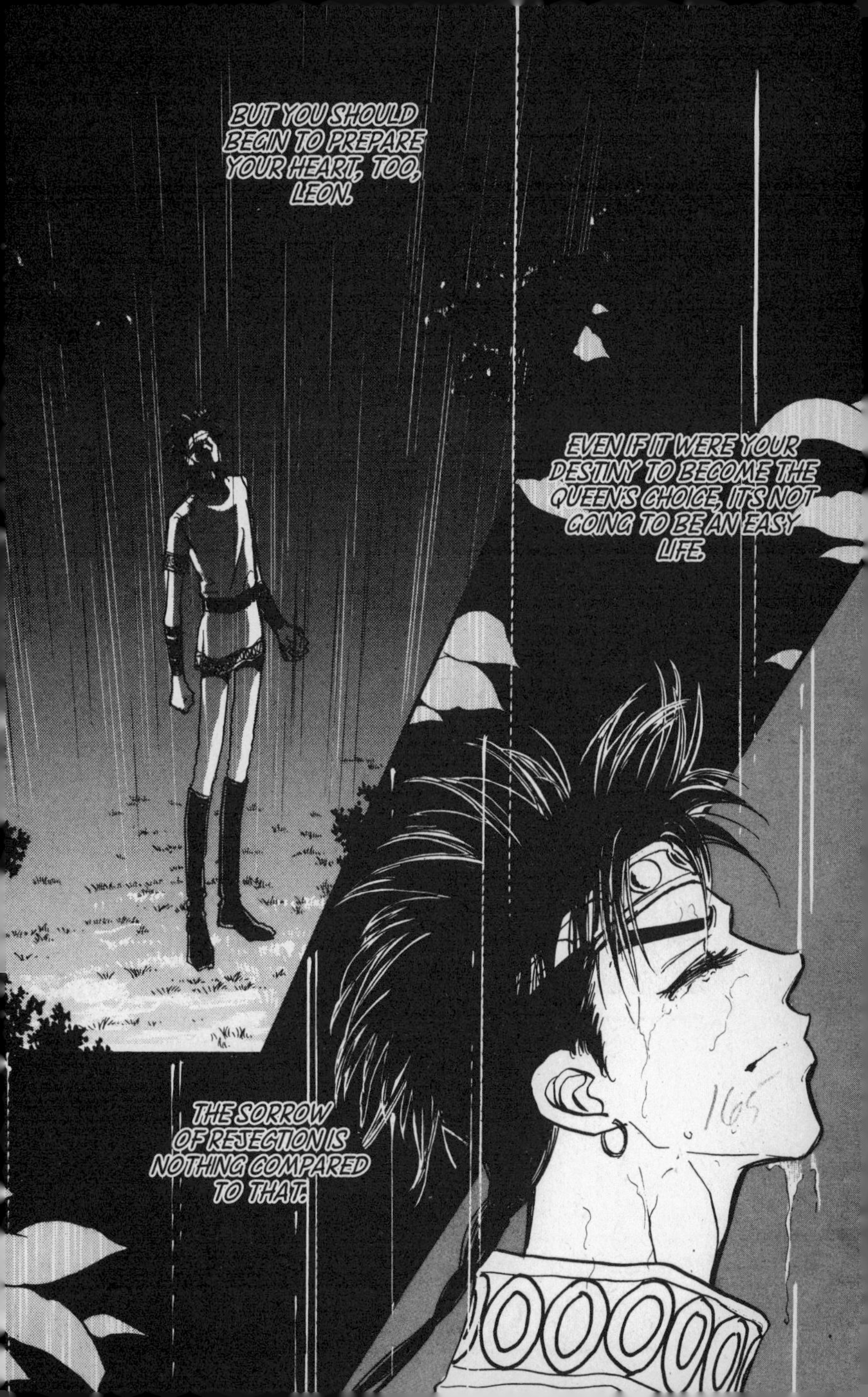
BUT YOU SHOULD BEGIN TO PREPARE YOUR HEART, TOO, LEON.
EVEN IF IT WERE YOUR DESTINY TO BECOME THE QUEEN'S CHOICE, IT'S NOT GOING TO BE AN EASY LIFE.
THE SORROW OF REJECTION IS NOTHING COMPARED TO THAT.

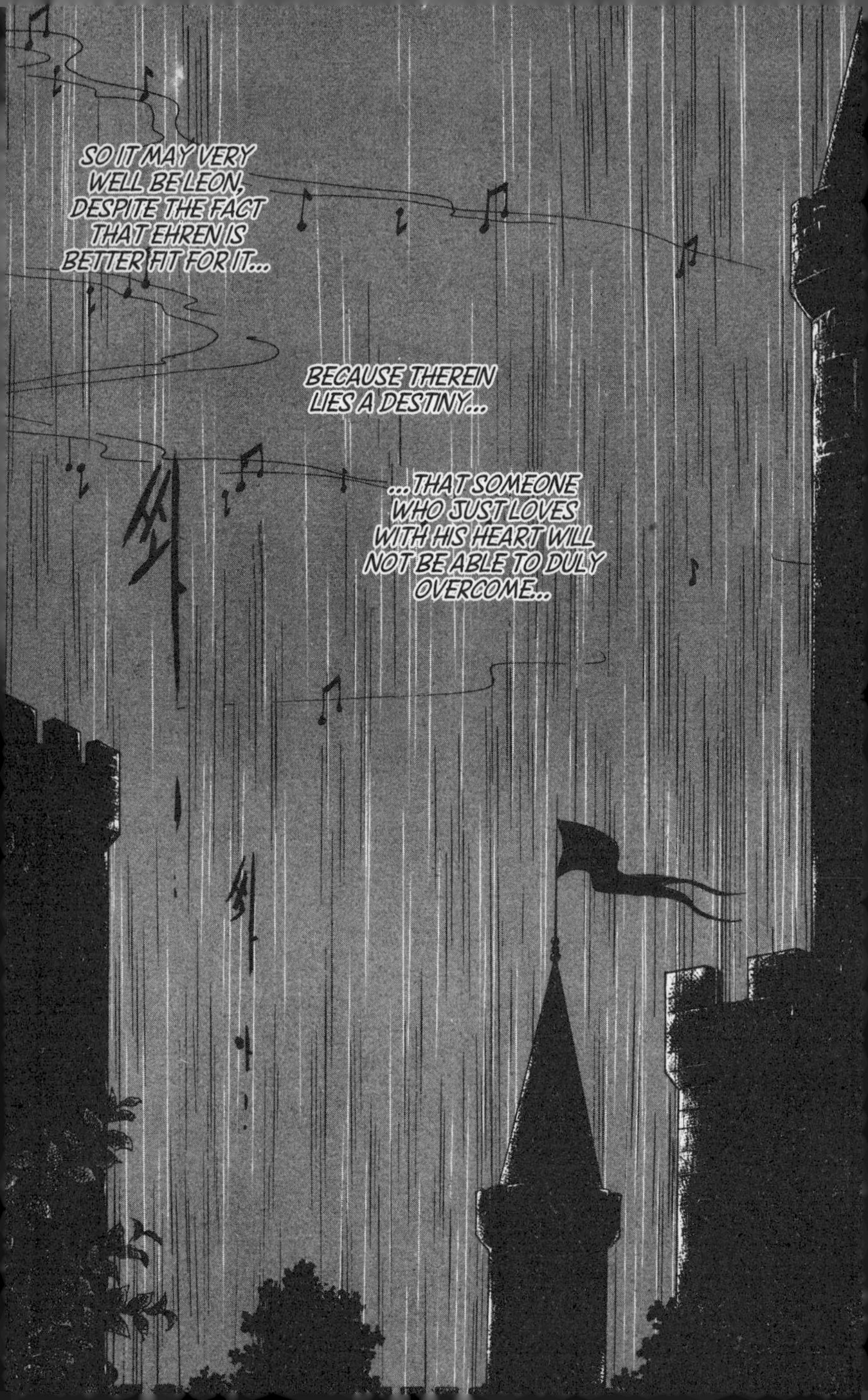
SO IT MAY VERY WELL BE LEON, DESPITE THE FACT THAT EHREN IS BETTER FIT FOR IT...
BECAUSE THEREIN LIES A DESTINY...
...THAT SOMEONE WHO JUST LOVES WITH HIS HEART WILL NOT BE ABLE TO DULY OVERCOME...

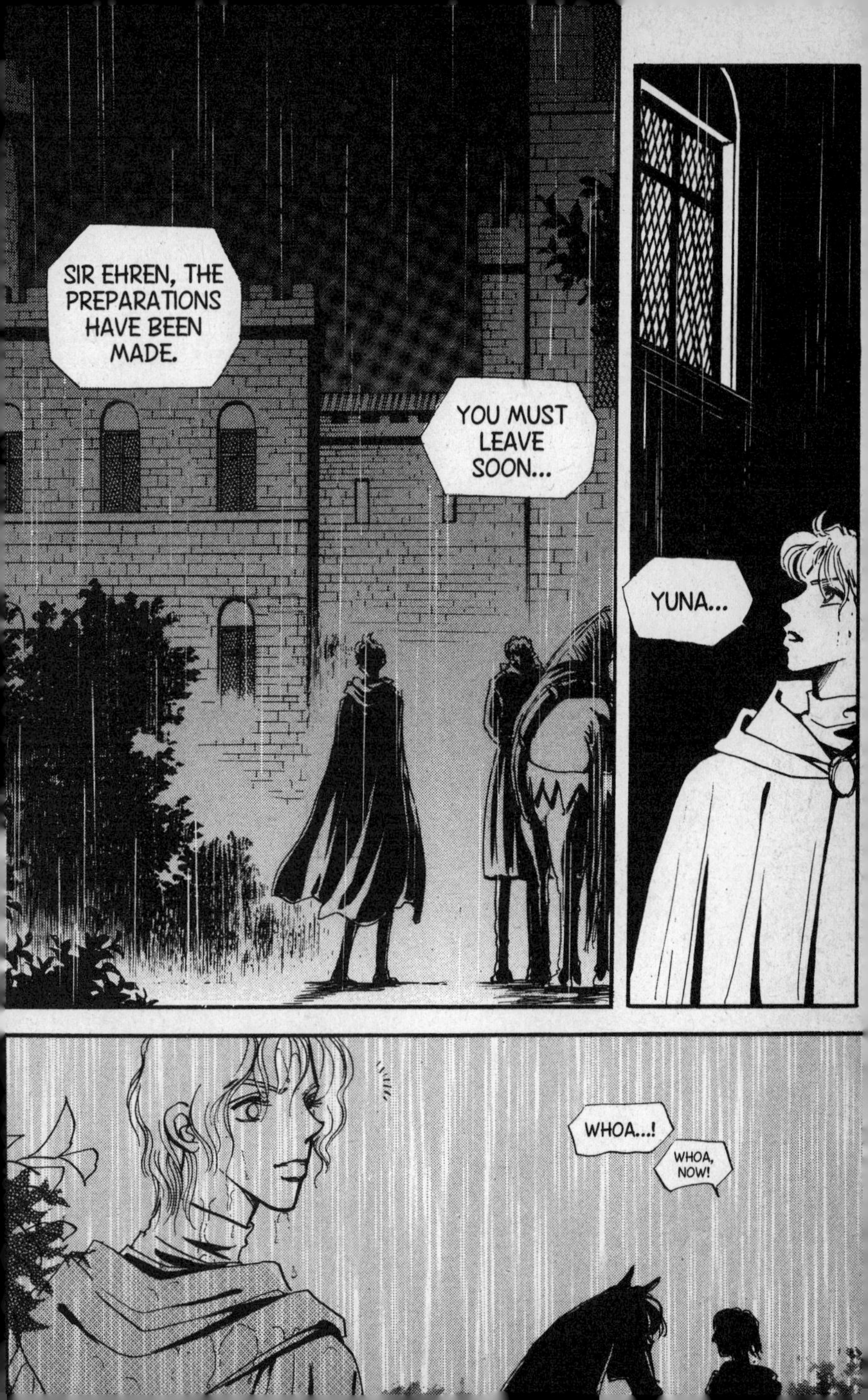
SIR EHREN, THE PREPARATIONS HAVE BEEN MADE.
YOU MUST LEAVE SOON...
YUNA...
WHOA...!
WHOA, NOW!

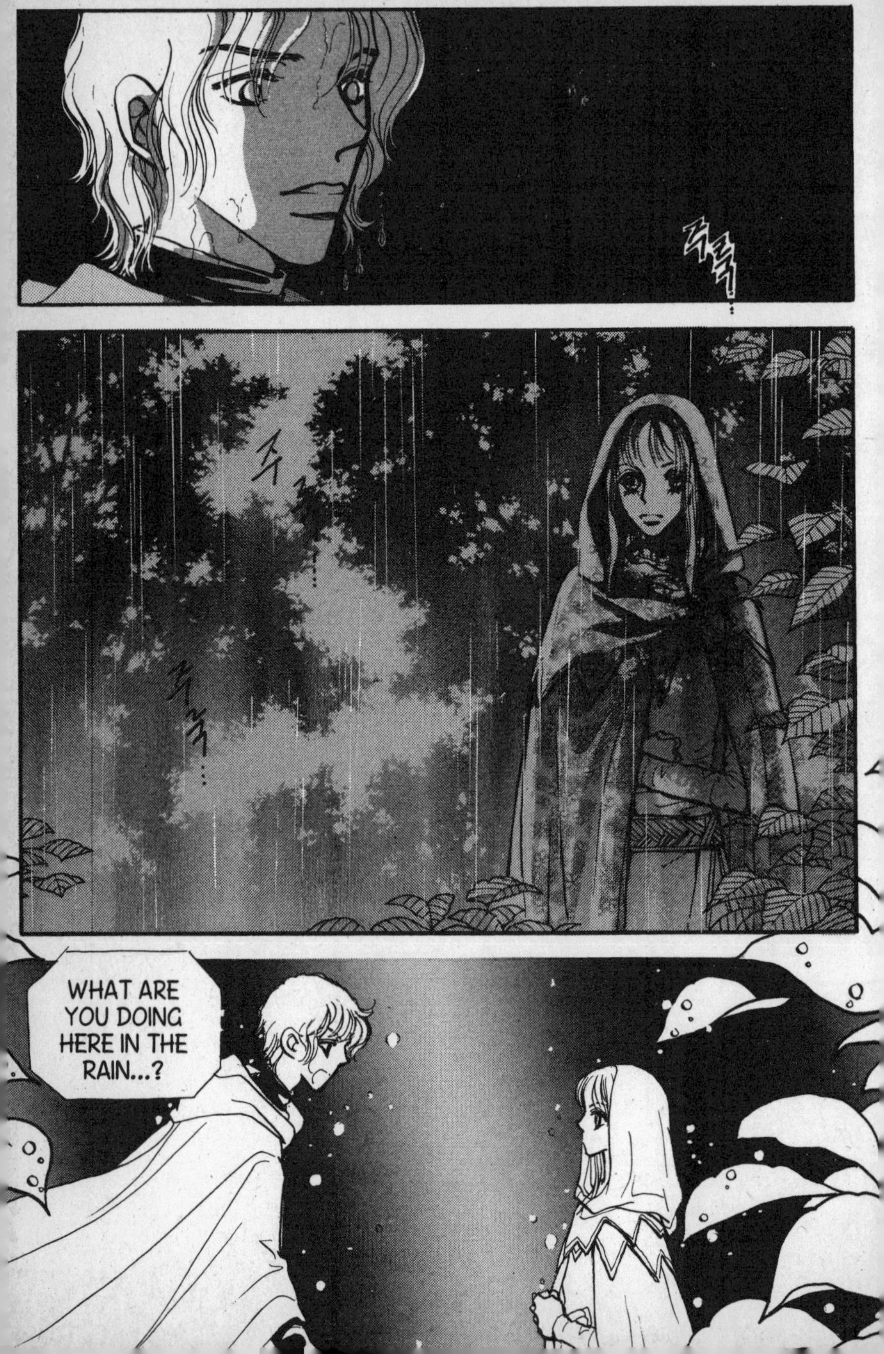
WHAT ARE YOU DOING HERE IN THE RAIN...?

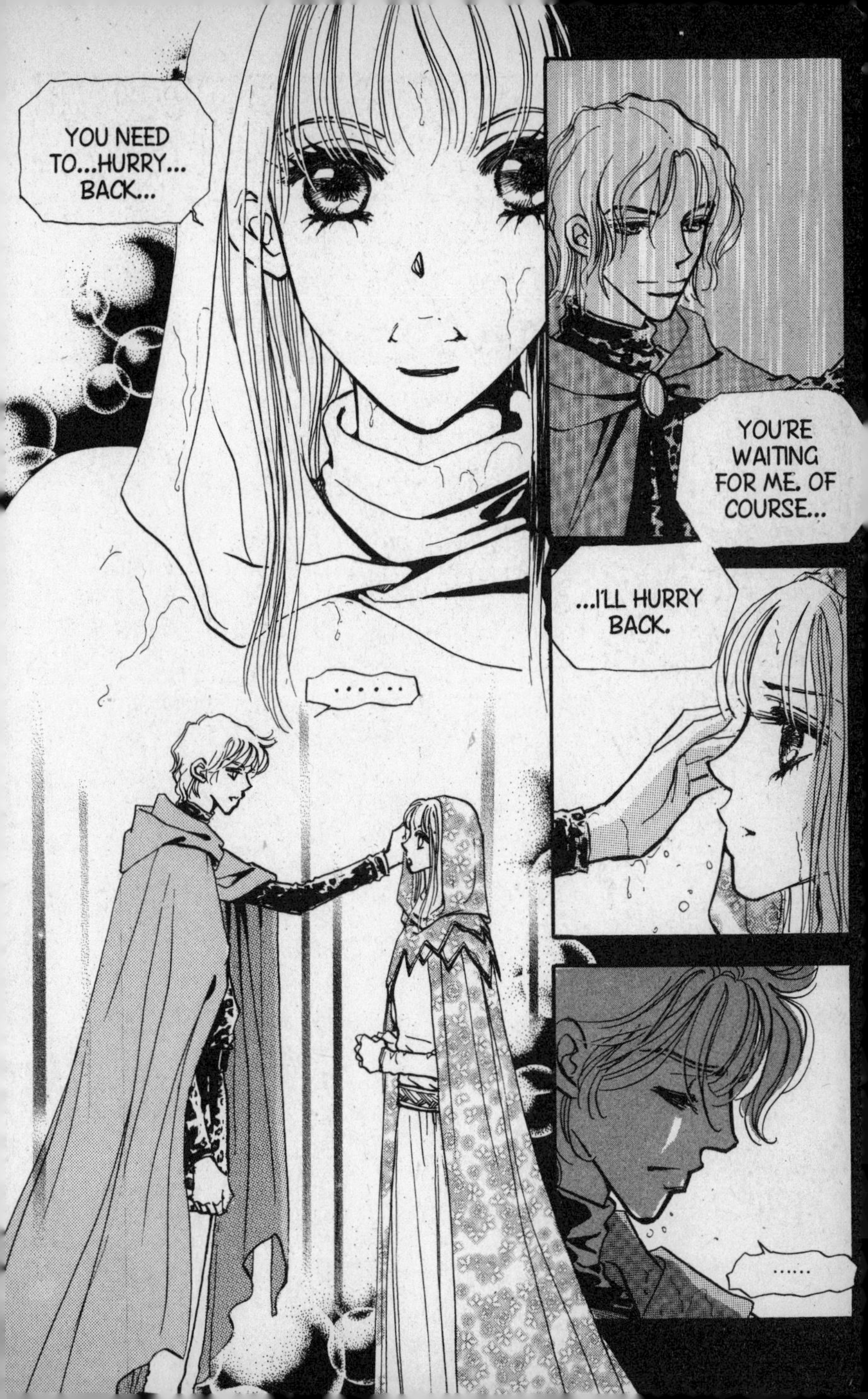
YOU NEED TO...HURRY... BACK...
......
YOU'RE WAITING FOR ME. OF COURSE...
...I'LL HURRY BACK.
......

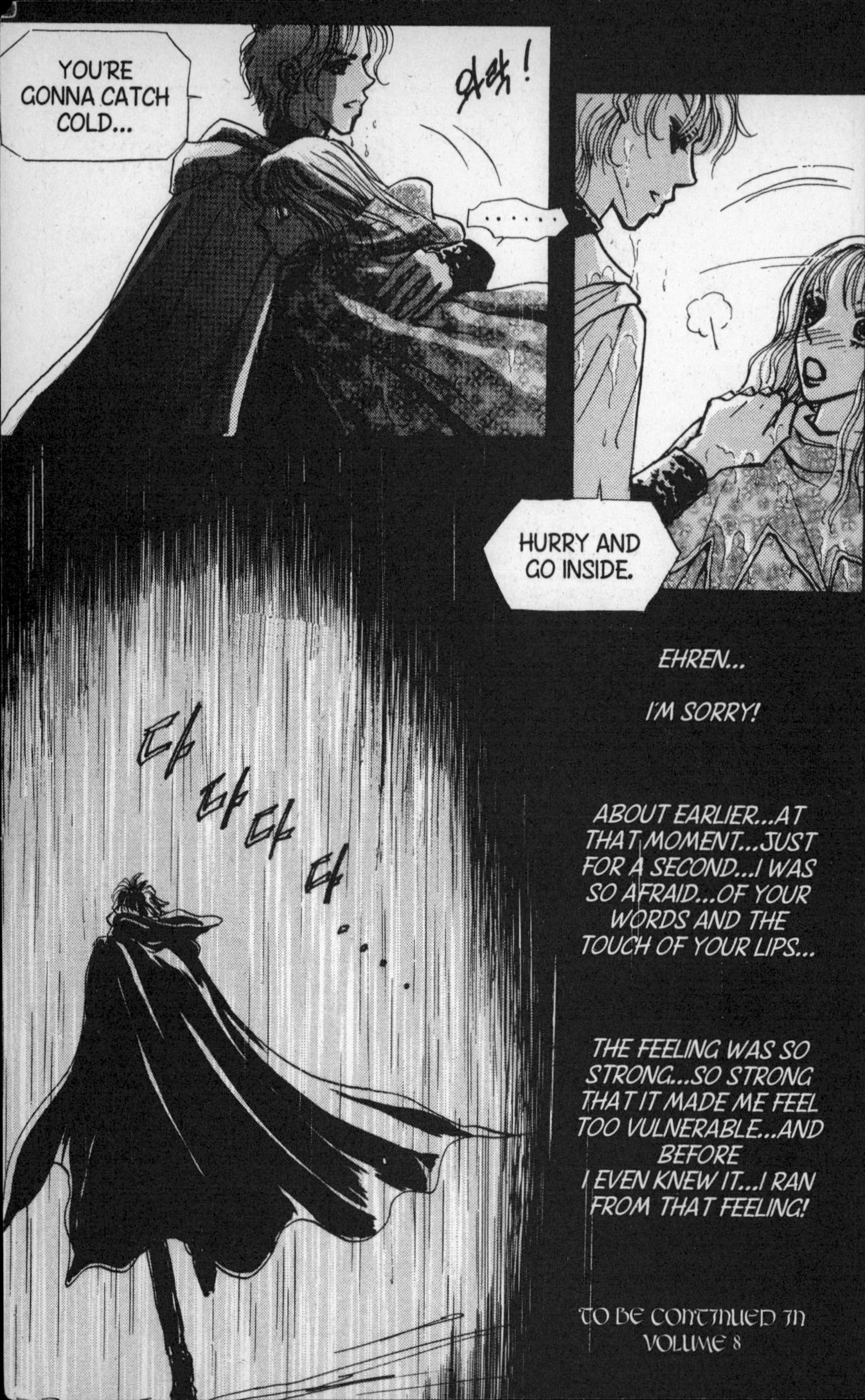
YOU'RE GONNA CATCH COLD...
......
HURRY AND GO INSIDE.
EHREN...
I'M SORRY!
ABOUT EARLIER...AT THAT MOMENT...JUST FOR A SECOND...I WAS SO AFRAID...OF YOUR WORDS AND THE TOUCH OF YOUR LIPS...
THE FEELING WAS SO STRONG...SO STRONG THAT IT MADE ME FEEL TOO VULNERABLE...AND BEFORE I EVEN KNEW IT...I RAN FROM THAT FEELING!
TO BE CONTINUED IN VOLUME 8

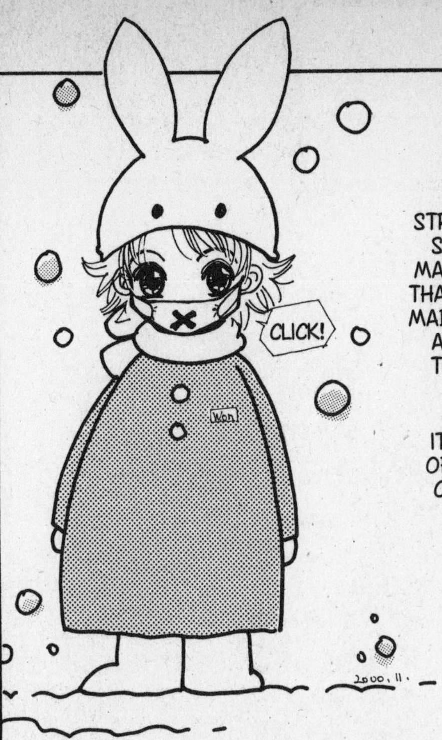
CLICK!
Won
2000. 11.

HELLO EVERYONE!

STRENGTHENED BY ALL YOUR LOVE AND SUPPORT...THE QUEEN'S KNIGHT HAS MADE IT ALL THE WAY TO VOLUME 7! IN THAT TIME, OUR MAIN CHARACTERS HAVE MADE MANY NEW FRIENDS...FAN CLUBS... AND EVEN FAN PAGES...AND THANKS TO ALL OF YOU, I, TOO HAVE MADE A HOMEPAGE!

IT IS A PLACE IN CYBERSPACE THAT ALL OF YOU WHO LOVE *THE QUEEN'S KNIGHT* CAN COME TOGETHER TO SHARE YOUR THOUGHTS.
HTTP://PHANTASMA.COM.NE.KR

And...!

IN JANUARY OF 2000, WE HELD A SURVEY TO RATE EACH CHARACTER'S POPULARITY. I RECEIVED MANY LETTERS AS WELL AS MANY COMIC STRIPS ILLUSTRATING THE BEHIND THE SCENES STORIES OF *THE QUEEN'S KNIGHT.* NOW WE ARE READY TO FINALLY REVEAL THEM. THIS ONE IS FROM SANG HEE PARK IN DAE JUN.

UNFORTUNATELY... IT WAS IMPOSSIBLE TO PUBLISH IT AS IT WAS...SO I REDREW IT. (THE ORIGINAL ONE FROM SANG HEE PARK IS MUCH BETTER.)

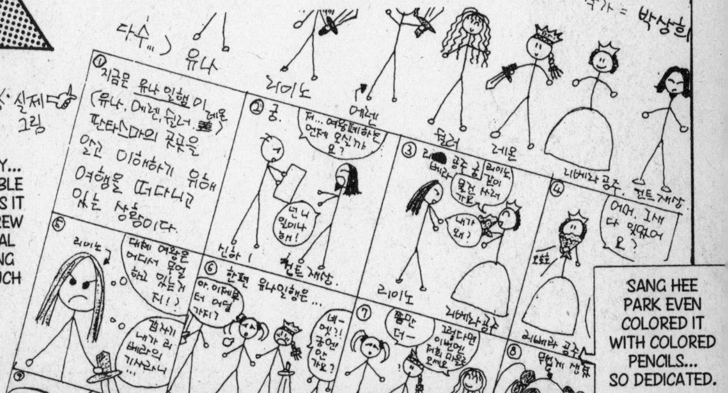

SANG HEE PARK EVEN COLORED IT WITH COLORED PENCILS... SO DEDICATED.

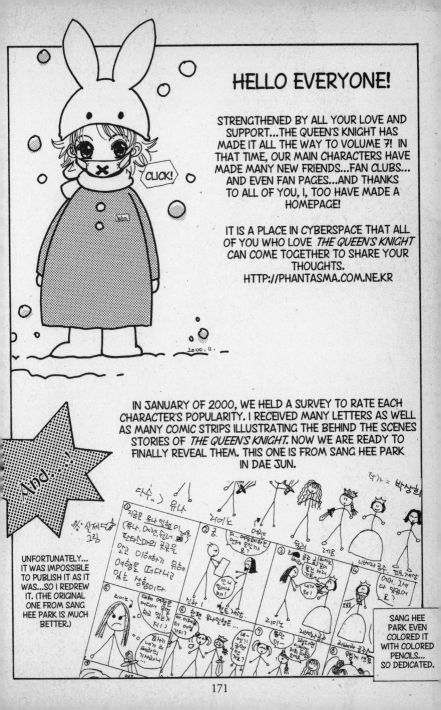

The Behind the Scenes Story of Queen's Knight, Simplified Pictures and All...

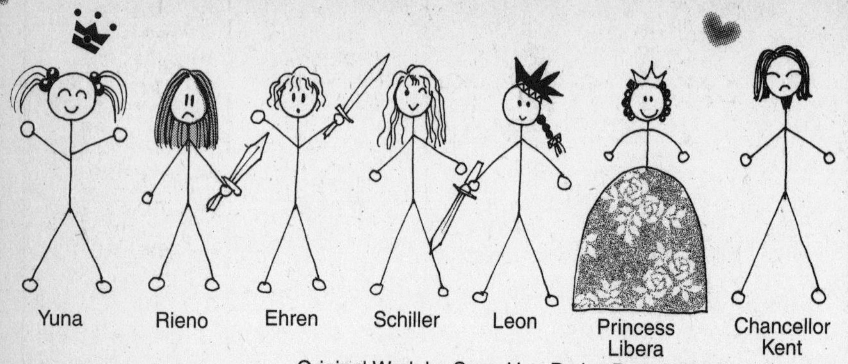
Yuna
Rieno
Ehren
Schiller
Leon
Princess Libera
Chancellor Kent

Original Work by Sang Hee Park Recopied by Kang Won Kim

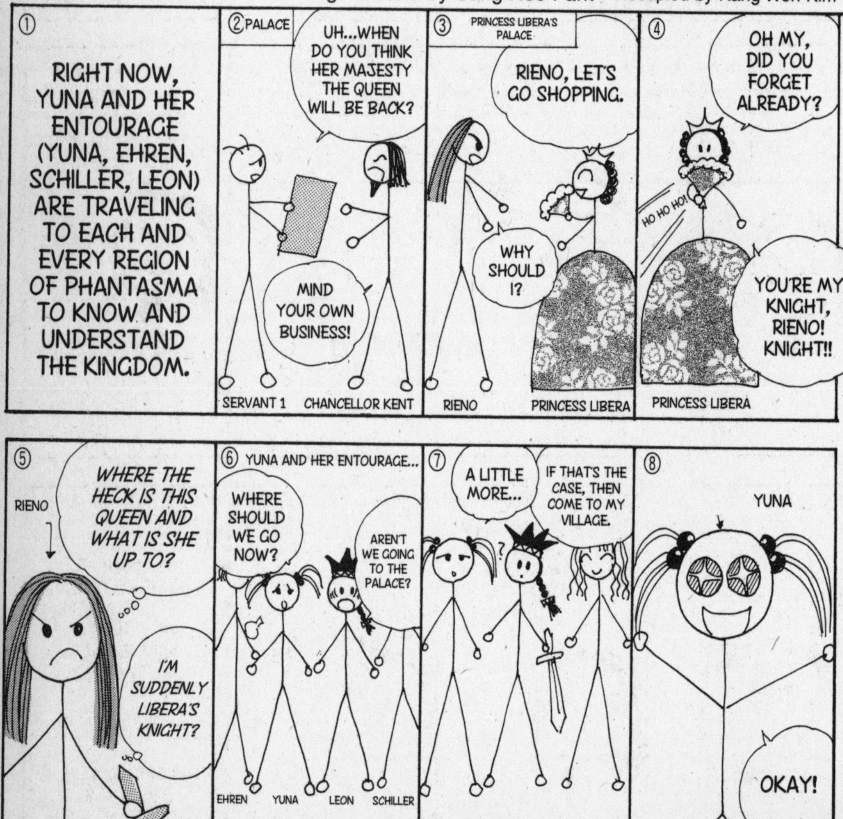
①
RIGHT NOW, YUNA AND HER ENTOURAGE (YUNA, EHREN, SCHILLER, LEON) ARE TRAVELING TO EACH AND EVERY REGION OF PHANTASMA TO KNOW AND UNDERSTAND THE KINGDOM.
② PALACE
UH...WHEN DO YOU THINK HER MAJESTY THE QUEEN WILL BE BACK?
MIND YOUR OWN BUSINESS!
SERVANT 1
CHANCELLOR KENT
③ PRINCESS LIBERA'S PALACE
RIENO, LET'S GO SHOPPING.
WHY SHOULD I?
RIENO
PRINCESS LIBERA
④
OH MY, DID YOU FORGET ALREADY?
HO HO HO!
YOU'RE MY KNIGHT, RIENO! KNIGHT!!
PRINCESS LIBERA
⑤
RIENO
WHERE THE HECK IS THIS QUEEN AND WHAT IS SHE UP TO?
I'M SUDDENLY LIBERA'S KNIGHT?
⑥ YUNA AND HER ENTOURAGE...
WHERE SHOULD WE GO NOW?
AREN'T WE GOING TO THE PALACE?
EHREN
YUNA
LEON
SCHILLER
⑦
A LITTLE MORE...
IF THAT'S THE CASE, THEN COME TO MY VILLAGE.
?
⑧
YUNA
OKAY!

THE ABOVE WORK HAS BEEN COPIED EXACTLY BY THE AUTHOR FROM SANG HEE PARK'S ORIGINAL WORK. THE ORIGINAL WORK WAS IMPOSSIBLE TO PUBLISH. (I TRIED TO CONVEY THE EXACT NATURE OF THE ORIGINAL WORK... ^^;

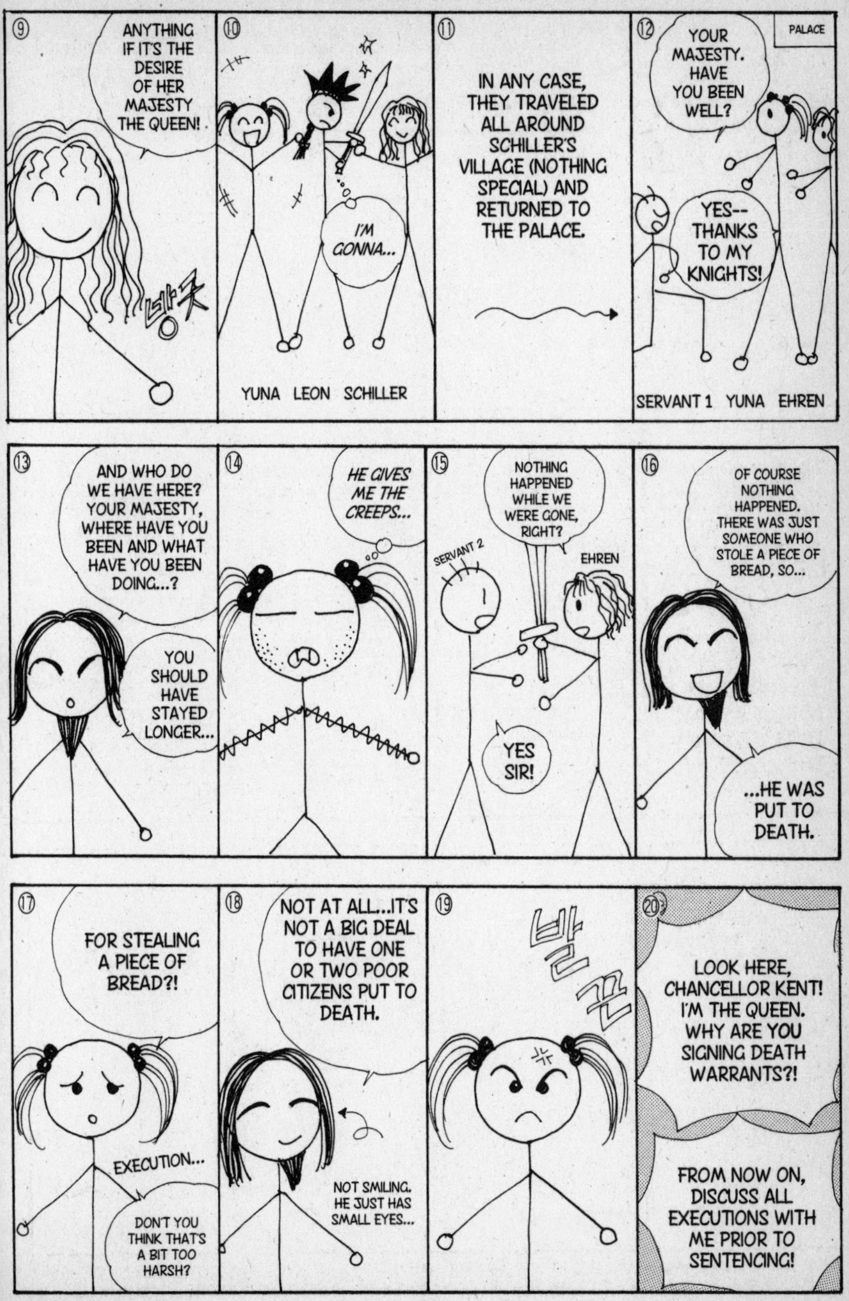
⑨
ANYTHING IF IT'S THE DESIRE OF HER MAJESTY THE QUEEN!
방긋
⑩
I'M GONNA...
YUNA LEON SCHILLER
⑪
IN ANY CASE, THEY TRAVELED ALL AROUND SCHILLER'S VILLAGE (NOTHING SPECIAL) AND RETURNED TO THE PALACE.
⑫
PALACE
YOUR MAJESTY. HAVE YOU BEEN WELL?
YES-- THANKS TO MY KNIGHTS!
SERVANT 1 YUNA EHREN
⑬
AND WHO DO WE HAVE HERE? YOUR MAJESTY, WHERE HAVE YOU BEEN AND WHAT HAVE YOU BEEN DOING...?
YOU SHOULD HAVE STAYED LONGER...
⑭
HE GIVES ME THE CREEPS...
⑮
NOTHING HAPPENED WHILE WE WERE GONE, RIGHT?
SERVANT 2
EHREN
YES SIR!
⑯
OF COURSE NOTHING HAPPENED. THERE WAS JUST SOMEONE WHO STOLE A PIECE OF BREAD, SO...
...HE WAS PUT TO DEATH.
⑰
FOR STEALING A PIECE OF BREAD?!
EXECUTION...
DON'T YOU THINK THAT'S A BIT TOO HARSH?
⑱
NOT AT ALL...IT'S NOT A BIG DEAL TO HAVE ONE OR TWO POOR CITIZENS PUT TO DEATH.
NOT SMILING. HE JUST HAS SMALL EYES...
⑲
발끈
⑳
LOOK HERE, CHANCELLOR KENT! I'M THE QUEEN. WHY ARE YOU SIGNING DEATH WARRANTS?!
FROM NOW ON, DISCUSS ALL EXECUTIONS WITH ME PRIOR TO SENTENCING!

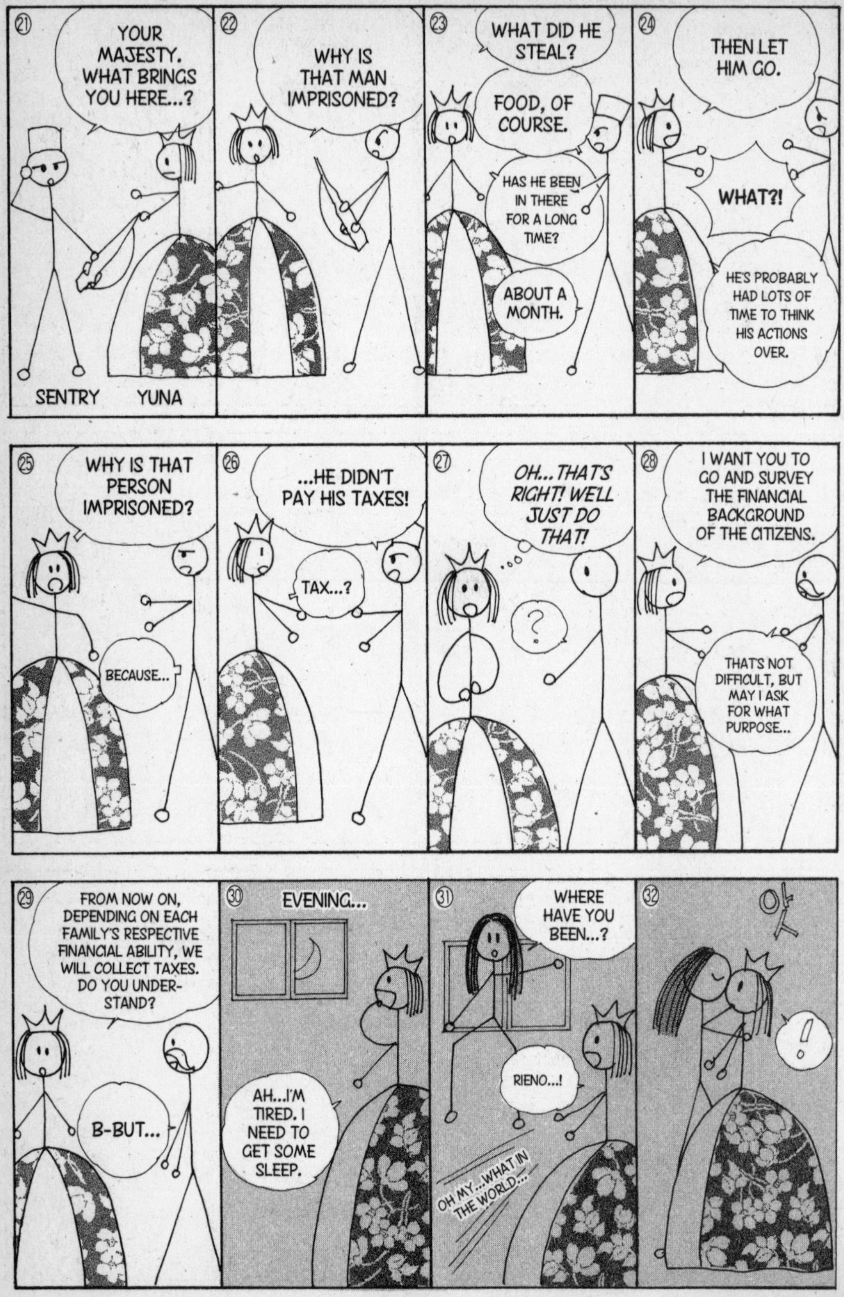
YOUR MAJESTY. WHAT BRINGS YOU HERE...?
SENTRY
YUNA
WHY IS THAT MAN IMPRISONED?
WHAT DID HE STEAL?
FOOD, OF COURSE.
HAS HE BEEN IN THERE FOR A LONG TIME?
ABOUT A MONTH.
THEN LET HIM GO.
WHAT?!
HE'S PROBABLY HAD LOTS OF TIME TO THINK HIS ACTIONS OVER.
WHY IS THAT PERSON IMPRISONED?
BECAUSE...
...HE DIDN'T PAY HIS TAXES!
TAX...?
OH...THAT'S RIGHT! WE'LL JUST DO THAT!
?
I WANT YOU TO GO AND SURVEY THE FINANCIAL BACKGROUND OF THE CITIZENS.
THAT'S NOT DIFFICULT, BUT MAY I ASK FOR WHAT PURPOSE...
FROM NOW ON, DEPENDING ON EACH FAMILY'S RESPECTIVE FINANCIAL ABILITY, WE WILL COLLECT TAXES. DO YOU UNDERSTAND?
B-BUT...
EVENING...
AH...I'M TIRED. I NEED TO GET SOME SLEEP.
WHERE HAVE YOU BEEN...?
RIENO...!
OH MY...WHAT IN THE WORLD...
!

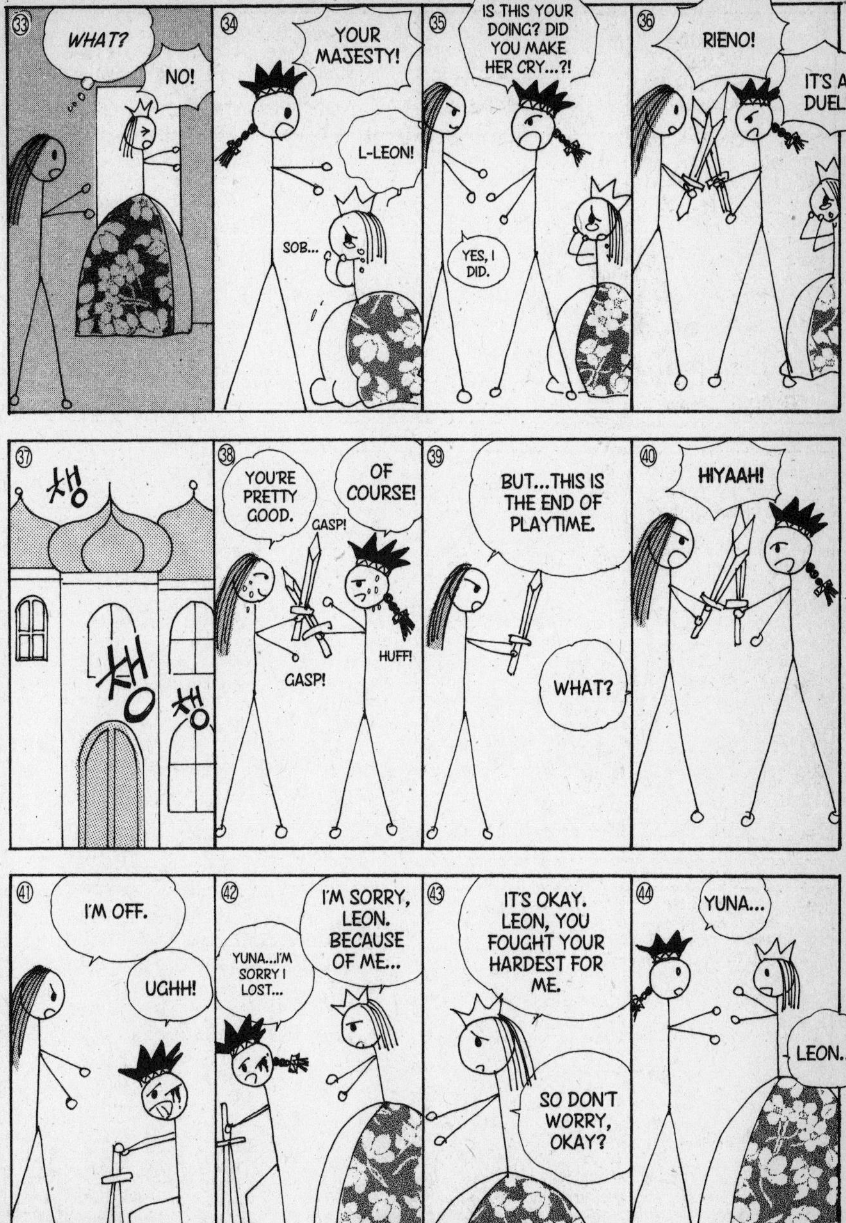

33
WHAT?
NO!
34
YOUR MAJESTY!
L-LEON!
SOB...
35
IS THIS YOUR DOING? DID YOU MAKE HER CRY...?!
YES, I DID.
36
RIENO!
IT'S A DUEL!
37
챙
챙
챙
38
YOU'RE PRETTY GOOD.
OF COURSE!
GASP!
HUFF!
GASP!
39
BUT...THIS IS THE END OF PLAYTIME.
WHAT?
40
HIYAAH!
41
I'M OFF.
UGHH!
42
YUNA...I'M SORRY I LOST...
I'M SORRY, LEON. BECAUSE OF ME...
43
IT'S OKAY. LEON, YOU FOUGHT YOUR HARDEST FOR ME.
SO DON'T WORRY, OKAY?
44
YUNA...
LEON...

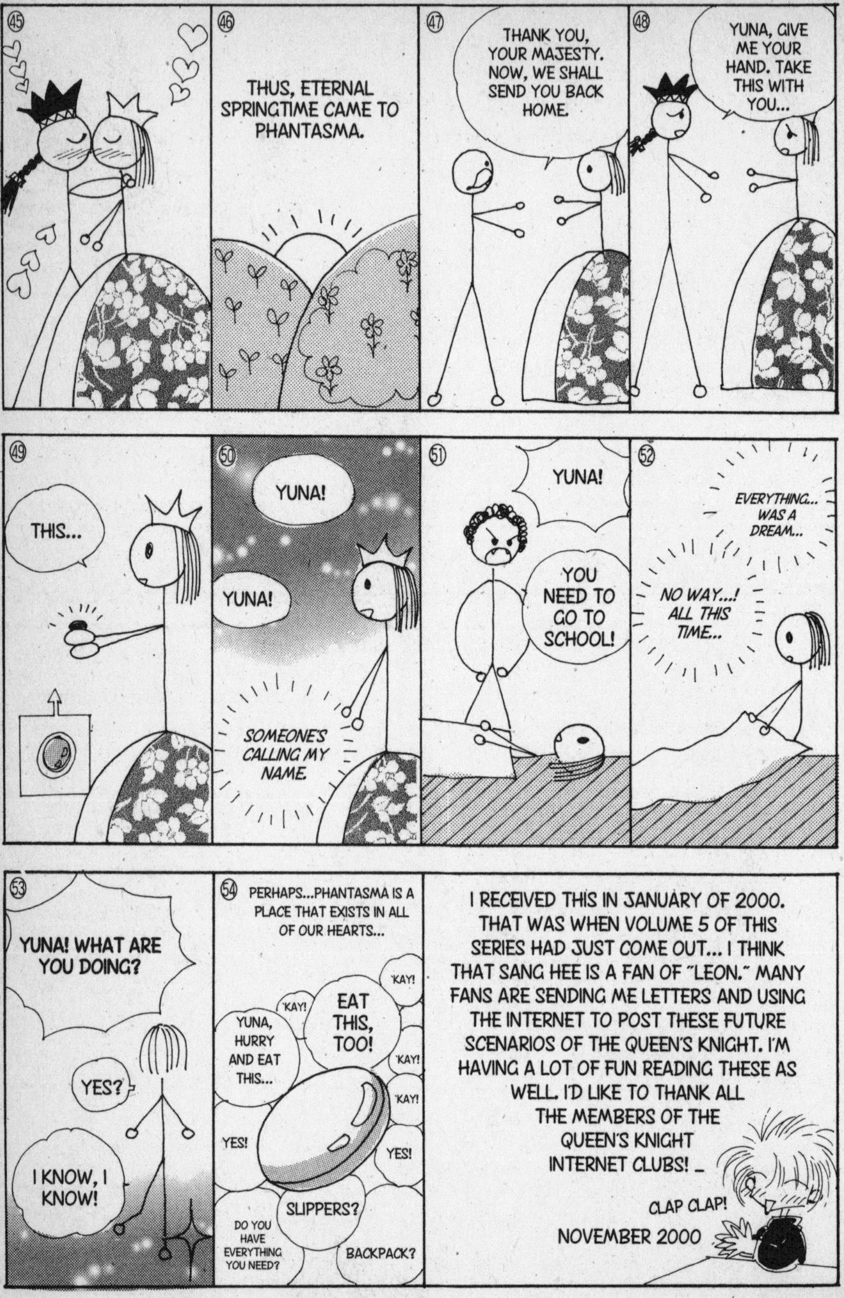
45
46
THUS, ETERNAL SPRINGTIME CAME TO PHANTASMA.
47
THANK YOU, YOUR MAJESTY. NOW, WE SHALL SEND YOU BACK HOME.
48
YUNA, GIVE ME YOUR HAND. TAKE THIS WITH YOU...
49
THIS...
50
YUNA!
YUNA!
SOMEONE'S CALLING MY NAME.
51
YUNA!
YOU NEED TO GO TO SCHOOL!
52
EVERYTHING... WAS A DREAM...
NO WAY...! ALL THIS TIME...
53
YUNA! WHAT ARE YOU DOING?
YES?
I KNOW, I KNOW!
54
PERHAPS...PHANTASMA IS A PLACE THAT EXISTS IN ALL OF OUR HEARTS...
'KAY!
'KAY!
EAT THIS, TOO!
YUNA, HURRY AND EAT THIS...
'KAY!
'KAY!
YES!
YES!
SLIPPERS?
DO YOU HAVE EVERYTHING YOU NEED?
BACKPACK?
I RECEIVED THIS IN JANUARY OF 2000. THAT WAS WHEN VOLUME 5 OF THIS SERIES HAD JUST COME OUT... I THINK THAT SANG HEE IS A FAN OF "LEON." MANY FANS ARE SENDING ME LETTERS AND USING THE INTERNET TO POST THESE FUTURE SCENARIOS OF THE QUEEN'S KNIGHT. I'M HAVING A LOT OF FUN READING THESE AS WELL. I'D LIKE TO THANK ALL THE MEMBERS OF THE QUEEN'S KNIGHT INTERNET CLUBS! _
CLAP CLAP!
NOVEMBER 2000

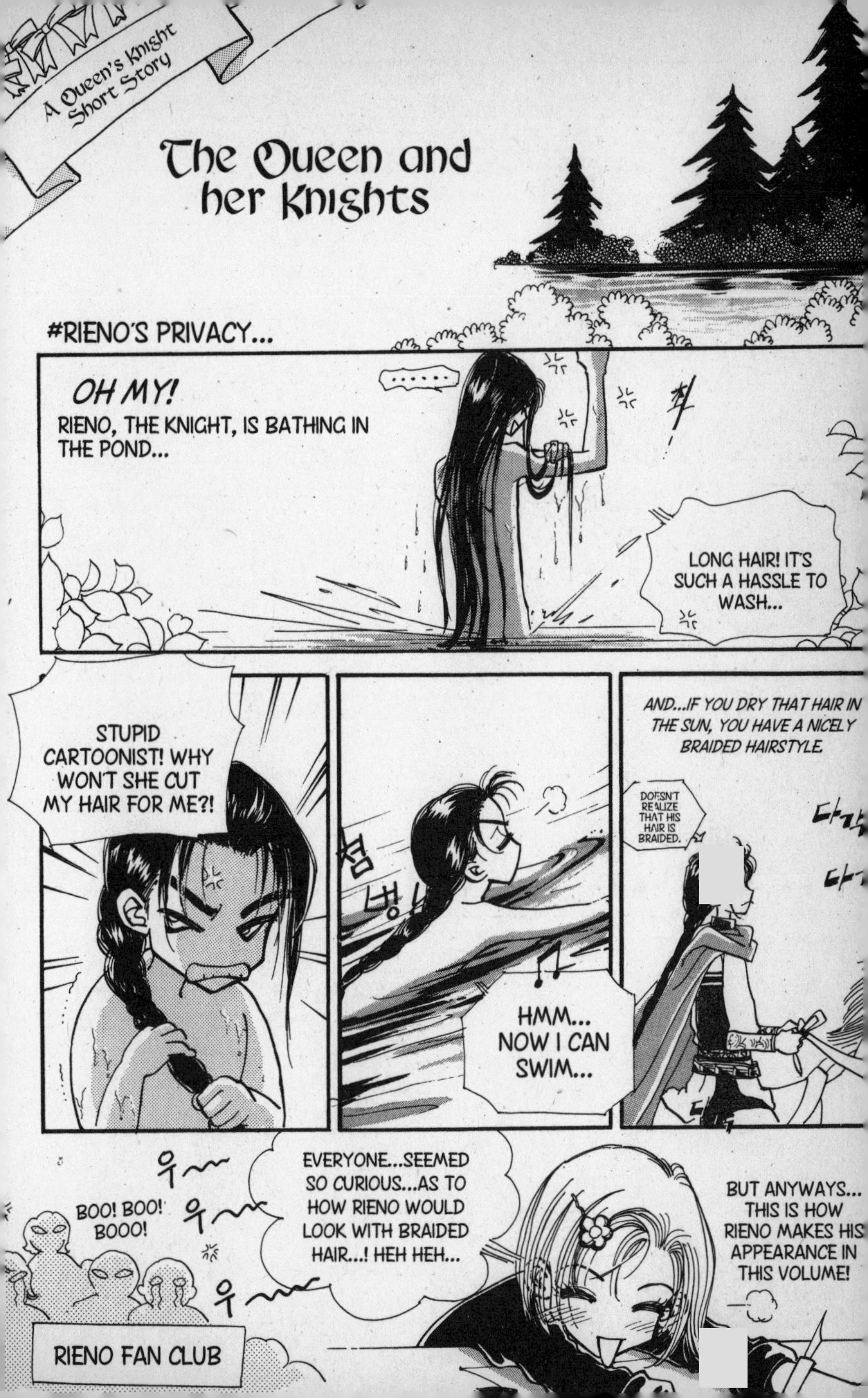
A Queen's Knight Short Story
The Queen and her Knights
#RIENO'S PRIVACY...
......
OH MY!
RIENO, THE KNIGHT, IS BATHING IN THE POND...
LONG HAIR! IT'S SUCH A HASSLE TO WASH...
STUPID CARTOONIST! WHY WON'T SHE CUT MY HAIR FOR ME?!
HMM... NOW I CAN SWIM...
AND...IF YOU DRY THAT HAIR IN THE SUN, YOU HAVE A NICELY BRAIDED HAIRSTYLE.
DOESN'T REALIZE THAT HIS HAIR IS BRAIDED.
우~
BOO! BOO! BOOO!
우~
우~
EVERYONE...SEEMED SO CURIOUS...AS TO HOW RIENO WOULD LOOK WITH BRAIDED HAIR...! HEH HEH...
BUT ANYWAYS... THIS IS HOW RIENO MAKES HIS APPEARANCE IN THIS VOLUME!
RIENO FAN CLUB

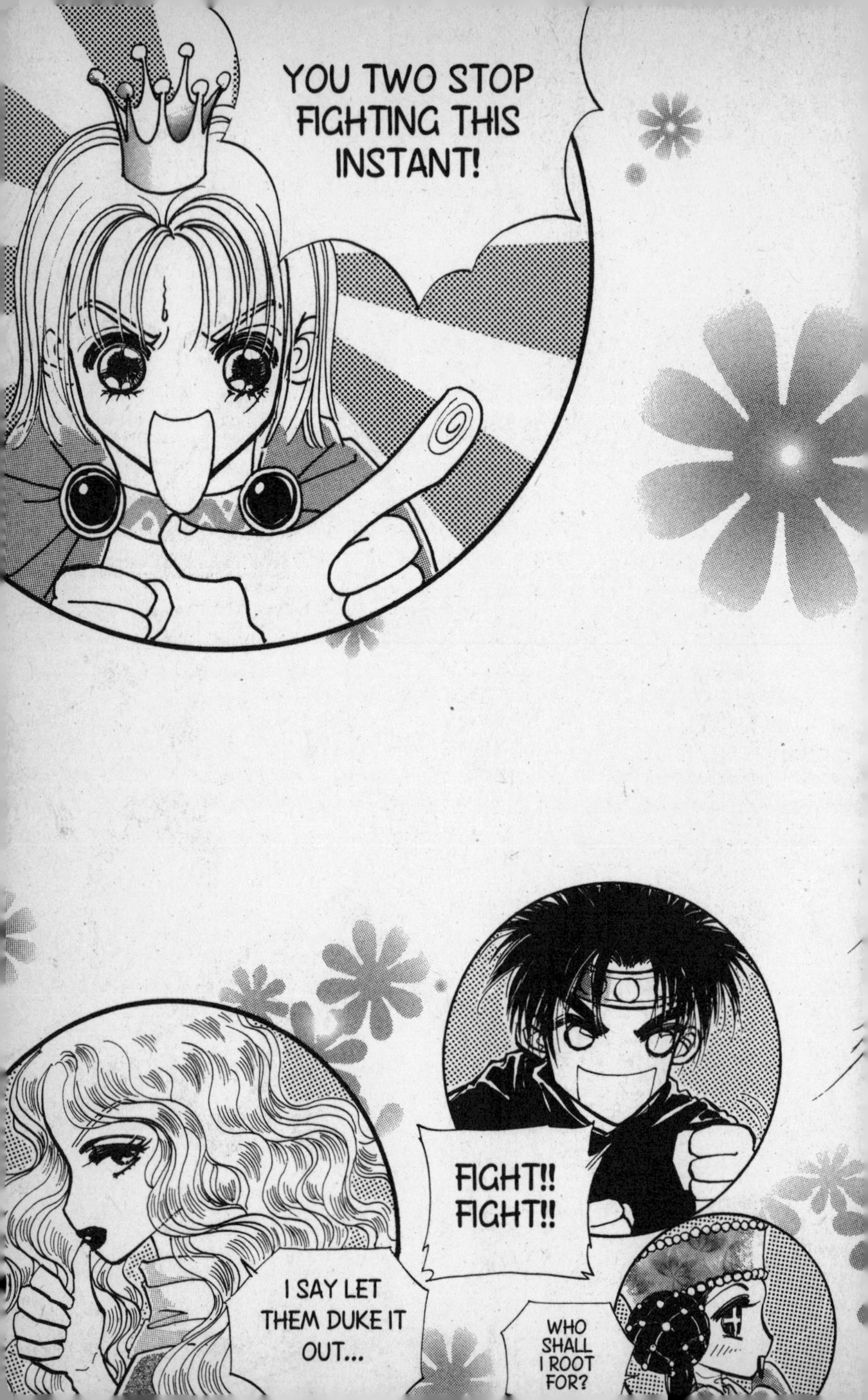
YOU TWO STOP FIGHTING THIS INSTANT!
I SAY LET THEM DUKE IT OUT...
FIGHT!! FIGHT!!
WHO SHALL I ROOT FOR?

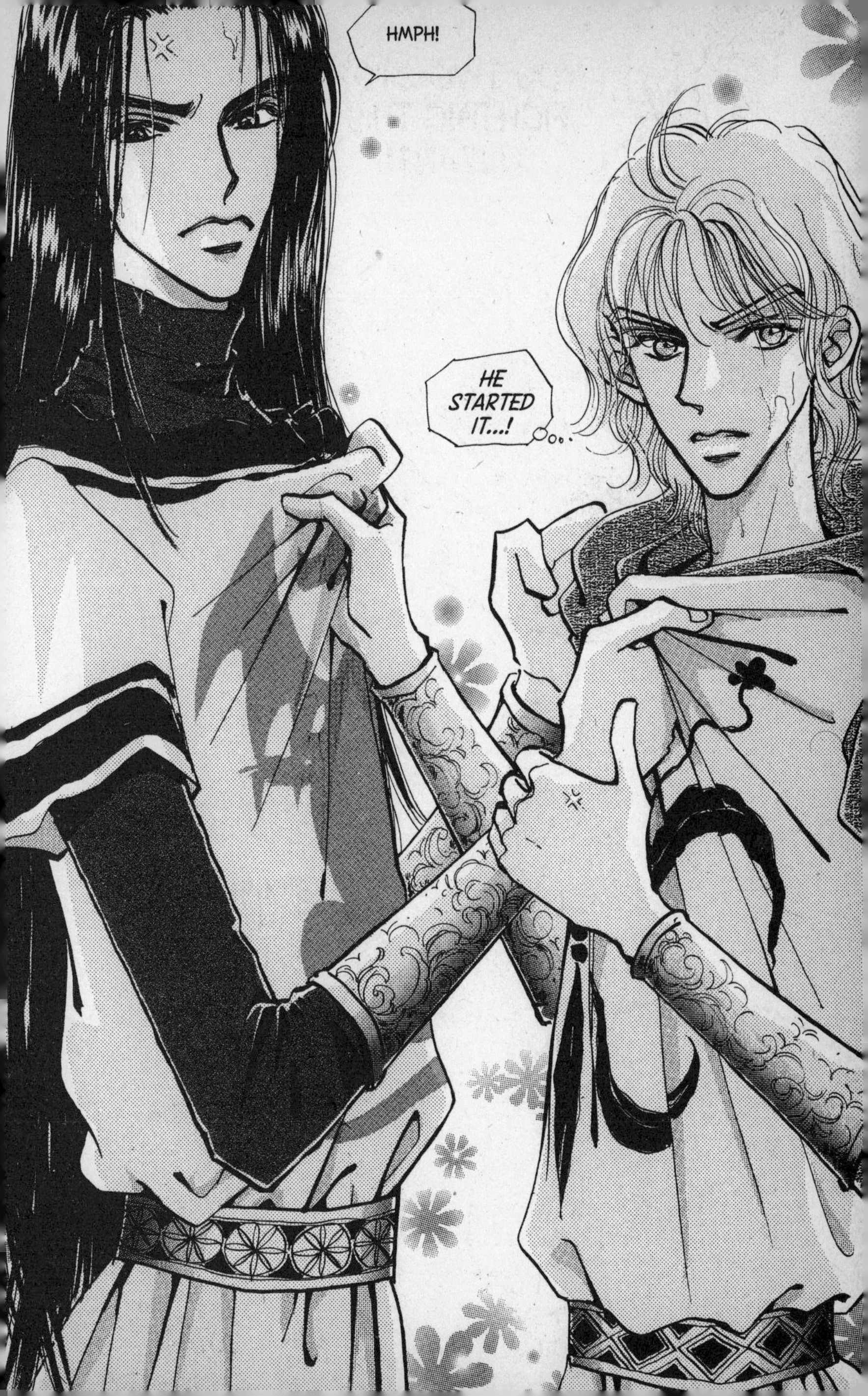
HMPH!
HE STARTED IT...!

IN THE NEXT VOLUME OF...
THE QUEEN'S KNIGHT

THE MYSTERIOUS CONNECTION BETWEEN THE QUEEN'S LOVE AND SPRING IS REVEALED WITH A SHOCKING REVELATION ABOUT REINO'S BIRTH. IN LIGHT OF THIS NEW INFORMATION, EHREN FINDS HIMSELF FACED WITH CHOOSING BETWEEN THE LOVE OF COUNTRY AND THE LOVE OF A WOMAN. EITHER WAY, YUNA'S AND PHANTASMA'S FATE HANGS IN THE BALANCE!

COMING SOON!

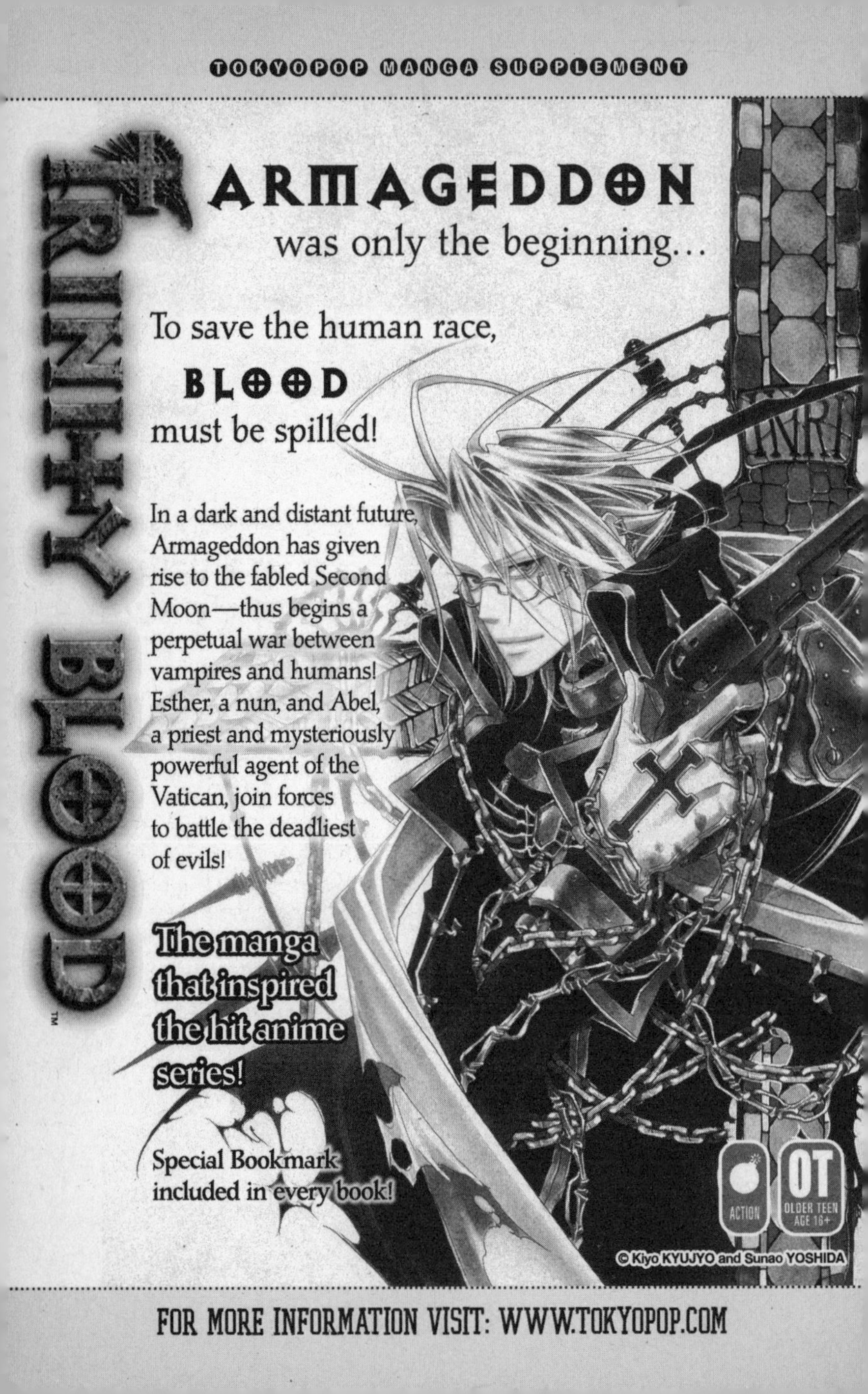

ELEMENTAL GELADE VOL. 2
BY MAYUMI AZUMA

ELEMENTAL GELADE

A SKY PIRATE MANGA BOUND TO HOOK YOU!

Rookie sky pirate Coud Van Giruet discovers a most unusual bounty: a young girl named Ren who is an "Edel Raid"—a living weapon that lends extraordinary powers to humans. But just as he realizes Ren is a very valuable treasure, she is captured! Can Coud and Arc Aile join forces and rescue her without killing themselves…or each other?

THE MANGA THAT SPARKED THE HIT ANIME!!

ACTION

T
TEEN
AGE 13+

© MAYUMI AZUMA

MLib
3/0?